Stephanie Adair
The Aesthetic Use of the Logical Functions in Kant's Third *Critique*

Kantstudien-Ergänzungshefte

Im Auftrag der Kant-Gesellschaft
herausgegeben von
Manfred Baum, Bernd Dörflinger
und Heiner F. Klemme

Band 202

Stephanie Adair

The Aesthetic Use of the Logical Functions in Kant's Third *Critique*

DE GRUYTER

ISBN 978-3-11-071025-0
e-ISBN (PDF) 978-3-11-057607-8
e-ISBN (EPUB) 978-3-11-057492-0
ISSN 0340-6059

Library of Congress Control Number: 2018946471

Bibliographic information published by the Deutsche Nationalbibliothek
The Deutsche Nationalbibliothek lists this publication in the Deutsche Nationalbibliografie;
detailed bibliographic data are available in the Internet at http://dnb.dnb.de.

© 2020 Walter de Gruyter GmbH, Berlin/Boston
This volume is text- and page-identical with the hardback published in 2018.
Printing and binding: CPI books GmbH, Leck

www.degruyter.com

To my mother and her love of Degas, Monet, Van Gogh and Renoir.

Acknowledgement

I would most especially like to thank Dr. Jennifer Bates for her close engagement with each chapter. The opportunity to respond to her careful comments and challenging counter arguments allowed me to gain not only crucial insights into the project, but also into the process of philosophical writing, itself. Dr. Dan Selcer's feedback not only on the dissertation itself but also on the prospectus was instrumental in shaping this project. I also want to thank Dr. Claudia Bickmann for the opportunity to attend her seminars on Kant while writing the dissertation. They provided a constant source of stimulation and discussions with her were always fruitful.

Contents

List of Abbreviations —— XIII

Introduction —— 1
I	Reflective Aesthetic Judgment —— 1	
II	Statement of the Problem —— 8	
II.A	The Logical Functions and Moments of the Judgment of Taste —— 9	
III	Project Overview —— 12	
IV	Chapter Outline —— 14	
IV.A	Chapter One: Renegotiating Kantian Constraints: Intuiting without Concepts —— 15	
IV.B	Chapter Two: Logical Functions of Judgment and the Layered Solution —— 16	
IV.C	Chapter Three: Pleasure Without Interest: Affirming a Negated Interest Through the Infinite Logical Function of Quality —— 17	
IV.D	Chapter Four: The Universal Validity of a Singular Judgment —— 18	
IV.E	Chapter Five: Disjunctivity and the Form of Purposiveness —— 18	
IV.F	Chapter Six: A Subjective, Exemplary Necessity —— 19	
V	Delving into the Details of Kant's Logic —— 20	
VI	A Terminological Note: Object —— 22	
VII	The Uniquely Human Judgment of Taste —— 26	

Chapter One: Renegotiating Kantian Constraints, Intuiting without Concepts —— 28
I	Intuitions and Objects —— 33	
II	Pure and Empirical Concepts —— 37	
II.A	The Strong View: Aesthetic Encounter Without Concepts? —— 38	
II.B	The Limiting View: Turning Back to Let in the Categories —— 62	
III	The "Higher Meaning" in Engagement with the Beautiful —— 71	
IV	Conclusion —— 73	

Chapter Two: Logical Functions of Judgment and the Layered Solution —— 75
I	Setting the Ground Work for a Layered Solution —— 79	
II	The Layered Solution —— 83	
II.A	An Illustrative Analogy: Dancing Between the Layers —— 88	
II.B	Aesthetic Judgment as Underlying Both Observation and Creation —— 91	

II.C	Intuitional Excess —— 92
II.D	Aesthetic Harmony and the Logical Functions —— 98
II.E	Allison's View —— 102
II.F	The Functioning of Logical Functions —— 110
II.G	The Transcendental Concept —— 111
III	An Analysis According to Moments —— 115
III.A	*Moments* in the first *Critique* —— 115
IV	How Logical Functions Guide the Analysis of Moments for Aesthetic Judgment —— 123
IV.A	The Interrelation of Logical Functions in General —— 128
V	Conclusion —— 129

Chapter Three: Pleasure Without Interest: Affirming a Negated Interest Through the Infinite Logical Function of Quality —— 133

I	The Logical Functions of Quality —— 134
I.A	Qualitative Complications —— 135
I.B	The Interrelation of Logical Functions in Quality —— 139
II	The First Moment of Aesthetic Judgment: Pleasure without Interest —— 141
II.A	Competing Readings —— 142
II.B	Quality before Quantity —— 145
II.C	Separating Existence from Essence: Kant's Hundred Possible Thalers —— 147
II.D	Disinterest —— 152
II.E	Different Ways of Taking Existence into Account: the Agreeable and the Moral —— 154
III	The First Moment and the Risk of Indexlosigkeit —— 161
III.A	Harmony, Mood and Free Play —— 167
IV	One Remaining Puzzle —— 170
IV.B	The Faculty-Interest —— 170
V	Conclusion —— 174

Chapter Four: The Universal Validity of a Singular Judgment —— 176

I	The Logical Functions of Quantity —— 177
I.A	Quantity in the first Critique —— 180
II	The Second Moment of Aesthetic Judgment —— 184
II.A	The Curiosity of the Second Moment —— 188
II.B	The Peculiar Intertwinement of Quantitative Functions in Aesthetic Judging: Singularity Equated with Universality in Aesthetic Judgment —— 192

II.C	The Singular Judging Subject —— 194	
II.D	Universal Communicability —— 197	
II.E	Section 9 —— 201	
III	Why Does Aesthetic Judgment Involve the Singular and Universal Instead of the Particular? —— 204	
III.A	The Fundamental Particularization made by Kant's System at the Outset —— 211	
IV	Conclusion: The Universal Voice —— 212	

Chapter Five: Disjunctivity and the Form of Purposiveness —— 215

I	The Logical Functions of Relation —— 217
I.A	Matter —— 218
I.B	Form —— 218
I.C	Modality —— 219
I.D	Hierarchy —— 220
I.E	Correspondence Between the Disjunctive Logical Function and Categories of Community —— 221
II	The Third Moment —— 225
II.A	Purposiveness with a Purpose —— 225
II.B	Taking the Purpose out of Purposiveness —— 230
II.C	What Purposiveness without a Purpose Means —— 233
III	Layers —— 249
IV	Conclusion —— 253

Chapter Six: An Exemplary, Conditioned Necessity —— 255

I	The Logical Functions of Modality —— 258
I.A	The Problematic, Assertoric and Apodictic —— 259
II	The Fourth Moment of Aesthetic Judgment —— 265
II.A	Exemplary Necessity —— 267
II.B	Conditioned Necessity —— 267
II.C	The Subjective Principle of Common Sense —— 273
II.E	The Proportion Sensed by the *Sensus Communis Aestheticus* —— 280
II.F	The Common Sense and the Representation of Subjective Necessity as Objective —— 283
III	Conclusion: Modality in Terms of the Layers —— 285

Concluding Remarks —— 287

I	The Project —— 287
II	Looking Back —— 287

III   Looking Ahead —— 290

Works Cited —— 292

Abstract —— 296
　　　　　The Aesthetic Use of the Logical Functions in Kant's Third *Critique* —— 296

Index —— 297

List of Abbreviations

Major Texts by Kant.

Critique of the Power of Judgment
Critique of the Power of Judgment. Translated by P. Guyer and E. Matthews. Cambridge: Cambridge University Press, 2000.

Critique of Practical Reason
Critique of Practical Reason. Translated by Mary Gregor. Cambridge: Cambridge University Press, 2005.

Critique of Pure Reason
Critique of Pure Reason. Edited and translated by P. Guyer and A. Wood. Cambridge: Cambridge University Press, 1997.

Groundwork of the Metaphysics of Morals
Groundwork of the Metaphysics of Morals. Translated by H. J. Paton. New York: Harper & Row, 1964.

Jäsche Logic
Jäsche Logic. The Jäsche Logic, Lectures on Logic. Translated by Michael Young, 521–640.

Prolegomena to any Future Metaphysics
Prolegomena to any Future Metaphysics. Translated by Lewis White Beck. Indianapolis: Bobbs-Merrill, 1950.

Introduction

The cognitive judgments of the first *Critique* determine an intuition by subsuming it under a concept, but the aesthetic judgments of the third reflect upon an intuition without subsuming it under a concept. My project centers on the reflective judgment of taste. Thus, it is worthwhile to establish at the outset an understanding of what it means for a judgment to be reflective. Before laying out the central problem of my project—the role of the logical functions in the merely reflective judgment of taste—here, I discuss how Béatrice Longuenesse and Rudolf Makkreel read merely reflective judgment. Through this engagement with their readings, I develop my own conception of reflective judgment as akin to an Aristotelian *praxis*. I then give a brief overview of how the following six chapters work to decipher the aesthetic operation of the logical functions.

I Reflective Aesthetic Judgment

Before presenting my project, let us look into what exactly Kant means by using the term "reflective" to describe the form of judgment with which he is concerned in the third *Critique*. Kant gives us his definition of the term: "[t]o reflect (to consider), however, is to compare and to hold together given representations either with others or with one's faculty of cognition, in relation to a concept thereby made possible."[1] Let us lay this definition of reflection alongside his description of how reflective aesthetic judgment operates to generate:

> [that] sensation which the harmonious play of the two faculties of cognition in the power of judgment, imagination and understanding, produces in the subject insofar as in the given representation the faculty of the apprehension of the one and the faculty of the presentation of the other are reciprocally expeditious[…].[2]

The reflective activity of aesthetic judgment thus involves the comparison between the faculties of cognition. The imagination offers up an intuition, stimulating the understanding to seek a concept under which this intuition could be subsumed. A peculiarity of the *merely* reflective aesthetic judgment is that in holding together the faculties and comparing them, no concept is "thereby made possi-

---

[1] *Critique of the Power of Judgment*, First Introduction, V, 20: 211.
[2] *Critique of the Power of Judgment*, First Introduction, VIII, 20: 224.

ble."³ This form of judgment "can never provide a determinate concept of the object."⁴ No concept of the understanding emerges to subsume the imagination's intuition and bring this harmonious free-play to a halt. Suspended in this indeterminate, reflective state, the faculties are enlivened by the endless search.⁵ This aesthetic free-play is "optimal for the animation of both powers of the mind (the one through the other) [...]."⁶

In *Kant and the Capacity to Judge* (1998), Béatrice Longuenesse maintains that the truly novel contribution of the third *Critique* is the introduction of judgments that are merely reflective. Longuenesse suggests that every judgment includes an initial moment of reflection, during which an appropriate concept is sought for subsuming the particular intuition at hand.⁷ Unlike determinative judgment, which eventually does subsume an intuition under a concept, aesthetic judgment merely searches for a concept, but never does find one.⁸

Rudolf A. Makkreel offers a different reading of what makes aesthetic judgments reflective in "Reflection, Reflective Judgment, and Aesthetic Exemplarity."⁹ He disputes Longuenesse's interpretation that reflective judgment serves as an initial stage for determinative judgment as well, contending that this would render aesthetic judgment something inferior and incomplete, as it would merely amount to the first two synthetic acts, of apprehension and reflection, stopping short of recognition. He argues that reflective judgment's work

---

3 *Critique of the Power of Judgment*, First Introduction, V, 20: 211.
4 *Critique of the Power of Judgment*, First Introduction, X, 20: 239.
5 *Critique of the Power of Judgment*, Bk. I, § 9, 5:219.
6 *Critique of the Power of Judgment*, Bk. I, § 21, 5:238.
7 Béatrice Longuenesse, *Kant and the Capacity to Judge* (Princeton: Princeton UP, 1998), 163–4. She writes, "[...] Kant was careful to characterize the judgments on which he focused in the third *Critique* (aesthetic judgments and teleological judgments) as *merely* reflective judgments (*nur reflektierende, bloß reflektierende*). This restrictive modifier is meant to deny that these judgments are in any sense determinative; they are *purely* reflective. They differ in this regard from other judgments relating to the sensible given, which are not *merely* reflective, but determinative *as well* [...]. Thus, the peculiar feature of aesthetic and teleological judgments is not that they are reflective judgment (*for every judgment on empirical objects as such is reflective*); it is rather that they are *merely* reflective judgments in which reflection can never arrive at conceptual *determination*."
8 "What makes judgments *merely* reflective is that in them, the effort of the activity of judgment to form concepts *fails*. And it fails because it *cannot* succeed. This is the case in "merely reflective" *aesthetic* judgment, where the agreement of imagination and understanding is of such a nature that it cannot be reflected under any concept" (Longuenesse, *Kant and the Capacity to Judge*, 164).
9 Rudolf Makkreel, *Imagination and Interpretation in Kant*, (Chicago, IL: University of Chicago Press, 1990).

goes beyond the simple search for a concept, functioning in a "coordinative," rather than determinative, manner. He focuses on the distinction that Kant draws between reflective judgments, which go from particular to universal, and determinative judgments, which go from universal to particular. Makkreel argues that Longuenesse misaligns reflective judgment with the function of reflection in three-fold synthesis. He writes, "[s]ince determinant judgment proceeds from a given universal to particular, it clearly involves a *subordinating* mode of thought."[10] This he contrasts to reflective judgment "which tends to begin with particulars," and thus has "a *coordinating* mode of thought."[11] Does this difference, however, mean that the two forms of judgment cannot both share in a reflective moment? I do not believe so.

Let me take the opportunity, here, to defend Longuenesse's interpretation against Makkreel's criticisms and show that understanding both determinative and merely reflective judgment as sharing a reflective moment does not reduce the former to an incomplete version of the latter, nor does it block merely reflective judgment from having further "merely reflective" characteristics, which are not developed by determinative judgment.

My first defense addresses Makkreel's objection that the difference of the direction that each judgment takes when moving between particular and universal rules out the possibility that the course of these judgments may overlap in a moment of reflection. My second defense will address Makkreel's allegation that conceiving of reflective judgment as a judgment which does not complete the last of the three acts of synthesis (recognition in a concept) would condemn it to be nothing more than an incomplete, and thus inferior, form of determinative judgment. While I agree that it would be incongruent with the status Kant accords to reflective aesthetic judgment if it were to amount to a mere precursor to determinative judgment, Longuenesse's view does not necessitate such a reading. Instead, it makes greater sense to understand the paths of reflective and determinative judgment as converging for a certain segment—this moment of convergence not being the final state for either form of judgment.[12]

I do not dispute that Kant differentiates between reflective and determinative judgments in terms of the direction taken between particulars and universals.

---

[10] Rudolf Makkreel, "Reflection, Reflective Judgment, and Aesthetic Exemplarity," In *Aesthetics and Cognition in Kant's Critical Philosophy*. edited by Rebecca Kukla. (Cambridge: Cambridge University Press, 2006), 223.
[11] Makkreel, "Reflection, Reflective Judgment, and Aesthetic Exemplarity," 223.
[12] Indeed, my layered judgment solution in chapter two will address the fully discursive acts of judging that are incited by the ineffable, harmonious free-play, suggesting that they occur in a different layer.

This can, however, be reconciled with the idea that the two forms of judgment share a reflective moment if we allow that the stages leading into and out of this moment differ. For reflective judgments, this search would naturally follow upon an intuition being reproduced by the imagination. For determinative judgments, however, the reflective moment would be something like a *second* beginning.

It is almost as if determinative judgments start on both ends. This idea of two beginnings should not be altogether surprising, because Kant acknowledges it right at the beginning of the first *Critique* when he writes, "[a]s far as time is concerned, then, no cognition in us precedes experience, and with experience every cognition begins."[13] On the one hand, the pure concept (i.e. category) which will subsume the intuition already resides in the understanding, constituting the "first beginning" of determinative judgment. On the other hand, "as far as time is concerned" a particular intuition must be given to us in experience before anything can be subsumed under this concept.[14] Thus, this encounter with an actual particular constitutes what I am calling the second "beginning." It is *temporally* prior to the recognition of this particular in the universal concept, but, the judgment "does not on that account [...] arise from experience,"[15] and this confers a certain priority upon the other starting point of possessing the universal.[16]

---

13 *Critique of Pure Reason*, B1.
14 The pure concepts of the understanding are already present a priori as the conditions for the possibility of encountering such a particular. The identification of the "beginnings" in this structure is, however, further complicated if we consider that the particular intuition may also be organized under an empirical concept, which may not yet have been acquired. The formation of empirical concepts is a fascinatingly complicated issue in Kant. W. H. Walsh discusses concept formation as arising through a proleptical awareness that foreshadows the emergence of a determinative object (Walsh, W. H., *Kant's Criticism of Metaphysics* [Edinburgh: Edinburgh University Press, 1975]). For the sake of differentiating reflective from determinative judgment, however, I am discussing a determinative judgment with an "achieved" concept, i.e., a concept that has already been formed. To address determinative judgments in which the concept that subsumes the intuition first emerges at this point would only confuse the contrast that Kant draws between reflective and determinative judgments in the first *Critique*. For a discussion of how reflection works in the process of forming a new empirical concept see Longuenesse, *Kant and the Capacity to Judge*, 115–122.
15 *Critique of Pure Reason*, B1.
16 Bickmann gives a helpful description of this complicated structure, when she writes "...unser Gemüt muss solche Initialstrukturen in sich ausprägen können, die selbst unfraglich, *in* – aber nicht *durch* – die Erfahrung gegeben sind" ("Die eingebettete Vernunft in Kants "Kritik der Urteilskraft": Wechselintegrationen vereint-entgegengesetzter Sphären." In *Philosophische Schrifte*,

With this in mind, we could describe a determinative judgment as running in the following manner. We encounter a particular that "stimulate[s] our senses," awakening our cognitive faculty and throwing it into a reflective moment in which it reaches out for a concept to subsume the intuition.[17] In this case, however, it *does* find such a universal, because this universal concept already resided in the mind of the judging subject before the particular was encountered, although the particular could not be cognized as a determination of the universal until it had been encountered, prompting, in turn, the understanding to reach out for a concept under which it could be understood. Hence, in a determinative judgment knowledge of the particular arises from the universal, but regarding how the judgment is temporally ordered, the particular must first be encountered before it can be thought under the universal. We might say that the universal is the judgment's epistemic causal beginning, whereas the particular is its practical, or immediate, causal beginning. Hence, the idea that "as far as time is concerned" the encounter of a particular is immediately followed by a reflective moment, in which the understanding searches for the appropriate universal concept, does not contradict the idea that the epistemic causal order of a determinative judgment runs from universal to particular.

In a determinative judgment the recognition of a concept follows right on the heels of this reflective moment. In a merely reflective judgment, however, this reflective moment leads the faculties of imagination and understanding into a state of harmonious free-play. Although determinative judgment does entail a concord of the faculties with one another, in which a concept is recognized as being adequate to the intuition, this is not to be confused with the enlivening harmony that aesthetic judgment reaches.

Makkreel's reading of Longuenesse's interpretation is unnecessary. The latter does not necessitate that the harmonious free-play of the faculties be posited as an initial stage for all sorts of judgments, with the only difference being that determinative judgments find a way out of this harmonious state, while reflective judgments are stuck there. Makkreel's own insistence on how merely reflective judgment operationally differs from the synthetic act of reflection appears to be the answer. Suppose all judgments have a reflective moment in which they search for the concept that fits with the intuition that has been apprehended and produced.[18] Whereas determinative judgments move from this stage into rec-

---

Band 68, edited by Reinhard Hiltscher, Stefan Klingner and David Süß, (19–39. Freiburg/Br.: Germany, 2006), 26).

[17] *Critique of Pure Reason*, B1.

[18] This would appear to involve a productive, not reproductive, use of the imagination in accordance with Kant's remark about figurative synthesis as "distinct from the intellectual synthe-

ognition in a concept, merely reflective judgments take a *different* route, in which the harmonious free-play "strengthens and reproduces itself" without a concept.[19]

It is at this point that the paths of determinative and reflective judgment diverge once again. It is not simply that they move on to different points, but also that they move on *in different ways*, because as Makkreel agrees, they function differently. But it is once the reflective search for a concept has begun that this difference fully surfaces. We might compare the different modes of functioning that makes these two forms of judgment so divergent to Aristotle's description of the different ways that an aim can relate to an action:

> But the ends [that are sought] appear to differ; some are activities, and others are products apart from the activities. Wherever there are products apart from the actions, the products are by nature better than the activities.[20]

In determinative judgment, reflection is an action engaged in as a process of production (*poiesis*), that is, carried out in order to generate the satisfying product of a conceptually subsumed intuition. We might compare this to Aristotle's description of a process as something that "takes time, and aims at some end, and is complete when it produces the product it seeks."[21] He adds that a process is "incomplete during the processes that are its parts."[22] This would work well as a description of the way that a determinative judgment aims at the finished product of subsumption. If this is thwarted, then only feelings of frustration and not

---

sis without any imagination merely through the understanding. Now insofar as the imagination is spontaneity, I also occasionally call it the productive imagination, and thereby distinguish it from the reproductive imagination, whose synthesis is subject solely to empirical laws, namely those of association, and that therefore contributes nothing to the explanation of the possibility of cognition *a priori*, and on that account belongs not in transcendental philosophy but in psychology" (*Critique of Pure Reason*, B152). He observes this in the third *Critique*, writing, "But if in the judgment of taste the imagination must be considered in its freedom, then it is in the first instance taken not as reproductive, as subjected to the laws of association, but as productive and self-active (as the authoress of voluntary forms of possible intuition) [...]" (*Critique of the Power of Judgment*, § 22, 5:240).

19 *Critique of the Power of Judgment*, Bk. I, § 12, 5: 222. I will further describe the path I see this route to take when I present my layered structure in chapter two.

20 Aristotle, *Nicomachean Ethics*, *Nicomachean Ethics*. Translated by Terence Irwin. (Indianapolis: Hackett Publishing, 1999)1094a4–6.

21 Aristotle, *Nicomachean Ethics*, 1174b20.

22 Aristotle, *Nicomachean Ethics*, 1174b22.

pleasure will ensue.²³ This aligns with Kant's remarks about how "[t]he attainment of every aim is combined with the feeling of pleasure."²⁴ It is important to note that this does not necessarily mean that every pleasure involves the attainment of an aim, but rather that whenever an aim is attained, pleasure ensues. In the determinative function of judgment, the act of reflection is a process, a means to an end. Its aim is to enable the subsumption of the particular under a universal. Thus, a successful determinative judgment achieves this end and is combined with a feeling of pleasure while a thwarted determinative judgment is accompanied by frustration or displeasure.

In reflective judgment, however, the act of reflection becomes an Aristotelian activity (*praxis*). As such, it is "complete at any time, since it has no need for anything else to complete its form by coming to be at a later time."²⁵ Thus, the inability to find a concept does not result in the sort of mental frustration that it would yield in a determinative judgment, because a reflective aesthetic judgment functions as an activity. The harmonious free-play that the faculties enter in the search for a concept is both the action and the product, meaning that it is complete at every moment.

My suggestion that reflective aesthetic judgment functions as a *praxis* is only further supported by the fact that Aristotle takes pleasure to be an activity, because it is complete in itself and engaged in for its own sake.²⁶ For Kant this aligns well with the type of pleasure that he describes as "[t]he consciousness of the causality of a representation with respect to the state of the subject, **for**

---

23 It is because aesthetic judgment has something *more* than concepts can capture, a sort of intuitional surplus, if you will, that the failure to find a concept is felt in a different way. A failed determinative judgment, such as the inability to remember the name of a song, has an intuitional content which would fit perfectly under the concept *if* the concept could be offered. The intuitional content of an aesthetic judgment, on the other hand—that elusive element that makes the song so beautiful and enlivens one's thoughts—is unable to be subsumed. Thus, the suspension in a pleasant free play instead of a frustrating nonattainment. Guyer illustrates this difference well, when he writes, "To be sure, one can imagine that *some* such experiences are pleasing, as reveries or daydreams sometimes are; but then again, the experience of ranging over an indeterminate multitude of possible concepts for an object without being able to settle on a determinate one for the object at hand is sometimes frustrating, indeed a nightmare – just imagine, or remember, going back and forth among several answers to an exam question, each of which seems plausible without one seeming conclusively correct" (Paul Guyer, "The Harmony of the Faculties Revisited," in *Aesthetics and Cognition in Kant's Critical Philosophy*, ed. Rebecca Kukla [Cambridge: Cambridge University Press, 2006], 177).
24 *Critique of the Power of Judgment*, Introduction, VI., 5:187.
25 Aristotle, *Nicomachean Ethics*, 1173b15.
26 see *Nicomachean Ethics*, Book X, Chapter 4.

maintaining it in that state."²⁷ The activity of reflection brings the judging subject into a state that is pleasurable in and of itself. Hence, the judging subject does not seek any further product external to this activity of reflection, but rather seeks only to maintain this state, "linger[ing] over the contemplation of the beautiful."²⁸

The mode of engagement is what enables us to distinguish between processes and activities. One person may eat carrots simply for the joy of the activity itself, without any thought to the additional ends that the eating of carrots may help achieve. Another person, who has a distinct hatred of the vegetable, but a vitamin A deficiency, might choke down the carrots as a mere means to a desirable end. Thus, if we understand the key difference between the modes of thought involved in reflective and determinative judgments as playing out along these lines, then both may be seen as involving the same action of reflection (just as the two individuals both engage in the same action of eating carrots). The way that one engages in this action, however, differs. And it is this difference of engagement, not a difference of the mental acts involved, which differentiates the one from the other.²⁹

II Statement of the Problem

Now that we have a better idea of what sort of judging activity is specified by the term "reflective," let us turn to the particular sort of merely reflective judgment with which the third *Critique* begins: the judgment of taste. The *Critique of the Power of Judgment's* Analytic of the Beautiful, does not have its own introductory paragraph. Rather, Kant begins directly with the "First Moment of the judgment of taste,* concerning its quality." The footnote attached to this title, however, contains the orientating remarks that would have appeared in an introductory paragraph, describing the methodology Kant followed in writing the Analytic of the Beautiful. Here Kant writes:

> The definition of taste that is the basis here is that it is the faculty for the judging of the beautiful. But what is required for calling an object beautiful must be discovered by the analysis of judgments of taste. In seeking the moments to which this power of judgment

---

27 *Critique of the Power of Judgment*, Bk. I, § 10, 5:220, emphasis original. Kant's conception of pleasure and how exactly it fits into aesthetic judgment in the third *Critique* is a matter of great debate. I offer my reading of this in chapters four and five.
28 *Critique of the Power of Judgment*, Bk. I, § 12, 5:222.
29 In chapter four I will develop in more detail the reason for this difference in engagement.

attends in its reflection, I have been guided by the logical functions for judging (for a relation to the understanding is always contained even in the judgment of taste). I have considered the moment of quality first, since the aesthetic judgment on the beautiful takes notice of this first.[30]

Over the course of the following chapters I will return to this footnote a number of times, scrutinizing various implications that these remarks have for Kant's following analysis. The claim that Kant makes here, which is of the most fundamental interest to my project, is that he used the logical functions from the table of judgments to guide his inquiry. When we compare the logical functions to the resulting moments, however, it is unclear exactly how this is to be understood. A number of commentators fail to see an important relation between the logical functions and moments of the judgment of taste. My project is to bring this relation to light. It is my thesis that the richly complex moments of the judgment of taste can only take shape through an equally complex relation to the logical functions. I detail how the production of each perplexing moment requires that more than one of the logical functions in the corresponding quadrant be engaged.

II.A The Logical Functions and Moments of the Judgment of Taste

Let us first take a look at the difficulty one initially encounters when attempting to understand how the logical functions relate to the judgment of taste. The logical functions, presented in the first *Critique*'s table of judgments, are as follows:

1. Quantity of Judgments
Universal
Particular
Singular

2. Quality
Affirmative
Negative
Infinite

3. Relation
Categorical
Hypothetical
Disjunctive

4. Modality
Problematic
Assertoric
Apodictic[31]

---

30 *Critique of the Power of Judgment*, § 1, 5:203, footnote.
31 *Critique of Pure Reason*, A70/B95.

One cannot help but be surprised to find that following the lead of these logical functions has brought Kant to the following four moments of aesthetic judgment:
- disinterested pleasure (Quality);
- universality without a concept (Quantity);
- purposiveness of form (Relation);
- necessary satisfaction (Modality).

Although universality does appear on the table above, aesthetic universality takes a subjective shape. Subjective universality has a contradictory ring to it and thus necessitates further interpretative work. Necessity may *prima facie* seem to correlate with apodictic modality, but the fourth moment of the judgment of taste reveals this not to be the case: "Since an aesthetic judgment is not an objective and cognitive judgment, this necessity cannot be derived from determinate concepts, and is therefore not apodictic."[32] As for disinterested pleasure and purposiveness of form (i.e., the first and third moments, respectively), they are clearly nowhere to be found on the table of judgments.

Kant's opening footnote to the Analytic of the Beautiful gives one the feeling that his orienting use of the logical functions ought be a straightforward matter. The literature, however, has found this to be far from the case. Some scholars dismiss Kant's decision to use these functions to guide his analysis. Paul Guyer even goes so far as to argue that this infelicitous decision obscures Kant's intended argument, remarking:

> Since the logical functions of judgment describe difference in the contents of judgments, and the moments of aesthetic judgment describe quite different features of the status and ground of judgments, there is no reason why the order or even the number of the former should provide and appropriate framework for the analysis of the latter. In fact, Kant's sequential arrangement of the four moments as four "definitions" of the judgment of taste obscures the difference in function between those describing the requirement of intersubjective acceptability and those describing criteria by which such a requirement may be judged to be fulfilled.[33]

Jens Kullenkampff brushes off the need for any in-depth engagement with the table of judgments, despite having given his commentary the inviting title *Kants Logik des ästhetischen Urteils*. Kullenkampff remarks that "such a sub-

---

32 *Critique of the Power of Judgment*, § 18, 5:237.
33 Paul Guyer, *Kant and the Claims of Taste*, Second Edition, (Cambridge, MA: Harvard University Press, 1997), 115.

sumption under the Kantian formal determinations of judgment is so unproblematically possible, that an extensive analysis does not at all arise."[34]

Even Henry Allison, who reads each of the four moments as serving a special purpose for Kant's argument, gradually pushes aside the notion that each of these moments has a crucial relation to the logical functions from the table of judgments. His analysis of the first and second moments of the judgment of taste attests to the important relation the moments have to the logical functions. For the third moment, however, this expectation quickly diminishes. Allison introduces his analysis of the third moment with the following remark:

> Following the "guiding thread" of the table of judgments in the *Critique of Pure Reason*, the third moment in the Analytic of the Beautiful is that of relation. Unlike the logical functions of relation or the relational categories, however, the relation in question is between the judging subject and the object judged and/or its representation.[35]

Allison's comments here display the temptation to stop reading the moments of aesthetic judgment as relating to the logical functions in a way that is significant for how this activity itself is intrinsically constituted. I do not dispute that the relation between the judging subject and the object judged is important to understanding aesthetic judgments, however, I contend that the relation of purposiveness without a purpose described in the third moment must be understood through the logical function that relates different elements within this judgment.[36] More specifically, nature and art must be held together in the activity of pure aesthetic judging, and the logical function of relation describes what sort of holding this is to be. Accordingly, for each of the four moments I examine how the logical functions of relation allow us to better describe the relational dynamic intrinsic to the judgment of taste.

---

34 Jens Kulenkampff, *Kants Logik des ästhetischen Urteils* (Frankfurt am Main: Vittorio Klostermann, 1978), 28, my translation. To quote the passage more fully: "Die Titel der vier Momente benennen nun Charaktere der logischen Form im engeren Sinn, und es macht keinerlei Schwierigkeiten, das Urtiel über das Schöne in der paradigmatischen Form "dieses x ist schön" unter die Titel der Urteilstafel zu subsumieren und zu bestimmen: es ist der Quantität nach einzeln, der Qualität nach bejahend, der Relation nach kategorische und der Modalität nach assertorisch. Eine solche subsumation unter die kantischen Formalbestimmungen von Urteilen ist so problemlos möglich, dass sich eine ausgebreitete Analytik gar nicht ergibt."
35 Henry Allison, *Kant's Theory of Taste*, 119.
36 The idea of a purposiveness without a purpose was greatly influential for post-Kantians, particularly Hegel. The question of how post-Kantians have made transformative use of Kant's ideas lays, however, outside of the scope of my project.

III Project Overview

My project concentrates on carefully detailing the relation between the table of judgments and the moments of the judgment of taste. This is a task that catches us up in a further curiosity of the third *Critique*. Throughout the Critique of the Aesthetic Power of Judgment Kant repeatedly casts aside concepts. For instance, Kant tells us that:

> The aesthetic power of judgment is thus a special faculty for judging things in accordance with a rule but not in accordance with concepts.[37]

This in turn means that:

> [...] the judgment of taste is merely contemplative [...]. But this contemplation itself is also not directed to concepts; for the judgment of taste is not a cognitive judgment (neither a theoretical nor a practical one), and hence it is neither grounded on concepts nor aimed at them.[38]

Indeed, the concept-independence of the judgment of taste is even stipulated in the definitions of the beautiful that result from the latter three moments. The first moment describes pure aesthetic judgment as involving a satisfaction "without any interest,"[39] unlike judgments of the agreeable and the good. Once this has been established, the remaining three definitions all entail a reference to the concept-independence of the judgment of taste. The definition to be derived from the moment of quantity is: "That is beautiful which pleases universally *without a concept*."[40] The definition derived from relation is: "Beauty is the form of the purposiveness of an object, insofar as it is perceived in it *without representation of an end*."[41] Here, the stipulation of concept-independence is somewhat imbedded in the definition, but comes clearly to light when one considers that "*an end is the object of a concept* insofar as the latter is regarded as the cause of the former."[42] The modality of the judgment of taste yields the following definition: "That is beautiful which is cognized *without a concept* as the object of

---

[37] *Critique of the Power of Judgment,* Introduction VIII, 5:194.
[38] *Critique of the Power of Judgment,* § 5, 5:209. See also: *Ibid.,* FI XII, 20:250; § 6, 5:211; § 17, 5:231; § 40, 5:296; § 42 5:300.
[39] *Critique of the Power of Judgment,* § 5, 5:211.
[40] *Critique of the Power of Judgment,* § 9, 5:219, emphasis added.
[41] *Critique of the Power of Judgment,* § 17, 5:236, emphasis added.
[42] *Critique of the Power of Judgment,* § 10, 5:220, emphasis added.

a necessary satisfaction."[43] Thus, we cannot ignore Kant's remarks about the concept-independence of the judgment of taste, "the faculty for the judging of the beautiful."[44]

A complication, however, arises insofar as empirical objects are constituted for Kant by subsuming an intuition under a concept.[45] Thus, if aesthetic judgments are to be "neither grounded on concepts nor aimed at them,"[46] then they should neither be based on an empirical object nor further determine one. Thus, in investigating the relation between the logical functions and aesthetic judgment, I also examine the role played by the empirical object in the judgment of taste and how this may occur without violating the stipulation of aesthetic concept-independence.

I focus on two specific ways that this concept-independence complicates our attempts to understand Kant's theory of the judgment of taste and regard the logical functions for judging as essential for breaking out of these interpretative difficulties. First, if pure aesthetic judgments involve a harmonious free-play of the faculties of imagination and understanding, then both of these faculties must be operative. To bar the concepts of the understanding from any central role in this activity of judgment would seem to exclude the understanding. I show, however, that this is not the case. A logical function belongs to the understanding but is not a concept. Rather, it is "the form of the concept alone."[47] Hence, by detailing the crucial role that the logical functions play in the judgment of taste, I describe how this free play involves the understanding without thereby becoming a determination through concepts.

Second, Kant's adamance that the judgment is "neither grounded on concepts nor aimed at them"[48] must be reconciled with the various ways in which concepts *do* appear to be involved in the judgment of taste. There are three ways, in particular, that this arises. First, Kant's account of aesthetic judgment is rooted in form. Form requires formal determinations, which can only be supplied through a determinately cognized object. At minimum this must involve the pure geometrical concepts discussed in the schematism of the first *Critique*.[49]

---

43 *Critique of the Power of Judgment*, § 22, 5:240, emphasis added.
44 *Critique of the Power of Judgment*, § 1, 5:203, footnote.
45 For Kant, an object is defined as "that in the concept of which the manifold of a given intuition is united" (*Critique of Pure Reason*, B137, emphasis added). Thus, where there is no concept, there can be no object.
46 *Critique of the Power of Judgment*, § 5, 5:209.
47 *Critique of Pure Reason*, A245/B302.
48 *Critique of the Power of Judgment*, § 5, 5:209.
49 See: *Critique of Pure Reason*, A137/B176.

Second, the judgment proclaiming the aesthetic value of an empirical object requires that it be subsumed under an empirical concept, so that it may occupy the subject position in the judgment. Third, our understanding of aesthetic judgment needs to be amenable to how "nature figuratively speaks to us in its beautiful forms."[50] Attempts to cut aesthetic judgment off from conceptual thinking altogether are thwarted by Kant's remarks that the feeling involved in pure aesthetic judgment "contain[s] a language that nature brings to us and that seems to have a higher meaning."[51]

I respond to this second set of difficulties with a layered solution that contextualizes pure aesthetic judging within a larger judgmental process. Although it is the concept-independent harmonious free play that characterizes pure aesthetic judgment, the faculties are not aesthetically enlivened in a cognitive vacuum. Rather, the harmonious free play of the faculties occurs within the context of judgment's normal, determinative activity. In this manner two layers of determinative judgment form around the purely aesthetic activity of judging, giving aesthetic judgment a layered structure.[52] I use these layers to explain how the properly aesthetic harmony of the faculties relates to the empirical object constituted on the first layer and incites the thinking of the third without becoming a determinate, cognitive judgment in the process.

IV Chapter Outline

Much has been written about the perplexing characteristics that the moments of the Analytic of the Beautiful describe. This is true not only for contemporary scholarship on Kant, but also for the works of post-Kantian philosophers, who were greatly influenced by how Kant develops these moments in the third *Critique*. My project, however, is not simply to understand these moments as they are developed in the third *Critique*. It is, rather, to understand each of these moments specifically through their relation to the logical functions on the table of

---

50 *Critique of the Power of Judgment*, § 42, 5:301.
51 *Critique of the Power of Judgment*, § 42, 5:302.
52 The resulting three layers roughly correspond with what Nicolai Hartmann picked out as the "essential aspects" of the act of observing beauty, which are intuition, enjoyment and assessment, see Hartmann, *Aesthetics*, trans. Eugene Kelly (Berlin/Boston: de Gruyter, 2014), 16. Although Hartmann mentions it only in passing, he also sees a "unification of all three sides of aesthetical receptivity" in Kant's aesthetics, the problem being that "too little was done to differentiate them" (*Ibid.*, 17).

judgments in the first *Critique*.⁵³ I am, as of yet, unaware of a book-length analysis that elaborates the moments in this way.⁵⁴

I begin chapters three through six by investigating what the corresponding quadrant of the table of judgments describes and how its logical functions operate. In doing so, I make regular use of the *Jäsche Logic* to supplement my engagement with the first *Critique*. Whereas the latter text discusses all four quadrants and twelve logical functions in one section (§ 9), the former dedicates ten sections (§ 21 – § 30) to a more detailed analysis.

IV.A Chapter One: Renegotiating Kantian Constraints: Intuiting without Concepts

In chapter one, I show that the judging activity involved in pure aesthetic judgment must be more complex than a simple statement of aesthetic value ("This x is beautiful"). To demonstrate this, I trace the difficulties that arise when we attempt to understand Kant's insistence that pure aesthetic judgment does not rely on concepts. The main challenge is to find a way of understanding this that nevertheless permits an empirically cognized object with determinate features to occasion the judgment. Moreover, Kant describes the beautiful as able to "dispose the mind" to thick moral concepts, such as innocence, audacity and candor.⁵⁵ For this to be possible, aesthetic judgment must have an array of concepts at its disposal. Otherwise it could not incite the meaningful contemplation of moral concepts. In this manner the first chapter establishes that an interpretative path for circumventing these difficulties is required to understand how pure aesthetic judgments of taste do and do not involve concepts. This prepares the way for my stratified interpretation of the judgment of taste as a layered process.

---

53 The key role that the connection between the first and third Critiques plays for my project, via the table of judgments, limits my engagement with post-Kantian philosophers who read the third *Critique* as a departure from the first.
54 Béatrice Longuenesse does take this approach in: Longuenesse, Béatrice. "Kant's Guiding Thread," in *Aesthetics and Cognition in Kant's Critical Philosophy*, edited by Rebecca Kukla (Cambridge: Cambridge University Press, 2006). Longuenesse's article has been instructive for my work here. But, as would be expected in a book-length project, I delve more deeply into each moment than she does in this article. Furthermore, our readings of which logical functions are operative do not always coincide, particularly for the first and third moments.
55 *Critique of the Power of Judgment*, § 42, 5:302.

IV.B Chapter Two: Logical Functions of Judgment and the Layered Solution

Chapter two presents my layered solution to the problems described in chapter one. I propose separating the activity of judging that uses concepts into a different layer than that which does not. The resulting layers resolve the difficulties described in chapter one by contextualizing pure aesthetic judging within a larger judgmental process. I recognize three distinct activities of judging involved in the overall process of aesthetic judgment, each located in a distinct layer. On the first layer, an object is given to knowledge through a judgment of experience. The empirical cognition of this object generates an intuitional excess that cannot be subsumed under a concept. This excess is taken up by the power of judgment in a properly aesthetic manner on the second layer, throwing the faculties of imagination and understanding into a harmonious, non-conceptual free-play. The third layer, then uses an aesthetically inspired vocabulary to relate the feeling perception of the second layer to the basic empirical judgment of the first. In this manner a layered solution places the properly aesthetic element of the second layer on a determinative base and allows meaningful discursive thinking to be aesthetically inspired. At the same time, however, it preserves the indeterminate, non-conceptual, purely aesthetic aspect of judgments of taste.

The motivation behind understanding aesthetic judgment as a process involving layers is not to designate certain layers as more complete, or "higher", than others. Rather, I streamline the process in this way so as to understand how aesthetic judgment can be "neither grounded on concepts nor aimed at them"[56] while still relating to objects, producing judgments about objects and inciting "much thinking."[57] Each layer's judging accomplishes something different. The judging of the first layer constitutes the raw sense data as an empirical object with determinate qualities. The second layer engages with the aesthetic excess that escaped the empirical judgment of this object, basking in the aesthetic pleasure that comes from the enlivening effect that contemplation of the excess has on the faculties. Although the reflection of this in the third layer gestures toward what escaped the first and was enjoyed—but not cognized—in the second, even in the last layer this excess remains something "no language fully attains or can make intelligible."[58] The intuitional surplus of an aesthetic judgment is in perpetual excess, "stimulat[ing] so much thinking that it can never be grasped in a determinate concept."[59] It stirs up a new set of vibrant, aesthetically inspired

---

[56] *Critique of the Power of Judgment*, § 5, 5:209.
[57] *Critique of the Power of Judgment*, § 49, 5:315.
[58] *Critique of the Power of Judgment*, § 49, 5:314.
[59] *Critique of the Power of Judgment*, § 49, 5:315.

terms, but leaves one with the perpetual feeling that when lingering over the beautiful, there is always something left to say.

IV.C Chapter Three: Pleasure Without Interest: Affirming a Negated Interest Through the Infinite Logical Function of Quality

Chapter three begins my analysis of the four moments of the judgment of taste in relation to the logical functions from the four corresponding quadrants in the table of judgments. Here I analyze the *Quality* of the judgment of taste, clarifying what is being affirmed in pure aesthetic judgment and what is being negated. Unlike scholars who have read aesthetic judgment as "affirmative,"[60] I find that what is affirmed here is a negation, namely, that of negated interest. Hence, I argue that the quality of pure aesthetic judgment is to be understood as an *infinite* form of judgment.

Disinterested pleasure presents us with quite a riddle. On the one hand, the feature of disinterest allows Kant to "bypass the faculty of desire,"[61] a move that is quite useful for separating aesthetic pleasure both from the gratification of agreeableness (involving pathological interest) and from the pleasure one takes in esteeming the good (involving practical interest).[62] Yet, that which is judged beautiful is not a mere phantasm conjured up by the subject. This implies that one would have an unavoidable interest in the existence of this beautiful object, simply insofar as it must exist outside of the subject in order to trigger a pleasurable aesthetic judgment. In this chapter, I not only show that the quality of aesthetic judgment should be understood as infinite, but also how understanding it as infinite allows us to pin-point the specific type of interest that is to be negated, while allowing other sorts of interests to be affirmed. I close by offering an alternative reading to Jens Kulenkampff's interpretation that the disinterestedness of aesthetic judgment severs the judging subject from the aesthetic pleasure so as to render aesthetic judgments devoid of indexicality (*indexlos*). On the contrary, I find that by reading disinterestedness through the logical function of infinite judgment, we can affirm the negation of a specific sort of interest, which by no means eliminates the subject's connection to the judgment.

---

[60] See: Crawford, Donald W. *Kant's Aesthetic Theory* (Madison: University of Wisconsin Press, 1974); Longuenesse, "Kant's Guiding Thread."
[61] Bernstein, Jay. "The Bernstein Tapes." The New School for Social Research, New York, NY. Lecture Recording from *10.17.2007.* Course Title: GPHI 6030 Kant's *Critique of Judgment*. Online.
[62] *Critique of the Power of Judgment*, § 5, 5:209.

IV.D Chapter Four: The Universal Validity of a Singular Judgment

Chapter four considers the *Quantity* of the judgment of taste. In an important sense, aesthetic judgment is both singular and universal, providing what Kant terms "the universal validity of a singular judgment" (*CPJ*, § 31, 5:281). This chapter accordingly traces the process of how a singular judgment becomes subjectively universal in the pure aesthetic. The singular aesthetic judgment does not simply run parallel to the universal aesthetic judgment. Rather, there must be a point of fusion, or transformation, between these two functions. To universalize one's singular judgment that a rose is beautiful into the statement that *all* roses are beautiful, however, would be to transform an aesthetic judgment into a logical judgment. This is not the sort of universality that Kant seeks.[63] I detail how a singular aesthetic judgment acquires a concept-free universal validity that ascribes a singular judgment to all judging subjects through the feeling of transcendental pleasure.

Guyer has taken issue with Kant's argument in the second moment. He objects that Kant overlooked the possibility that the singular judgment could apply to a particular group of *some* judgers, instead of to *all*.[64] This objection is interesting to me, since it speaks to the question of which logical functions are at work in the second moment. Thus, I respond to Guyer, showing how only a subjective universal validity could emerge from the path Kant describes pure aesthetic judgment to take. Moreover, I show that in pure aesthetic judgment the elements that would allow this to break off into particularity are absent.[65] I go on to identify one way in which pure aesthetic judgment picks out the judging subject as a particular sort of human among all humans in general, but this quickly shows itself to be far from the sort of particularization Guyer is after.

IV.E Chapter Five: Disjunctivity and the Form of Purposiveness

Chapter five examines the *Relation* of the judgment of taste. Many have taken the relation to be categorical, but such a reading would shed no light on purposiveness without a purpose, which is the term central to the third moment of the

---

[63] *Critique of the Power of Judgment*, § 8, 5:215.
[64] Guyer, *Kant and the Claims of Taste*, 117.
[65] This is in line with Allison's response to Guyer. Allison points out that all of the examples that Guyer offers for how an aesthetic judgment could hold for only a particular group of people "fall under the general rubric of the agreeable" (Allison, *Kant's Theory of Taste: A Reading of the Critique of Aesthetic Judgment*, 101).

judgment of taste. I argue that clarity is brought to this curious purposeless purposiveness if we understand it to emerge from a disjunctive relation in which the two mutually exclusive complements of art and nature are held together to constitute the sphere of beauty. Thus, the tulip is judged as beautiful when viewed as nature appearing *as if* it were art. This beauty, however, would be lost if it simply *were* nature appearing as nature, or art appearing *as* art. Art is only beautiful when it can be seen *as if* it were nature. The art/nature dichotomy contains mutually exclusive but complementary components that must be disjunctively held together for a pure aesthetic judgment of beauty to arise.

Kant gives further attention to purposiveness in the Critique of the Teleological Power of Judgment. Thus, in the process of examining the *forma finalis* of purposiveness, I draw upon his discussion of the final cause (*nexus finalis*) and effective cause (*nexus effectivus*) in § 65.[66] This not only allows the contrast between a purposiveness with and without purpose to crystalize, but it also gives me the opportunity to make a suggestion about how The Critique of Aesthetic Judgment relates to The Critique of Teleological Judgment.

IV.F Chapter Six: A Subjective, Exemplary Necessity

Chapter six pertains to the *Modality* of the judgment of taste. The modality of a judgment tells us nothing about the content of the judgment itself, but rather how "the relation of the whole judgment to the faculty of cognition is determined."[67] Hence, the fourth moment pronounces subjective universality with an exemplary, conditioned necessity. I examine how subjective necessity is "represented as objective under the presupposition of a common sense,"[68] by investigating what is *common* about the common sense. The subjective principle assuming the existence of the common sense is what allows pure aesthetic judgment to take up its position of necessity within the cognitive landscape. By laying claim to the status of an exemplary judgment through subjective necessity, the transformation that began in the second moment—from singular to universal—completes itself.

Kant's analysis of the fourth moment begins with a discussion cast in terms of the possible, actual and necessary from the table of the categories rather than in the modal terms that appear on the table of judgments.[69] I examine why the

---

[66] *Critique of the Power of Judgment*, § 10, 5:220.
[67] *Jäsche Logic*, § 30, 604.
[68] *Critique of the Power of Judgment*, § 21, 5:239.
[69] *Critique of the Power of Judgment*, § 21, 5:236.

relation between the logical functions and categories, of explainer and explained, is reversed in the quadrant of modality. I find that the key to this reversal lies in the fact that modality positions the already constituted judgment as a whole, rather than determining the content of the judgment itself. This intertwining of the categories and logical functions, thus, does not threaten Kant's remarks about the concept-independence of aesthetic judgments, because it does not pertain to how the judgment intrinsically functions.

V Delving into the Details of Kant's Logic

This project is greatly concerned with the logical functions. Thus, chapters three through six all begin with a detailed investigation into the operations of the logical functions from the relevant quadrant of the table of judgments. In the first *Critique,* Kant's discussion of how the logical functions operate spans just over three pages. This is enough to supply a rough outline of the key features and to touch on any noteworthy logical peculiarities, but it does not supply the more nuanced, detailed description that this project requires. As Huaping Lu-Adler notes, "the direct discussions of logic in the writings Kant himself prepared for publication are sparse and may very well be limited by the specific philosophical concerns attached to those publications."[70] For this reason, I have used the *Jäsche Logic* to fill in the details for the outline sketched by the first *Critique*. The *Jäsche Logic* is not one of Kant's own published texts, but rather a work that Kant commissioned his student Gottlob Benjamin Jäsche to compile for him from his lecture notes. In the preface, Jäsche reports that Kant expressed a "special, honorable confidence in [him], that, being acquainted with the principles of [Kant's] system in general, [he] would easily enter into the course of [Kant's] ideas, that [he] would not distort or falsify [Kant's] thoughts, but rather would present them with the required clarity and distinctness."[71]

This text is a great resource, because it supplies detail on issues that Kant's published works do not fully flesh out. It must, however, be used with caution. First, since Kant did not compile it himself there can be places where Jäsche made choices in the presentation of the ideas that are not the choices that Kant would have made. For this reason, the text should not be used in isolation from Kant's other works. Rather, the text should be employed to flesh out ideas

---

[70] Huaping Lu-Adler, "Constructing a Demonstration of Logical Rules, or How to Use Kant's Logic Corpus," in *Reading Kant's Lectures*, ed. Robert Clewis (Berlin: Walter de Gruyter, 2015), 139.
[71] *Jäsche Logic*, Preface 3.

that are already seen in abbreviated form in Kant's own published works. Should Kant's published works come into an irreconcilable conflict with something reported in the *Jäsche Logic*, the published works should take precedence on this point and the *Jäsche Logic* be set aside.

Another issue that arises with this text is the fact that Jäsche was working with notes from Kant's logic course, not notes on Kant's own original philosophy. This suggests that the *Jäsche Logic* may not be sensitive to issues where Kant departed from the standard view of the time. To this objection I have two responses. First, if Kant needed to differentiate his understanding of a certain logical term from that of his contemporaries, then we are likely to find a passage in his published works where he explicitly addresses this break. Second, if we look at Jäsche's report of why Kant chose him for this task, it was not because Jäsche showed a particular propensity for logic in general, but rather because Kant felt that Jäsche "would easily enter into the course of his [Kant's] ideas, that [he] would not distort or falsify his [Kant's] thoughts, but rather would present them with the required clarity and distinctness."[72] This gives us reason to believe that Jäsche's task was not simply to put together a logic textbook, but rather a book that would convey what Kant found to be the superior understanding of logic. Thus, the *Jäsche Logic* may be more general than a text that would report only Kant's own insights into logic and must be used carefully with attention to the fact that Jäsche may have made choices in the presentation of the material that can lead us away from Kant's own position. That said, it can still serve as an important resource for teasing out points of detail that seem to be assumed as the background of Kant's own published works and are for that reason not discussed outright in those works.

J. Micheal Young, English translator of the Cambridge Edition of *Lectures on Logic* (which includes the *Jäsche Logic*), cautions that, "[t]he manual must be interpreted with care [...] and it has to be appraised in light of other available materials."[73] The same conclusion is reached by Huaping Lu-Adler in her article "Constructing a Demonstration of Logical Rules, or How to Use Kant's Logic Corpus" (2015). She begins by setting out the problem that neither Kant's own published remarks on logic, nor the *Jäsche Logic*, nor the transcribed logic lectures, nor Kant's handwritten notes on logic "can alone represent Kant's view on logic in a way that is at once reliable, precise, and complete."[74] Lu-Adler does not find

---

72 *Jäsche Logic*, Preface 3.
73 Young, 2004, xviii.
74 Lu-Adler, "Constructing a Demonstration of Logical Rules, or How to Use Kant's Logic Corpus," 137.

that "Jäsche's problematic editorial methods" discredit the work.[75] She finds instead that the text "is indispensible – albeit alone insufficient – for our understanding of Kant's view on logic."[76] This aligns with Terry Boswell's observation in his article "On the Textual Authority of Kant's *Logic*" (1988) where he concludes that, "[w]hat is questionable from a philological point of view would be the exclusive use of this one document."[77] Thus, I have followed Lu-Alder's recommendation of citing the *Jäsche Logic* in order to "articulate fully certain points that are already contained in the writings Kant himself prepared for publication."[78]

VI A Terminological Note: Object

The German language provides two terms that can both be translated into English as "object" (*Gegenstand*, *Objekt*). This presents a certain difficulty for discussing German philosophy in English, and even more so for translating it. T. F. Geraets, W. A. Suchting, and H. S. Harris discuss Hegel's technical use of these two terms in the comments on terminology at the beginning of the English translation of Hegel's *The Encyclopedia Logic*:

> In the technical sense, *Gegenstand* contrasts with *Objekt*, which designates objectivity in general, independence of the subject, *Gegenstand* signifying (as its etymology suggests) an object of consciousness, mediated by and thus changing in relation to it.[79]

---

[75] Lu-Adler, "Constructing a Demonstration of Logical Rules, or How to Use Kant's Logic Corpus," 137.
[76] Lu-Adler, "Constructing a Demonstration of Logical Rules, or How to Use Kant's Logic Corpus," 137.
[77] Terry Boswell, "On the Textual Authority of Kant's *Logic*." In *History and Philosophy of Logic* 9–2 (1988: 193–203), 201.
[78] Lu-Adler, "Constructing a Demonstration of Logical Rules, or How to Use Kant's Logic Corpus," 140.
[79] T.F. Geraets, W. A. Suchting and H. S. Harris, *Translators' Preface*, in *The Encyclopaedia Logic: The Encyclopaedia of Philosophical Sciences 1 with the Zusatze*. trans. and eds. Theodore F. Geraets, W. A. Suchting & H. S. Harris, (Indianapolis: Hackett Publishing, 1991), xliii. This bears a certain resemblance to the way that Allison differentiates between the two for Kant. He designates *Objekt* as the "judgmental or logical conception of an object" in contrast to *Gegenstand* which is the weightier "'real' sense of object" that connects to "the notion of objective reality," and thus is an object "in the sense of an actual entity or state of affairs (an object of possible experience)" (1983, 136; 135).

Aside from the complications that such terms can present, for Hegel scholars they also open up a special avenue for interpreting the text. That is, they create the possibility of working through a given philosophical issue in terms of the object's status. In Kantian scholarship, Henry Allison uses this terminological distinction to argue that,

> [...] in the Transcendental Deduction, objective validity and objective reality are connected with different conceptions of an object. Since it is linked to judgment, objective validity goes together with a judgment or logical conception of an object (an object in *sensu logico*). This is an extremely broad sense of 'object', which encompasses anything that can serve as the subject in a judgment. The term that Kant generally uses (at least in the Deduction) for an object in this sense is *Objekt*. Correlatively, the notion of objective reality is connected with a "real" sense of object, that is, with an object in the sense of an actual entity or state of affairs (an object of possible experience). Kant's term for an object in this sense is *Gegenstand*.[80]

Note Allison's parenthetical remark "at least in the Deduction," indicating his recognition that Kant does not always invoke these terms in a clearly delineated technical manner. In his article "Six Perspectives on the Object in Kant's Theory of Knowledge," S. R. Palmquist expresses a similar sentiment. He writes:

> Kant's use of the word 'object' (*Objekt* or *Gegenstand*) is a potential source of much confusion and ambiguity. Sometimes he employs it as a general term either nontechnically to refer to an ordinary 'thing' which is met in experience, or technically to mean something like 'a thing which stands in some kind of relation—potential, actual or necessary—to some kind of subject'. Yet at other times he employs it as a more specific term referring to one or another of the particular stages in the process of determining a thing to be an object. Consequently, its meaning is not always evident when Kant uses it without a qualifying adjective [cf. B2:76 and G3:778]. This ambiguity results, no doubt, from the fact that he explains the role of the object in his theory of knowledge primarily by implementing six other 'object-terms' (as I shall call them).[81]

Palmquist proceeds to develop an interpretation of "Kant's six object-terms" arguing that "the terms 'positive noumenon,', 'negative noumenon' and 'phenomenon' are the empirical correlates of the transcendental terms 'thing in itself', 'transcendental object' and 'appearance', respectively [...]."[82]

---

[80] Henry Allison, *Kant's Transcendental Idealism: An Interpretation and Defense* (New Haven: Yale University Press, 1983) 135.
[81] Palmquist, S. R., "Six Perspectives on the Object in Kant's Theory of Knoweldge," *Dialectica* 40, no. 2 (1986): 121–151; 122.
[82] Palmquist, "Six Perspectives on the Object in Kant's Theory of Knoweldge," 142.

Moreover, for the set of concerns I will be investigating in Kant's third *Critique*, designating the object as either an *Objekt* or *Gegenstand* does not necessarily clarify the matter. The issue interrogated in my first chapter, for instance, is not whether the aesthetic object that occasions the judgment of taste is purely logical or "real". According to the terminological distinction that Allison suggests for interpreting the Deduction, whatever occasions the judgment of taste will admittedly have more to do with a *Gegenstand* than an *Objekt*, because it centers on the intuitional reception of sense data and not empty "logical concepts of an object."[83] This is not the salient distinction for understanding what it is that occasions the judgment of taste. The primary question I will be investigating in relation to the aesthetic object is, rather, whether it is an unconceptualized or conceptualized intuition. Thus, the key distinction is not between the two German terms that can both be translated into English as "object," but rather between two different types of object that Kant discusses, appearance (*Erscheinung*) and phenomenon (*Phänomen*). I find the object that occasions the activity of aesthetic judgment to arise in the tension between phenomenon and appearance. In the first *Critique*, Kant distinguishes between these two:

> [...] there are two conditions under which alone the cognition of an object is possible: first, intuition, through which it is given, but only as appearance; second, concept, through which an object is thought that corresponds to this intuition.[84]

Longuenesse draws on this passage to differentiate appearance from phenomenon:

> When Kant, in the text quoted previously, writes that "the object is given, *but only as appearance,*" this restrictive formula may first be intended to distinguish the appearance from the object in itself, outside all representation, and thus to restrict spatial and temporal forms to appearances or "indeterminate objects of empirical intuition." But it is also intended to distinguish, *within the realm of representation,* between the object "only as" appearance and the object "as" object. In other words, it is intended to distinguish the object that might be called "preobjective" (the indeterminate object of empirical intuition, prior to any distinction between the representation and the object of representation) from the "objective" object, or the object "corresponding to" intuition. For this distinction to be possible, and therefore "for the cognition of an object *as object,*" a second type of representation is required: concepts.[85]

---

83 Allison, *Kant's Transcendental Idealism: An Interpretation and Defense*, 135.
84 *Critique of Pure Reason*, A92–3/B125.
85 Longuenesse, *Kant and the Capacity to Judge*, 24.

She proceeds to show how this differentiation between appearances and phenomena as two sorts of objects can be seen as early as Kant's *Inaugural Dissertation*. In this manner we can distinguish between "*apparentia* and *phaenomenon*" as "the object 'simply as appearance' (the indeterminate object of an empirical intuition) and the object 'as object,' 'corresponding to intuition.'"[86] Longuenesse later summaries these as, "(1) the object as *appearance (apparentia,* according to the *Dissertation)* or the "indeterminate object of an empirical intuition"; and (2) the object as *phenomenon,* or the empirical object as *determined by concepts.*"[87]

In chapter two I will put forward my layered reading of the judgment of taste, suggesting that the experience of an empirical object occasions such a judgment, but that it is not something cognized in this object (i.e., as *phenomenon*) that throws the faculties into the harmonious free play of the judgment of taste. Rather, this free play is occasioned by reception of an intuitional excess that accompanies this empirical object (i.e. as mere *appearance*) and is a part of the intuition that can never be cognized in the object, because it can never be subsumed by a concept (can never become a *phenomenon*). Thus, that which specifically triggers a pure aesthetic judgment of taste is the uncognizable intuitional excess that accompanies a cognized empirical object. To put this in the object terms just discussed, I understand the cognized object as a phenomenon (or, as Longuenesse puts it, the object as object) and the intuitional excess as an appearance (the pre-cognized object). These two are received together as the empirical object that occasions the judgment of taste.

---

[86] Longuenesse, *Kant and the Capacity to Judge,* 25. This also aligns with how Mark Okrent distinguishes between these terms writing, "There is no question that Kant makes the distinction between the appearance, the object of mere intuition, and the phenomenon, or the object which is thought corresponding to this intuition" (Okrent, Mark, "Acquaintance and Cognition," in *Aesthetics and Cognition in Kant's Critical Philosophy,* ed. Rebecca Kukla [Cambridge: Cambridge University Press, 2006], 93). Okrent thus entertains a two-object solution to the question of how animals experience the world: "We represent 'phenomena' (*Phaenomena*), both intuitively and conceptually, as well as intuitively representing appearances; animals represent only 'appearances' (*Erscheinungen*)" (Okrent, "Acquaintance and Cognition," 93). He does not, however, find that it provides a satisfactory picture for animal sapience. Orkent's treatment of this issue is engaged with in more detail in chapter one.
[87] Longuenesse, *Kant and the Capacity to Judge,* 107–8.

VII The Uniquely Human Judgment of Taste

One theme of particular interest that continually weaves through my project is the special dimension of human meaning and feeling described by the third *Critique*. We first begin to see this in Kant's description of the judgment of taste as something that can only arise in a human judging subject. In the first moment of the judgment of taste this surfaces in the comparative analysis Kant uses between the satisfaction that pure aesthetic judgment involves and other sorts of satisfaction: the agreeable and the good. Whereas the agreeable is experienced by all embodied creatures (animals and humans alike) and the good is esteemed by rational beings (humans and spirits),

> [...] beauty is valid only for human beings, i.e., animal but also rational beings, but not merely the latter (e.g., spirits), rather as beings who are at the same time animal [...].[88]

This demarcates beauty as a uniquely human terrain. Over the course of my analysis we see how the world is not simply cognizable by us as described in the first *Critique*, but furthermore how this world that we cognize becomes meaningful in a way that is specifically compelling for human feelings. In aesthetically judging the world, we feel it to be infused with spirit. Kant explains, while remarking on artistic works that demonstrate academic skill but lack "spirit":

> Spirit, in an aesthetic significance, means the animating principle in the mind. That, however, by which this principle animates the soul, the material which it uses for this purpose, is that which purposively sets the mental powers into motion, i.e., into a play that is self-maintaining and even strengthens the powers to that end. Now I maintain that this principle is nothing other than the faculty for the presentation of aesthetic ideas; by an aesthetic idea, however, I mean that representation of the imagination that occasions much thinking though without it being possible for any determinate thought, i.e., concept, to be adequate to it, which, consequently, no language fully attains or can make intelligible. – One readily sees that it is the counterpart (pendant) of an idea of reason, which is, conversely, a concept to which no intuition (representation of the imagination) can be adequate.[89]

Thus, in the process of pure aesthetic judging, one's faculties are animated by spirit, so that aesthetic ideas may be presented, occasioning "much thinking" without settling into "any determinate thought," and thus inspiring us to ideas that go beyond what words can capture.

---

[88] *Critique of the Power of Judgment*, § 5, 5:210.
[89] *Critique of the Power of Judgment*, § 49, 5:313–314.

Aesthetic judgments of taste do not reveal something behind appearances, but rather add a layer of specifically human significance to them. Gazing upon the determined empirical object but judging in accordance with taste, a human feeling takes hold on the transcendental level. It is this feeling, in turn, that incites "much thinking." The first *Critique* having already sufficiently investigated how experience is possible, we might say that the third *Critique* looks at how the feeling of spirit is possible. It shows that empirical objects are not condemned to blight under determinative cognition, but that beauty may grace their surfaces as the judging subject lingers in contemplation.

Chapter One:
Renegotiating Kantian Constraints, Intuiting without Concepts

What happens to a judgment, if there is no concept to act as its determining grounds? From the standpoint of Kant's first *Critique*, such a judgment would seem to be so meaninglessly blind that we might hesitate to call it a judgment at all. Knowledge can only occur where both of the two key mental components are involved: intuition and concept.[1] As Kant famously declares,

> Without sensibility no object would be given to us, and without understanding none would be thought. Thoughts without content are empty, intuitions without concepts are blind.[2]

The intuitions without concepts, which are so easily dismissed here, reemerge in the third *Critique* as unexpectedly purposive for our faculties. Far from dissolving into a meaningless abyss of caprice, we find in aesthetic judgment that

> [the] inner relationship [between the faculties of imagination and understanding] is optimal for the animation of both powers of the mind [...] and this disposition cannot be determined except through the feeling (*not by concepts*).[3]

Thus, aesthetic judgment presents us with a bit of a riddle—a mode of judgment that does not operate through concepts and yet boasts an optimal animation of the faculties. The high status of aesthetic judgment is further illustrated in Kant's discussion of how an aesthetic idea "occasions much thinking, though without it being possible for any determinate thought, i.e., concept, to be adequate to it."[4] Not only is a concept not determining this idea, but what is aesthetically stirred up in it reaches beyond our conceptual grasp.[5] Thus, we "linger over the consid-

---

[1] *Critique of Pure Reason*, A74/B50.
[2] *Critique of Pure Reason*, A51/B75.
[3] *Critique of the Power of Judgment*, Bk. I, § 21, 5:239, emphasis added. The concept independence of aesthetic judgment is repeatedly remarked on by Kant. For instance, "The aesthetic power of judgment is thus a special faculty for judging things in accordance with a rule but not in accordance with concepts" (Introduction, IIX., 5: 194).
[4] *Critique of the Power of Judgment*, Bk. I, § 49, 5:314.
[5] It is interesting, here, to note that what Kant means by judging without determinative concepts differs from the way that Hegel describes going beyond the determined concept in the *Geistesphilosophie*. With a close reading of Fragment 17, Jennifer Ann Bates explains that, for Hegel, the reason to break out of the determinative concept is to escape from becoming fixed

eration of the beautiful," and in doing so "this consideration strengthens and reproduces itself."⁶

This chapter lays out the set of concerns that lead me to offer a layered interpretation of how Kant's aesthetic judgment functions. Kant describes aesthetic judgment as a mode of merely reflective judgment that does not depend on concepts in the way that determinative judgments do. As Kant tells us in the First Introduction, aesthetic judgment is a "judgment which precedes all concepts of the object," and as such it "has its determining ground in the power of judgment, unmixed with any other faculty of cognition."⁷ Attempts can be made to understand this quizzical feature of aesthetic judgment in one of the following three ways: 1. concepts are altogether absent, 2. concepts are present but severely limited in their operations, 3. concepts are present but function in a very different manner than in determinative judgments. For instance, Béatrice Longuenesse takes the first view in "Kant's Leading Thread in the Analytic of the Beautiful" where she writes, "But Kant is adamant that judgments of taste are *not* cognitive judgments, and that *as* aesthetic judgments, they do not rest on categories."⁸ I will be calling this the strong view. The second view, which I will be calling the limiting view, often takes the form of the suggestion that the pure concepts are operative, while empirical concepts are not. Rudolf Makkreel gives voice to this view in his article "Reflection, Reflective Judgment, and Aesthetic Exemplarity" where he argues that since the categories are a priori and formal, "categories such as substance and causality are applicable to all possible phenomenal objects. No special reflective or technical skill is necessary for their application."⁹ This would make the categories already operative before the reflective moment

---

on one side of the dialectic, the intellectual side. Thus, Hegel proposes to off-set the determined concept by "acknowledging the 'thereness'" of the thing conceptualized (Bates, *Hegel's Theory of Imagination*, 24). Bates further elaborates that this does not involve positing the thing in itself, because to do so would be to posit a determinative concept of what is determined (Ibid.). Although Kant's move away from determinative concepts in the third *Critique* does not appear *prima facie* to be a move toward the object, but rather burrows deeper into the workings of the faculties in the subject, his shift away from determinative concepts eventually does raise questions similar to Hegel's about the object in an unconceptualized mode of "thereness," as the thing *about which we have* a determinative concept.

6 *Critique of the Power of Judgment*, Bk. I, § 12, 5:222.
7 *Critique of the Power of Judgment*, First Introduction, XI., 20:243.
8 Longuenesse, "Kant's Leading Thread in the Analytic of the Beautiful." In *Aesthetics and Cognition in Kant's Critical Philosophy*. edited by Rebecca Kukla (Cambridge: Cambridge University Press, 2006), 195.
9 Makkreel, "Reflection, Reflective Judgment, and Aesthetic Exemplarity," 225.

Longuenesse identifies with the reflection of aesthetic judgment.[10] Lewis White Beck takes a similar position, writing "The concepts which Kant holds do *not* play a role in the construction of (pure) aesthetic experience are not categorial concepts but empirical."[11] The third view according to which there is a different conceptual operation in the judgment of taste is held by Henry Allison, who writes "that the beautiful is the exhibition of an indeterminate concept of the *understanding*."[12] He takes this to be in accordance with the way that the judgment of taste "is a judgment of mere reflection, that is, one not issuing in cognition, which would require a determinate concept."[13] As Allison takes the indeterminate concept exhibited in the beautiful to be of the understanding, he concludes that:

> An indeterminable concept of the understanding would be one that is not schematizable, which means that it is merely the form of a concept, not an actual concept. Consequently, we must take Kant's point here to be that the beautiful is that which has the form of the exhibition of *some concept or other* (it being undetermined which one), and this is fully in accord with the accounts in the Introductions and the Analytic of the Beautiful considered in the first two parts of this study.[14]

I will ultimately be arguing for a specific sort of limiting view that does not fall neatly into any of the three options listed above, but does incorporate elements of each. The view I put forward in chapter two will address the difficulties presented in chapter one by limiting the involvement of concepts to certain layers of the activity of judging. The first layer is a normal determinative cognition of an object where the concept determines an intuition, but with a part of the intuition unable to be determined in this way. Thus, the subsumptive activity of the concepts is complete for the part of the intuition subsumed, but there remains a part of the intuition that is unable to be subsumed. The second layer exhibits an activity of judging that is as close as one can come to what the strong view describes. Here, neither empirical concepts nor the categories are operative, although there is the involvement of an "indeterminate concept of the understand-

---

10 Makkreel further elaborates on his account of how the categories may be operative in aesthetic judgment without empirical concepts in Makkreel, *Imagination and Interpretation in Kant: The Hermeneutical Import of the Critique of Judgment Imagination and Interpretation in Kant*.
11 Lewis White Beck, *Essays on Kant and Hume*, (New Haven: Yale University Press, 1978), 56.
12 Henry Allison, *Kant's Theory of Taste: A Reading of the Critique of Aesthetic Judgment* (Cambridge, MA: Cambridge University Press, 2001), 308.
13 Allison, *Kant's Theory of Taste: A Reading of the Critique of Aesthetic Judgment*, 308.
14 Allison, *Kant's Theory of Taste: A Reading of the Critique of Aesthetic Judgment*, 308.

ing" that can never yield cognition.¹⁵ It is then in the third layer that we see the discursive activity that is inspired to conceptually grasp after the feeling of pure aesthetic pleasure, unable to ever subsume it under any of the possible determinate concepts that suggest themselves.¹⁶

Over the course of this chapter, I will investigate the first two of these possible interpretations—the strong view and the limiting view, respectively—to show that on their own they do not paint a satisfactory picture of aesthetic judgment. The view that concepts function differently in aesthetic than determinative judgments will be discussed in the next chapter where I lay out my layered solution. Kant has two competing criteria for aesthetic judgment. On the one hand,

---

15 *Critique of the Power of Judgment*, § 23, 5:245.
16 My idea of bringing together the strong and limiting views is similar to Guyer's idea of bringing together what he terms the precognitive and multicognitive views through his inauguration of a metacognitive view in his article: Paul Guyer "The Harmony of the Faculties Revisited," In *Aesthetics and Cognition in Kant's Critical Philosophy*, edited by Rebecca Kukla. (Cambridge: Cambridge University Press, 2006). At the same time, however, my layered solution stratifies the activity of judging in a way that Guyer's metacognitive view does not. The similarities and differences between my view and his are detailed in the next chapter. The view Guyer describes as 'precognitive' is similar to the strong view: "[...] on this interpretation, the harmony of imagination and understanding would be a state of mind that satisfies all the conditions for cognition except the final condition [application of a determinate concept] that would transform it into actual cognition" (*Ibid.*, 165). Guyer identifies some of the proponents of this view to be Dieter Henrich ("Kant's Explanation of Aesthetic Judgment," 1992, 38), Donald Crawford (*Kant's Aesthetic Theory*, 90), Ralf Meerbote ("Reflection on Beauty," in *Essays in Kant's Aesthetics*, eds. Cohen, Ted & Paul Guyer [Chicago, IL: University of Chicago Press, 1982], 55–86), and even himself in his previous works (Allison, *Kant and the Claims of Taste*, 66). Guyer goes on to describe how: "An alternative class of interpretations maintains that the free play of the faculties does not satisfy all but one of the normal conditions for cognition, but rather that it satisfies all of them, although only in an indeterminate way: Instead of suggesting *no* determinate concept for the manifold of intuition that it furnishes, a beautiful object suggests an indeterminate or open-ended *manifold* of concepts for the manifold of intuition, allowing the mind to flit back and forth playfully and enjoyably among different ways of conceiving the same object without allowing or requiring it to settle down on one determinate way of conceiving the object. We can call such interpretations 'multicognitive' in order to convey that on this sort of account the free play is precisely among a multiplicity of possible concepts and hence cognitions suggested by the beautiful object" (Guyer, "The Harmony of the Faculties Revisited," 165–166). Here, the concepts are prevented from carrying out determinative subsumption and hence limited in their function. Thus this view represents the form of what I have called the limiting view in which the concepts function differently. Guyer cites the following as examples of a multicognitive interpretation: Seel "Über den Grund der Lust an schönen Gegenständen: Kritische Fragen an die Ästhetik Kants,"1988, 344; Rush, "The Harmony of the Faculties," 2001, 52; Allison, *Kant's Theory of Taste: A Reading of the Critique of Aesthetic Judgment*, 2001, 171; Budd, "The Pure Judgment of Taste as an Aesthetic Reflective Judgment," 2001, 255.

it is somehow not to involve the subsumption of an intuition under a concept. On the other hand, it is both about objects of experience, and able to lead to a rich contemplation of "aesthetic ideas."[17] We will see that these two stipulations, ultimately, cannot be met without the use of concepts. For this reason, I will argue that the best way to make sense of this is if aesthetic judgment is understood as a streamlined process with distinct acts of judging occurring on three different layers, the first and the third yield discursively articulable judgment statements ("This is a tulip" and "This tulip is beautiful", accordingly). Meanwhile, the middle layer will be what I call properly aesthetic. Here, the act of judging operates in accordance with the logical functions, but with no object involved to be determined by concepts.

The objective of this chapter is to show why such a layered reading is necessary, and this will be done by tracing out the struggle that we find ourselves in if an unstratified picture of aesthetic judgment is assumed. Flattened conceptions of aesthetic judgment often treat it as if it were driven by the aim to produce the statement that proclaims the object's aesthetic value, "This x is beautiful." Over the course of this chapter, it will become clear why such a presumption —assumed both by the strong and by the limiting view—is mistaken.

According to the strong view, Kant has re-imagined the role of concepts in aesthetic judgment, entirely eliminating them so as to give us a form of judgment that is free of concepts, altogether. I will test out this reading by investigating whether there would even be a way of observing something beautiful without concepts mediating the encounter. I work through the possible modes of awareness in which one could encounter the beautiful (experience, acquaintance, perception and representation without consciousness), ultimately determining that the first three involve concepts and although the final mode might be without concepts, it is also without consciousness, and thus too weak to support aesthetic judgment.

At this point I turn to the reading of the concepts as having a limited involvement in aesthetic judgment. If the limiting view is to be seriously entertained, then one must first determine which mode of encounter limits the operation of concepts to the greatest extent without impinging upon other aspects of how Kant describes aesthetic judgement. Following this line of questioning, I work through the previously discussed modes of encounter, but in reverse (representation without consciousness, perception, acquaintance, experience). At the end of the chapter, this investigation may appear to have brought us full cir-

---

17 *Critique of the Power of Judgment*, § 49, 5:314.

cle. Be that as it may, the circle is hermeneutic, not vicious.[18] Each time we touch upon the modes of encounter, we do so differently, and the conclusion that one encounters the beautiful in the mode of experience means something different at the close of the chapter than it would have initially.

Moreover, this conclusion signals only another beginning. While at this point it will have, on the one hand, become clear that the process of aesthetic judgment must begin with the experience of an aesthetic object, it will also have become clear that aesthetic judgment must go beyond this experience. The conclusion that one aesthetically judges an object of experience is, on its own, unsatisfactory. Although it accounts for certain aspects of Kant's aesthetic theory, if it is left at this, then all peculiarities about the role of concepts vanish in the process. Thus, once we have worked our way from conceptualized experience to representation without consciousness, and back again, it will have become clear why we should consider an entirely different interpretive route—one that understands aesthetic judgment to involve not just one, but three, layers of judging. This layered solution will then be carefully laid out in chapter two.

I Intuitions and Objects

The strong view would be a reading in which Kant's remarks are taken to mean that concepts, cannot be involved in aesthetic judgment at all. This view will ultimately be rejected, because it would corner us into a framework that can neither support aesthetic judgment as pertaining to some singular thing ("This flow-

---

18 Martin Heidegger comments on how philosophical inquiries tend toward circular constructions, which, unlike a meaningless circular argument, actually acquire greater meaning over their course: "We have indeed already shown, in analyzing the structure of understanding in general, that what gets censured inappropriately as a 'circle', belongs to the essence and to the distinctive character of understanding as such. In spite of this, if the problematic of fundamental ontology is to have its hermeneutical situation clarified, our investigation must now come back explicitly to this 'circular argument'[...]. Or does this pre-supposing have the character of an understanding projection, in such a manner indeed that the interpretation by which such an understanding gets developed, will let that which is to be interpreted *put itself into words for the very first time, so that it may decide of its own accord whether, as the entity which it is, it has the state of Being for which it has been disclosed in the projection with regard to its formal aspects*? Is there any other way at all by which an entity can put itself into words with regard to its Being? We cannot ever 'avoid' a 'circular' proof in the existential analytic, because such an analytic does not do *any* proving *at all* by the rules of the 'logic of consistency'" (Martin Heidegger, *Being and Time*, trans. Macquarrie and E. Robinson. [New York: Harper & Row, 1962] 362–363/314–315).

er"[19]), nor inspire aesthetic ideas.[20] For this study, however, it is meaningful to investigate precisely how the strong view fails, as doing so will give us a better picture of how aesthetic judgment operates and what elements of Kant's cognitive machinery from the first *Critique* can be involved. First, let us get the lay of the land for the strong view by considering what complications it would need to resolve regarding intuitions and objects in order to stand firm as an adequate interpretation of Kant's aesthetic theory.

In "Acquaintance and Cognition," Mark Okrent tackles a strikingly similar problem when he asks what it is that the Kantian framework would claim his dog, Mac, to see when he sees a bus.[21] Animals, according to Kant, lack the discursive abilities necessary to conceptualize their experiences. Thus, with this question, Okrent is, like us, seeking a mode of engagement that does not depend on concepts and, furthermore, investigating what an entirely unconceptualized encounter would be like, if, indeed, such a thing should prove itself even to be possible. Kant regards dogs as lacking the ability to employ concepts altogether, and thus having no choice in experiencing the world in a concept-independent manner. Humans, on the other hand, may not be employing the conceptual ability that they *do* have when making aesthetic judgments. For this reason, Okrent's account of Kant's view of animal sapience illuminates the complications faced by a strong view of aesthetic judgment. His analysis can serve ours as a sort of control group study, which gives a straightforward picture of how this could work for a case in which Kant's system does not even allow for the possibility of employing concepts. Thus, the Kantian view of animal sapience affords us a clarity that we do not get with aesthetic judgment. In aesthetic judgment concepts *could* still turn out to be in play, and in evaluating the strong view our task is to determine whether or not they must.[22]

The strong view would draw a certain parallel between a person stimulated to judge aesthetically and a dog stimulated to bark at a bus. Both cases raise the

---

19 *Critique of the Power of Judgment*, § 32, 5: 282.
20 *Critique of the Power of Judgment*, § 49, 5:314.
21 Okrent, "Acquaintance and Cognition." In this article Okrent is not interested in the issue of animal sapience in its own right, but only in how it would be conceived in a Kantian framework. For a consideration of this issue in its own right, see: Robert W. Lurz, *The Philosophy of Animal Minds* (Cambridge: Cambridge University Press, 2009).
22 By saying that Kant is clearer on the non-involvement of concepts in animal consciousness than he is on the status of their involvement in aesthetic judgment, I do not mean to claim that Kant's (meager) account of animal consciousness is satisfactory, let alone more satisfactory than his theory of aesthetic judgment. Indeed, after various attempts to make Kant's account work, Okrent's concludes that Kant will need to give up the premises that prevent us from being able to view animals as cognizing objects (Okrent, "Acquaintance and Cognition," 107).

same problem of whether the object to which one responds can be experienced without concepts. As Okrent summarizes the issue:

> So any subject, such as my dog Mac, who lacks this ability to cognize or recognize things *as* this or that, also lacks the ability to have thoughts [...]. Kant suggested that thought requires the use of concepts [...] and that the use and acquisition of concepts require reflection, or self-consciousness [...]. To cognize something as something is to recognize that the thing belongs to a type, and this recognition just *is* the application of a concept [...]. But it appears that the only way to acquire such a concept so as to be able to apply it is to reflect on the relations among one's various representations, and the ability to do this in turn appears to depend upon the ability to represent various representations in a single mental act. So any agent who lacks this reflective ability lacks the ability to think of things as this or that, and with this disability, also lacks the capacity to think at all.[23]

Dogs appear not to have a discursive human understanding that can provide the concepts under which their intuitions may be subsumed. In the first *Critique*, Kant tells us that "[a]n object, however, is that in the concept of which the manifold of a given intuition is united."[24] Without the concept in which the manifold must be united so as to be experienced as an object, it would seem that a dog cannot experience the bus as an object. Okrent does not contest this interpretation of Kant's view, although he questions whether it accurately reflects how we see dogs behaving:

> From our armchairs, we have come to the conclusion that Mac has no perceptions of objects. But this can't be right. In our dealings with our dogs we count on their object recognition abilities all of the time. Mac's behavior around the bus suggests both that he responds to it as an object [...] and that his ability to recognize the object depends upon a capacity to use the partial presence of the bus's sensory properties as *marks* for the presence of the object that is the bus.[25]

Dissatisfied with a simple dismissal of Mac's ability to experience an object, Okrent further investigates what avenues of engagement Kant does leave open to animals. The question of *animal sapience* in Kant can provide helpful insight into what sort of mental engagement would be possible for our engagement with the beautiful under the strong view, that is, if concepts are taken to be barred from aesthetic judgment. As opposed to the case of humans—where we are concerned with disentangling conceptual from non-conceptual processes—with animals no careful sorting is necessary, because we are presented with creatures

---

23 Okrent, "Acquaintance and Cognition," 87–88.
24 *Critique of Pure Reason*, B137.
25 Okrent, "Acquaintance and Cognition," 88.

that Kant presumes have no access to concepts or conceptual processes in the first place.

Okrent cuts straight to the heart of the issue. If we take animals to have no concepts, then all they will have are intuitions. These intuitions, however, cannot be of objects, because having an intuition of an object

> depends not only on the synthetic activity of imagination, but also on the reflective capacity of the understanding to explicitly represent the unitary, rule-governed character of that activity [to take this position] is to assert that no agent who is incapable of such reflection, such as my dog, is capable of perceiving, or intuiting, objects at all.[26]

As Okrent points out, in the *Jäsche Logic* Kant seems to think that intuitions do relate to objects ("All cognitions, that is, all representations related with consciousness to an object, are either *intuitions* or *concepts*"[27]) and that animals "are *acquainted* with objects too, but they do not *cognize* them,"[28] meaning that they acquire this acquaintance with objects only through intuition.

This predicament is quite similar to the one that faces us in the third *Critique*. Kant repeatedly casts concepts aside in his theory of aesthetic judgment. Two prime examples of this can be found in the following passages:

> The aesthetic power of judgment is thus a special faculty for judging things in accordance with a rule but not in accordance with concepts.[29]

And then again:

> Hence the judgment of taste is merely contemplative [...]. But this contemplation itself is also not directed to concepts; for the judgment of taste is not a cognitive judgment (neither a theoretical nor a practical one), and hence it is neither grounded on concepts nor aimed at them.[30]

And yet he clearly intends for an object to be involved in the process of aesthetic judgment. Describing how such a judgment is carried out, he writes, "I must immediately hold the object up to my feeling of pleasure and displeasure [...]."[31] In-

---

26 Okrent, "Acquaintance and Cognition," 92–93.
27 *The Jäsche Logic*, § 1, 589
28 *The Jäsche Logic*, VIII, 570
29 *Critique of the Power of Judgment*, First Introduction, II., 5:194.
30 *Critique of the Power of Judgment*, § 5, 5: 209.
31 *Critique of the Power of Judgment*, § 8, 5: 215.

deed, at times, he even discusses this judgment's independence from concepts *and* the "determination" of an object in the very same breath:

> Now the judgment of taste, however, determines the object, independently of concepts, with regard to satisfaction and the predicate of beauty.[32]

In this manner, we see that in both Kant's account of *animal sapience* and aesthetic judgment the same tension arises between an intuition without concepts and the need for an object to be involved.

II Pure and Empirical Concepts

Before continuing, let us briefly pause to investigate precisely what is to be understood through the term "concept." A number of commentators readily take Kant's insistence that aesthetic judgment does not involve concepts to mean that it involves neither empirical concepts nor the pure concepts of the understanding (the categories).[33] Some have attempted to understand this as only disallowing empirical concepts and not the pure concepts.[34] Since the categories have a determinative function, however, it does not seem possible for an indeterminate form of judgment pertaining to a sensible intuition to makes use of them without this becoming a determining judgment in the process. Moreover, as Paul Guyer points out, the Transcendental Dialectic is set up in such a manner that the categories cannot be applied to a sensible intuition without invoking the rest of the apparatus, which includes empirical concepts. Guyer writes,

> [...] Kant cannot have thought that beautiful objects are those to which we apply the categories without applying any determinate concepts to them, since he clearly thought that the categories are only the forms of determinate concepts and can be applied to intuitions only through determinate concepts.[35]

Thus, there can be two different versions of the strong view. According to the strictest version of this view, Kant intends for concepts to play no role whatsoever in aesthetic judgment, and this goes for the pure concepts of the understanding, just as well as for empirical concepts. The weaker version of this view would

---

[32] *Critique of the Power of Judgment*, Bk. I, § 9, 5: 219.
[33] See Longuenesse, "Kant's Leading Thread in the Analytic of the Beautiful," 195.
[34] See Makkreel, "Reflection, Reflective Judgment, and Aesthetic Exemplarity," 225 and Lewis White Beck, *Essays on Kant and Hume*, 1978, 56.
[35] Guyer, "The Harmony of the Faculties Revisited," 180–181.

contend that no empirical concepts are operative, but allow for the involvement of the categories. In this manner the weaker version of the strong view bleeds into what I have termed the limiting view, i.e., concepts are involved, but there is a limitation on what *sorts* of concepts can be involved. For this reason, let us begin by examining the strongest version of the strong view, according to which neither pure, nor empirical concepts can be involved, reserving the weaker version, which would permit the involvement of the categories, for our discussion of the limiting view.

II.A The Strong View: Aesthetic Encounter Without Concepts?

Can the strong view reconcile intuitions without concepts to Kant's tendency to relate aesthetic judgment to an object? To do so would require that there be a way in which one's faculties could be stimulated into the harmonious freeplay of aesthetic judgment without this very form of stimulation occurring through concepts. Typically we would describe the encounter that stimulates one into an aesthetic judgment as an "experience" of an "aesthetic object," however, since both "experience" and "object" are specialized Kantian terms—and moreover ones whose appropriate application here quickly comes under question—I will avoid confusion by employing more general language and not commit us to any particular specialized term until that term has been deemed appropriate. Thus, in this section I write of modes of "encountering" and "engaging" with "the beautiful", rather than *experiencing* an aesthetic *object*.

"Experience" will be the first mode of engagement scrutinized, since it is what we would initially expect to stimulate an aesthetic judgment. I will proceed by examining modes of engagement in order of descending objectivity to determine if there is one that satisfies our criteria of providing an intuition of something without using concepts to do so. I will follow the lower levels "[i]n regard to the objective content of our cognition in general" as Kant lays them out in the *Jäsche Logic* § VIII, 569. The progression will thus take the following course: empirical cognition (*Erkenntnis*); acquaintance (*kennen*); perception (*Wahrnemung*); mere representation (*sich etwas vorstellen*). As the objective conceptual framework unravels, however, we will see that a new concern arises. Supposing we do find a mode of encounter that satisfies the strong view's requirement of concept independence, would such a mode be robust enough to support the complex happening of aesthetic judgment?

II.A.1 Experience

For Kant, experience is a type of empirical cognition. Thus, experience is something that must first be produced. The Introduction of the A Edition immediately remarks on this, opening with the observation that: "Experience is without doubt the first product that our understanding brings forth as it works on the raw material of sensible sensations."[36] In the B Edition the discussion quickly turns to how the understanding must "work up the raw material of sensible impressions into a cognition of objects that is called experience."[37] This further accords with Kant's remarks that "we can represent nothing as combined in the object without having previously combined it in ourselves."[38] To have the sort of seamless, coherent experience with which we are familiar, the "raw material of sensible impressions" must be synthesized. Synthesis is described as "the action of putting different representations together with each other and comprehending their manifoldness in one cognition [*Erkenntnis*]."[39] Since "[a]ll judgments are accordingly functions of unity among our representations,"[40] bringing about synthesis, this, in turn, means that experience for Kant is decidedly judgmental.[41]

> Experience is an empirical cognition [*Erkenntnis*], i.e., a cognition [*Erkenntnis*], that determines an object through perceptions. It is therefore a synthesis of perceptions, which is not itself contained in perception but contains the synthetic unity of the manifold of perception in one consciousness, which constitutes what is essential in a cognition of objects of the senses, i.e., of experience (not merely of the intuition or sensation of the senses).[42]

Here we see that experience occurs on a more objective level of cognition than perception—a level on which the object becomes determinate. In experience the object of the senses is cognized, whereas in perception only "the intuition or sensation of the senses" was given.

---

36 *Critique of Pure Reason*, A1.
37 *Critique of Pure Reason*, B1.
38 *Critique of Pure Reason*, B 130.
39 *Critique of Pure Reason*, A77/B103.
40 *Critique of Pure Reason*, A69/B94.
41 Allison links this to the discursive nature of human knowledge, emphasizing that "...it should be kept in mind that all human knowledge is judgmental for Kant (as opposed to being intuitive)" (Allison, *Kant's Transcendental Idealism: An Interpretation and Defense*, 27). In the Guyer/Wood translation, *Erkenntnis* is translated as "cognition," whereas other translations waffle between this rendition and "knowledge." In Kant, the term is meant to correlate with the Latin term *cognitio*. For a detailed exploration of the difficulties in translating this term, see Rolf George, "Vorstellung and Erkenntnis in Kant," in *Interpreting Kant*, ed. Moltke S. Gram (Iowa City: University of Iowa Press, 1982), 4; 34.
42 *Critique of Pure Reason*, A 176/B 218–9.

This cognitive, determinative judgment "constitutes what is essential in a cognition of an object of the senses," and it is this that yields experience.

As an empirical cognition of the object, determined by the understanding to yield knowledge, experience is the product of the *fifth* grade of cognition presented in the *Jäsche Logic*:

> The *fifth: to understand* something (*intelligere*), i.e., to cognize something *through the understanding by means of concepts,* or to *conceive.*[43]

From this we see that aesthetic *experience*, as a form of experience independent of concepts, is impossible right from the outset. For the Transcendental Deduction is dedicated to demonstrating that "through the categories alone is experience possible; only by means of them can any object of experience be thought [...]."[44] With the very same stroke the possibility of contemplating an aesthetic *object* is eliminated, since an object is defined as "that in the *concept* of which the manifold of a given intuition is united."[45]

This presents us with what may seem to be a false dilemma: either concepts are involved in aesthetic experience in some way, or there is no such thing as aesthetic experience. On the face of it this would seem to be no choice at all. Things are, however, not as hopeless for the strong view as they may seem, because "experience of an object" is not our only option.[46] Perhaps we should let

---

43 *The Jäsche Logic*, VIII, 65.
44 *Critique of Pure Reason*, A93/B126.
45 *Critique of Pure Reason*, B137, emphasis added.
46 It might be objected here that if the strong view will not allow us to have aesthetic experience of objects, then this line of inquiry ought to be abandoned from the outset, because aesthetic judgment does appear to make judgments about objects—something for which one could argue from the very grammatical form that such judgments take ("This flower is beautiful"). Although this concern will be addressed in due time, there are two reasons not to cast the strong view aside just yet. First, there are still other modes available for encountering something beautiful. Namely, the object [*Phänomen*] may be downgraded to a mere appearance [*Erscheinung*], and the act of cognition to mere acquaintance, perception or representation without consciousness. Thus the demand of thoroughness obliges us to investigate whether any of these can meet the strong view's requirements of concept independence, before turning to the complications that arise from the fact that despite Kant's comments about concept non-involvement, he also suggests that aesthetic judgment can take a discursive form: "This flower is beautiful". The undeniable fact that this statement involves two conceptual terms ("flower" and "beautiful") is one of the complications that I will argue is best solved through a layered solution. That is, however, an issue that needs to be worked up to by first establishing whether the strong view even gets off the ground with an adequate mode of encounter. Second, in my layered solution, I will be arguing that the properly aesthetic layer of judging involves a cognitive act on a lower grade than that of experience. Thus, a thorough investigation of how these lower modes function, par-

the cognition of an object fall aside and explore whether one of the other forms of awareness Kant describes could be the proper subjective mode of engagement to provide the stimulus for aesthetic judgment, meeting the strong view's criteria of concept-independence.

In the Introduction, I discussed the two types of objects that are relevant to this inquiry: appearances (unconceptualized intuitions) and phenomena (conceptualized intuitions). Put in these terms, if that which occasions the judgment of taste is an intuition that is not subsumed under a concept, then it is an appearance. It is clear from the first *Critique* that Kant does not deny that there are such appearances.[47] The question to be dealt with in this chapter is thus not whether an unconceptualized intuition is possible, but rather whether an unconceptualized intuition could function as the aesthetic object that occasions the judgment of taste. Thus, my focus will not be to work through this issue in terms of the object's status. I will, instead, cast my analysis in terms of the differing levels of awareness, because our question pertains more to the *mental acts* that are performed in pure aesthetic judgment, than to a particular group of objects that can be set apart from all other objects as beautiful. Indeed, as Kant observes in the Introduction to the third *Critique*, the power of judgment "can claim no field of objects as its domain."[48] In general, I will use the term object to indicate what Longuenesse has called "the "objective" object,"[49] that is, the intuition that has been subsumed by a concept. It is this to which Kant refers when he defines an object as "that in the concept of which the manifold of a given intuition is united."[50] The "the indeterminate object of empirical intuition, prior to any distinction between the representation and the object of representation,"[51]

---

ticularly in relation to concepts, will serve our later analysis well. Our investigation into these lower modes is not to be understood as an effort to trace out a genealogical story of concept generation. The concern is not how one's acquaintance with something could *transform* into the experience of a conceptualized object. Rather, we are investigating whether the way that a subject is stimulated when being acquainted with, or perceiving, something circumvents the employment of concepts (concepts which the subject both has a priori and acquires empirically) so as to fit the requirements of the strong view.

47 See *Critique of Pure Reason*, A92–3/B125.
48 *Critique of the Power of Judgment*, Introduction, III, 5:177.
49 Longuenesse, *Kant and the Capacity to Judge*, 24.
50 *Critique of Pure Reason*, B137. We see this definition alluded to in the third *Critique* as well when Kant writes, "Now there belongs to a representation by which an object is given, in order for there to be cognition of it in general, **imagination** for the composition of the manifold of intuition and **understanding** for the unity of the concept that unifies the representations" (§ 9, 5:217).
51 Longuenesse, *Kant and the Capacity to Judge*, 24.

which Longueness calls the 'pre-objective' object, will not typically be referred to as an object by me, but rather as intuition, a part of which will prove to be of great importance in the form of what I call "intuitional excess."[52] I will use the term "empirical object" to designate the way that I ultimately find these two both to be present in that which occasions a judgment of taste. In this manner, what sets an object apart is that, whether *Phänomen* or *Erscheinung*, it is constituted through a cognitive process that yeilds *Erkenntnis*, whereas feelings are not objects and they are simply felt in a noncognitive manner.

Hence, I would like to focus our attention on the mental process through which one is aware of something, as this is what determines the status of the object for Kant's transcendental idealism. It is this mental process that constitutes the object *as* an appearance or phenomenon in the first place. Kant clarifies this in the third *Critique* when he writes:

> However, the set of all objects to which those concepts are related, in order where possible to bring about a cognition of them, can be divided in accordance with the varying adequacy or inadequacy of our faculties for this purpose.[53]

It is the "adequacy or inadequacy" of our faculties in the attempt to cognize objects that constitutes the status of these objects, and thus serves as the measure responsible for divisions among different classes of objects. For example, if it turns out that we encounter something beautiful in the mode of experience, then this beautiful thing will, thus, be constituted as a phenomenon. With this in mind, my inquiry will focus on identifying the status of the mental process of encounter. Thus, when possible, I will leave the status of the object open, referring to it as the "beautiful thing" until the process has been decided upon so as to fix its objective status. When I do use the term 'object', the meaning of this term will be clarified by indicating the form of awareness through which this object is perceived, since for Kant it is this that designates differing statuses among 'objects'. When I refer to objects of experience, cognized objects or cognition of an object, this is to underscore the aspect of objects most important to my analysis—namely, that such an object is generated through the subsumption of an intuition under a concept, making it not only determinative, but also something of which one has knowledge. Occasionally I will use the term 'object' in a purely

---

[52] See the next chapter.
[53] *Critique of the Power of Judgment*, Introduction, II, 5:174.

logical sense. In such cases, this will be highlighted either directly in the passage where the term arises, or in a footnote.[54]

In the *Jäsche Logic* Kant differentiates between the forms of awareness, laying out the degrees of objectivity to which a cognition can be graded.[55] The experience of an object, which was discounted above, would correspond to the fifth grade. But we may still consider the four other grades of less objectivity descending from it:

> The *first* degree of cognition is: *to represent* something;
> The *second:* to represent something with consciousness, or *to perceive* (*percipere*);
> The *third:* to be acquainted with something (*noscere*), or to represent something in comparison with other things, both as to *sameness* and as to *difference*;
> The *fourth:* to be acquainted with something *with consciousness*, i.e., to *cognize* it (*conoscere*). Animals are *acquainted* with objects too, but they do not *cognize* them.[56]

At this point, the objection might be raised that if our goal is to locate a form for mentally engaging with something that is not determined by the categories, then this list is futile, because right from the start these are described as degrees of cognition (*Erkenntnis*) and cognition is defined as the subsumption of an intuition under a concept so as to yield knowledge. It must be noted, however, that the *act* of cognition itself only first arises in the *fourth* grade, before which the modes of engagement are described as acquaintance, perception and representation. Cognition does not enter these levels as a verb describing the activity

---

54 For a further discussion of how the terms *Gegenstand* and *Objekt* are to be understood in Kant, see my footnotes 98 (regarding how Allison differentiates between them) and 123 (regarding *Gegenständlichkeit*) below.
55 As I noted in the Introduction, I will be using the *Jäsche Logic* in order to "articulate [more] fully certain points that are already contained in the texts Kant himself prepared for publication" (Lu-Adler, "Constructing a Demonstration of Logical Rules, or How to Use Kant's Logic Corpus," 140). Kant's hierarchy of the grades of cognition is not presented in his published works in a manner that is as cut and dry as it is in the *Jäsche Logic*. From the way that consciousness is discussed in his published works, however—particularly in the first *Critique*, third *Critique* and *Prolegomena*—it is clear that Kant takes there to be cognitions of different degrees of objectivity. Thus, I use the hierarchical structure of the *Jäsche Logic* to structure my analysis, but in interrogating how these different grades of consciousness function and the sort of mental activity that they are able to support, I rely on Kant's published works. Interestingly, this use of the *Jäsche Logic* in the first chapter is an inversion of how I use it in chapters three through six. Here, the *Jäsche Logic* outlines a structure, which is understood more fully by engaging with Kant's published works. In later chapters, Kant's first *Critique* outlines the key features of the logical functions, while the *Jäsche Logic* supplies us with points of detail so that what was outlined in the first *Critique* can take a clear shape.
56 The *Jäsche Logic*, VIII, 65.

(to cognize), but only as the subject whose gradations are being laid out. Thus, this passage describes the intensive spectrum in which cognition manifests. Kant titles these *grades of cognition,* not because each level describes a different sort of cognition, but because cognition is what is coming into being.

To understand better how Kant sees this grades of cognition working, let us turn to his discussion of gradation in the Anticipations of Perception in the first *Critique.*[57] Here he is concerned with the sensation of a given perception, describing how,

> the empirical consciousness can grow in a certain time from nothing = 0 to its given measure, thus it has an intensive magnitude, corresponding to which all objects of perception, insofar as they contain sensation, must be ascribed an intensive magnitude, i.e., a degree of influence on sense.[58]

We are not here concerned with the degree of sensation in a perception. Indeed, the gradation in the *Jäsche Logic* is, in a way, measuring along the inverse scale, since it is concerned with the degree to which the sensation provided by the lower faculties is subordinated to the higher faculties. Despite this difference in what is being measured, however, the scale provided in the *Jäsche Logic* also measures an increasing "degree of influence"—the influence that the higher faculties have on what is presented by the lower. Thus, the scale could similarly be described as moving "between reality and negation" with "a continuous nexus of many possible intermediate" points.[59] As degrees of cognition, these points show us how cognition may "decrease and thus gradually disappear."[60] Thus, cognition in its most objective form represents the "magnitude" towards which the gradations lead with increasing intensity. Representation without consciousness is the point on the scale lying closest to "0" or complete negation. It must pass from the first to the fourth grade before it can be cognized, and to the fifth before it can become *cognition* proper.

Understood in this manner, it appears that not all of the scale's grades of cognition are truly cognitions. They are referred to in this manner, because this is the "reality" toward which the scale is oriented, *not* because they all already achieve the level of cognition, in and of themselves. It would be best only to apply the status of cognition beyond the point at which the action of *cognizing (erkennen)* becomes possible. There is no mention of cognizing in the first

---

57 *Critique of Pure Reason,* B207/A165- B211/A169.
58 *Critique of Pure Reason,* B208/A165.
59 *Critique of Pure Reason,* B209/A168.
60 *Critique of Pure Reason,* A168/B210.

grade through the third, while each of the following grades is carefully described in terms of a cognitive act. The fourth grade is described plainly as *"erkennen (cognoscere),"* the fifth as *"durch den Verstand vermöge der Begriffe erkennen oder konzipieren,"* the sixth as *"etwas durch die Vernunft erkennen oder einsehen (perspicere),"* and the seventh and final grade as *"in dem Grade durch die Vernunft oder a priori erkennen."*[61] Thus, let us recommence our search for a mode of mental engagement that does not make use of the categories at the grade right before *erkennen* becomes the key action.

II.A.2 Acquaintance

Kant's description of acquaintance in the Jäsche *Logic* is initially appealing for the strong view as a possible mode of encounter to stimulate an aesthetic judgment, because it would have us "represent something in comparison with other things, both as to *sameness* and as to *difference*."[62] This talk of comparison resonates with aesthetic judgment's reflective comparison of the faculties.[63]

Okrent discusses acquaintance at length. The idea of formulating a Kantian solution to the question of animal sapience by describing the intuiting of objects that they perform as *kennen*, in contrast to the cognizing of objects that humans perform (*erkennen*), is similarly appealing at the start, particularly because Kant states outright that "[a]nimals are *acquainted* with objects too, but they do not *cognize* them."[64] Hence, Okrent primarily situates his attempt to solve the problem of *animal sapience* within the Kantian framework on this level.[65] As he scrutinizes it further, however, some quite unsatisfactory implications begin to arise:

---

61 *Jäsche Logic*, VIII, 65.
62 *Jäsche Logic*, VIII, 65.
63 "To reflect (to consider), however, is to compare and to hold together given representations either with others or with one's faculty of cognition, in relation to a concept thereby made possible" (*Critique of the Power of Judgment*, First Introduction, V., 20: 211).
64 *Jäsche Logic*, VIII, 65.
65 In addition to inquiring into the mode of awareness that his dog could have in Kant's system, Okrent briefly entertains a "two-object" solution, which explores whether his dog could be seeing the bus as a Kantian object with a different status than fully cognized objects of experience. He does so, by making use of the distinction that Longuenesse draws in *Kant and the Capacity to Judge*, according to which there are "two sorts of intentional objects, a 'pre-objective' object and an 'objective' object" (Okrent, "Acquaintance and Cognition," 94). The former are mere 'appearances' [*Erscheinungen*] whereas the latter are 'phenomena' [*Phänomene*]. Okrent finds two reasons why this differentiation fails to solve the problem, however. First, the way that the "pre-objective indeterminate object of empirical intuition" is characterized, renders it an *"impossible object"* (*Ibid.*, 95). That is, for such a pre-objective appearance, there would be "no distinction *within the realm of representation* between the sensory representation and the object represented

As laid out here, the notion of *kennen*, or acquaintance with things, straddles the canonical distinction in the *Critique* between subjective modifications of a subject's states, or sensation, and *Erkenntnisse*, or *objective* perceptions. But Kant can't have it both ways. Either *kennen*, as opposed to *erkennen*, involves representing an object as distinct from the representation of the object, or it doesn't. If it doesn't, then how does the fact that animals are capable of *kennen*, and thus can represent objects, square with the claim that representation with consciousness and the ability to form judgments is necessary for intending objects? The problem is that intuition differs from mere sensation precisely insofar as it is apprehension of an *object* and to be an object is to be distinct from the representation of the object. But cognition, as a type of representing, is the representing of an object. So one can't be acquainted with an *object* without having a cognition of an object.[66]

As Okrent points out, the status of acquaintance regarding conceptualized objects is quite complicated. The concepts necessary for intending objects as objects (i.e., *Phänomene*) are missing, and yet reference to an object is still made. This raises the question of how aesthetic judgment relates to objects. Is a conceptualized object (*Phänomen*) truly necessary for aesthetic judgment, or might the object play only the causal role of stimulant? If it is the latter, then it would only be necessary that something be encountered for an aesthetic judgment to ensue, but not that an object be thought through this encounter.[67] If this is so, then the strong view gains some footing, because the object would not

---

by that representation" (*Ibid.*, 95). If this is the case, then, Okrent challenges, "in what sense, if any, are the sensory representations representations of an *object* at all?" (*Ibid.*, 95). Second, Okrent contends that we would still have great difficulty characterizing appearances as anything but "identical with phenomena" (*Ibid.*, 96). "Let us assume for a second that the class of object of intuition (let's call it O_1) was disjoint form the class of the objects of judgments (O_2). In this case, it is hard to see how any empirical intuition we might have of appearances, the class of objects belonging to O_1, could ever be relevant to our judgments concerning the objects in O_2. It is only because the members of these classes are identical, and are intended as identical by the one who judges, that the empirical content of our intuitions could be, and be intended to be, evidence for our judgments about the objects of thought" (*Ibid.*, 96–97). Whereas this distinction is not helpful for understanding what a dog experiences, it does ultimately prove to be helpful for understanding the judgment of taste. Here, the idea of an *Erscheinung* representing an "impossible object" fits nicely with the way that Kant repeatedly brackets objects in the judgment of taste. Moreover, our judgments about something's beauty is by no means "relevant" for that object in the way that a judgment that determines a property of the object would be. The universality of pure aesthetic judgments is thus subjective, pertaining to the sphere of judging subjects and not the objects judged.
66 Orkent, 2006, 100.
67 I am not maintaining that the relation to the object is *indeed* merely causal in the manner described, but rather entertaining this possibility so that the cognized object of experience may recede a bit more into the background, allowing us to further pursue the mode of encounter.

need to be encountered *as* an object; it would merely need to be encountered as a source of sensible stimuli.

Earlier I cited two passages from the third *Critique* in which Kant refers to aesthetic judgment as involving an object.[68] Reading the object's role as limited to that of an unconceptualized stimulus would surely work for the first passage, in which, to judge aesthetically, "I must immediately hold the object up to my feeling of pleasure and displeasure [...]." [69] The key element in this passage may not be the "object," but rather the action of "holding" through which one directly encounters that which is to be judged. Such a reading is even further encouraged when we lay the above passage alongside the following:

> Whether a garment, a house, a flower is beautiful: no one allows himself to be talked into his judgment about that by means of any grounds or fundamental principles. One wants to submit the object to his own eyes, just as if his satisfaction depended on sensation [...].[70]

The object must be subjected to my senses, generating feelings of pleasure or displeasure, because my feelings supply the measure for the judgment. We could then cast this in the terms of the *Prolegomena*. To judge the beauty of a flower, I must "hold [it] up to my feeling of pleasure and displeasure" just as in judgments of perception I must physically enter a room to perceive that it is warm, or place sugar on my tongue to perceive its sweetness, or alternatively wormwood and its nastiness.[71] None of these demand a conceptualization of the object, but rather a mere encounter between the object and my senses, so that I may perceive how I am affected. Kant writes of perception, observing that

> [a]ll that such a judgment does is to connect two sensations to a single subject (myself) at a particular time; they aren't intended to be valid of the object.[72]

If we take the object as fulfilling merely the role of sensual stimulus, then perception might be a more fitting mode for encountering it. Moreover, acquaintan-

---

68 These were the following: "[...] I must immediately hold the object up to my feeling of pleasure and displeasure [...]." (Ibid, Bk. I, § 8, 5: 215) and "Now the judgment of taste, however, determines the object, independently of concepts, with regard to satisfaction and the predicate of beauty" (Ibid, Bk. I, § 9, 5: 219).
69 *Critique of the Power of Judgment*, § 8, 5:215.
70 *Critique of the Power of Judgment*, § 8, 5: 216.
71 These perceptual examples are chosen because they are Kant's own from the *Prolegomena*, "[t]hat the room is warm, sugar is sweet, wormwood is nasty, are merely subjectively valid judgments" (§ 19).
72 *Prolegomena*, § 19.

ce's relation to concepts was questionable, given its awkward attempt to "straddle the canonical distinction in the *Critique* between subjective modifications of a subject's states, or sensation, and *Erkenntnisse*, or *objective* perceptions,"[73] as Okrent notes. If we move one rung lower on our list of the candidate modes of encounter from the *Jäsche Logic*, then this should place us squarely in a concept-independent realm of intuition.

II.A.3 Perception

Although the object must encounter the judging subject's sense organs in order to provide the sense data perceived, the foregoing analysis suggests this may be no more than the crude matter of having one's senses confronted with an object that need not be cognized *as* an object in the process, thus circumventing the involvement of concepts. In the *Prolegomena*, Kant acknowledges such an encounter to be possible when observing that even in judgments of perception:

> The object in itself always remains unknown; but it gives us perceptions through our sensibility, and these are connected [...].[74]

If a concept of the understanding *were* to settle on it, then,

> the result [would be] an objective judgment—something that doesn't merely report on perceptions but says things about an object.[75]

In perceptions, and even judgments of perception, this does not occur, and this is what differentiates such judgments from those of experience. Even more interestingly, however, Kant tells us in a footnote that the judgments of perception listed above (the warmth of a room, the sweetness of sugar, the nastiness of wormwood),

> could never become judgments of experience, even if a concept of the understanding were added. They refer merely to feeling, which is incurably subjective and can never become objective. Still, they serve my immediate purpose of illustrating judgments that are merely subjectively valid, involving no relation to an object.[76]

---

73 Okrent, "Acquaintance and Cognition," 100.
74 *Prolegomena*, § 19.
75 *Prolegomena*, § 19.
76 *Prolegomena*, § 19.

With this it becomes even more attractive to take perception as the mode of encounter that leads to aesthetic judgment. Not only is perception immune to conceptualization (due to its foundation on feeling), but it also presents a case where there is an undeniable encounter with an object that works as a stimulant, and yet, "involv[es] no relation to an object." This resonates with Kant's third *Critique* acknowledgement that we often,

> speak of the beautiful as if beauty were a property of the object and the judgment logical (constituting a cognition of the object through concepts of it), although it is only aesthetic and contains merely a relation of the representation of the object to the subject [...].⁷⁷

The differentiation between aesthetic judgments of sense and pure aesthetic judgments of reflection only strengthens the case for moving towards a mode of engagement which "involv[es] no relation to an object." Kant differentiates between the two in the following manner:

---

77 *Critique of the Power of Judgment*, Bk. I, § 6, 5: 211. There is something odd about the fact that Kant designates as subjective both aesthetic judgments and the judgments of warmth in the *Prolegomena*. That is, insofar as each of these gives rise to a discursively articulable judgment statement (i.e.: when I touch the stone, I feel warmth; the flower is beautiful), they do in fact make use of concepts. One might contend that the very communicability of these judgments already constitutes the judgment as "objective" in the sense that it is put into the terms of a shared language. There are two ways of responding to these concerns. First, Kant distinguishes between subjectively and objectively valid judgments in terms of that in which the "representations are combined" (*Critique of Pure Reason*, B142). Objectively valid judgments occur when the "representations are combined in the object" (Ibid). Those that combine the representations in the subject are subjectively valid. Hence, the former "bring[s] given cognitions to the objective unity of apperception [...] distinguish[ing] the objective unity of given representations from the subjective" (*Ibid.*, B141–142). This is to contrast with judgments of "only subjective validity, e.g., in accordance with laws of association" (*Ibid.*, B142). Thus, the way that these terms are differentiated within Kant's system does not directly pertain to whether the judgment can be put in a discursively articulable form. Rather, the deciding factor is whether the representations are combined in the idea of the object or the idea of the subject. The second response is that this objection ties in with the set of concerns that will motivate my layered solution in the next chapter. There, I will be distinguishing between three layers so that the second layer will be about the *activity* of the mental processes of judging, while the universally communicable judgment, stating the object's beauty, is only generated in the third layer. Thus the capacity of aesthetic judgment to produce a discursively articulable judgment statement need not indicate that the workings of aesthetic judgment are entirely subsumed under the discursive term "beauty". In the next chapter I will describe how a certain aesthetic excess escapes the conceptualization of the aesthetic object on the first layer and motivates "much thinking" on the third (*Critique of the Power of Judgment*, Bk. I, § 49, 5:314).

> Thus an aesthetic judgment is that whose determining ground lies in a sensation that is immediately connected with the feeling of pleasure and displeasure. In the aesthetic judgment of sense it is that sensation which is immediately produced by the empirical intuition of the object, in the aesthetic judgment of reflection, however, it is that sensation which the harmonious play of the two faculties of cognition in the power of judgment, imagination and understanding, produces in the subject insofar as in the given representation the faculty of the apprehension of the one and the faculty of presentation of the other are reciprocally expeditious, which relation in such a case produces through this mere form a sensation that is the determining ground of a judgment which for that reason is called aesthetic and as subjective purposiveness (without a concept) is combined with the feeling of pleasure.[78]

With the description this passage provides, we see that both pure and impure aesthetic judgments could be understood in terms of perception. In impure aesthetic judgments of sense, this would be a perception *of* an object, which is not perceived *as* an object, but rather merely perceived insofar as the object immediately produces a sensation. In pure aesthetic judgments, the sensation being perceived is produced by "the harmonious play of the two faculties of cognition in the power of judgment." Like perceptions, the foundation lies in the subject's feeling that arises from these, not in the subject's cognizing something in the thing encountered (i.e. the object or the harmony).

Earlier there were two passages offered which could be used to support the idea that aesthetic judgment must involve an 'objective object' (i.e., a phenomenon). I have already argued that the first passage could be dealt with by understanding the object that I must "hold up to my feeling of pleasure and displeasure" as providing a perception, not cognition. Let us now turn to the second challenging passage from the third *Critique* to determine whether it necessitates a cognition of the object in aesthetic judgment.

This passage may initially appear more daunting, but, when taken in context it need not present an insurmountable obstacle to leaving the perceived object uncognized in a concept, so that perception may serve as the mode of encountering the beautiful for the strong view's reading of aesthetic judgment. To quote the passage under concern more fully, it reads:

> Now the judgment of taste, however, determines the object, independently of concepts, with regard to satisfaction and the predicate of beauty. Thus that subjective unity of the relation can make itself known only through sensation. The animation, of both faculties (the imagination and the understanding) to an activity that is indeterminate but yet, through the stimulus of the given representation, in unison, namely that which belongs to a cognition in general, is the sensation whose universal communicability is postulated by the judgment

---

[78] *Critique of the Power of Judgment*, First Introduction, VIII., 20:225.

of taste. Of course, an objective relation can only be thought, but insofar as it is subjective as far as its conditions are concerned it can still be sensed in its effect on the mind; and further, in the case of a relation that is not grounded in any concept (like that of the powers of representation to a faculty of cognition in general), no other consciousness of it is possible except through sensation of the effect that consists in the facilitated play of both powers of the mind (imagination and understanding), enlivened through mutual agreement.[79]

Given Kant's clear commitment to preserving the indeterminate nature of aesthetic judgment, we must infer that "determining" something through a feeling functions quite differently than doing so through a concept in a determinative judgment. [80] Otherwise, the reflective nature of aesthetic judgments would be in jeopardy. Kant's very phrase "determines the object" is misleading, as a determination through feeling cannot yield the "the distinctness that one can rightly demand elsewhere, namely from a cognition in accordance with concepts."[81] Considering how this quickly becomes a discussion of the animating harmony to be found in the subjective relation of the faculties, his reference to determination actually appears to be somewhat ironic. That is, whereas objects of experience are determined through concepts and become objects of knowledge, in aesthetic judgment the closest thing to any determining activity that is to be found is supplied by,

---

79 *Critique of the Power of Judgment*, § 9, 5:219, emphasis added.
80 This accords with Kant's remark in the First Introduction to the third *Critique* that, "if in the general division of the powers of the mind overall the faculty of cognition as well as the faculty of desire contain an objective relation of representations, so by contrast the feeling of pleasure and displeasure is only the receptivity of a determination of the subject, so that if the power of judgment is to determine anything for itself alone, it could not be anything other than the feeling of pleasure [...]" (20:208).
81 *Critique of the Power of Judgment*, Preface to the first edition (1790), 5:170. It might be argued that since we are able to give a name to this feeling, organizing it under the term "pleasure", it is, indeed, conceptualized. At this point in my analysis, the point to be made is that, according to how Kant characterizes subjective and objective judgments, the communicability of the predicate does not tell us whether it is combined with the subject in the representation of the subject or object. Hence, this is not a factor that determines whether the judgment is subjective or objective within Kant's framework. Moreover, in chapter two I will understand the relation between the conceptual term "pleasure" and the feeling of pleasure by separating these into two different layers of aesthetic judgment. I will argue that this linking of the feeling of pleasure to the discursive term "pleasure" is a correlation, in which the term "pleasure" (which arises on the third layer) does not fully capture the activity of judging that occurs on the second, properly aesthetic, layer. That is to say, the conceptual term does not subsume the intuition of the feeling. In chapter four, where I discuss the second moment of aesthetic judgment, I will suggest that one of the peculiarities of aesthetic judgment is its claim to "universal communicability" of the uncommunicable—the ineffable perception of pleasure on the second layer.

a feeling of pleasure (or displeasure) and a satisfaction that accompanies the representation of the object and serves it instead of a predicate.[82]

It is hardly a determination of an object if, as subjective, the relation can only be "sensed in its effect on the mind." Thus, this passage does not stand in the way of letting the cognized object fall aside and explore the possibility that a perception is the proper subjective mode of engagement that can provide the stimulus for aesthetic judgment.

Now that these preliminary obstacles to seeing aesthetic judgment as stimulated by a perception have been cleared away and some commonalities between aesthetic judgment and perception have been outlined, let us test whether this mode of encounter truly meets the strong view's criteria: Are concepts, both pure and impure, truly inoperative in perceptions that stimulate one into an aesthetic judgment? Our hope was that the lower position perceptions occupy on Kant's list of cognitive functions in the *Jäsche Logic* would assure no concepts to be operative. As we look further into the matter, however, we quickly find that perception begins to cloud up with issues similar to those that Okrent detailed regarding acquaintance (*kennen*).

Like aesthetic judgments, Kant aligns perceptions fully with the lower faculties of intuition and sense, in contradistinction to the higher faculty of understanding:

> So experience is a product of the senses and of the understanding, and we have to discover how these two faculties combine to produce it. One of them is simply intuition of which I am conscious, i.e. perception, which belongs merely to the senses.[83]

According to this, it sounds as though one is having a perception of the senses when one is conscious of an intuition, but not cognizing through this perceptual state. As discussed above, this offers the benefit that it does not involve perceiving an object *as* an object. Rather the object would be simply encountered, and the way that it affected the senses would be perceived. Kant's description of judgments of perception in the *Prolegomena* confirms this:

> There are two kinds of judging. (1) I may merely compare perceptions and conjoin them in a consciousness of my state. (2) I may conjoin them in consciousness in general. What I have in (1) is merely a judgment of perception, a subjectively valid connecting of perceptions in my mind, without reference to an object.[84]

---

82 *Critique of the Power of Judgment*, Bk. I, § 36, 5:288.
83 *Prolegomena*, § 20
84 *Prolegomena*, § 20

II Pure and Empirical Concepts — 53

What is really telling for our purpose is his description of how a judgment of perception can become a judgment of experience:

> To turn perception into experience, therefore, we need (2) a different kind of judging. An intuition (or perception) *must be brought under a pure a priori concept of the understanding*; this concept settles what kind or form of judgment can be made about this intuition; thus it connects the individual person's intuition with a frame of mind that anyone must be in when making judgments about such intuitions; and in this way it provides the empirical judgments with universal validity. Such a concept, I repeat, merely fixes a general way in which judgments can be brought to bear on the intuition.[85]

If perceptions "must be brought under a pure a priori concept of the understanding" in order to be turned into experience, then it would seem that *as* perceptions they were not subsumed under the categories. Have we found our concept-independent mode of engagement?

As promising as perception may look for those seeking to give the strong view a foothold, others have found this same aspect troublesome. If the categories do not have a determinative role in perception, then how can one become aware of perceiving at all? No matter how subjective and indeterminate we are willing to conceive of perception, if we undercut the unity of consciousness, which is dependent upon the categories, then we end up with a mode of engagement of which one is unaware, and thus, no true mode of engagement at all. As stated in no uncertain terms in the first *Critique*:

> The I **think** must **be able** to accompany all my representations; for otherwise something would be represented in me that could not be thought at all, which is as much as to say that the representation would either be impossible or else at least nothing for me.[86]

This combined with the description of perception above, threatens to render perception either impossible or, at least, imperceptible ("nothing to me"), which would, in turn, lead to an equally impossible imperceptible-perception. Is there a unity of consciousness to which a perception could be attached so as to avoid this fate?

Henry Allison remarks on this, writing that it is "striking" that,

> judgments of perception are presented as lacking two properties which, in the Second Edition of the *Critique*, Kant holds to be essential to all judgments [...]. [That is, that they] are merely subjectively valid and occur without the use of any categories [...and] involve a con-

---

85 *Prolegomena*, § 20, emphasis added.
86 *Critique of Pure Reason*, B132, emphasis original.

nection of perceptions 'in a consciousness of my particular state' [rather than] 'consciousness in general' that occurs in an objectively valid judgment of experience.[87]

He tackles this problem by pointing to sections, like the one above, where perception is described as being "conjoin[ed] [...] in a consciousness of my state," which is juxtaposed to how experience is "conjoin[ed] [...] in consciousness in general," characterizing the former as a subjective unity of consciousness and the latter as an objective unity of consciousness. He develops his interpretation of the consciousness of which perceptions are capable through a reading of § 18 and § 19 in the first *Critique*'s *Transcendental Deduction*, describing this "as remnants of the inadequate doctrine of the *Prolegomena*,"[88] suggesting that:

> The distinction in the *Critique* between subjective and objective unity may be seen as a corrective to the earlier distinction between two kinds of judgment. The necessity for such a corrective stems from the theory of judgment made explicit in the Second Edition, according to which objective validity is an inherent trait of all judgments.[89]

As we can see, there is good reason to draw this parallel between perceptions and the subjective unity of consciousness:

> The **transcendental unity** of apperception is that unity through which all of the manifold in an intuition is united in a concept of the object. It is called objective on that account, and must be distinguished from the **subjective unity** of consciousness, which is a **determination of inner sense**, through which the manifold of intuition is empirically given for such a combination.[90]

Perceptions are clearly meant to be something of which one can become aware and thus combined with some sort of "consciousness of my state." It seems right to follow Allison's lead and identify this consciousness with the first *Critique*'s subjective unity of consciousness. To become conscious of one's state would align perfectly with a form of consciousness that is a determination of inner senses, since this is the pure form of intuition through which one intuits one's states. The further distinction between objective and subjective unity of consciousness parallels that between perception and experience, with the former consisting only of the intuition of empirical data received through the senses, which can then, in turn, be processed by the understanding to yield the latter,

---

[87] Allison, *Kant's Transcendental Idealism: An Interpretation and Defense*, 149.
[88] Allison, *Kant's Transcendental Idealism: An Interpretation and Defense*, 149
[89] Allison, *Kant's Transcendental Idealism: An Interpretation and Defense*, 148
[90] *Critique of Pure Reason*, B139

an experience involving the objective unity of consciousness. As Kant observes in the *Prolegomena* "experience itself is nothing but a continual joining together of perceptions."[91] Our question is now whether the identification of the subjective unity of consciousness as the sort of consciousness that is combined with perceptions—a move necessary to prevent perceptions from deteriorating into an imperceptible impossibility—requires that concepts be operative. The following analysis will show the answer to be 'yes'. Let us investigate this by turning to Allison's analysis of how the subjective unity of consciousness functions. Allison identifies the use of the categories to determine an object as operative in objective judgments, but not in subjective judgments. As his analysis develops, however, he reveals that although the categories may not be operative in this manner in subjective judgments, they are still operative in a more fundamental manner. Thus, the hope that perception will provide the strong view with a concept-independent mode of encounter is initially encouraged, but ultimately disappointed.

Allison characterizes the subjective unity of consciousness as "not less, but other than a dream."[92] He suggests that we could understand any judgment of perception as one of two types. Either it is the sort of perception that could ultimately be translated into an objectively valid judgment of experience *if* the categories were introduced—for example, the perception that "when the sun shines on the stone, it becomes warm" could become a causal claim that "the sun warms the stone"—or the perception could be so thoroughly subjective that the categories could not be introduced to effect such a change. The perception that "in touching the stone I sense warmth"[93] is "inherently subjective, because [it] refer[s] to feeling states that cannot be attributed to the object."[94] Insofar as the subjective judgment reports only how the representations are being combined in the subject, these representations are not being brought under the objective unity that the categories provide, leaving them to be merely contingently associated with each other, unable to acquire the necessary unity that is only provided when the categories are used to combine the representations in the object.[95] Allison elaborates on how this works, explaining that *Sinnenanschauungen* pertain to "a play of representations which affect our feelings and desires."[96] As such, their unity does not represent an object, but only a feeling. This entirely side-steps the specific application of the categories to representations that com-

---

91 Kant, *Prolegomena*, § 5.
92 Allison, *Kant's Transcendental Idealism: An Interpretation and Defense*, 152.
93 *Jäsche Logic*, § 40, 609.
94 Allison, *Kant's Transcendental Idealism: An Interpretation and Defense*, 149.
95 See *Critique of Pure Reason*, B141–142.
96 Allison, *Kant's Transcendental Idealism: An Interpretation and Defense*, 154.

bines them in the representation of an object—this sort of combination in accordance with the categories being the one that allows our experience of objects to obtain necessity. In the play of *Sinnenanschauungen* nothing (or, no *thing*—no object) is represented to us, meaning that insofar as we are "knowing beings," such subjective perceptions are "nothing to us," but insofar as we are feeling, desiring beings they *are* something to us.[97] Allison writes:

> By such a judgment, Kant means perceptual awareness itself, not a reflective judgment about this awareness. To return once more to Kant's examples, my perceptual consciousness of the bitterness of wormwood and the sweetness of sugar (the "seemings" themselves) are the actual judgments of perception. They are regarded as judgments because they are modes of consciousness with their peculiar "subjective objects" (appearances). Nevertheless, as judgments about such "subjective objects" (appearances) they are radically distinct from judgments of experience.[98]

The role played by the categories is to "convert subjective judgments into objective judgments." In stubbornly subjective judgments of perception, the categories are unable to latch on to the judgment and convert it in this way, because that which is being judged is a feeling which cannot be "unified in a way that is independent of my perceptual state."[99] Such a shift from a judgment that takes the subjective perceptions of the subject as its basis to one that is not based upon the perceptions of the subject can only be carried out if there is an object that can take up the foundational position vacated by the subject. In judgments about feelings, however, the object cannot serve this role, thus, their inconvertible nature. For this reason, Allison concludes that perceptions involve,

> a unity or connection of representations through which nothing is represented, not even our subjective states [...] no object (Objekt) can be represented by means of this order or connection, and this must include a subjective object. For this reason it appears that the term 'subjective' is somewhat of a misnomer, and that 'nonobjective' or 'nonrepresentational' would be more appropriate.[100]

---

97 Allison, *Kant's Transcendental Idealism: An Interpretation and Defense*, 153.
98 Allison, *Kant's Transcendental Idealism: An Interpretation and Defense*, 152.
99 Allison, *Kant's Transcendental Idealism: An Interpretation and Defense*, 150.
100 Allison, *Kant's Transcendental Idealism: An Interpretation and Defense*, 154. In this quotation, one may note Allison's specification of the object as an *Objekt*. He differentiates between this and *Gegenstand* as follows, "in the Transcendental Deduction, objective validity and objective reality are connected with different conceptions of an object. Since it is linked to judgment, objective validity goes together with a judgment or logical conception of an object (an object in *sensu logico*). This is an extremely broad sense of 'object', which encompasses anything that can serve as the subject in a judgment. The term that Kant generally uses (at least in the Deduction) for an object in this sense is *Objekt*. Correlatively, the notion of objective reality is connected with

II Pure and Empirical Concepts — 57

The characteristic that gives perception its uniquely subjective quality is the absence of an object, or rather, the fact that it does not involve the unity of an object, but rather the unity of the consciousness of a feeling.[101] Without an object in play, Allison concludes that there is nothing to be represented.

In § 26 of the first *Critique*, Kant equates perception with empirical consciousness through the synthesis of apprehension:

> …by the **synthesis of apprehension** I understand the composition of the manifold in an empirical intuition, through which perception, i.e., empirical consciousness of it (as appearance), becomes possible.[102]

Thus we can summarize that perception is empirical consciousness of an appearance, which is united by the subjective unity of consciousness and synthesized in apprehension. Kant writes of the synthesis of apprehension, clarifying that,

> this synthetic unity can be none other than that of the combination of the manifold of a given **intuition in general** in an original consciousness, in agreement with the categories, only applied to our **sensible intuition.** Consequently all synthesis, through which even perception itself becomes possible, stands under the categories, and since experience is cognition through connected perceptions, the categories are conditions of the possibility of experience, and are thus also valid *a priori* of all objects of experience.[103]

Although, the idea that perceptions combined with the subjective unity of consciousness initially seemed to present a promising concept-independent mode of encounter for the strong view, this section makes it abundantly clear that

---

a "real" sense of object, that is, with an object in the sense of an actual entity or state of affairs (an object of possible experience). Kant's term for an object in this sense is *Gegenstand*" (1983, 135). See the Introduction for my explanation as to why I highlight the difference between objects in terms of *Phänomen* and *Erscheinung* instead of *Gegenstand* and *Objekt*.

101 The fact that people can talk to each other about their feelings does not present problems for the sort of distinction that Kant is making, here, between subjective and objective judgments, because the distinction pertains to the way that these judgments organize the subject's perceptions, that is, that when the subject perceives the warmth of the stone, then she associates the representation of the feeling and of the stone in her representation of her own subjective state. If she is, then, to turn to remark on this feeling to another person, so as to tell them "This stone feels warm to me," then her ability to name and communicate her contingent association does not change the subjective way that she "merely conjoin[s] [the perceptions] in a consciousness of [her] state" (*Prolegomena*, § 20). In the next chapter this structure will be further clarified through my layered solution, which streamlines the process of aesthetic judgment so that we may see that three distinct acts of judging are involved.

102 *Critique of Pure Reason*, B160.

103 *Critique of Pure Reason*, B161.

the first *Critique* does not actually support such hopes. As for Allison's reading of the subjective unity of consciousness as not involving an object—a reading which initially seemed to suggest a way around the categories by getting us around their use to determine objects of experience—we now find that what actually motivated Allison to characterize perceptions in this manner, was his ultimate intention to argue that their subjective status does *not* stem from somehow avoiding the involvement of the categories, but rather from this categorical involvement not determining an object.[104] With a close analysis of § 17–20, Allison argues that Kant sought to prove that the categories are necessary conditions for the possibility of experience, by showing that their necessity enters the equation at the level of perception (that of which experience consists), in this manner

---

104 The argument that the categories must be operative on a certain level in judgments of perception—because this is the only way for such judgments to acquire the requisite unity of a manifold in one consciousness through the "logical connections of perception in a thinking subject" (Allison, *Kant's Transcendental Idealism: An Interpretation and Defense*, 152)—becomes even more evident when we consider the case of dreams. Taking up the description of intuitions without concepts as "less than a dream," L. W. Beck investigates what the status of dreams would be in Kant, specifically focusing on the status of dream objects in his essay "Did the Sage of Königsberg have No Dreams?" He concludes that "A dream is a subjective object. In a dream I dreamingly-see a three-headed monster. To dreamingly-see it, unlike to-see-it-*sans-phrase*, does not imply that there *is* a three-headed monster. But I say, 'Last night I dreamt I saw a three-headed monster,' and my judgment about *that* event is as objective as the judgment that I slept in my bed and makes just as valid a claim on your credence. You cannot verify it by inspection, but the occurrence of the dream, unlike the monster in the dream, falls under the Second Postulate of Empirical Thought, fulfilling the criteria of existence […]. The categories do not differentiate veridical from non-veridical experience; they make the difference between dumbly facing chaos without even knowing it—'less even than a dream'—and telling a connected story, even if it is false" (Beck, "Did the Sage of Königsberg have No Dreams?" 54). Allison reflects on Beck's example, observing that even in a dream "I must make use of the categories" (Allison, *Kant's Transcendental Idealism: An Interpretation and Defense*, 152). That is namely because the dream objects are located "in the spatiotemporal framework of a dream world" thus they "stand in connection with other object in the dream world" and "involve the conscious awareness of such imaginary object" (*Ibid.*). The categories must be involved in order for the spatiotemporal framework of the dream world to be synthesized, objects to appear within this dream world as spatial and temporal and for the dreamer to be conscious of all of them within the dream. Allison uses Beck's argument to bolster his own, stating that subjective objects (those that are only experienced within the subject such as feelings, tastes and dreams) "involve conscious awareness" and thus "involve the categories" (*Ibid.*). Thus, it is the intuition which "does not conform to the conditions for the unity of apperception" which makes no use of the categories and is thus regulated to the status of being even less than a dream (*Ibid.*). Subjective objects, however are *not* less than a dream. Indeed, dream objects are numbered among the subjective objects and, just like any other spatiotemporal object of conscious awareness, these must involve the categories.

their necessity has already been carefully woven-in, even before the level of experience has been reached—thus demonstrating that the categories pertain to all modes of consciousness, proving their necessity and universality.[105]

Undeniable evidence emerges in § 20, demonstrating that for Kant any attempt to find a mode of consciously encountering sensible intuitions that is independent from the categories will be bound to fail. Right from the very title, this is evident: *§ 20. All sensible intuitions stand under the categories, as conditions under which alone their manifold can come together in one consciousness.* The paragraph long section spells this out in no uncertain terms:

> The manifold that is given in a sensible intuition necessarily belongs under the original synthetic unity of apperception, since through this alone is the **unity** of the intuition possible (§ 17). That action of the understanding, however, through which the manifold of given representations (whether they be intuitions or concepts) is brought under an apperception in general, is the logical function of judgments (§ 19). Therefore all manifold, insofar as it is given in **one** empirical intuition, is **determined** in regard to one of the logical functions for judgment, by means of which, namely, it is brought to a consciousness in general. But now the **categories** are nothing other than these very functions for judging, insofar as the manifold of a given intuition is determined with regards to them (§ 13). Thus the manifold in a given intuition also necessarily stands under categories.[106]

While one must admire the philosophical acumen of proving the categories by intertwining them with the very consciousness necessary for any sort of awareness, this does not bode well for the strong view. Indeed, it cuts off what looked like the last promising in-road. Perception is already saturated with the pure concepts of the understanding.

Let us test whether this truly is the case, by investigating whether it can square with the passage in the *Prolegomena* that appeared to provide the strongest proof for the categories not operating in perceptions. This was the section, above, detailing how judgments of perception could be transformed into judgments of experience:

> To turn perception into experience, therefore, we need (2) a different kind of judging. An intuition (or perception) **must be brought under a pure a priori concept of the understanding** [...].[107]

---

[105] Allison, *Kant's Transcendental Idealism: An Interpretation and Defense*, 167.
[106] *Critique of Pure Reason*, B143.
[107] Kant, *Prolegomena*, § 20, emphasis added.

The requirement to bring the intuition of a perception under a category initially makes it sound as if the intuition is *not* under any category until this is done. Upon further scrutiny, however, it appears that this passage can be reconciled with the idea that the categories were already operative in the perceptual judgment before its conversion into a judgment of experience. Later in the same section Kant provides an example of a converted judgment of experience.

> ([...] But if I say 'The sun warms the stone', which means that the sun causes the stone to become warm, the concept of cause is added to the perception and connects the concept of warmth necessarily with the concept of sunshine.) If all our objectively valid synthetic judgments are analyzed, it turns out that they never consist in mere intuitions that are brought together in a judgment through mere comparison [...]. Always, a pure concept of the understanding has been added to the concepts that are abstracted from intuition.[108]

What always needs to be added is "*a* pure concept of the understanding" not *the* pure concept*s* of the understanding. It is not that something which utterly lacked categorial determination is first brought under the categories, but rather that a further determination is added to the categories already operative in perceptual judgment. This expansion of the category's role in the transition from subjective to objective unity of consciousness is well described in § 19:

> [...] a judgment is nothing other than the way to bring given cognitions to the **objective** unity of apperception. That is the aim of the copula **is** in them: distinguish the objective unity of given representations from the subjective. For this word designates the relation of the representations to the original apperception and its **necessary unity** [...].

As a contingent empirical subjective judgment, the perception already related to the necessary unity of original apperception, with the operation of the categories limited to bringing consciousness to the representation's combination with a feeling in the subject. As a judgment of experience, however, the feeling is exchanged for the representation of a property that can belong to an object and a category is introduced that relates these two representations as "combined in the object."[109] Thus, in the subjective perception of the warmth of a stone, the subject lays her hand on the stone and the representation of the stone (as an appearance) is combined with the immediate feeling of warmth in the subject. In an objective judgment of experience, however, the subject abstracts from this feeling, converting it into the concept of warmth as a property of the object. In the concept of the object she then combines the representation of

---

108 Kant, *Prolegomena*, § 20
109 *Critique of Pure Reason*, B142.

this property (warmth) with the representation of the stone, and accordingly judges the stone to be warm. As combined in the object, this judgment holds "regardless of any difference in the condition of the subject," and hence does not concern "something merely found together in perception."[110]

If the categories must be operative in order for even a feeling to be brought to consciousness, then the peculiarity of perceptions is not that the categories are *not* operative in them, but rather that the categories are not operating so as to combine representations in the object. Rather, the categories are combining a feeling with consciousness in perceptions, and with a representation of an appearance in judgments of perception. Hence, the categories are operative in judgments of perception, so as to allow the subject to consciously perceive a feeling. At this point it is becoming increasingly clear that the categories (and thus concepts) will need to be permitted a limited operation in the apparatus of aesthetic judgment. For the sake of thoroughness, however, let us take a cursory look at the lowest mode of cognition: representation without consciousness.

II.A.4 Representation without Consciousness

Perception was representation combined *with* consciousness, the second rung up on the ladder of cognition in the *Jäsche Logic*. On the lowest rung we find "The *first* degree of cognition [...]: *to represent* something." Consciousness has been stripped away in the transition from the second to the first degree, leaving us only with mere representation. Kant further elaborates on representations that are not united with consciousness in the following section from the first *Critique:*

> An **object,** however, is that in the concept of which the manifold of a given intuition is **united.** Now, however, all unification of representation requires unity of consciousness in the synthesis of them. Consequently the unity of consciousness is that which alone constitutes the relation of representations to an object, thus their objective validity, and consequently is that which makes them into cognitions on which even the possibility of the understanding rests.[111]

For our current purposes, we can invert this passage to see that it is the "unification of representations" which requires consciousness, not the representations

---

110 *Critique of Pure Reason*, B142. Admittedly, this is not what all philosophers mean when distinguishing between subjective and objective judgments. However, a close reading of the text gives us good reason to believe that this is, indeed, the way that Kant distinguishes between the two, regardless of how dissatisfactory this may be for those who want to get at something else with theories of the subjective.
111 *Critique of Pure Reason*, B137.

themselves. This representation bears absolutely no relation to an object, because there is no unity of consciousness operating to establish such a relation.[112] By taking up the strong view of aesthetic judgment, we initially set out in search of something that might be encountered in a mode that does not involve any concepts. We have now found that thing, but by virtue of fitting our criteria it also proves to be incapable of being encountered. In the process of casting away concepts, we have also cast away the consciousness which is the only avenue for something to become anything "to us." Through its independence, however, it wins nothing more than a state of absolute blindness. Hence, what we have here is fully unencounterable—"less than a dream."[113]

II.B The Limiting View: Turning Back to Let in the Categories

My goal in working through the possible modes of encounter was not to provide a genealogy of how concepts are formed, but rather to determine whether the strong view of concept independence in aesthetic judgment can even get a foothold by identifying a mode for encountering the beautiful that fits its criteria. At this point we can conclude that it does not. Without subsumption under any concept, an intuition fails to meet the conditions for the possibility of conscious awareness in the first place. I conclude that there is no mode of encountering the beautiful (i.e., of being stimulated into reflective aesthetic judgment) that could occur in total isolation from the categories. As seen above, in Allison's discussion of perception, a cognitive process that is carried out in isolation from the

---

[112] Longuenesse draws out the distinction between representations with and without consciousness in terms of whether the representation has or has not been the object of the synthesis of apprehension. She indicates that representations without consciousness should be understood as representations to which the "I think" *could* attach, but has not yet done so. She explores the examples that Kant offers of such representations without consciousness in the *Anthropology* as "the features of a house seen from afar, individual notes of a chord struck in the course of a musical improvisation" (Longuenesse, *Kant and the Capacity to Judge*, 65).

[113] At this point, it is interesting to note that for Kant the beautiful must be encountered in a conscious mode, although things might play out quite differently, if his discussions of aesthetic judgment seemed to be open to involving an unconscious pleasure. Alas, as notoriously obscure as Kant's discussion of pleasure becomes in § 9 of the third *Critique*, it is clear that the subject is conscious of the pleasure involved in aesthetic judgment, otherwise it could not serve as the grounds for the judgment. Hence there will, at this point, be no attempt to read Kant's account through Jacques Lacan's notion of *jouissance* (see: Jacques Lacan, *On Feminine Sexuality: the Limits of Love and Knowledge: Encore.*1972–1973, ed. Jacques-Alain Miller. Trans. Bruce Fink. [New York: Norton, 1998]).

categories would be barred from the unity of apperception, making it something upon which one cannot reflect. It was for this reason that Allison concluded that even if subjective judgments of perception do not utilize the categories to determine an object, their combinations of the representations in the subject does involve the transcendental unity of apperception, and, thus, the categories. This is not entirely surprising, considering how Kant's Transcendental Deduction hinges on the idea that the use of the categories is a necessary condition for the possibility of experience. For aesthetic judgment it means that the categories must be involved in some manner. Thus, at this point, we should discard the strong view and explore the limiting view instead. The limiting view assumes that Kant's discussion of concepts aims to limit, not eliminate, their operation in aesthetic judgment.

In testing the limiting view, the leading question will be which mode of encounter limits the operation of concepts most greatly without undermining other aspects of how aesthetic judgment operates. Thus, I will now work backwards through our grades of cognition, choosing the one that satisfies these criteria while also offering a magnitude closest to zero.[114] Over the course of this analysis, the types of awareness that are less objective than experience will reveal themselves not to be robust enough to support two key elements of Kant's theory of aesthetic judgment, namely, that we make this judgment about a clearly delineated object and that this judgment "occasions much thinking."[115]

II.B.1 Perception and Acquaintance: Revisited

Representation without consciousness was already discounted not for any suspected use of the categories, but more so, because consciousness is necessary for other aspects of Kant's description of aesthetic judgment. Hence, I will begin directly with the second grade, *perception*. Just to quickly summarize the above, before this grade was discounted due to the involvement of the categories, perception appeared to be a promising mode of encountering something beautiful, because Kant's description it in § 19 of the *Prolegomena* provides us with the following characteristics which align nicely with Kant's characterization of aesthetic judgment:
- The object remains unknown, and hence uncognized;
- Perceptions come through sensibility;

---

[114] *Critique of Pure Reason*, B208/A165.
[115] *Critique of the Power of Judgment*, Bk. I, § 49, 5:314.

- The "objects"[116] of certain perceptions (such as the sweetness of sugar) can never become objects of experience, because what is perceived is a feeling, not a cognized object;
- Perceptions are subjectively, not objectively valid;
- Despite the fact that no object is cognized in a perception, an object is most certainly encountered.

Characterized in this fashion, perception appears to be the perfect mode of encountering something that is to be aesthetically judged. In order to test whether it truly is, however, let us look more closely into its primary difference from experience—that it does not cognize an object—and explore whether this would present any problems for Kant's aesthetic theory.

In the context of a discussion about the A Deduction's three-fold synthesis and what would result from a mere invocation of the synthetic acts of apprehension and reproduction without recognition in a concept, J. M. Bernstein offers some informative remarks that help us think about what it is like to encounter something as a mere perception:

> [B]y themselves, apprehension and reproduction constitute the possibility of minimum cognitive awareness. We have access to some "x", we are geared to it cognitively, that is we are responding to it, which is to say that information about it is present to the mind such that my behavior with respect to it can be explained only by how it is represented not how it actually is [...]. Recognition in a concept adds this *what* of what it is to which I am attending. It is not some fuzzy blob in the sky, but it is a "bird." The crux here is that nothing but a concept will tell me what sort of complex happening I am responding to. For example, like last week, hearing Big Ben. I must not only hold the rings in mind, but I must hold them in mind as rings of a clock. Otherwise it is just big noise. The point is that we have got to conceptualize it as not just noises, not just tones—some noises can be in rhythm and melody, e. g. church bells do a certain tune prior to ringing the time. You have to know the difference between listening to the tune and then counting the rings of the time. These are two different acts. Each is a listening to the bells but under different conceptual descriptions. Therefore discriminating the way in which I counted the tones, whether I bother counting them,

---

116 More specifically, the object would be the feeling of sweetness in the subject and since Kant holds that feeling is not used for the cognition of an object, this would be an *Erscheinung*: "Now even though we are also used to calling this feeling (in accordance with this designation) a sense (modification of our state) for the lack of another expression, yet it is not an objective sense, whose determination would be used for the **cognition** of an object (for to intuit something with pleasure or otherwise cognize it is not a mere relation of the representation to the object, but rather a receptivity of the subject), which contributes nothing at all to the cognition of the object" (*Critique of the Power of Judgment*, VIII 20:222)

whether I synthesize them as a tune, etc. Without those activities, what we have is simply orderly noise. But concepts make that noise into song or a string of the time or whatever.[117]

Bernstein's description here also works as a description of a perception that is not made into an experience, falling nicely in line with Allison's remark that the subjective aspect of perception could be better captured by the idea of a "non-objective" consciousness, because it gives no object to consciousness. Thus, a perception fails to support a "complex happening." But is this sufficient for the way that Kant talks about aesthetic judgment? Is it really accurate to say that it was merely a perception of "big orderly noise" that brought one to revel in the beauty of Beethoven's 9th?

Let us assess whether limiting the involvement of concepts in the way that they are limited in perception would impinge upon other aspects of Kant's theory of aesthetic judgment. To conceive of aesthetic judgment as involving the inability to apply empirical concepts to perceptual objects would imbue aesthetic judgment with a non-discursive nature. Since aesthetic judgment is described as a merely reflective judgment, reflective activity would appear to be of great importance. This prohibition on cognizing an object, and resultant inability to apply empirical concepts, would not present a problem for the special sort of reflectivity that designates aesthetic judgments as reflective. According to our earlier discussion of what Kant means by calling this form of judgment "reflective," this reflectivity need not be discursive. Here, "reflective" designates two essential characteristics. First, there is a movement in which the particular is given. Second, the universal is sought in such a manner that the faculties of imagination and understanding are thrown into a harmonious state of free-play, felt to be pleasant by the judging subject.[118] For the first characteristic, discursive conceptualization of an intuition is unattainable. For the second, where reflective judgment subsists in the suspended state of harmonious free play, it is *felt*— not discursively articulated.[119] In this manner, we see that neither of the essential

---

117 Bernstein, Jay. "The Bernstein Tapes." The New School for Social Research, New York, NY. Lecture Recording from 3.8.2006, 17:30–26:00. Course Title: GPHI 6065 Kant's *Critique of Pure Reason*. Online.
118 Over the course of the following chapters I will be drawing out two sorts of harmonious free play that occur in two different layers: between the faculties on the second and a possible further harmony in the discursive free play among indeterminate concepts on the third.
119 Later, I will consider the significance of the fact that the proclamation of an aesthetic judgment ("This flower is beautiful") *is* a discursive statement. At this point, however, our concern is to establish that the harmonious free play of the faculties that designates a judgment as reflective must not, itself, be discursively conceptualizable.

characteristics of aesthetic judgment's reflective nature requires the use of concepts for discursivity. The reflective activity that aesthetic judgment performs appears to be located in a non-conceptual, non-discursive, operation of the faculties. In this manner, the way that the absence of concepts from aesthetic judgment would prevent the reflective activity of this judgment from becoming discursively articulable presents no obstacle, because the type of reflection involved *is* of a specifically non-conceptual, non-discursive sort in which the faculties are held up to one another.

Furthermore, to conceive of aesthetic reflection as non-discursive actually supports the general sense of the third *Critique* that the properly aesthetic can *only* be felt first hand and *not* discursively impressed on others through, for instance, the elaboration of rules "established as proofs."[120] The most that one can do, is to present others with the object one takes to be beautiful and encourage them to submit it to their own faculty of judgment, perhaps recommending certain especially pleasing aspects to their senses. But no mere recommendation of an object to others as beautiful can suffice, because, as Kant illustrates through an analogy to gastronomical taste,

> I am deaf to all these grounds, I try the dish with **my** tongue and my palate, and on that basis (not on the basis of general principles) do I make my judgment.[121]

This emphasis on the necessity of submitting a singular object to one's own faculty of judgment in order to make an aesthetic judgment about it would work well with the idea that the reflective activity entailed in such judging is based upon feeling, not any cognition of an object, and as such unable to be discursively captured.[122] In this manner it appears that the absence of concepts does not threaten the characteristic that makes aesthetic judgment a merely reflective judgment.

But is this the only sort of reflection that occurs? In addition to the non-discursive reflective activity, characteristic of aesthetic judgment, there appears to be a secondary *discursive* reflection involved in one's engagement with the aes-

---

[120] *Critique of the Power of Judgment*, § 33, 5:284.
[121] *Critique of the Power of Judgment*, § 33, 5:285.
[122] This is not to say that the judging never becomes discursive, but only that the harmonious play of the faculties that designates aesthetic judgment as reflective is not discursive. I will later address how this free play can eventually motivate a discursive judgment. With this issue we begin to see the reasons for streamlining the process of aesthetic judgment into distinct acts of judging, so that the non-discursive harmony may motivate, but not be subsumed under, a discursive judgment that states something's aesthetic value.

thetic. By this I mean the sort of reflection to which Kant refers in this passage, leading into his discussion of moral ideas. He tells us that in beautiful nature:

> the modifications of the light (in the coloring) or of the sound (in tones) [...] are the only sensations which permit not merely sensory feeling but also reflection on the form of these modifications of the senses, and thus as it were contain a language that nature brings to us and that seems to have a higher meaning.[123]

Even if, for the moment, we set aside Kant's remark that it is as if these modifications contain a language, to conceive of a "reflection on the form of these modifications of the senses" without the use of empirical concepts would lead us into a number of puzzling situations.

To suppose that we encounter beauty in the mode of a perception, where the categories are operative, but no empirical concepts determine that which is perceived, would mean that one could only ever speak of having encountered beauty, but never be able to identify its form with an empirical concept and say *what* the beautiful thing was. As one's eye happens across a masterfully beautiful painting, one would simultaneously be overcome by its beauty and unable to identify it *as* a painting.[124] The same would occur just as well when, walking in the garden, one happened across a bit of especially lovely foliage or, Kant's beloved example of natural beauty, the tulip. An inability to apply empirical concepts to beautiful things would put the judging subject in a situation where one was not only unable to pick out any determinate features, but also unable to name it.

This unravels into ever increasing absurdity the more seriously we take it. Imagine an artist in the process of creating a beautiful statue. At the outset, it would be a mere lump of clay, but as she skillfully shaped it and the lump began to acquire beauty, the artist would begin failing to be able to cognize the shape of what is manifesting before her. The clay would acquire beauty as it assumed a beautiful form. If beauty cannot entail cognition of an object, however, then the artist would begin with a fully cognizable lump of clay, but, as the statue took shape, the clay would become decreasingly cognizable, losing its objectness[125] over to beauty. Not only is this absurd, but it directly contradicts

---

123 *Critique of the Power of Judgment*, Bk. I, § 42, 5:302.
124 Later analysis will reveal the problem here to be that one is lacking the first layer of the layered solution I will present in the next chapter. That is to say, no determined object is given to one in experience.
125 With the term "objectness" I mean to indicate its status as a determinate, spatio-temporal *Gegenstand*, in Allison's interpretation of the term discussed above (see footnote #98). My rea-

Kant's description of beauty as existing specifically through form and shape. As Richard N. Manning observes, Kant is "preoccupied [...] with what to make of sensible contents with form, but to which no concept is applied or perhaps even adequate."[126]

At the beginning of the Transcendental Aesthetic, Kant describes how we may, in our minds, strip from the representation of a body,

> everything the understanding thinks about it, such as substance, force, divisibility, etc., as well as that which belongs to sensation, such as impenetrability, hardness, color, etc. [...].

This would leave us with simple "extension and form" which "belong to the pure intuition."[127] Such a pure intuition would be, however, insufficient to stimulate an aesthetic judgment. This sort of form "must all lie ready for it in the mind *a priori*, and can therefore be considered separately from all sensation,"[128] but the form of something beautiful is given *a posteriori* as a determination of matter that governs the shape it takes *as* extended in the pure forms of space and time, not being these pure forms themselves. As Kant explains in the third *Critique*:

> All form of the objects of the senses (of the outer as well as, mediately, the inner) is either shape or play: in the latter case, either play of shapes (in space, mime, and dance), or mere play of sensations (in time) [...] drawing in the former and composition in the latter constitute the proper object of the pure judgment of taste [...].[129]

---

sons for not regularly relying on this term are discussed in the introduction. We might also call this its *Gegenständlichkeit*, or concreteness.
126 Manning, Richard N., "The Necessity of Receptivity: Exploring a Unified Account of Kantian Sensibility and Understanding," in *Aesthetics and Cognition in Kant's Critical Philosophy*, ed. Rebecca Kukla (Cambridge: Cambridge University Press, 2006), 81.
127 *Critique of Pure Reason*, A20–21/B34–35.
128 *Critique of Pure Reason*, A20/B34.
129 *Critique of the Power of Judgment*, First Introduction, VIII., 5:225. Also: "The beautiful in nature concerns the form of the object, which consists in limitation" (*Critique of the Power of Judgment*, § 23 5:244). If there is not enough determination—or an absence of the right kind of determination—then the imagination is given to "invent" and "the mind entertains itself" with "fantasies" (*Ibid*. General Remark 5:243–4). This occurs in "the changing shapes of a fire in a hearth or of a rippling brook, neither of which are beauties, but both of which carry with them a charm for the imagination, because they sustain its free play" (*Ibid*). Alternatively, the judgment of the sublime is also pure aesthetic but "to be found in a formless object insofar as limitlessness is represented in it [...] and yet it is also thought as a totality" (*Ibid*. § 23 5:244). For a discussion of how this issue of determination applies to abstract art see footnote #139 below.

For the statue to have a spatially determined form, the schematized pure concepts of the understanding must be operative, enabling us to observe the striking posture of Degas' *La Petite Danseuse de Quatorze Ans*,

> [w]ith her shoulders back and her head held high and slightly upturned, her posture is erect and dignified, even haughty, a bearing emphasized in ballet training, but here particularly poignant.[130]

We see how the sharp angle of her chin plays against the delicate curve of her calves, juxtaposed to the tension in her downward stretched arms, fingers interlaced behind her back. To take all of this in, the intuition must be brought under pure geometrical concepts, giving the intuition a determinate shape.[131] Otherwise, the form of the statue would be lost, disappearing into the sort of blurry play of perceptual stimuli that newborns are thought to experience before they learn to organize the visual field.

As Claudia Bickmann points out, the "free interplay of the two faculties of mind is not without criteria."[132] The freedom of this free play is in accord with the "inner criteria" of "the spatio-temporal constitution of our sensible experience."[133] It is, rather, the way that the imagination remains free from the rules

---

[130] National Gallery of Art. (2015, April 15). *Little Dancer Aged Fourteen: Explore this Work*. Retrieved from: http://www.nga.gov/content/ngaweb/Collection/highlights/highlight110292.html.

[131] In the Schematism, Kant discusses the necessity of relating intuitions of spatial determinations to geometrical concepts, so as to intuit their shape, writing, "Thus the empirical concept of a plate has homogeneity with the pure geometric concept of a **circle,** for the roundness that is thought in the former can be intuited in the latter" (*Critique of Pure Reason*, A137/B176). Without relating the intuition to the concept of a circle, one would be unable to distinctly recognize the fact that objects, to which the empirical concept "plate" apply, have a roundness to them, their spatial extension taking a characteristically curved form. On could not *think* the roundness of the plate.

[132] Bickmann, "Kants "Sinnliches Scheinen der Idee" Die Einheit von Ethik und Ästhetik in Kants Kritik der Urteilskraft." In *Das Geistige und das Sinnliche in der Kunst. Ästhetische Reflexion in der Perspektive des deutschen Idealismus*, edited by Dieter Wandschneider, 13–27 (Würzburg: 2005), 16, my translation.

[133] *Ibid.*, my translation. The original reads, in full, "Im diesem Wechselspiel zwischen Einbildung und Verstand wird zugleich die Interpretationsgrundlage von Kants Ästhetik als Ästhetik der Autonomie greifbar. Doch ist dieses freie Zusammenspiel der beiden Gemütskräfte nicht maßstablos. Als inneres Maß gilt die raum-zeitliche Beschaffenheit unserer sinnlichen Erfahrung. Diese setzt, quasi von unten her, der frei spielenden Einbildungskraft enge Grenzen. Unfrei gegenüber den Sinnen bleibt die Einbildungskraft gleichwohl frei gegenüber dem Verstand, weshalb der Geschmack keine Vorschriften und Regeln gestattet, weil es hier die Einbildungskraft ist, die die Gesetze gibt, und diese frei ist." Bickmann also comments on this in an earlier article, where she writes: "Dieses freie Zusammenspiel beider Gemütskräfte ist für Kant nicht maßstab-

of the understanding that provides for the freedom of the interplay. Rebecca Kukla concurs, "when we judge an object to be beautiful, it is not as though we cease to be able to also judge it to have various determinate properties by subsuming it under concepts."[134] This makes it look as though aesthetic judgment needs to encounter the intuition of the object to be judged in a mode that offers more determination than mere perception. But is the next mode up, acquaintance, any better?

Even when considering acquaintance—a cognitive act with a higher level of objectivity than perception—Orkent runs into similar problems for working out how Kant would imagine that his dog, Mac, encounters the bus. With acquaintance still falling short of fully cognizing an object, empirical concepts cannot be applied to the intuition. Hence, when the bus passes by, in the mode of acquaintance, Mac would merely undergo:

> loud, abrasive mechanical noise, smell of diesel fuel, yellow patch, spinning wheels, and so on [...]. But nowhere in this sensed complex is there any element that displays an *object*, that is, something that perdures, or continues identical with itself through time and can have properties that change only if they are caused to change.[135]

Likewise, even if being acquainted with something beautiful would allow us to experience temporal and spatial determinations, there is an important dimension to our engagement with an aesthetic object that would be lost if all we saw were: "slight curve," "sharp angle," "downward cast straight lines"—without recognizing that it is a *chin* that is angled upward and *arms* that are thrust downward, and even more so, that it is a young ballet dancer who is represented in this haughty posture. Okrent does not find acquaintance to be a satisfactory explanation of how his dog experiences a bus.[136] We should be only less eager

---

slos. Der innere Maßstab für das ästhetisch aufgenommene Objekt wird vielmehr durch die raum-zeitliche Beschaffenheit unserer sinnlichen Erfahrung direkt diktiert. Diese setzt quasi "von unten her" der frei spielenden Einbildungskraft enge Grenzen" (Bickmann, "Das unskeptisches Fundament der Erkenntniskritik. Kants "schlechterdings notwendige Voraussetzungen" bei den wesentlichen Zwecken der menschlichen Vernunft." In *Transzendentalphilosophie heute*, edited by Andreas Lorenz, (Königshausen & Neumann: Breslauer, 2004), 145). Here Bickmann emphasizes how the inner criteria that spatio-temporal constitution places on aesthetic judgment assures that the judgment is not arbitrary.

134 Kukla, 2006, 13
135 Okrent, "Acquaintance and Cognition," 88.
136 More specifically, Okrent finds that this does not accord with how his dog both appears to respond to the bus as a persisting object, and "takes the partial presence of the bus's sensory properties as marks for the presence of the object that is the bus" ("Acquaintance and Cognition," 88).

to take it up as an adequate mode to encounter something beautiful.Let me further develop the reason why, by bringing into view something that has thus far been regulated to the side-lines: aesthetic judgment's capacity to give us something that presses beyond what concepts can capture.

III The "Higher Meaning" in Engagement with the Beautiful

One would expect the encounter with something beautiful to reach a level of complexity not only greater than "orderly noise," but also beyond the stale cognition of an object through a concept in experience. This does not simply reflect how people generally talk of their engagement with aesthetic objects, but also how Kant does in the third *Critique*. Thus far we have been narrowly focused on how the aesthetic fits into Kant's cognitive apparatus, but we also need to account for the cognitive mechanics of aesthetic judgment in a way that aligns with the role that Kant accords to it in relation to human meaningfulness. Kant's treatment of beauty as something much deeper than any sort of mere sensory pleasure comes clearly to the fore when he discusses its relation to moral ideas:

> The charms in beautiful nature, which are so frequently encountered as it were melted together with the beautiful form, belong either to the modifications of the light (in the coloring) or of the sound (in tones). For these are the only sensations which permit not merely sensory feeling but also reflection on the form of these modifications of the senses, and thus as it were contain a language that nature brings to us and that seems to have a higher meaning. Thus the white color of the lily seems to dispose the mind to ideas of innocence, and the seven colors, in their order from red to violet, to the ideas 1) of sublimity, 2) of audacity, 3) of candor, 4) of friendliness, 5) of modesty, 6) of steadfastness, and 7) of tenderness. The song of the bird proclaims joyfulness and contentment with its existence. At least this is how we interpret nature, whether anything of the sort is its intention or not.[137]

If the beautiful is to "dispose the mind" to thick moral concepts, such as those of innocence, audacity, candor, friendliness, modesty, steadfastness and tenderness, then a mere perceptual encounter along the lines of "some fuzzy blob" would be inadequate to support such a stirring contemplation of beauty. Furthermore, if aesthetic judgment merely judges a perception, then we would have difficulty making sense out of Kant's remark that:

---

[137] *Critique of the Power of Judgment*, Bk. I, § 42, 5:302.

we consider coarse and ignoble the thinking of those who have no feeling for beautiful nature (for this is what we call the receptivity to an interest in its contemplation) [...].[138]

Without something more robust than perception as the stimulus for aesthetic judgment, there does not seem to be any grounds for saying that a person who prefers to spend her time in another manner, say, playing racquetball rather than contemplating perceptions, is "coarse" and "ignoble."

A further manner in which empirical concepts play a decisive role in aesthetic judgment is made apparent in the following passage:

> But this interest, which we here take in beauty, absolutely requires that it be the beauty of nature; and it disappears entirely as soon as one notices that one has been deceived and that it is only art, so much so that even taste can no longer find anything beautiful in it or sight anything charming. What is more highly extolled by poets than the bewitchingly beautiful song of the nightingale, in a lonely stand of bushes, on a still summer evening, under the gentle light of the moon? Yet there have been examples in which, where no such songbird was to be found, some jolly landlord has tricked the guests staying with him, to their complete satisfaction, by hiding in a bush a mischievous lad who knew how to imitate this song (with a reed or a pipe in his mouth) just like nature. But as soon as one becomes aware that it is a trick, no one would long endure listening to this song, previously taken to be so charming; and the same is true with every other songbird.[139]

Here Kant brings out how nature harbors beauties which are more remarkable and suited to our aesthetic judgment than human products, illustrating this with how the tone that is found "bewitchingly beautiful" immediately becomes something that "no one would long endure" upon the discovery that what was taken to be a "birdsong," really is coming from "a mischievous lad" hidden in the bush with a reed in his mouth. For our purposes this shows that the concept under which one organizes "this *what* of what it is to which I am attending" [140] actually does influence the aesthetic judgment. If aesthetic judgment were merely stimulated by a perceived sensation, in total isolation from the cognition of an object, then the same tone would occasion the same aesthetic judgment regardless of what a judgment of experience would identify as its source. In this passage, however, we see this not to be the case. As a birdsong, the tone is beautiful, as a human song orchestrated by "some jolly landlord," this beauty "disappears entirely [...] so much so that even taste can no longer find anything beautiful in

---

138 *Critique of the Power of Judgment*, Bk. I, § 42, 5:302.
139 *Critique of the Power of Judgment*, Bk. I, § 42, 5:302.
140 Bernstein, Jay. "The Bernstein Tapes." The New School for Social Research, New York, NY. Lecture Recording from *3.8.2006*, 17:30–26:00. Course Title: GPHI 6065 Kant's *Critique of Pure Reason*. Online.

it." Thus, it is inadequate for our mode of encounter to provide us only with the sensation which is to be aesthetically judged. Rather, empirical concepts must be involved, so as to supply the "*what* of what it is" I am sensing.

There must be enough of Kant's cognitive apparatus in play for an aesthetic judgment to involve a "complex happening." To do so, the judgment cannot simply be stimulated by a perception of, or acquaintance with, "orderly noise", but rather must be stimulated by an *experience* of "music." This, however, requires much more than simply letting the categories operate so as to connect a feeling with consciousness (as they do in perception). This means having the categories operate in a cognition of an object and applying an empirical concept ("music") to this object, so as to name it. Thus, not only the pure concepts of the understanding, but also empirical concepts, have come tumbling back in.

IV Conclusion

The foregoing analysis has shown the admission of concepts, empirical and pure alike, to be a necessary and justified step. Instead of finding that aesthetic judgment pulls away from all forms of conceptualization, we have revealed that it actually depends upon encountering beauty in a mode that permits two significant forms of conceptualization. First, the object to be judged must be experienced as a fully conceptualized object with basic qualitative determinations (ex: straight, curved, angled, red, and so forth). Second, the object must be able to be organized under higher order empirical concepts, if such concepts are available for the object. Hence, one does not just experience a definite shape, but also identifies this shape as that of a tulip.[141] Our last pass through the gradation of modes of

---

[141] Even abstract art, which resists determination in many ways, involves a certain, very basic sort of determination, in order to be an object of experience for us. Many aspects of abstract art may remain indeterminate, however this indeterminacy is predicated upon a certain unproblematic determination. For example, even if the art piece is non-representational and thus it does not seem possible to supply a higher order empirical concept under which it should be organized, certain fundamental determinations (straight, curved, red, blue, circle) are in play so as to constitute the experience of the artwork in the first place. Even in works without geometrical determinations, colors are determined. And even in works where the colors are indistinct, so that one may find oneself asking "Is that red, or is it violent? Or...maybe...orange?" the very fact that there are colors in the painting functions as a determination enabling these questions to be asked. Furthermore from a Kantian standpoint one would expect any experience of an art-object to be constituted through determinations, because experience is constituted through determinative judgments. Thus, the determination of the empirical object should not be understood as *complete* determination. In my layered solution I will argue that the key factor allowing

awareness has revealed only experience to be robust enough to support both the basic qualitative and empirical forms of conceptualization. We cannot, however, simply conclude that aesthetic judgments *are* judgments of experience, because to do so would sacrifice the conceptual peculiarities that Kant describes this form of judgment as offering. Indeed, the need for concepts to be involved in aesthetic judgment in the ways just described is in tension with this form of judgment's thoroughly subjective characteristic:

> The green color of the meadows belongs to objective sensation, as perception of an object of sense; but its agreeableness belongs to subjective sensation, through which no object is represented, i.e., to feeling, through which the object is considered as an object of satisfaction (which is not a cognition of it).[142]

This passage would seem to indicate that even the perception of certain sensations ("the green color of the meadows") can be too objective for aesthetic judgment's taste. For this reason, I find that the best solution is to identify three distinct activities of judging that are at work in aesthetic judgment. How such a layered solution can effectively deal with these difficulties will be laid out in the next chapter. This solution will allow pure and empirical concepts to be operative in the process of aesthetic judgment without threatening its indeterminate character. This will involve a reconceptualization of what the indeterminate character involves.

---

aesthetic judgments to be occasioned by an empirical object is a certain intuitional aesthetic excess that escapes this determination. That said, surely there are some abstract artworks held in high regard today that Kant would not call beautiful. His system *can* account for the aesthetic value of much more contemporary art than one may have expected, however, there are bound to be some styles of art that have arisen since his time which will not be judged beautiful under his system. For three of Kant's own examples of how an absence of determination can disqualify something from being judged beautiful, see note #129 above. The empirical object that is to be judged beautiful must demonstrate a careful balance between the *Erscheinung* of the aesthetic excess that inspires our faculties and the fundamental determinations that govern the form of the *Phänomen* of the aesthetic object as object.

142 *Critique of the Power of Judgment*, Bk. 1, § 3, 5:206.

Chapter Two:
Logical Functions of Judgment and the Layered Solution

According to the foregoing analysis, experience (giving an object to knowledge through empirical consciousness) is the best mode for encountering that which stimulates the subject into making an aesthetic judgment. Only the experience of an object can allow us to encounter something that takes a distinct form and can give rise to the "higher meanings" stirred up by contemplation of the beautiful in the judging subject.

As one works carefully through Kant's Critique of Aesthetic Judgment, tensions begin to arise between the subjective and objective nature of aesthetic judgment, threatening to become outright contradictions if an interpretative way of circumventing them is not found. For example, the disinterested nature of aesthetic judgment, laid out in the first moment of the analytic of the beautiful, does not readily cohere with Kant's later comments in § 41:

> The beautiful interests empirically only in society; [...] For himself alone a human being abandoned on a desert island would not adorn either his hut or himself, nor seek out or still less plant flowers in order to decorate himself; rather, only in society does it occur to him to be not merely a human being, but also, in his own way, a refined human being [...].[1]

The fact that Kant describes the beautiful as something that "interests" us does not, in and of itself, signify an unavoidable contradiction, since the disinterestedness [*Interestlosigkeit*] of the first moment is a technical term that denotes an absence of interest *in the existence* of something—or, even more specifically, one does not seek to employ this existing thing to achieve any practical end. What is more worrisome, however, are the other elements in this passage, which *do* seem to indicate that our interest in the beautiful is caught up with a desire for the existence of certain things. This surfaces in the way that the beautiful becomes important when one is empirically (i.e., existing) in society and, furthermore, that such an interest in the beautiful leads one even to "plant flowers in order to decorate himself," signifying both an interest in the *existence* of the beautiful object (flowers) and a desire to enjoy the use of this object through the adornment of one's own, *existing*, body. Since Kant does not strike down empirical interest in the beautiful as a false appearance of beauty, or designate it as an impure aes-

---

[1] *Critique of the Power of Judgment*, Bk. I, § 41, 5: 296–7.

thetic judgment (which he does do for judgments of gratification), the threat of contradiction is quite real.

I find that streamlining the process of aesthetic judgment into layers provides the best interpretive solution to contradictions of this kind. Indeed, Kant's own introductory remarks to § 41 encourage such a reading:

> That the judgment of taste, by which something is declared to be beautiful, must have no interest for its determining ground has been adequately demonstrated above. But from that it does not follow that after it has been given as a pure aesthetic judgment no interest can be combined with it. This combination, however, can always be only indirect, i.e., taste must first of all be represented as combined with something else in order to be able to connect with the satisfaction of mere reflection on an object a further pleasure in its existence (as that in which all interest consists).[2]

Here Kant not only acknowledges the risk of running into contradiction when elucidating the social importance of the beautiful, but furthermore, he pushes this danger aside by explaining that this empirical interest is something that is added "after [the judgment] has been given as a pure aesthetic judgment."[3] As such this "further pleasure in [an object's] existence" comes after the "mere reflection," relating to it in a manner that "can always be only indirect."[4]

In my layered solution, I not only take up the distinction between a judgment of experience and the pure aesthetic judgment of taste (the necessity of which was indicated by the previous chapter), but also the distinction between pure aesthetic judgment and the way that this "sets the faculty of intellectual ideas (reason) into motion,"[5] giving "more to think about than can be grasped and made distinct in it."[6] The empirical object is cognized on the first layer, while the properly aesthetic activity of judging takes place on the second layer, and the social importance of the beautiful comes discursively to the fore on the third layer.

This approach of picking out different parts, or levels, to aesthetic judgment, is not altogether unprecedented. In negotiating the tension between a "disinterested satisfaction and given rule of our faculty of reason," Claudia Bickmann explains that the two are "not incompatible" aspects, but rather, "merely concern

---

2 *Critique of the Power of Judgment*, § 41, 5: 296.
3 *Ibid.*
4 *Ibid.*
5 *Critique of the Power of Judgment*, § 49, 5:315.
6 *Ibid.*

different levels of approaching the aesthetic phenomenon."[7] She argues that the autonomy of aesthetic reflection pertains to "the level of aesthetic experience" while "the connection to truth" concerns "the horizon of a philosophical aesthetic in which aesthetic experience is comparatively and distinctively fit into our theoretical, just as into our practical, connection to the world [Weltbezug]."[8] Whereas Bickmann writes of different levels, Paul Guyer's multicognitive view, which will be discussed shortly, picks out two distinct parts of aesthetic judgment with differing conceptual involvement. He permits concepts into the judgmental subject of aesthetic judgment, but keeps them out of the predicate. Thus, the "rose" is a conceptualized object, whereas it's beauty indicates a non-conceptualized feeling. This sections the two sides of the judgment off from each other enough for them to function in different ways.

These observations ready the ground for my own layered solution. In my solution, the division between the subject and predicate that Guyer acknowledges in his multicognitive view will be separated into different layers: the determinate subject being conceptualized on the first layer, the feeling of the predicate generated on the second, and the discursive judgment (that "X is beautiful") proclaimed on the third. The first level of aesthetic experience, to which Bickmann refers, will have strong parallels with my second layer, whereas her level of the aesthetic experience as it fits into our theoretical and practical connection to the world will correspond with my third level. [9]

---

[7] Bickmann, "Kants 'Sinnliches Scheinen der Idee.' Die Einheit von Ethik und Ästhetik in Kants Ethikotheologie," 19, *my translation*. The original reads: "Für Kant gilt beides: Interessloses Wohgefallen und vorgegebene Regeln unserer Vernunftvermögen sind für Kant nicht unverträglich, sondern betreffen allein unterschiedliche Ebenen der Annäherung an das ästhetische Phänomen."

[8] *Ibid.*, my translation. "Das Autonomie-Argument betrifft die Ebene der ästhetischen Erfahrung. Die Wahrheitsanbindung betrifft demgegenüber den Horizont einer philosophishen Ästhetik, in der die ästhetische Erfahrung in unseren theorethische wie praktischen Weltbezug vergleichend und unterscheidend eingegliedert wird."

[9] I also find affinity between my layered solution and the way that Christopher Janaway lays out aesthetic judgment (Christopher Janaway,"Kant's Aesthetics and the 'Empty Cognitive Stock,'" in *Kant's Critique of the Power of Judgment: Critical Essays*, ed. Paul Guyer [Lanham: Rowman and Littlefield, 2003]). Here he describes two moments of experience in relation to an aesthetic object, as well as a first and second judgment, in the process of arguing that even within Kant's framework specialized knowledge of an art form can allow one to better appreciate the aesthetic object judged (see 84f). The diagram of aesthetic judgment he presents on page 81 bears similarity to my layered solution, particularly insofar as he identifies three stages feeding into one another. The difference is that my layered solution is conceived so that there is a layer on which no concepts are operative, this layer being purely aesthetic. Furthermore, I would adjust his analysis to so that the specialized knowledge ("cognitive stock") to which he refers comes

In this chapter I first elaborate my layered solution. I then take the final steps in preparation for our analysis of the moments of aesthetic judgment by investigating how we should understand the term "moment" and, thus, what we are to expect from an analysis of *moments*.

The preceding chapter gave us reason to believe that a layered solution is necessary for aesthetic judgment to do everything Kant describes it as doing without fully collapsing into the determinative framework of a judgment of experience. When encountering complications such as this, one may be tempted to regard the difficulty as a demonstration that certain parts of Kant's system simply fail. Given Kant's remarkable philosophical achievements and recognition as a central figure in modern philosophy, however, I find that it is incumbent upon the reader first to pursue interpretive solutions, thoroughly investigating whether there is a way to make Kant's theory coherent. To conclude prematurely that this great philosophical mind was not intuitively developing a theory that could be coherent, even if all of the complicating elements were not yet sufficiently addressed, would be to do him a great disservice. That said, the development of an interpretive solution is also a delicate matter, because it will not be something that Kant clearly presented in some hidden portion of the text. Nor will it necessarily be something that Kant must have been thinking, but just never got around to stating outright. Rather, it may very well be something that was not fully worked out in Kant's text. In the case at hand, what I propose is an interpretive clarification of how we could understand aesthetic judgment to work, so as to sacrifice neither the curious limitation on concepts, nor the meaningfully discursive dimension that these judgments open up. Given the solution at which I have arrived and the way that it does not demand one to sacrifice any part of the system he lays out (but only clarifies them), I find it to be a sufficiently Kantian solution to a problem that Kant did not address. Thus, it *may* even be the solution that was intuitively assumed by Kant. Since Kant does not clearly address this issue, however, I do not go so far as to claim that it *is* the solution Kant would have offered if he had sought to address the problem. Although I will regularly draw on passages that gesture towards such a solution, like § 41 above, my task will not be to demonstrate that my layered solution is actually laid out by Kant in a cryptic form. Rather, the bulk of the support for my reading will

---

into play on the third layer of aesthetic judgment, whereas the first layer centers on the constitution of the empirical object and escape of the intuitional aesthetic excess. The higher level appreciation with which he concerns himself in this essay speak to the way that the third layer brings the feeling of the second layer and the specialized third layer knowledge this feeling triggers into relation with the first layer, using it to recognize the empirical object on a higher level—as not just spatio-temporal, but also purposive (*zweckmäßig*).

come from showing how it allows us to make sense out of the nearly contradictory description that Kant provides of how aesthetic judgment works.

I Setting the Ground Work for a Layered Solution

A number of commentators have similarly reached the conclusion that whatever Kant's insistence on aesthetic judgment as independent of concepts may mean, it cannot be given the most extreme interpretation, i.e., that the entire aesthetic apparatus is utterly devoid of concepts, lest we thereby render aesthetic judgment ultimately impossible. Allison, for example, suggests that a concept is involved "as the exhibition of the form of a concept in general" through which the imagination "stimulates the understanding by occasioning it to entertain fresh conceptual possibilities, while, conversely, the imagination, under the general direction of the understanding, strives to conceive new patterns of order."[10] It remains indeterminate which would be an adequate concept for the intuition. This cannot, however, be the full story of how aesthetic judgment functions. To only view aesthetic judgment as stirring up an indeterminable concept would still leave us with the problem that bars aesthetic judgment from relating to an object, as discussed in the previous chapter. One can only appreciate the clean contours of a statue, relate the feeling this stirs to moral ideas and engage in aesthetic criticism, if the object and its qualitative features have been determinatively thought through concepts. Without such determination, the aesthetic object would be an unsteady, indeterminable swirling of feeling, unable to support the higher level processes of moral appreciation and art criticism.[11] These are the concerns to which the first and third layer of my solution attend.

Paul Guyer's reading bears a number of similarities to mine. In "The Harmony of the Faculties Revisited" he addresses the question of how concepts may and may not be operative in aesthetic judgments. He begins by organizing the interpretations dealing with the involvement of concepts into three views: 'precognitive', 'multi-cognitive' and 'meta-cognitive'.[12] Both the precognitive and multi-cognitive views read the harmony of the faculties in aesthetic judgment

---

10 Allison, *Kant's Theory of Taste*, 171.
11 As noted in the previous chapter (footnote #139) abstract art does not escape this issue, for even if its indeterminacies cause the observer to question many things in the artwork (i.e. What is that?), the posing of these questions is predicated upon some determination in the work, be it a grouping of distinct lines, certain colors, or even simply the fact that there are colors in the painting, although the observer has difficulty identifying exactly which colors these are.
12 Guyer, "The Harmony of the Faculties Revisited," 165–170.

as "not involv[ing] any determinate concepts."[13] According to the precognitive view, aesthetic judgment encounters the object in the mode of perception and "satisfies all of the conditions for normal cognition of an object *except for that of the actual application of a determinate concept to the manifold*."[14] The multi-cognitive view, on the other hand, sees aesthetic judgment as satisfying all of the conditions for normal cognition, "although only in an indeterminate way."[15] According to this interpretation it is not that there is *no* concept in play, but only that there is no *determinate* concept in play.

As we have seen above, however, it is deeply problematic to understand aesthetic judgment as unable to relate to determinate concepts in *any* way. Guyer focuses on the problem that such a reading would cause for the grammatical form that aesthetic judgments are to take:

> An aesthetic judgment does not have the form "This is beautiful" but rather "This *F* is beautiful": this hummingbird, this sunset, this painting, this symphony, this part of the garden (but not the other), this façade of the building (but not its other elevations), or the public space of this hotel (but not its guest rooms). And these objects or parts of objects cannot be individuated without concepts [...]. [This] is certainly evident in Kant's examples of aesthetic judgments: In spite of his insistence that the judgments are in some sense independent of determinate concepts, he always supposes that they are about particular objects, which can only be individuated by means of such concepts [...]. Thus, while Kant may well have thought that we can abstract from *some* concepts that we would ordinarily apply to possible objects of taste, in particular concepts of their intended *use* or *end* (*CPJ*, § 15, 5:226–7, 5:229–31), his own examples of paradigmatic judgments of taste suggest that he could not very well have thought that we could assess our aesthetic responses to objects or even respond to them at all without individuating them by means of ordinary concepts such as 'triangle' or 'plate', 'hummingbird' or 'painting.'[16]

Guyer goes on to highlight how Kant's insistence that there are no concepts in play is targeted at the predicate, not at the subject.[17] He does this through what he terms his preferred 'meta-cognitive' view, which offers a helpful inroad for my layered solution. According to this view, Guyer sees aesthetic judgment as having both an ordinary cognitive aspect and an aspect that "seems to satisfy the understanding's general requirement of unity and coherence in some further way, which is not specified by such determinate concepts."[18] He supports this

---

13 Guyer, "The Harmony of the Faculties Revisited," 178.
14 Guyer, "The Harmony of the Faculties Revisited," 165.
15 Guyer, "The Harmony of the Faculties Revisited," 165.
16 Guyer, "The Harmony of the Faculties Revisited," 179–180.
17 Guyer, "The Harmony of the Faculties Revisited," 184.
18 Guyer, "The Harmony of the Faculties Revisited," 187.

view by citing passages where Kant refers to a determinative aspect that is involved in aesthetic judgments, although it is not what imbues such judgments with their properly aesthetic quality. For instance, Kant observes that in the judgment of taste, it is

> nevertheless [...] still quite conceivable that the object can provide it with a form that contains precisely such a composition of the manifold as the imagination would design in harmony with the lawfulness of the understanding in general if it were left free by itself.[19]

Accordingly, it sounds as if what is properly *aesthetic* about aesthetic judgment is this further form of unity that such a judgment is able to achieve (or feel to be achieved), going beyond the sort of unity that cognitive judgments seek. Guyer suggests that,

> the precognitive and multicognitive approaches to the harmony of the faculties can in the end be taken to characterize specific ways in which our experience of unity and coherence in the manifold presented to us by particular objects can go beyond the conditions necessary for ordinary cognition – although it should be implied precisely by the fact that the harmony of the faculties must be a free play that there can be no single, concrete description of this state, so that these approaches cannot be more than abstract descriptions of some ways in which objects might yield a metacognitive harmony.[20]

If I put my view into Guyer's framework, then the primary difference is that whereas Guyer regards the normal determinative and the additional aesthetic aspects as belonging to the same judgment, I take these to be two separate activities of judgment, taking place on separate layers. Within the framework of my solution, the conceptualization of the judgmental subject is accounted for by the first, basic empirical layer, which generates an object of experience. The second layer takes up the additional aesthetic aspects which throw the faculties into a harmonious free play. This feeling incites a third-layer attempt to articulate the

---

19 *Critique of the Power of Judgment*, Bk. I, § 22, 5: 241. Further support for this view is offered by a passage from the First Introduction, "For in the power of judgment understanding and imagination are considered in relation to each other, and this can, to be sure, first be considered objectively, as belonging to cognition (as happened in the transcendental schematism of the power of judgment); but one can also consider this relation of two faculties of cognition merely subjectively, insofar as one helps or hinders the other in the very same representation and thereby affects the *state of mind* [...]" (First Introduction, VIII., 20: 223). This passage speaks particularly in favor of my layered solution, since it does not simply suggest that there is an objective way and subjective way of considering the relation of understanding and imagination, but furthermore, that the objective consideration occurs *before* the subjective.
20 Guyer, "The Harmony of the Faculties Revisited," 187.

feeling of the subject in relation to the empirical object (cognized in the first layer judgment) inspiring "much thinking."

Guyer, however, does not streamline the process into separate layers.[21] Instead, he attempts to deal with these same issues while keeping the process of aesthetic judgment one-dimensional. He treats aesthetic judgment as a singular act of judging that aims entirely at generating the verdict on the aesthetic value of the object, i.e., "This x is beautiful." Thus, he supposes these issues to be solved if concepts are admitted into the judgmental subject, but not the predicate. That is to say, that concepts allow one to put the fully cognized object "rose" in the subject position, but the feeling of pleasure, with which the judgment states that this rose is combined, is not determined by concepts.[22] As suggested in the footnotes in chapter one,[23] this is problematic, because as ineffable and uncognizable as the feelings of pleasure that motivate this judgment may be, the term that occupies the position of predicate, "beautiful," is just as much a concept as the grammatical subject, "rose." Thus, if there is truly to be an unconceptualized space for feeling in aesthetic judgment, then we need to move away from the assumption that the final judgment statement exhausts the activity of aesthetic judging. The sentence declaring a thing to be beautiful is no more the essence of aesthetic judgment, than the singular personal pronoun "I" used to designate one's perspective on the world *is* the transcendental unity of apperception.[24] To mistake the one for the other is to confuse the empirical with the transcendental. In this manner, my layered solution improves upon Guyer's 'meta-cognitive' view, because it does not assume that aesthetic judgment culminates in the statement "This tulip is beautiful," and thus simultaneously side-steps the complications presented by the fact that the predicate

---

21 Guyer, "The Harmony of the Faculties Revisited."
22 Guyer, "The Harmony of the Faculties Revisited," 179–180. Although under his meta-cognitive view Guyer allows that the harmonious lack of conceptual determination can either take the pre-cognitive or multi-cognitive route (either involving no concepts or only indeterminate concepts), he does not address the fact that the grammar of the aesthetic judgment, which he uses to solve problems that arise if the object judged is indeterminable, commits us to an equally grammatically conceptualized predicate.
23 See n77, n81, n101 and n122.
24 This parallel builds off of Claudia Bickmann's discussion of the transcendental unity of apperception, which "als das Akzentrum und Prinzip aller Verknüpfung nur bestimmungsfrei und einfach sein [kann]. So lässt es sich auch nicht als die erste "Person singularis" in einer offenen Satzform beschreiben, denn als Teil einer Relation – der verknüpften Vorstellungen in unserem Urteil – kann es ihr Prinzip nicht sein" (Bickmann, "Das unskeptisches Fundament der Erkenntniskritik. Kants "schlechterdings notwendige Voraussetzungen" bei den wesentlichen Zwecken der menschlichen Vernunft," 135–136).

"beautiful" is no less a concept than the subject "tulip." Furthermore, the third layer allows the aesthetic excess that escapes a determinative judgment of the object on the first layer to affect the subject in a manner that is taken up discursively, inciting higher meanings. Guyer's model does not offer a natural segue into this sort of discursive contemplation.

That said, Guyer's view provides an important point of departure for my own. Not only does he show that determinative judgments of experience can be involved without violating the terms Kant has set out, but my view also profits from Guyer's insight that there need not be an exclusive choice between the pre-cognitive and multi-cognitive views of aesthetic harmony. Rather, the harmony could sometimes only occur without concepts being involved, but sometimes go beyond this to offer a further multi-cognitive "harmonious play among images and thoughts [...] a free play that itself seems to satisfy the understanding's demand for coherence but that is not dictated by any determinate concepts of the objects and cannot generate any such determinate concepts."[25] I agree that we see both a harmony of the faculties without concepts and a discursive free-play with concepts. Through my layered solution, however, I would like to separate each form of harmony onto a separate layer of aesthetic judgment. The harmony that occurs without conceptual determination is the harmony of the free-play of the faculties on the second layer of aesthetic judgment. When this leads to a further harmony that occurs in the free play of concepts, where there is only ever an indeterminable concept, this is the discursive harmony of the third layer. Guyer makes it clear that we must conceive of aesthetic judgment in a manner that allows for both kinds of harmony. The absence of concepts from the one and presence in the other indicates that these two forms of harmony function in distinct manners. In my layered solution there is, thus, one layer without concepts and one layer with concepts, and these two types of harmony very naturally fall so that the one that is concept independent is located on the second layer, and the one that is discursive is on the third.

II The Layered Solution

With a layered solution, we can allow for one to encounter the object to be judged in the mode of experience without sacrificing the indeterminate character of aesthetic judgment. The properly aesthetic element needs to be placed on a determinative base. Aesthetic judgment proper must not be the only sort of judg-

---

25 Guyer, "The Harmony of the Faculties Revisited," 188.

ment involved in encountering the beautiful. Rather, there are three distinct activities of judging involved. An object is given to knowledge through a judgment of experience on the first layer. An aesthetic excess is received in the empirical cognition of this object, and it is this which is taken up by the power of judgment in a properly aesthetic manner on the second layer. The third layer, then attempts to relate the feeling perception of the second layer to the basic empirical judgment of the first through a new aesthetic vocabulary. In this manner, the two forms of conceptual employment are separated out so that the basic constitution of an object of experience is performed in the first layer and the "higher meanings" are contemplated in the third. These three layers correspond to what Nicolai Hartmann picked out as the "essential aspects" of the act of observing beauty, which are intuition, enjoyment and assessment.[26] Although Hartmann only mentions it in passing, he believes there to be a "unification of all three sides of aesthetical receptivity" in Kant's aesthetics, the only problem being that "too little was done to differentiate them."[27] Due to the analysis of the foregoing chapter, it appears that the best way to make sense out of Kant's aesthetics is by taking on the interpretative task of differentiating these elements. And this is what my layered solution will accomplish.[28]

The first and third layers of aesthetic judgment are constituted by judgments of experience, but with very different aims. The first layer is a basic judgment of experience, constituting an empirical object ("This is a tulip"), while the third layer discursively expands upon this, which can take a variety of forms, but minimally it states the aesthetic value of the object cognized in the first layer ("This tulip is beautiful"). In the second, middle layer the object has already been established and the concern is turned inward, focused on the interplay of the faculties and feelings of the subject. Although the empirical judgment supplies the determination necessary to permit the properly aesthetic judgment to discursively relate to an object of experience, there must be an unsubsumed element of the intuition that escapes the empirical judgment, inciting an act of aesthetic judging. This intuitional surplus is felt, but not made into a determination of the em-

---

26 Hartmann, *Aesthetics*, 16.
27 Hartmann, *Aesthetics*, 17.
28 This reading falls in line with Kant's frequent reference to judgments judging judgments. We see this, for instance, in the first *Critique* where Kant describes how one judgment may serve as the subject for another judgment. Under "Relation" in the table of judgments it is actually only categorial judgments that involve "two concepts […] considered to be in relation to each other," while hypothetical judgments relate "two judgments" and disjunctive judgments relate "several" (*Critique of Pure Reason*, A73/B98). The idea that one judgment may feed into another in the layered solution is, thus, in accordance with how Kant describes judgments to function.

pirical object.²⁹ It is the *je ne sais quoi* that cannot be discursively grasped, but inspires a certain stimulation of the faculties.³⁰ Although it escapes our conceptual grasp, it still exerts an influence on one's state.³¹ This reading is supported by Kant's remark that "the satisfaction in beauty, however, is one that presupposes no concept, but is immediately combined with the representation through which the object is given (not through which it is thought)."³² Here Kant acknowledges that something is given in the representation, which gives us the empirical object, but this *something* is not part of the empirical object, because to be part of the empirical object it would have to be thought *in* this object. That cannot be the case, however, because this *something* is not even thought.

---

29 My project is focused on judgments of the beautiful and not those of the sublime; however, seeing as they are both pure aesthetic judgments, I am encouraged by the way that the sublime can also be easily read as beginning with an intuitional excess. Aside from this commonality in their point of departure, however, these two types of pure aesthetic judgment take very different paths. Whereas the intuitional excess of the judgment of taste brings the faculties of imagination and understanding into a harmonious free play, the intuitional excess of the sublime proves to be more than either the imagination or the understanding can handle (depending on whether it is the mathematical or the dynamical sublime). Thus, "the taste for the beautiful presupposes and preserves the mind in **calm** contemplation" (*Critique of the Power of Judgment*, § 24, 5:247, bold original), bringing with it "a feeling of the promotion of life, and hence is compatible with charms and an imagination at play" (*Ibid.*, § 23, 5:244–5). In the judgment of the sublime, in contrast, we are confronted with an intuitional excess that is "contrapurposive for our power of judgment," even "doing violence" to our faculties of mind (*Ibid.*, § 23, 5:245). Here a pleasure "arises only indirectly, being generated, namely, by the feeling of a momentary inhibition of the vital powers and the immediately following and all the more powerful outpouring of them" (*Ibid.*). This occurs in the mathematical sublime when nature presents us with something absolutely great, revealing "the very inadequacy of our faculty for estimating the magnitude of the things of the sensible world," (*Ibid*, § 25, 5:250) or alternatively in the dynamical sublime, where the "all-destroying violence" of nature "make[s] our capacity to resist into an insignificant trifle in comparison with [its] power" (*Ibid*, § 28, 5:261). For more on how my layered structure of interpretation could be applied to the sublime, see the Conclusion ("Looking Ahead").
30 Here, one might be tempted to compare my view to that of Karl Ameriks, who contends that it is "special objects" of features of objects that are responsible for the judgment of beauty (Karl Ameriks, "How to Save Kant's Deduction of Taste." *Journal of Value Inquiry* 16 (1982): 295–302, 299). My view differs from this in a crucial way. What stimulates the faculties into a harmonious free play, thus occasioning a judgment of beauty, is something special about the intuition that is cognized into an object, but it is not the part of this intuition which is cognized into an object that provides for this special attribute. This special attribute is provided by the part of the intuition that escapes cognition. Thus, in my view, it would be wrong to say that the *object* (i.e., the objectified intuition) stimulates an aesthetic judgment.
31 For a more detailed description this intuitional excess, see section II. C. of this chapter entitled Intuitional Excess.
32 *Critique of the Power of Judgment*, Bk. I, § 16, 5:230.

I will show there to be a common aesthetic thread that runs through the layers, passing from the intuitional surplus of the first to the free play enlivening the faculties on the second and then to the incitement of a discursive verdict on the object's aesthetic value, which may be accompanied by a further discursive harmony on the third. Tracing this thread, we see the second layer to be where the characteristics Kant underscores as unique to pure aesthetic judgment surface most distinctly. On the second layer there is no object, but only a feeling, given to the subject through the harmonious free play of the faculties, and this feeling is "merely conjoin[ed]" with the inner perception of the free play "in a consciousness of my state."[33] Thus, it is here that the peculiar concept-independent act of judging surfaces. I will, accordingly, refer to this as the *properly aesthetic layer*.

In the previous chapter we looked at how Kant describes the possible transformation of a judgment of perception into a judgment of experience, relating the feeling that the subject perceives to the object that stimulated this feeling in the subject, and thus concluding that the object possesses a certain property. The third layer involves the generation of cognitive judgements that are incited by the second layer's act of perceptual judging and relates this to the empirical object, judged by the first layer. The third layer is inspired by the feeling perception of the free-play to communicate something that will bring the object of the first layer together with the feeling of the second. The initial step in doing so is to generate an aesthetic judgment statement, such as "This tulip is beautiful." This statement objectifies the perception, so that the feeling of the second layer may be treated as if it were a property of the object.[34] This opens the gate to further intellectualization of the aesthetic perception. Thus it is on this layer that the discursively reflective and intersubjective practices of art criticism and philosophical aesthetic contemplation are carried out.

It is not that the higher layers are completer or truer versions of the lower layers. Each layer involves a different sort of judging. The first layer judges the

---

33 Prolegomena, § 20.
34 Admittedly, there is a certain tension here. While necessary for the higher meanings that beauty is to inspire, such an objectifying move grates with Kant's remarks on the technical inaccuracy of attributing beauty to the object (see *Critique of the Power of Judgment*, § 6). His insistence that this is due to our way of talking about beauty, is more telling than it might initially seem. Only through such objectification of the second layer's perception may the higher meanings beauty inspires become discursively contemplable. By no means is this to indicate that the third layer is the truth of the second. The sensation of aesthetic pleasure perceived in the second layer is somehow linked to the terms it motivates in the third layer. But neither the term "beautiful" nor any of the higher meanings can capture, determine or subsume the aesthetic pleasure of the second layer, itself.

raw sense data to be a certain object with certain qualities. The second layer engages with the aesthetic excess, which escaped the empirical judgment of the object, throwing the faculties into a perceptible, but not cognizable, harmonious free-play. Although the reflection of this in the third layer gestures towards what was ineffably perceived in the second, it does not, however, conceptually capture what occurred there. The harmonious free-play of the faculties, and feeling perception thereof, can neither be subsumed by the concepts of the first layer, nor by those of the third. In the third layer, it stirs up a new set of aesthetic terms but still escapes being determined by these terms, leaving one with the unshakable feeling that when lingering over the beautiful, there is always something left to say. Thus, the intuitional excess which could not be subsumed under the concept of the object on the first layer re-emerges on the third level in a new form.

The location of what is aesthetic differs on each layer. On the first layer the aesthetic subsists in that which escapes, in the second layer it subsists in the play, and then in the third layer the aesthetic subsists in the incitement to meaningful thinking. Thus, we see that in the first and third layers the aesthetic is located at the outskirts of the determinative cognitive activity, escaping or inciting it, while the second layer, which involves nothing foreign to aesthetic judgment, may be considered purely aesthetic. In chapter five, I will investigate the possibility that the common aesthetic thread running through these layers and allowing them to influence one another is *Zweckmäßigkeit, aber ohne Zweck*.[35] In the Preface Kant remarks that the faculty for judging,

> has to provide a concept itself, through which no thing is actually cognized, but which only serves as a rule for it, but not as an objective rule to which it can conform its judgment, since for that yet another power of judgment would be required in order to be able to decide whether it is a case of the rule or not.[36]

This, principle emerges as the purposiveness of nature, which is "a special *a priori* concept that has its origin strictly in the reflecting power of judgment."[37] Aesthetic judgment tells the story of how a sense of purposiveness takes hold in the first place. It is this curious sense of a purposiveness without purpose that escapes the empirical cognition of the first layer, throws the faculties into a pleasurable free-play on the second, and inspires a flurry of meaningful thinking on

---

[35] *Critique of the Power of Judgment*, Bk. I, § 15. B46/A46 [5:228]. That is to say, purposiveness without a purpose.
[36] *Critique of the Power of Judgment*, Bk. I, Preface, 5:169.
[37] *Critique of the Power of Judgment*, Bk. I, Preface, 5:181.

the third. Thus, it begins as fully unconceptualized, exerting an increasing influence upon our cognitive faculties in the process of the layers.

II.A An Illustrative Analogy: Dancing Between the Layers

Now that my layered solution has been sketched out, let us take a closer look at how the layers relate to one another through an analogy to dance. The second layer is characterized by dynamicity. Here, acts of thinking operate, but no object or determinative quality is generated through this. We might draw an analogy between how this layer functions and how a trained dancer moves when dancing for his own enjoyment without any choreography. With no professional obligation determining his movements, he glides freely about the floor. Only the feeling that the music stirs in him guides his movements. The music may very well have words, and these words may contribute to the way that he feels the music, and thus in a certain sense to the way that he moves, but this is not a direct, constraining influence, for the dance is not aimed at telling the story of the lyrics through movements. Rather, the driving force of the dance is an impulse to: *"Feel! Move! Feel!"* The dancer is not consciously calculating his movements to the beats of the music, and yet somehow, without thinking about it, he anticipates an acceleration of the tempo, sensing a musical change that is about to take hold.

We can relate this to the interaction between the layers of my solution in the following manner. For the dancer, it is clear that both a pre-established knowledge and concurrently cognized experience have a bearing on what he is doing. Thus, we can see how the dance training and musical determinations, on the one hand, and the object constituted through empirical judgment, on the other, both have what I would like to call a deactivated, enabling presence. Just as the empirical judgment that determines the aesthetic object to be a statue with a set of determinate properties falling under a certain empirical concept enables the harmonious free play of the faculties on the second layer of aesthetic judgment, so too do the properties of the music and the dancer's previous training play a role in enabling him to freely dance from feeling. The dancing is not *about* the steps previously learned, nor is aesthetic judgment *about* the determination of the object, although both the judging activity in the properly aesthetic layer and the dancing carry out their activity upon the foundation that each of these provides.[38] Admittedly, it is the aesthetic excess that escapes determination in the

---

[38] The way that this dancer proceeds has strong parallels to Carolyn Dicey Jennings' descrip-

first layer, which throws the faculties into a harmonious free play in the second layer, but this does not mean that the first layer becomes of no consequence.

The first-layer determinations of the object may inspire a certain sort of feeling or movement of the faculties, just as the determinations of the music inspire a particular feeling on the part of our dancer, encouraging him towards a certain style of movement. In this manner the first layer, and its determinations, feed into the second layer, without the second layer being *about* these determinations—rather, this layer is about the feelings and movements inspired. This is an important point of distinction, because it means that the concepts involved in the first layer influence and inspire the second layer, but the second layer is not about processing them or determining them further. The second layer is about the activity of judging in a pure aesthetic manner. Fueled by the feelings perceived, this judging is far more concerned with the act of judging itself than with producing a "judgment" as a product. It lingers "over the consideration of the beautiful because this consideration strengthens and reproduces itself."[39]

The analogy to dance is also instructive for understanding how the second layer relates to the third. According to my layered solution, the third layer of aesthetic judgment is the flurry of discursive activity that the second layer's feeling act of judging motivates. It is thus on the third layer that a proclamation of the object's aesthetic value is issued and aesthetic ideas are contemplated. Although this proclamation (i.e., "This tulip is beautiful") is one of the key products of aesthetic judging, it would be wrong to take it as the summation of aesthetic judgment altogether. It is merely a judgment statement that the workings of the second layer inspire, but it does not subsume the process of judging—to see it in such a manner would be to overlook the actual *dancing* of our dancer.

In our analogy, the third layer would be comparable to whatever discursive results the dancing might yield for our dancer. Perhaps through his dancing he acquired greater reflective insight into how he is feeling, allowing formerly in-

---

tion of "entrained consciousness" in *Consciousness Without Attention*. This form of consciousness involves both "the experience of being entrained to a task despite performing that task without the aid of attention" and "requires focus" (Carolyn Dicey Jennings, "Consciousness without Attention," Journal of the American Philosophical Association 1, no. 2 [2015]: 276 – 295; 288). She further draws this out as a contrast between attunement and attention. In entrained consciousness one is "attuned to an object, process, or activity" in such a way that one is "not thinking about oneself, one's surroundings, or one's future," but rather "skillfully responding to particular visual stimuli without invoking the top-down biasing of attention" (289f). Interestingly, Jennings also elaborates this form of consciousness as characterized by "the lack of a divide between subject and object" (Jennings, "Consciousness without Attention," 290).

39 *Critique of the Power of Judgment*, § 12, 5:222.

choate feelings to manifest discursively. Perhaps he uses his free-form dance to create a choreography by turning back to conceptualize the movements he naturally found himself performing. This parallels aesthetic judgment's third-level attempt to conceptualize the movements of the faculties in the properly aesthetic layer. Engaged in such conceptualization, the art critic will talk of how the bright color of the woman's cap draws attention upward, suggesting notions of loftiness and nobility with its point, while the cap's reflection in the pond below also allows it to resonate with a sense of one's inescapable humanity. Thus, it is on the third level that one not only engages in art criticism, but also philosophizes about aesthetics—both being attempts to grasp at the ineffable experience of the second layer. Although the third layer cannot capture the second, the latter does incite "much thinking" in the former. It should, however, also be noted that the third layer's attempt at conceptualization is somewhat alienated from the movement of the second that incites it. Nicolai Hartmann makes a very similar point when he comments on how aesthetics is alienated from art:

> For its part, aesthetics is also no continuation of art. It is not a stage above it, to which art must or even could rise. Aesthetics is not such a thing, any more than literature is psychology or sculpture is anatomy. Its task is in a certain sense just the opposite. Aesthetics attempts to remove the veils from the mystery that is carefully preserved by the arts. It attempts to analyze the act of beholding that enjoys its object, which can continue as long as it is not disrupted and disturbed by thinking. It makes into an object what is not an object in this act and cannot become one, the act itself. For that reason also the art object is something different for aesthetics, i.e., an object of reflection and inquiry, which it cannot be for aesthetical beholding. Here is found the reason why the attitude of the aesthetician is not an aesthetical attitude, such that it naturally follows the latter; it subordinates itself to it, but does not place itself within it, and *a fortiori* does not place itself in a position inferior to or above it.[40]

The motivation behind talking about this in terms of layers is not to designate certain layers as more complete, or "higher," than others. Rather, the goal of streamlining the process of aesthetic judgment in this way is to separate different activities of judging involved in aesthetic judgment from one another. Thus, the fact that the third layer comes after the second, being incited into discursive activity by it, is not to indicate that the third layer accomplishes something that the second layer attempted but failed. This division indicates instead that very different sorts of judging activity take place on each of these layers. The first layer carries out a judgment of experience, so as to give us an object. This supplies the conditions for the possibility of the other layers, avoiding the difficulties dis-

---

[40] Hartmann, *Aesthetics*, 5.

cussed in the first chapter, but in and of itself this first layer judgment of an object successfully completes its task of generating an object of experience. The aesthetic excess that this layer generates is something that cannot be captured by an object of experience. It cannot be cognized through subsumption under a concept and thus cannot even be thought of as part of the object of experience. The second, properly aesthetic, layer is the pure activity of judging, done freely and for its own sake and without thought to anything else. The third layer represents what the second layer awakens on a discursive level within the subject. The discursive, and thus conceptual, nature of this layer alienates it to a certain extent from the properly aesthetic layer that incites it. But, for Kant as opposed to Hartmann, this separation does not go so far as to render aesthetics a matter *entirely* removed from aesthetic pleasure.

II.B Aesthetic Judgment as Underlying Both Observation and Creation

This analogy also brings to light a further point of interest about Kant's aesthetic theory. In a number of ways, Kant's theory of aesthetic judgment appears to be much more about observing beauty than creating it. Aside from the sections on genius, the creative artistic process often seems to be pushed aside in Kant's system of aesthetic judgment. This becomes even more the case, if the second layer is not separated from the third. A failure to separate these two would allow the proclamation of something's beauty ("This x is beautiful") to eclipse the properly aesthetic activity of judging, itself.[41] It is, however, in this act on the second layer that the judging of the subject and the creative process of the artist coincide. Here one is concerned with perceiving the aesthetic feelings of the faculties in their harmonious free play. These could very well be supposed to be the sorts of feelings that also guide the creation of art. After acquiring fundamental facili-

---

[41] Kristi Sweet similarly emphasizes the importance of drawing "a distinction between a judging (attempted) of the *object*, and the *judgment of taste*" (Sweet, Kristi, "Reflection: Its Structure and Meaning in Kant's Judgments of Taste." *Kantian Review* 14, no. 1 [2009]: 53–80; 63). She elaborates, "The object of a judgment of taste is our feeling, or aesthetic response to an object in nature – the feeling's quality, cause relation, etc. Thus pleasure is the nexus of judgment; a result of an attempt to determine the object in nature (or unintentional reflection) by which we might say, 'this object occasions pleasure in me', but pleasure is also the object and ground of the judgment of taste, by which in saying 'this object is beautiful' we make a claim not only about our relation to the object, but more substantively about the universal conditions of judging and thus the relation of others to this object" (63–64).

ty with the instrument or medium, musicians and visual artists alike turn their attention to sensing and feeling. Nicolai Hartmann remarks on this as well,

> a fourth element makes a powerful entrance in the background of the receptive attitude, that of autonomous engagement or of spontaneous achievement [...] and the receptive act seems thereby to approach the act of the productive artist. In Kant, this took the form of a reactive engagement, a 'play of the powers of the mind,' [...] an inward re-creation of the original creation of the artist, but re-created solely in the act of beholding.[42]

Thus, the creation of art could be understood along the lines of a similarly stratified process. The first stage involves learning the techniques, scales and movements necessary for the material production of the art. Once these skills have been acquired, however, and become a sort of "second nature" to the artist, they may fall back into a deactivated, enabling role so that the true creation of the art may be led by the feeling of aesthetic pleasure. The real creation of art would then take place on the second layer and the third layer would be when the artist pulls back to think discursively about her creation. Since artistic genius lies in the ineffable creative stage (second layer), upon entry into this discursively reflective layer the artist's ability to talk about her work may very well not be on par with her non-discursive creative abilities.[43]

II.C Intuitional Excess

Although Kant does not, himself, use the term "intuitional excess" or "intuitional surplus" it is clear that pure aesthetic judgment involves an intuition that is not subsumed under a concept.[44] I understand such an intuition to be an intuition

---

42 Hartmann, Aesthetics, 17.
43 We might compare this to Socrates' remarks in Plato's *Apology*, "I discovered, then, very soon about the poets that no wisdom enabled them to compose as they did, but natural genius and inspiration; like the diviners and those who chant oracles, who say many fine things but do not understand anything of what they say" (Plato, *Plato: Five Dialogues: Euthyphro, Apology, Crito, Meno, Phaedo*. Translated by G. M. A. Grube [Indianapolis: Hackett Publishing, 2002], 23B).
44 Kant first observes the possibility of intuition without concepts in the Introduction, where he writes, "representation belonging to the faculty of cognition can also be an intuition, pure or empirical, without concepts" (*Critique of the Power of Reason*, XI, 20:245). Over the course of his remarks in the Analytic of the Beautiful it becomes clear that judgments of taste are based on just such an intuition without concepts. Kant writes, "But if the question is whether something is beautiful, one [...wants to know] how we judge it in mere contemplation (intuition or reflection)" (*Ibid*, § 2, 5:204). In contrast, Kant observes that in objects that are regarded as having some determinate purpose "there is also no immediate satisfaction at all in their intu-

that *exceeds* what can be cognized. Rather than make repeated reference to "intuition without a concept," I have given a name to this, a move that allows me to discuss intuitional excess more effectively, tracing its role in the judgment of taste.

Let us describe this intuitional excess a bit further. The intuitional excess of objects that are judged beautiful occasions the transcendental free play of the imagination and the understanding so as to generate a pleasure that is not based on any private grounds, but rather on the transcendental arrangement of the faculties.[45] I take this to be a *specific* sort of intuitional excess, and *not* the *only* sort of intuitional excess possible. To understand the intuitional excess that leads to the judgment of taste, it can be helpful to begin by examining a simpler example of an intuitional excess that can arise through the accumulation of personal experience. After doing so, I will use this as a point of entry for discussing the specifically pure aesthetic intuitional excess.

Since intuition is not cognitive, an intuitional excess will be something that is felt but not thought, although it may incite a flurry of thoughts in an attempt to grasp this feeling conceptually, albeit unsuccessfully. The reader is likely familiar with how an excess of feeling can be stirred up by looking upon an object of great sentimental value. For example, imagine that you are cleaning out the attic when you suddenly happen upon your favorite stuffed animal from childhood. The simple well-worn bear opens up a fount of memories, meanings and feelings. It might be that your mind quickly fixes upon one specific memory, but perhaps it does not and instead you gaze upon the bear basking in the inchoate glow of its significance. Perhaps there is someone else there with you and, upon your discovery of this beloved bit of synthetic fibers and textile, words rush to your lips, "Oh, my goodness. I can't believe it. That was my favorite teddy bear when I was a child..." These meager statements only gesture at the uncanny feeling that has taken hold. So you try again, "I took him with me just about everywhere for a number of years... I used to loop my thumb through

---

ition. A flower, by contrast, e. g., a tulip, is held to be beautiful because a certain purposiveness is encountered in our perception of it which, as we judge it, is not related to any end at all" (*Ibid*, § 17, 5:236 note). And as for the tulip that pleases in its intuition, we know too that "Flowers, free designs, lines aimlessly intertwined in each other under the name of foliage, signify nothing, do not depend on any determinate concept, and yet please" (*Ibid*, § 4, 5:207). In this manner the judgment of the beautiful is occasioned by an intuition and yet "neither grounded on concepts nor aimed at them" (*Ibid*, § 4, 5:209). This intuition without a concept is what I call the intuitional excess.
45 This is described in more detail in chapter four, see section II. The Second Moment of Aesthetic Judgment.

the tag on his back and carry him upside-down..." This specificity still fails to capture how the now dilapidated toy is working upon you to bring up all of the smells and tastes of childhood, the feeling of being simultaneously protected and thwarted by infantile powerlessness, the joy offered by an imaginative world of play. But even this description only grasps at the feeling of intuitional excess that strikes you when looking upon the bear. The feeling of intuitional excess itself is "something else, which gives the imagination cause to spread itself over a multitude of related representations, which let one think more than one can express in a concept determined by words."[46] Bearing this in mind, the purpose of my description is to allow the reader to identify the sort of feeling I am talking about and not to actually encapsulate the feeling in discursive terms, since that is by definition impossible. With *intuitional excess* I essentially mean a feeling that there is a manifold of content replete with meaning, while all attempts to articulate this content through concepts only pale in comparison to the feeling itself.[47] It "gives more to think about than can be grasped and made distinct in it."[48]

The intuitional excess that occasions a pure aesthetic judgment of beauty is of a specific sort. We may hone in on it by first narrowing our view with the observation that it is not generated by every judgment of experience. If it were, then it would have to be possible to judge everything given to us in experience as beautiful. We have two reasons to conclude that this is not the case. First, judgments of beauty are not the only type of pure aesthetic judgment that responds to intuitional excess. A pure aesthetic judgment in which the intuitional excess is so great that the judging subject finds it to be "a formless object insofar as limitlessness is represented in it,"[49] is *not* a judgment of the beautiful, but rather, of the sublime. Thus, intuitional excess does not always lead to a judgment of beauty. Second, there are two places where Kant specifically mentions an aesthetic judgment of beauty to be inappropriate. When he describes guests who discover that what they took for a charming birdsong was actually "a mischievous lad who knew how to imitate this song" hidden in the bush, then although they had "previously taken [the song] to be so charming" it quickly becomes some-

---

[46] *Critique of the Power of Judgment*, § 49, 5:315.
[47] One might venture that all feelings involve an intuitional excess of some sort. I find such a claim plausible. Whether or not all feelings involve such an excess, however, does not impact my reading of the intuitional excess that gives rise to the judgment of taste, because I already concede that this is a specific type of intuitional excess.
[48] *Critique of the Power of Judgment*, § 49, 5:315.
[49] *Critique of the Power of Judgment*, § 23 5:244.

thing "no one would long endure."⁵⁰ Something that cannot be endured clearly does not stimulate the pure aesthetic pleasure that causes one to linger over the beautiful. Furthermore, Kant writes of a young poet who "does not let himself be dissuaded from his conviction that his poem is beautiful by the judgment of the public nor that of his friends," but only later "when his power of judgment had been made more acute by practice does he depart from his previous judgment of his own free will."⁵¹ In both of these cases Kant holds that a judgment of beauty is not appropriate and if someone believes herself to have made a judgment of beauty in the cases described above, then she is either not clear on what it is she is judging (as with the guests) or has yet to develop an acute power of judgment. The fact that there would be cases in which something would not be judged beautiful by someone with exemplary taste indicates that not all *Phänomen* are accompanied by the *Erscheinung* of the specific intuitional excess that occasions the judgment of beauty.⁵²

Let us now investigate what we know about this specific type of intuitional excess. The judgment of taste is grounded upon an intuition that is not subsumed by a concept,⁵³ and hence such judgments are occasioned by that which I call intuitional excess. This means that the judging subject is receptive to something that is not cognized in the object. The subject's mode of being receptive to this is through feeling, as feeling is neither something that can be cognized of the object, nor something that needs to be discursively (i.e., conceptually) thought in order to be felt. It "arouses a multitude of sensations and supplementary representations for which no expression is found."⁵⁴ The feelings of the subject compound as the activity of judging gets underway. On the first layer, the subject is receptive to something in the *Erscheingung* that exceeds the cognized *Phänomen*. How exactly this occurs and *what* exactly it is remains

---

50 *Critique of the Power of Judgment*, § 42 5:303.
51 *Critique of the Power of Judgment*, § 32 5:282.
52 The question of whether judgments of experience always involve a part of the *Erscheinung* not being cognized in the *Phänomen* is not something that my project can answer. I allow that the sort of intuitional excess that can occasion pure aesthetic judgments is not the only sort of intuitional excess possible. In addition to this, there could be not only the psychological intuitional excess discussed, but also an excess regarding that which is given to the senses in intuition, a sort of 'excess of *aisthesis*' (a term for which I am ingratiated to Daniel Selcer). An excess of this sort could represent an excess that is generated by every judgment of experience. The intuitional excess to which I refer in this project is, however, specifically that which occasions the judgment of taste by inspiring the faculties into the requisite harmonious free play.
53 See chapter two, footnote #44, above.
54 *Critique of the Power of Judgment*, § 49, 5:316.

somewhat mysterious in Kant's text, and how could it not? If the intuitional excess cannot be subsumed under the concepts necessary for cognizing it, then the theorist is bound to encounter a certain difficulty in *thinking* this excess, let alone explicating it. A satisfactory analysis that parses out what exactly this uncognizable excess is and lays bare its mode of functioning does not seem possible. Thus, what can be done is more a description from the outside of what it feels like when one is receptive to it and an observation about what sorts of things seem to trigger it.

Concerning the first point (i.e. what it feels like), the subject is receptive to the intuitional excess that leads to a judgment of beauty through a potent sense of meaningfulness without any determinate meaning—or, to put it in properly Kantian terms, a sense of purposiveness without any determinate purpose, *Zweckmäßigkeit, aber ohne Zweck*.[55] I take this to be why Kant identifies purposiveness without a purpose as the principle of pure aesthetic judgment.[56]

Now let us turn to the question of what allows this excess to be received by the judging subject. In stark contrast to the excess generated by an accumulation of personal experiences described above, the excess that occasions the pure aesthetic judgment of taste must be something that is not just found in a given individual subject, but holds universally for all judging subjects. Kant seeks to secure this by identifying judgments of beauty as *pure:* "A judgment of taste is thus pure only insofar as no merely empirical satisfaction is mixed into its determining ground."[57] The problem is that a judgment of taste declares beautiful something that is empirically given. Kant responds to such objections, arguing that it is not the empirical matter of these things to which one responds with a judgment of beauty, but rather the pure form:

> A mere color, e.g., the green of a lawn, a mere tone (in distinction from sound and noise), say that of a violin, is declared by most people to be beautiful in itself, although both seem to have as their ground merely the matter of the representations, namely mere sensation, and on that account deserve to be called only agreeable. Yet at the same time one will surely note that the sensations of color as well as of tone justifiably count as beautiful only insofar as both are **pure**, which is a determination that already concerns form, and is also the only thing that can be universally communicated about these representations with certainty: because the quality of the sensations themselves cannot be assumed to be in accord in all subjects, and it cannot easily be assumed that the agreeableness of one color in prefer-

---

55 How exactly this can arise is the central topic of chapter five.
56 *Critique of the Power of Judgment*, § 15, 5:228.
57 *Critique of the Power of Judgment*, § 14, 5:224.

ence to another or of the tone of one musical instrument in preference to another will be judged in the same way by everyone.[58]

Thus, the point of juncture between the cognized *Phänomen* and the intuitional excess that stimulates the free play of the faculties appears to be the pure form structuring the empirical object. The form is what we cognize as we are swept over by this sense that something is replete with an indeterminate purposiveness.[59] The connection between this and form will come more into view in chapter five where I investigate the idea of purposiveness without a purpose in its own terms. There I describe how a product of nature is judged to be beautiful insofar as its form makes it seem as if it were an artistic creation, intentionally shaped to serve a certain purpose, but as a product of nature it cannot be determined to have a purpose. Thus, I describe how there must be both a form that sparks this sense of purposiveness and something else that keeps this purposiveness in excess of any determinate purpose. This is what is meant by the "judging of forms without concepts and [...] finding a satisfaction in the mere judging of them."[60] For our current purposes, what can be said is that in contemplating the form one becomes receptive to an intuitional excess. On the first layer, one is receptive to the feeling that the empirical object represents more significance, more purposiveness than what is determinatively cognizable in the *Phänomen*. This "more" stimulates the faculties into a harmonious free play on the second layer. It is here that the properly aesthetic pleasure is generated through the transcendental arrangement of the the faculties.[61] On the third layer, one discursively

---

[58] *Critique of the Power of Judgment*, § 14, 5:224.
[59] Hence Kant finds that, "In painting and sculpture, indeed in all the pictorial arts, in architecture and horticulture insofar as they are fine arts, the **drawing** is what is essential, in which what constitutes the ground of all arrangements for taste is not what gratifies in sensation but merely what pleases through its form [...]. All form of the objects of the senses (of the outer as well as, mediately, the inner) is either **shape** or **play:** in the latter case, either play of shapes (in space, mime, and dance), or mere play of sensations (in time)." (*Critique of the Power of Judgment*, § 14, 5:225 emphasis original).
[60] *Critique of the Power of Judgment*, § 42, 5:300.
[61] Thus, it is not that the second layer is pure form, but that one of the things stimulating the faculties into the second-layer harmonious free play is the first-layer cognition of the empirical object's pure form. I regard the judgment of taste as part of a lager process of judging that spans all three layers and this activity of judging is a determinate activity, although it does not determine an object (*Phänomen*). This activity of judging is afforded its determinate form through the operation of the logical functions of judgment. The form that the activity of judging accordingly taken is, however, to be differentiated from the form that is cognized in the drawing of a painting, play of musical sensations in time, or dance of shapes in space. The latter belongs to the

grasps after the feeling of the second layer, and it is this grasping after that gives rise to an aesthetic idea:

> In a word, the aesthetic idea is a representation of the imagination, associated with a given concept, which is combined with such a manifold of partial representations in the free use of the imagination that no expression designating a determinate concept can be found for it, which therefore allows the addition to a concept of much that is unnameable, the feeling of which animates the cognitive faculties and combines spirit with the mere letter of language.[62]

Thus, even when thinking is stimulated on the third layer that which was not cognized on the first and second layers continues to exceed what can be conceptually grasped.

II.D Aesthetic Harmony and the Logical Functions

As discussed in the previous chapter, Kant is clear that one of the essential characteristics making an aesthetic judgment *aesthetic* is the harmony that it creates by putting the understanding into an indeterminate, yet enlivening, relation with the faculty of imagination. This is one of the reasons why I call the second layer, on which this occurs, *properly* aesthetic. Normally the faculties of imagination and understanding are brought together in judgment through the use of concepts [*Begriffe*]. One might say that it is through the understanding's ability to supply a concept that it is able to grab ahold of [*greifen*] the intuition that the imagination supplied. I have suggested, however, that the second layer of aesthetic judgment involves a judging of perception and not of experience. Thus, concepts do not determinatively seize up intuitions of an object, because, here, the only sort of intuition involved is that of a feeling. Although the indeterminate nature of the harmony between the faculties in aesthetic judgment suggests that the one faculty should not have too strong of a grip on the other, the very fact that there is a harmony implies a give and take which can only occur if the two are sufficiently in connection with one another. If concepts are not determining the relation of the understanding to the imagination in the second layer, however, then how are these two faculties able to come into contact with each other, so as to create the *harmony* that is to arise?

---

empirical object, while the former belongs to the activity of judging that is occasioned by that object.
62 *Critique of the Power of Judgment*, § 49, 5:316.

The table of judgments outlines the functions of judgment and it is from this table that the categories are derived. Kant describes the relation between the logical functions and the categories, writing:

> I will merely precede this with the explanation of the categories. They are concepts of an object in general, by means of which its intuition is regarded as determined with regard to one of the logical functions for judgment.[63]

The table of judgments is not suitable for application to empirical objects. That is why the table of categories emerges. These are the logical functions of judgment as they are applied *categorically* to objects, enabling one to "think an object."[64]

As Bickmann observes:

> Only in 'reflecting abstraction' can thinking become self-referential and the conditions of the form of thinking be made conscious. By placing it before the parentheses [*vor die Klammer setzt*], that particular object of thought—the "not-I" or the "transcendental Thingness"— our thinking will be freed to view the conditions of the form of thought. This is the method that underlies Kant's transcendental philosophical analysis. It is not so much concerned with objects, but rather with the way of knowing objects, insofar as this is possible a priori. In the 'Metaphysical Deduction' the forms of judgment are examined as the conditions of form for performing the connections [*als Forbedingungen solcher Verknüpfungsleitungen*] that make it possible for us to relate to objects in an empirical experience.[65]

Although the logical functions, as the conditions of the form of this connection, make it *a priori possible* "for us to relate to objects in an empirical experience," they do not, in themselves, *constitute* objects of experience. They relate more essentially to our "way of knowing objects" and the transcendental object of thought, i.e. the "transcendental Thingness".[66] The logical functions are a cru-

---

63 *Critique of Pure Reason*, B128.
64 *Critique of Pure Reason*, A80/B106.
65 Bickmann, "Das unskeptisches Fundament der Erkenntniskritik. Kants "schlechterdings notwendige Voraussetzungen" bei den wesentlichen Zwecken der menschlichen Vernunft," 132, my translation. The original reads, "Erst in "reflektierender Abstraktion" kann das Denken selbstbezüglich werden und die Formbedingungen des Denkens zu Bewusstsein bringen. Indem es das je besondere Objekt des Denkens—das "Nicht-Ich" oder die "transzendentale Sachheit"—vor die Klammer setzt, wird in unserem Denken der Blick frei für die Formbedingungen des Denkens als Tätigkeit. Es ist dies die Methode, die Kants transzendentalphilosophischer Analyse zugrunde liegt. In ihr ist nicht so sehr von den Gegenständen, als vielmehr von der Erkenntnisart der Gegenstände, insofern sie a priori möglich ist, die Rede. In der "metaphysischen Deduktion" werden die Urteilsformen als Formbedingungen solcher Verknüpfungsleitungen untersucht, die es möglich machen, uns auf Gegenstände in einer empirischen Erfahrung zu beziehen."
66 For more on this, see section II. G. below regarding the transcendental concept.

cial part of the cognitive structure that allows us to relate to empirical objects, but a further step must be taken for the enablement of this possibility to be realized. That is, the further connection of the categories must be performed upon the intuition of an empirical object for this to be not just about the constitution of our thinking, but also, about the constitution of objects. Bickmann writes:

> In the "Transcendental Deduction of the Pure Concepts of the Understanding" a further step of the process is to be undertaken, in order for this performance of the connection of our thinking [diese Verknüpfungsleistung unseres Denkens]—as the function of synthesis of the understanding—to be demonstrated in its object constituting function.[67]

Thus, the use of the categories represents a further step that takes us beyond the *Verknüpfungsleistung* of the logical functions, and it is here that the unitive function's ability to constitute empirical objects manifests. To consider the functions of judgment on their own, is to consider them apart from this "further step", and as such they belong entirely to the faculty of understanding.

Since no object is being cognized on the properly aesthetic layer, where the harmonious free play of the faculties occurs, the logical functions of judgment may operate in the act of judging this harmony without entailing conceptual determination. A logical function is not itself a concept, but rather "the form of the concept alone."[68] As pure form, the functions of judgment guide this act of judging, and thus afford the understanding a light hold on the imagination, so that the faculties may enter into a harmonious free play in their transcendental use. Indeed, when Kant tells us of his decision to use "the logical functions for judging" as his guide in the Analytic of the Beautiful, he immediately follows this with the parenthetical remark "for a relation to the understanding is always contained even in the judgment of taste."[69] Without such a relation, the "blind" intuition would collapse back into sensibility while the fantastical tendencies of the understanding took flight, escaping the narrow limits set upon them by the senses.[70] We would see an unhinging of the faculties, rather than harmo-

---

[67] Bickmann, "Das unskeptisches Fundament der Erkenntniskritik. Kants "schlechterdings notwendige Voraussetzungen" bei den wesentlichen Zwecken der menschlichen Vernunft," 132, my translation. The original reads, "In der "transzendentalen Deduktion der reinen Verstandesbegriffe" soll in einem weiteren Schritt der Versuch unternommen werden, diese Verknüpfungsleistungen unseres Denkens—als Synthesisfunktionen des Verstandes—in ihrer gegenstandskonstitutiven Funktion zu erweisen."
[68] *Critique of Pure Reason*, A245/B302.
[69] *Critique of the Power of Judgment*, Bk. I, § 1, Footnote: 5:203.
[70] The idea that a complete failure to connect intuitions to the understanding in any way would leave these intuitions in a stubbornly unthinkable state is supported by Kant's famous declara-

nious free-play. It is precisely the operation of the logical functions from the table of judgments in aesthetic judgment that guards against this.

Aesthetic judgment presents us with a certain gap that is maintained between imagination and the understanding. Normally this gap would be bridged by the vehicles of mediation that Kant carefully describes in the first *Critique*. Kant remarks on this disconnect in the third *Critique*, writing:

> If the given representation, which occasions the judgment of taste, were a concept, which united understanding and imagination in the judging of the object into a cognition of the object, then the consciousness of this relationship would be intellectual (as in the objective schematism of the power of judgment, which was dealt with in the critique). But in that case the judgment would not be made in relation to pleasure and displeasure, hence it would not be a judgment of taste. Now the judgment of taste, however, determines the object, independently of concepts, with regard to satisfaction and the predicate of beauty. Thus that subjective unity of the relation can make itself known only through sensation.[71]

The crucial point of juncture occurs when the imagination offers up the schematized intuition for the understanding to subsume under concepts. In aesthetic judgment, the imagination is still offering up intuitions that have been "schematized without a concept."[72] at this point that the schism between the imagination and understanding comes forward, since the understanding lacks the concepts for taking up this intuition. The logical functions mediate the relation between the faculties, however, providing just the right sort of indeterminate unity to the activity of aesthetic judging. This reading is supported by Kant's remark that,

> The faculty of concepts, be they confused or distinct, is the understanding; and although understanding also belongs to the judgment of taste, as an aesthetic judgment (as in all judgments), it does not belong to it as a faculty for the cognition of an object, but as the

---

tion that "Thoughts without content are empty, intuitions without concepts are blind" (*Critique of Pure Reason*, A51/B75). He describes the situation in which we would find ourselves if the understanding were to become unhinged from sensible intuitions when criticizing metaphysicians, such as Plato: "Captivated by such a proof of the power of reason, the drive for expansion sees no bounds. The light dove in free flight cutting through the air the resistance of which it feels, could get the idea that it could do even better in airless space. Likewise, Plato abandoned the world of the senses because it set such narrow limits for the understanding, and dared to go beyond it on the wings of the ideas, in the empty space of pure understanding. He did not notice that he made no headway by his efforts, for he had no resistance, no support, as it were, by which he could stiffen himself, and to which he could apply his powers in order to put his understanding into motion" (*Ibid.*, A5/B9).
71 *Critique of the Power of Judgment*, Bk. I, § 9, 5:218–219.
72 *Critique of the Power of Judgment*, Bk. I, § 35, 5:287. Here Kant remarks that "the freedom of the imagination consists precisely in the fact that it schematizes without a concept."

faculty for the determination of the judgment and its representation (without a concepts) in accordance with the relation of the representation to the subject and its internal feeling and indeed insofar as this judgment is possible in accordance with a universal rule.[73]

Thus, the role of the understanding is not to supply a concept, but to determine the act of judging, so that this can be a determinate act, although it does not generate a conceptual determination of the object. To better understand how this can work, let us take a closer look into what exactly the logical functions are, so that we may better understand the special unitive role they play in the properly aesthetic layer, enabling the harmony of the faculties peculiar to aesthetic judgment.

II.E Allison's View

According to our analysis in chapter one, perception is the mode of awareness that is subjectively, not objectively, valid in which one perceives a feeling, not a cognized object. For these reasons it makes sense to consider the second layer of aesthetic judgment as the judging of a perception. This is in accordance with how Kant characterizes aesthetic judgment as containing a subjective relation:

> Of course, an objective relation can only be thought, but insofar as it is subjective as far as its conditions are concerned it can still be sensed in its effect on the mind; and rather, in the case of a relation that is not grounded in any concept (like that of the powers of representation to a faculty of cognition in general), no other consciousness of it is possible except through sensation of the effect that consists in the facilitated play of both powers of the mind (imagination and understanding), enlivened through mutual agreement.[74]

From this we see that a subjective relation can still be present when an objective relation is lacking, because only "the powers of representation to a faculty of cognition in general" is under concern, and as such the relation "is not grounded in any concept." Here, the categories are not actively determining an object. What is at stake, instead, is something "sensed in its effect on the mind," this being the "sensation of the effect that consists in the facilitated play of both powers of the mind." It is the logical functions that facilitate the play of these powers by supplying the requisite form to the activity of judging, itself, so that it may be a distinct *activity*, even if it does not yield a determinate product. To

---

73 *Critique of the Power of Judgment*, Bk. I, § 15, 5:229.
74 *Critique of the Power of Judgment*, Bk. I, § 9, 5:218–219.

better understand how this works, we need to investigate the difference between the logical functions and categories. What does it mean for the former to be operative in a case where the latter find no object for their application? Is such a disentangling of the two even possible? I will argue that this is possible if we regard the logical functions as determining the activity of judging, and the categories as determining the product that can be produced through such judging.

In the previous chapter, we saw that Allison understands the categories as inoperative in judgments of perception, because they cannot determine an object that is not there. At the same time, he also observed that there must be certain "logical connections" to this "perception in a thinking subject."[75] Allison remarks that "it is difficult to see what such a logical connection could involve, if not a connection according to these concepts."[76] I contend, however, that this may be seen differently in special cases. In the second layer of aesthetic judgment, for instance, the "logical connections" could be understood as denoting how the logical functions govern the activity of judging. Allison does not give enough attention to the difference between the table of judgment and the table of categories to account for this case. Indeed, he describes the logical functions and categories as simply two sides of the same coin, appearing as either the one or the other depending upon the perspective from which the theorist views them. In many cases Allison's reading is appropriate, but the harmonious free-play of aesthetic judgment offers us an exception in which one "side" of the coin appears without the other.

Allison describes the categories and the table of judgment from which they are derived as "possessing a single characteristic activity, which they analyze at different levels."[77] He supports his analysis with a passage he calls the "nerve" of the metaphysical deduction's argument:

> The same function that gives unity to the different representations in a judgment also gives unity to the mere synthesis of different representations in an intuition, which, expressed generally, is called the pure concept of understanding. The same understanding, therefore, and indeed by means of the very same actions through which it brings the logical form of a judgment into concepts by means of the analytical unity, also brings a transcendental content into its representations by means of the synthetic unity of the manifold in intuition in general, on account of which they are called pure concepts of the understanding that pertain to objects a priori; this can never be accomplished by universal logic.[78]

---

75 *Prolegomena*, § 18.
76 Allison, *Kant's Transcendental Idealism: An Interpretation and Defense*, 152.
77 Allison, *Kant's Transcendental Idealism: An Interpretation and Defense*, 123.
78 *Critique of Pure Reason*, A79/B104–5.

From this Allison concludes that when this function "gives unity to the different representations in a judgment" it goes under the title "function of judgment" and when it "gives unity to the mere synthesis of different representations in an intuition" it is called a "category."[79] He states that the operation, itself, is one and the same, only the differing object causes one to call it by a different name. He summarizes:

> If we assume that the understanding has such a transcendental or objectifying function, and that it exercises it through the same operations by means of which it judges, then it follows that the logical functions of judgment, which are the forms in accordance with which the understanding unites its concepts in judgment, will also be the forms in accordance with which it unites the manifold of intuition in order to determine an object for judgment.[80]

I am willing to accept the idea that the logical functions and the categories bring the same sort of unity to two different things, but the differing object[81] of this activity alters the nature of the activity itself, and not just its name. Allison's reading makes it sound as though we could say that just as deer meat is venison, so are the logical functions of judgment the categories. This is, however, precisely the assumption that becomes questionable when aesthetic judgment is under concern. Kant's footnote at the beginning of the third *Critique* states that the logical functions guided his analysis of the beautiful.[82] How are we to reconcile the instructive role that the logical functions of judgment play here with the limitations Kant places on the operation of concepts in the judgment of taste, if there is no significant difference in how the two function? The reading of aesthetic judgment that I will offer is one in which the key aesthetic role of the logical functions is to give unity to the *activity* of judging, and not the representations in this judgment.

---

[79] This is not all that far from P. F. Strawson's suggestion in the Metaphysical Deduction, "We must take it that the categories are here derived simply by adding to the forms of logic the idea of applying those forms in making true judgments about objects of awareness (intuition) in general, whatever the character of our modes of awareness of these objects may be" (Strawson, P. F., *Bounds of Sense* [London: Methuen, 1966], 77).
[80] Allison, *Kant's Transcendental Idealism: An Interpretation and Defense*, 126.
[81] The word "object" here is meant in a grammatical sense as the direct object, designating the recipient of the unitive function of the logical functions and categories. In the case of the categories this would be an intuition, which becomes an object [Phänomen] through this process, whereas for the logical functions this would be the components of a judgment, which crucially do not become an object [Phänomen] in this manner.
[82] *Critique of the Power of Judgment*, Bk. I, § 1, 5:203.

The question of whether or not the unitive function is applied to an object of experience is of much greater significance than Allison anticipates, particularly when aesthetic judgments are under consideration. The very passage Allison uses in support of his thesis that the two are ultimately one and the same, signifies a difference not of perspective, but of *extent,*

> [the categories] are nothing but mere forms of judgment insofar as these forms are applied to intuitions [...] and that by such application our intuitions first of all obtain objects and become cognitions.[83]

The categories are the forms of judgment when these are applied to intuitions. But Kant reports that "an aesthetic judgment is of a unique kind, and affords absolutely no cognition (not even a confused one) of the object, which happens only in a logical judgment."[84] If the logical functions in aesthetic judgment are being applied to the process of judging itself, instead of to intuitions, then the categories, as intuition-modifiers, would not be operative. The categories enable the understanding to grab ahold of an intuition so as to obtain an object. In an inner perception, such as is found on the second layer of judgment—where there is no cognizable object—the understanding can still reach out to the intuition through the logical functions and enter a harmonious free play with it, a free play that is not to be anchored down in the cognition of an object.

Allison assumes that a difference of what is being modified can be admitted without affecting any significant difference in how the logical unity, itself, functions. However, passages from the first *Critique* call this assumption into question:

> I will merely precede this with the explanation of the categories. They are concepts of an object in general, by means of which its intuition is regarded as determined with regard to one of the logical functions for judgment. Thus, the function of the categorical judgment was that of the relationship of the subject to the predicate, e.g., "All bodies are divisible." Yet in regard to the merely logical use of the understanding it would remain undetermined which of these two concepts will be given the function of the subject and which will be given that of the predicate. For one can also say: "Something divisible is a body." Through the category of substance, however, if I bring the concept of a body under it, it is determined that its empirical intuition in experience must always be considered as subject, never as predicate; and likewise with all the other categories.[85]

---

[83] *Metaphysical Foundations of Natural Science,* AK. IV, 474.
[84] *Critique of the Power of Judgment,* Bk 1, § 15, 5:228.
[85] *Critique of Pure Reason,* B128–129.

This passage shows two things. First, it demonstrates that a "merely logical use of the understanding" is possible. Such a use of judgment is governed only by the logical functions. The involvement of the categories is not called for insofar as the judgment is not anchored in the cognition of an intuition. On the "merely logical" level it is just the logical connection between the components of the judgment that are in play, and this is acquired through the logical functions. Second, we see that a judgment is transformed when it goes from being "merely logical" to involving categorical determination. In the merely logical judgment the subject and predicate were interchangeable, but if the judgment becomes one in which the category of substance is operative, then only the judgmental component signifying the "empirical intuition in experience" can "be considered as subject." Thus, we see that although the unitive function of the logical functions and the categories may be very much the same, their difference of object causes judgments that involve categorical subsumption to have a much greater level of determination than those that merely remain "logical."

It is of further interest to note that the logical functions usually unite concepts whereas the categories provide unity to objects, making the second layer of aesthetic judgment a strange creature, indeed. For, here, there is no object to be united by categories, nor are there concepts to be unified. Rather, the feeling perception of a free play of the faculties is guided by the logical functions so that this activity may be harmonious, even if it is not the sort of action that generates a unified product. It is for this reason that Kant describes the relation of the faculties in aesthetic judgment as the one "in which they must stand in the power of judgment in general" and not "the relation in which they actually stand in the case of a given perception."[86]

Typically in "the merely logical use of the understanding" the logical functions would join together "two concepts" with it "remain[ing] undetermined which of these [...] will be given the function of the subject and which will be given that of the predicate."[87] In the second layer of aesthetic judgment, however, the two entities that are brought together in an undetermined relation through the logical functions are that of the imagination and understanding "considered

---

[86] *Critique of the Power of Judgment*, First Introduction, VII., 20:220. The full sentence reads, "But since in the mere reflection on a perception it is not a matter of a determinate concept, but in general only of reflecting on the rule concerning a perception on behalf of the understanding, as a faculty of concepts, it can readily be seen that in a merely reflecting judgment imagination and understanding are considered in the relation to each other in which they must stand in the power of judgment in general, as compared with the relation in which they actually stand in the case of a given perception."
[87] *Critique of Pure Reason*, B128–129.

in the relation to each other in which they must stand in the power of judgment in general."⁸⁸ In the first *Critique* Kant does indicate the possibility of considering the pure understanding in this transcendental use:

> if one does away with all conditions of sensibility that distinguish them as concepts of a possible empirical use, and takes them for concept of things in general (thus of transcendental use), then that is to do nothing more than to regard the logical functions of judgment as the conditions of the possibility of things themselves, without in the least being able to show whence they could have their application and their object, thus how in pure understanding without sensibility they could have any significance and objective validity [...].⁸⁹

This passage supplies further evidence that one may consider the logical functions of judgment on their own "as the conditions of the possibility of things themselves." Regarded in such isolation, one would have in view neither "their application and their object" nor any objective validity. Instead, this is only put in relation to the transcendental concept which provides the "concept of things in general" and will be discussed shortly. Hence, one only has in view the "transcendental use" of the logical functions which facilitates the activity of the understanding in general without pertaining to the content that may be determined by the faculties. Kant further describes this:

> But now what sorts of things those are in regard to which one must use one function rather than another remains hereby entirely undetermined: thus without the condition of sensible intuition, the synthesis of which they contain, the categories have no relation at all to any determinate object, thus they cannot define one, and consequently they do not have in themselves any validity of concepts.⁹⁰

This passage confirms that when regarding the logical functions in their transcendental use, the determining role of the categories would fall away, because there is "no relation at all to any determinate object" on this level. This unraveling of determinate roles might be precisely what is needed for the faculties to be freed up, so that their interaction may become one of play.⁹¹

---

88 *Critique of the Power of Judgment*, First Introduction, VII., 20:220.
89 *Critique of Pure Reason*, A239–241/B299–300.
90 *Critique of Pure Reason*, A246/B302.
91 In this second layer harmony, one is not *explicitly* conscious of the movements of the imagination and understanding in this free play, or the way that the judging activity receives its determinations from the logical functions. Indeed, for the subject to be able to pinpoint these things would require discursive concepts and thus defeat the the purpose of the second layer, which is conceived of as a special area in which concepts find no application. Christopher Janaway comments on the extent to which one can be said to be conscious of the harmonious free

This passage also supports the idea that "[i]f one does away with all conditions of sensibility" then the categories lose their application, but the logical functions remain operative.[92] Hence, it is not that all uses of the logical functions of judgment must involve the categories, but that all uses of the latter must involve the former.[93] This has a further implication, which Kant discusses in the following passage:

> The logical functions of judgment in general – unity and multiplicity, affirmation and negation, subject and predicate – cannot be defined without falling into a circle, since the definition would itself have to be a judgment and therefore already contain these functions of judgment. The pure categories, however, are nothing other than the representations of things in general insofar as the manifold of their intuition must be thought through one or another of these logical functions: Magnitude is the determination that must be thought only through a judgment that has quantity (*judicium commune*); reality, that which can be thought only through an affirmative judgment; substance, that which, in relation to the intuition, must be the ultimate subject of all other determinations.[94]

Whereas the categories can be defined through the logical functions, since they think the manifold of intuition through these functions, the logical functions cannot be similarly defined—they are the explainer that warrants no further explanation.[95]

---

play of the understanding and imagination, writing that, "presumably the subject need not be in possession of the concepts *imagination, understanding*, and so on. Kant says (§ 9) that "the relation that the presentational powers must have in order to give rise to a power of cognition in general" can be "sensed in the effect it has on the mind," and that this is "the only way we can become conscious of it." It simply feels good to be a mind having this consciousness of the ease and vitality of its own working" (Janaway,"Kant's Aesthetics and the 'Empty Cognitive Stock,'" 78).

92 *Critique of Pure Reason*, A239/B299.

93 Jay Bernstein remarks on this: "[Judgments] involve the application of categories, and the application of categories just is the spontaneously grasping of the manifold in an intuition as the presentation of an object. This is to say that it is not the case that every time we say "S is P" we are using the categories—that is plainly false. But it is to say that every time we grasp something as a substance with a property, it is tied up with the subject-predicate form of judgment. So it is the other way around" (Bernstein, Jay. "The Bernstein Tapes." The New School for Social Research, New York, NY. Lecture Recording from 4.12.2007, 7:00 – 8:00. Course Title: GPHI 6065 Kant's Critique of Pure Reason. Online.).

94 *Critique of Pure Reason*, A245–6/B302.

95 This holds for my analysis of quality, quantity and relation in connections with the first three moments of the judgment of taste; however, the roles of explainer and explained reverse themselves in the fourth moment when modality is under discussion. Why this occurs and how it does not undermine this analysis is discussed in detail in chapter six.

In lieu of Allison's comparison to a coin with two sides, let me suggest a limited grammatical analogy for understanding the interconnection and possible separation of the logical functions and categories. We might think of logical functions, considered on their own, as if they related to intransitive verbs. That is to say, they concern a (logical) action that does not take a phenomenon as object. The categories, then, would relate to transitive verbs, which can only be used with a phenomenon as object (or, rather, with an intuition that they determine into such an object).[96] As Bickmann points out, even reason must be able to be given to itself as an object so that it may be the "testing authority, as the faculty to be tested, simultaneously conceived as subject just as object of the observation."[97] This resonates with the heautonomy of the third *Critique*, through which the faculty of judgment "does not give the law to nature nor to freedom, but solely to itself."[98] Bickmann further describes reason's reflexivity:

> Reason, as a testing, analyzing, synthesizing, reflecting, etc. activity, is its own object; as object of the analysis it is that towards which it is directed with cognizing intent.[99]

There is, thus, a crucial distinction to be made between cognitive processes that are directed towards objects as phenomena and those that are directed toward "activity." In a similar vein to Bickmann's discussion of reason, I read the logical functions as directed at the activity of thinking, while the categories determine phenomena. This difference has a real effect on how each functions, because to "take" a phenomenon as its object signifies *constituting* and *determining* this object. In the properly aesthetic layer the logical functions have an intransitive role, they only concern the *act* of judging and, thus, take no phenomenon as object. Here, the judging subject is perceiving how the free play of the faculties brings about a feeling of pleasure. The characteristic features of this layer are

---

96 This analogy has a certain limit. The difference between logical functions and the categories is not that the former does not modify anything (i.e., grammatically take a direct object), but rather that the grammatical "object" that it takes cannot be an intuition which it makes into an objective object (i.e. *Phänomen*).
97 Bickmann, "Das unskeptisches Fundament der Erkenntniskritik. Kants "schlechterdings notwendige Voraussetzungen" bei den wesentlichen Zwecken der menschlichen Vernunft," 131, my translation. The original reads, "Prüfinstanz wie als das zu prüfende Vermögen, als subjekt wie als Objekt der Betrachtung zugleich aufgefasst."
98 *Critique of the Power of Judgment*, First Introduction, VIII, 20:225.
99 Bickmann, "Das unskeptisches Fundament der Erkenntniskritik. Kants "schlechterdings notwendige Voraussetzungen" bei den wesentlichen Zwecken der menschlichen Vernunft," 131, my translation. The original reads,"Vernunft als eine prüfende, analysierende, synthetisierende, reflektierende, etc. Tätigkeit ist ihr eigener Gegenstand; ist als Objekt der Analyse zugleich dasjenige, worauf sie in erkennender Absicht bezogen ist."

all activities (perceiving, playing and feeling) or actors (the faculties in their free play and the subject in a feeling-perception). There is no "thing" involved.

The passages from Kant discussed above[100] reveal that the involvement of an object of experience is a game changer. Once there is an object in play, the placement of the elements in the judgment become fixed in the categorical determination of the object. The empirical object takes up the position of judgmental subject and, as thought under the category of substance, it cannot become predicate. If the properly aesthetic layer concerns the pure activity of judging and the feeling of faculty harmony, then the unitive function is not operating in the applicative, determinative manner that involves categorical determination. This implies that the subject and predicate positions are interchangeable in such a free-play of the faculties, in general, guided only by the logical functions; the imagination and understanding dance in and out of different roles.

II.F The Functioning of Logical Functions

The logical functions of judgment "give unity to the different representations in a judgment" and do so by governing the act of judging. On their own the logical functions tell us the sorts of things that judgments can do, the categories then apply this ability to intuition. As Longuenesse puts it "[t]he logical forms of judgment guide the activity by which understanding elevates given representations to a discursive form—that is, reflects them under concepts."[101] Although these two roles are difficult to disentangle when they are both operative, we can understand the logical functions as guiding the activity of the understanding—the cognitive process—while the categories are the application of this activity to some thing—an intuition—which determines that thing as having a discursive form. The former guides the activity and the latter determines the product that comes about through this activity. Assuredly, when something is, in fact, there to be determined, then these *do* appear to be merely two sides of the same coin, as Allison suggested. But in the curious case of the aesthetic harmony of the faculties, when there is no empirical object that is being determined, then the one side appears without the other.

The possibility that the two sides of the coin can come apart in this manner is of great importance to aesthetic judgment. The "beauty" that the object is declared to have in the judgment made on the third layer is not actually to be prop-

---

[100] *Critique of Pure Reason*, B128–130 and A239–246/B299–302.
[101] Longuenesse, *Kant and the Capacity to Judge*, 11.

erly attributed to the object itself. When discussing the curiously universal nature of aesthetic satisfaction, Kant writes:

> Hence he will speak of the beautiful as if beauty were a property of the object and the judgment logical [...], although it is only aesthetic and contains merely a relation of the representation of the object to the subject, because it still has the similarity with logical judgment that its validity for everyone can be presupposed.[102]

Although we may tend to describe beauty as if it were a property of an empirical object, this is not accurate, because the beauty is in the harmonious free play of the faculties that takes place within the subject. If the categories are the unitive function in the objectification of an intuition, then their involvement in the properly aesthetic layer would jeopardize the "subjective"[103] nature of this judgment by shifting the beauty into the object.

II.G The Transcendental Concept

From the foregoing, we can see how the second layer avoids the involvement of both empirical and pure concepts insofar as there is nothing on this layer for such concepts to cognize. This is not, however, to mean that what Kant terms the transcendental concept is not in play. This becomes apparent in the Dialectic, where Kant turns his attention to the question of how the subjective universality of the judgment of taste can arise, so that "[i]t is possible to argue about taste (but not to dispute)."[104]

The antinomy that arises here concerns whether in the judgment of taste there is "hope of coming to mutual agreement," because if so,

> one must be able to count on grounds for the judgment that do not have merely private validity and thus are not merely subjective, which is nevertheless completely opposed to the fundamental principle **Everyone has his own taste.**[105]

These grounds are the transcendental arrangement of the faculties, discussed in greater detail in chapter four. Since this transcendental arrangement of the faculties does, however, involve what Kant terms the transcendental concept and

---

[102] *Critique of the Power of Judgment*, § 6, 5:211.
[103] That is, "subjective" as in unified in the subject's consciousness of itself, and not in that of the object.
[104] *Critique of the Power of Judgment*, § 56, 5:338.
[105] *Critique of the Power of Judgment*, § 56, 5:338.

the present chapter seeks to describe on which layers concepts are operative, I will discuss the transcendental concept at this point.

In Kant's critical system a non-private ground for mutual agreement is typically provided by concepts. Hence, Kant formulates the antinomy of taste as an issue of concepts:

> 1. **Thesis.** The judgment of taste is not based on concepts, for otherwise it would be possible to dispute about it (decide by means of proofs).
> 2. **Antithesis.** The judgment of taste is based on concepts, for otherwise, despite its variety, it would not even be possible to argue about it (to lay claim to the necessary assent of others to this judgment).[106]

The solution to this antinomy is not to affirm the thesis or antithesis, but rather to clarify the *sort* of concept that is involved in pure aesthetic judgment. This transcendental concept—involved in the harmonious transcendental free play of the faculties on the second, properly aesthetic layer of the judgment of taste—is *nothing* like any *determinate* concept. It is "in itself indeterminable and unfit for cognition."[107] The transcendental concept is *neither* an empirical concept *nor* a category. It cannot on its own subsume an intuition so as to generate a cognition. The transcendental concept, thus, allows Kant to achieve the careful balance that he takes the judgment of taste to require:

> The judgment of taste must be related to some sort of concept, for otherwise it could not lay claim to necessary validity for everyone at all. But it need not on that account be demonstrable **from** a concept, because a concept can be either determinable or else in itself indeterminate and also indeterminable. The concept of reason, which is determinable by means of predicates of the sensible intuition that can correspond to it, is of the first sort; of the second sort, however, is the transcendental concept of reason of the supersensible, which is the basis of all that intuition, and which thus cannot be further determined theoretically.[108]

Hence, it is nothing like the concept from which a proof could be demonstrated.[109] Rather the concept which supplies the necessary foundation for the subjective universality of the judgment of taste is a concept of reason. The "transcendental concept of reason of the supersensible" supplies "the basis of all [...] intuition," and thereby grounds our conception of an object *überhaupt:*

---

106 *Critique of the Power of Judgment*, § 56, 5:338–339.
107 *Critique of the Power of Judgment*, § 57, 5:340.
108 *Critique of the Power of Judgment*, § 57, 3:339.
109 Thus, arguments remain unable to be mobilized to convince others to agree with one's own judgment of taste.

> A concept of this kind, however, is the mere pure rational concept of the supersensible, which grounds the object (and also the judging subject) as an object of sense, consequently as an appearance.[110]

It does not supply the conceptual specificity that would allow me to experience, say, this ceramic cup. It functions, instead, on the transcendental level to allow me to conceive of anything as an object at all, so that I am not just receptive to random sense data, but unify this sense data as an object of sense—as an appearance that is given to me. The transcendental concept thus belongs to the transcendental structure that must be in place for concepts (both pure and empirical) to be used to cognize an object. It is a necessary but insufficient condition for cognition. In any cognition (at least) one category from each quadrant must be operative. But which of the three this is varies depending upon the representation (e. g., some things are cognized as a unity, while others are cognized as a plurality). There are, however, two things that are permanently in place and do not change depending upon the representation: the transcendental unity of apperception and the transcendental concept. These form the two poles of the cognitive structure through which the various representations pass.[111] The absence of an object for cognition on the second layer of pure aesthetic judgment does not shake this fundamental structure. Thus, the transcendental concept remains in place, even though the concepts for determining an object find no application. This "transcendental concept of reason of the supersensible" is a priori necessary as "the basis of all that intuition." It can neither "be further determined theoretically" itself , nor can it determine anything else if operative in isolation from other determinate concepts. Consequently, it does not subsume the intuitional excess. It only provides what is necessary for the reception "of all that intuition."[112] Hence, the involvement of this transcendental concept does not introduce anything that is at odds with my description of the properly aesthetic, second layer above.[113]

The transcendental concept is "a concept that **cannot** be determined by intuition, by which nothing can be cognized." [114] It is a permanent fixture in the transcendental arrangement of our faculties, and as such its involvement sup-

---

110 *Critique of the Power of Judgment*, § 57, 5:340.
111 For this reading, I am grateful to the diagrams that Claudia Bickmann used in her Kant seminars (Universität zu Köln, Cologne, Germany. 2014–2016).
112 *Critique of the Power of Judgment*, § 57, 3:339.
113 Thus, the argument of the first chapter remains unaffected, because there the determination of an object through a concept was under consideration, which is something that this transcendental concept could never do on its own.
114 *Critique of the Power of Judgment*, § 57, 5:340.

ports the extension of the pure aesthetic judgment of taste "as necessary for everyone."[115] For such extension the judgment "must [...] be based on some sort of concept," otherwise it would remain "an intuitive singular representation related to the feeling of pleasure, only a private judgment"[116] with "its validity [...] limited to the judging individual alone."[117] It is, thus,

> by means of this very concept [that the judgment of taste] acquires validity for everyone (in each case, to be sure, as a singular judgment immediately accompanying the intuition), because its determining ground may lie in the concept of that which can be regarded as the supersensible substratum of humanity.[118]

In terms of my layered solution, the involvement of this transcendental concept in the second layer prevents the intuitional excess from losing all connection to the representation of an object. It thereby enables the second layer feeling of transcendental pleasure to be related back to the first-layer empirical object. In this manner, the operation of the understanding on the third layer may grasp after the second-layer feeling in a re-cognition of the first-layer empirical object. This, in effect, allows the judgment discursively proclaimed on the third layer to be about the object of the first layer ("This *tulip* is beautiful") and not simply collapse into musings about one's own state ("I feel pleasure"; "I feel like my mind is working in harmony with itself").

We, however, remain severely limited in what we can say of this indeterminable transcendental concept of the supersensible, because "the explanation of the possibility of their concept [i.e. the concept that resolves the antinomy between the thesis and antithesis] exceeds our faculty of cognition."[119]

---

115 *Critique of the Power of Judgment*, § 57, 5:340.
116 *Critique of the Power of Judgment*, § 57 5:339.
117 *Critique of the Power of Judgment*, § 57 5:339.
118 *Critique of the Power of Judgment*, § 57, 5:340.
119 *Critique of the Power of Judgment*, § 57, 5:340. More specifically, the antinomy can be resolved if "we take the concept, on which the universal validity of a judgment must be based, in the same sense in both conflicting propositions, and yet we assert two opposed predicates of it. Thus, the thesis should say that the judgment of taste is not based on **determinate** concepts; but in the antithesis, it should say that the judgment of taste is still based on some, although **indeterminate** concept (namely, of the supersensible substratum of appearances); and then there would be no conflict between them" (*Ibid*, 5:340–341, bold original)

III An Analysis According to Moments

The foregoing discussion has revealed a special unitive role that the logical functions perform in the properly aesthetic layer, enabling the harmony of the faculties that is peculiar to aesthetic judgment. This sheds some light on the footnote attached to the title of the first moment in the Analytic of the Beautiful,

> In seeking the moments to which this power of judgment attends in its reflection, I have been guided by the logical functions of judgment (for a relation to the understanding is always contained even in the judgment of taste).[120]

There is, however, another key term here which warrants scrutiny. In order to understand how the logical functions are to guide us through the moments of aesthetic judgment, we must first get an idea of what the term "moment" [*Moment*] itself indicates. I will begin by looking at a few passages from the *Critique of Pure Reason* where this term arises, and use these to understand what it means to analyze aesthetic judgment in terms of its moments.

III.A *Moments* in the first *Critique*

In Kant's *Clue to the Discovery of all Pure Concepts of the Understanding*, he identifies the moments as the logical functions falling under the four titles in the table of judgments. This means that each quadrant contains three moments, giving us twelve moments in total. This, however, only supplies us with a starting point in investigating what it means to analyze something in term of its moments. It would be wrong to take this to indicate that an analysis of something in terms of its moments consists only of identifying which entry from each quadrant is in play. To use such a thin reading for our purposes would be to assume that the question of the operation of the logical functions could be reduced to the simple observation that the statement of the judgment "X is beautiful" is: affirmative, singular, categorical and assertoric. Under such a paltry notion of an analysis of moments, one would naturally underappreciate the import of Kant's remark that the logical functions guide his analysis of the moments of aesthetic judgment. Jens Kulenkampff takes this simplistic approach and thus concludes that "such a subsumption under the Kantian formal determinations of judgment is so unproblematically possible, that an extensive analysis does

---

[120] *Critique of the Power of Judgment*, Bk. I, § 1, 5:203.

not at all arise."[121] Of course, the grammatical statement itself *could* be brought into connection with the table of judgments in this way, but this is not what comprises an analysis of *moments*. The table of judgments is the "table of the moments of thinking in general."[122] Hence, as I will establish shortly, to analyze the moments of something is to look at how "the function of thinking"[123] governs the processes through which it takes shape. An analysis of moments leads us into a rich investigation of the mental processes underlying whatever is under scrutiny. This has direct implications for our analysis of aesthetic judgment, indicating that its moments are much more than the mere identification of which function is operative in statements proclaiming something to be beautiful.

Let us begin by looking at Kant's use of the term *Moment* at the beginning of "The Analytic of Principles." He opens up this section by contrasting merely formal logic with transcendental logic. It is in his description of formal logic that the term *Moment* arises. Formal logic "abstracts from all content of cognition [...] and concerns itself merely with the form of thinking."[124] He goes on to explain that the canon for reason can be included in the analytical part of formal logic, providing *a priori* insight "through mere analysis of the actions of reason into their moments, without taking into consideration the particular nature of the cognition about which it is employed."[125] Transcendental logic, however, follows a different route, because it "is limited to a determinate content, namely that of pure *a priori* cognitions alone."[126] From this passage, we learn the following. Formal logic acquires *a priori* insight by analyzing "the actions of reason into their moments," whereas the *a priori* element in transcendental logic is the "determinate content" of "pure *a priori* cognitions alone." This contrast suggests that a moment can provide a way of describing "actions of reason," having more to do with the analysis of mental acts (their form) than the content (their matter) in relation to which those acts are performed. This would explain why the third *Critique* discusses four moments "of the judgment of taste,"[127] or alternatively "of aesthetic judgment"[128] and not four moments of the beautiful.[129]

---

121 Kulenkampff, *Kants Logik des ästhetischen Urteils*, 28, my translation. The original reads, "Eine solche subsumation unter die kantischen Formalbestimmungen von Urteilen is so problemlos möglich, dass sich eine ausgebreitete Analytik gar nicht ergibt."
122 *Critique of Pure Reason*, A71/B96–7.
123 *Critique of Pure Reason*, A70/B95.
124 *Critique of Pure Reason*, A131/B170.
125 *Critique of Pure Reason*, A131/B170.
126 *Critique of Pure Reason*, A131/B170.
127 *Critique of the Power of Judgment*, Bk. I, § 1, 5:203.
128 *Critique of the Power of Judgment*, Bk. I, § 24, 5:247.

Kant is providing an analysis of the mental action of judging and not of the content judged, nor of the conclusion to which such judging leads, because it is the peculiarities of the mental act *itself* that designate it as aesthetic, not the object, nor the resulting proclamation of beauty.

The dynamic quality that is conveyed with the term "moment" comes to the fore in Kant's discussion of intuitive magnitudes under "Anticipations of Perception." He writes:

> Now I call that magnitude which can only be apprehended as a unity, and in which multiplicity can only be represented through approximation to negation = 0, intensive magnitude. Thus every reality in the appearance has intensive magnitude, i.e., a degree. If one regards this reality as cause (whether of the sensation or of another reality in appearance, e.g., an alteration), then one calls the degree of reality as cause a **"moment"**, e.g., the **moment** of gravity [*das Moment der Schwere*], because, indeed, the degree designates only that magnitude the apprehension of which is not successive but instantaneous. But I touch on this here only in passing, for at present I am not yet dealing with causality.[130]

This further supports the idea that moments are concerned with analyzing processes or acts. The "degree of reality as cause"[131] is designated as a *moment* and held in contrast to "the degree" as the specific intensive magnitude reached. The achieved degree of an intensive magnitude is reached through the driving force that pushes the magnitude along the scale between "0" (total negation) and some degree of existence. This driving force is the moment. The resulting degree of a magnitude exists as a product generated through the action of the moment. Whereas the moment, itself, pertains to the causal chain and, hence, is "successive", once this moment has brought about the degree of magnitude, this product is something that can be apprehended in an "instantaneous" manner.[132]

---

129 It might, here, be objected that although the term "moments of the beautiful" does not arise, the first book is, in fact, entitled the Analytic of the Beautiful. This observation does not, however, ultimately conflict with the point I seek to establish. In analyzing the experience of beauty, we are looking at the underlying mental function that allows one to experience the beautiful, which is the act of aesthetic judgment. It is this act of thinking which will be analyzed into its moments, not the product of this act, i.e., not the recognition of something as beautiful. In analyzing the beautiful we thus look at the act of thinking (aesthetic judgment), that is, at the condition for the possibility of an appearance of the beautiful. And, in doing so, we must investigate the specific functioning of this mental act by analyzing it into its moments.
130 *Critique of Pure Reason*, A168–9/B210, *bold added.*
131 *Critique of Pure Reason*, A168–9/B210.
132 *Critique of Pure Reason*, A168–9/B210.

It is informative to note that in the German language the term *Moment* has not only a number of meanings, but also both a masculine and neuter form.[133] In the masculine, *der Moment*, is an English cognate designating temporality as an instant in time. The *Deutsches Wörterbuch* from Jacob und Wilhelm Grimm (Leipzig 1854–1961) also lists a neuter entry, *das Moment*, which carries the meanings of momentum or elemental impulse ("*der bedeutung des beweggrundes, oder wesentlichen, ausschlag gebenden umstandes*"[134]). Indeed, not only does the passage cited above feature *Moment* in the neuter, but furthermore the Grimm brothers' *Deutsches Wörterbuch* cites Kant as the historical source for *das Moment*.[135] This indicates that Kant's use of the term does not fold up neatly into any pre-existing meanings of his time, but rather inaugurates a specialized use, tailored to Kant's own philosophical need. Thus, we must think through Kant's usage of the term to understand how the meanings of momentum and elemental impulse form a thick concept unique to his system. On the one hand, *momentum* highlights the dynamic character of the term, insofar as it pertains to the driving force of an active process. On the other hand, *das Moment* is used to analyze this act of thinking, picking out an *element* of it, or, as in the case of intensive magnitudes, indicating how it operates as an *elemental impulse* to yield a certain degree.

To stay with Kant's own example, gravity appears to be picked out as a *Moment*, because it is a force that can cause an object to obtain a certain degree on the scale of intensive magnitudes, and thus account for the qualitative differences we find among different types of matter. Kant brings this out more fully only a few pages later where he again makes reference to the "moment of gravity," but this time his concern is more properly with causality, and in particular, how a *sensation* is caused:

> Nearly all natural philosophers, since they perceive a great difference in the quantity of matter of different sorts in the same volumes (partly through the moment of gravity, or weight, partly through the **moment** of resistance against other, moved matter), unanimous-

---

133 The *Deutsches Wörterbuch* from Jacob und Wilhelm Grimm (Leipzig 1854–1961) lists the masculine entry for *Moment* as "augenblick, zeitpunkt; bewegendes, entscheidendes." In the neuter they report that *Moment* is taken "unmittelbar aus dem lateinischen und als neutr. entlehnt die philosophische und rechtssprache des vorigen jahrh. moment in der bedeutung des beweggrundes, oder wesentlichen, ausschlag gebenden umstandes."
134 See, Deutsches Wörterbuch from Jacob und Wilhelm Grimm (Leipzig 1854–1961).
135 "...ob die causalität zur wirklichkeit der objecte zulange oder nicht, .. macht in der praktischen aufgabe gar kein moment derselben aus. Kant 4, 150; vergl.hauptmoment theil 4 2 , 623" (Jacob and Wilhelm Grimm, *Deutsches Wörterbuch*, 1854–1961).

ly infer from this that this volume (extensive magnitude of the appearance) must be empty in all matter, although to be sure in different amounts.¹³⁶

Rather than settle for differing volumes being solely accountable in terms of extensive magnitudes, however, Kant provides an alternative explanation according to which this difference can be explained intensively,

> although equal spaces can be completely filled with different matters in such a way that in neither of them is there a point in which the presence of matter is not to be encountered, nevertheless everything real has for the same quality its degree (of resistance or of weight) which, without diminution of the extensive magnitude or amount, can become infinitely smaller until it is transformed into emptiness and disappears.¹³⁷

From this it appears that the diminishing of a thing's weight, signifies that gravity has less against which it may exert its force. The difference in the weights of two equal spaces is thus not necessarily to be explained by one space being "emptier" than the other, but rather may also be due to the spaces being filled with matters that are qualitatively different—involving matter with a different consistency and thus offering a different degree of resistance to the gravitational force. The fact that Kant's explanation of this is sprinkled with the term moment (gravity, resistance and weight all being described as such), underscores how an analysis of moments favors a dynamic explanation over a static one. Here, an analysis of moments does not explain the difference in volume between two equal spaces in the static terms of a presence or absence of objects, but rather in the dynamic terms of the increasing or decreasing strength of some force (the moments of gravity and resistance).¹³⁸ Whereas "gravity" is a general

---

136 *Critique of Pure Reason*, A173/B215, bold added.
137 *Critique of Pure Reason*, A174/B216.
138 Kant may appear to be waffling at B215 about whether the first moment should be designated as that of gravity or of weight. This could seem to betray an uncertainty about whether this moment is characterized by weight or gravity. Instead of reading it in this way, however, there is reason to believe that in this context Kant supplies both terms because they are such inseparable parts of this moment. In a certain sense, the force of gravity clings to the weight of the object. The two most prevalent Germanic terms for gravity are *Anziehungskraft* and *Schwerkraft* (also shortened to *Schwere*, as it is here), the former translates literally as "force of attraction," while the latter contains in it the word *schwer* and is thus along the lines of "the power of weight." This indicates the link between weight and gravity to be much more palpable in German than English. The original German text at B215 reads "teils durch das Moment der Schwere, oder des Gewichts, teils durch das Moment des Widerstandes gegen andere *bewegte* Materien." Here, the transition from gravity (*Schwere*) into weight (*Gewicht*) is not as jolting as it may seem in English. Rather, it appears to be a relatively natural passage, since weight

force, what is understood by looking at the "moment of gravity" is the determination of this force—that is, the specific degree of force exerted in a certain instance. Unlike, extensive magnitudes, which are apprehended through the addition of successive parts, intensive magnitudes supply their degree to apprehension as "instantaneous."[139] This measurement, however, does not pertain to the *Moment* itself, but rather, to the "momentary" degree that this *Moment* produces. Thus, the neuter meanings of *Moment* apply to the *Moment*, itself, while the masculine term with a temporal meaning pertains to that which the *Moment* produces for apprehension (i.e. the "degree"). To bring the four terms together in one definition, we could say that a *Moment* is a certain sort of impulse (*momentum*) in its *elemental* feature of being the *factor* and thereby causing what one is then able to *instantaneously* apprehend as a certain degree. In the affectation of an intensive magnitude, three primary elements are involved: the cause, the scale providing "a continuous nexus of possible realities"[140] that span between reality and negation, and the resulting degree. We could thus say that the *Moment* pertains to the causal side of this equation and the analysis of something's *Moments* is an analysis of the determinations characterizing the causal impulse (*Moment*) so that it can produce the effect that it does. To adopt Aristotelian terminology, we could say that an analysis of something's moments is the elaboration of the formal cause that shapes the efficient cause so as to produce this thing. I will be elaborating on this shortly, but presently we can see that, in Kant's example above, the analysis of the *Moment* allows the matter in a given space to be analyzed in terms of the degree (formal cause of the *Moment*) of gravitational force (efficient cause, and thus *Moment*) exerted upon it, which thus causes it to have a certain weight (the product).

An analysis of moments can unpack the dynamical connections that underpin a seemingly static appearance. We see this above, where the static appearance of weight (static) is identified as the product of gravitational force (dynamic), and this force is further analyzed in terms of its degree. Likewise, although aesthetic judgment concerns a state of pleasure and verdict of beauty, an analysis of the moments will concern the dynamical processes behind these, i.e. the *feeling* of pleasure and *judging* of beauty.

This interrelation of causal actions and moments comes even more clearly to the fore at the close of the Second Analogy, when Kant writes:

---

is constituted through the gravitational force and there must be some weighable object present upon which the gravitational force may exert itself in order for this force to be active.
139 *Critique of Pure Reason*, A168–9/B210.
140 *Critique of Pure Reason*, A169/B211.

> All alteration is therefore possible only through a continuous action of causality, which, insofar as it is uniform, is called a **moment**. The alteration does not consist of these **moments**, but it is generated through them as their effect.[141]

Thus, it is not that the moments *are* the alteration, but that they determine the alteration, allowing the alteration to take the form that it does and thus produce a particular appearance for us to apprehend. The moment is the "continuous action of causality."[142] In an Aristotelian vein, we might, again, think of moments as the efficient cause, which designates "the original source of change or rest."[143] In general, this is to be understood as how "a producer causes a product and a changer causes a change."[144] This efficient cause, however, can itself be analyzed to reveal the determinations governing its causal action. Thus, an *analysis* of *Moments* can be understood to reveal the formal cause[145] of the efficient cause that provides the alteration. Thus, in the case of the second analogy, an alteration arises from the causal moment of a uniform, continuous action. To analyze an alteration into its moments, is to scrutinize the causal action that gives rise to it in accordance with a rule. The Analogies are concerned with empirical cognitions, representing something objective. Hence, in this context, the analysis of moments consists in detailing the way that the mental processes of empirical cognition are guided by the categories. Although aesthetic judgment involves an initial empirical layer, the properly aesthetic layer of the judgment is not carried out through an active application of the categories in the determination of an object.[146] Thus, an analysis of the moments of *aesthetic judgment* will detail how the logical functions operate (formal cause) so as to determine an activity of thinking (efficient cause) to generate the verdict that something is beautiful, rather than how the categories operate to determine the experience that gives us an empirical object.

When Kant refers to something's moment, this designates the efficient cause that produces this thing. When he writes of analyzing this moment, I see this as

---

141 *Critique of Pure Reason*, A208–9/B254, bold added.
142 *Critique of Pure Reason*, A208–9/B254.
143 Aristotle, *Physics*, Physics. Translated by Robin Waterfield (Oxford: Oxford University Press, 1996), II.3:194b29.
144 Aristotle, *Physics*, II.3:194b29.
145 Formal cause is described in the *Physics* as "the form or pattern (i.e. the formula for what a thing is, both specifically and generically, and the terms which play a part in the formula)" (Aristotle, *Physics*, II.3:194b26).
146 As detailed in chapter one, the categories have what we may term a deactivated presence in aesthetic judgment, residing only in the empirical object that was constituted on the initial empirical layer.

an analysis of the determinations of the efficient cause which allow it to act as it does. I am not arguing that we should understand Kant's analysis of moments as pertaining only to empirical or transcendental analysis. An analysis of moments may detail how objects of experience act upon one another as cause and effect in nature, or how Kant's transcendental apparatus works to constitute cognitive processes. What I want to underscore is the way that an analysis of moments is an analysis of the formal causes determining an efficient cause, regardless of the level on which this may occur.

My analysis of Kant's use of the term *Moment* in the first *Critique* has revealed a certain ambiguity in its meaning—that is, even though Kant states in the *Clue to the Discovery of all Pure Concepts of the Understanding* that the logical functions are the moments,[147] and in the *Jäsche Logic* that something's moments are its quantity, quality, relation, modality,[148] given the array of meanings that the term may bear, it cannot always be assumed to refer directly to an analysis of the logical functions or titles of the table. For instance, in the Second Analogy[149] the discussion of the moments does not lead into any explanation of how something relates to the table of judgments, or categories. That said, there is an important point of commonality that surfaced in Kant's use of this term. An analysis according to moments was directed at a dynamic *process* or *impulse* (momentum), and not an *object*. The moment reveals the factors that give this process its form, and thus govern the act of imbuing the product of such a process with determinations. Thus, when aesthetic judgment is the process under scrutiny, then an analysis according to its moments will be concerned with the transcendental story of how the faculties operate—that is, the determinations of

---

[147] "If we abstract from all content of a judgment in general, and attend only to the mere form of the understanding in it, we find that the function of thinking in that can be brought under four titles, each of which contains under itself three moments. They can suitably be represented in the following table" (*Critique of Pure Reason*, A70/B95).

[148] "To acquaint us better with the essential differences that exist between the logical and the aesthetic perfection of cognition, not merely in the universal but from several particular sides, we want to compare the two with one another in respect to the four chief moments of quantity, quality, relation, and modality, on which the passing of judgment as to the perfection of cognition depends" (*The Jäsche Logic*, V, 38); "The distinction among judgments in respect of their form may be traced back to the four principal moments of *quantity, quality, relation,* and *modality,* in regard to which just as many different kinds of judgments are determined" (*The Jäsche Logic,* § 20, 102).

[149] Here Kant remarks that "[t]he ground of proof of this proposition, however, rests solely on the following moments," and referenced "the moment of gravity" (*Critique of Pure Reason*, A168–9/B210).

the *operation* of the faculties, not the determination of empirical objects *through* the workings of these faculties.

IV How Logical Functions Guide the Analysis of Moments for Aesthetic Judgment

Let us now take a closer look at how the moments can be expected to function for aesthetic judgment. We have already examined the footnote at the beginning of the Analytic of the Beautiful while focusing on the guiding role that the logical functions play in Kant's analysis. Let us return to this same footnote, but this time with an eye to what can be gleamed from it about the term *Moment*:

> But what is required for calling an object beautiful must be discovered by the analysis of judgments of taste. In seeking the moments to which this power of judgment attends in its reflection, I have been guided by the logical functions for judging (for a relation to the understanding is always contained even in the judgment of taste).[150]

The second sentence acknowledges that, as observed above, it is not immediately self-evident that an analysis of something's moments will be carried out in relation to the logical functions. Thus, it warrants mentioning that in an analysis of aesthetic judgment this will, in fact, be the case. This is not, however, all that we learn from this passage about what an analysis of moments will mean.

The first sentence tells us what the analysis of the moments of aesthetic judgment will yield. An "analysis of judgments of taste" seeks to discover "what is required for calling an object beautiful."[151] Such an analysis functions by "seeking the moments to which this power of judgment attends in its reflection." That to which judgment attends in its reflection manifests most clearly if we systematically analyze the powers of judgment in terms of its logical functions. Doing so will reveal the processes that are at work in aesthetic contemplation (i.e. in the act of aesthetic judging). Kant explains that such an analysis of moments by means of the logical functions will tell us "what is required for calling an object beautiful." From the foregoing, we can conclude that this is not to be taken as the generation of a set of criteria for the object, but criteria for

---

150 *Critique of the Power of Judgment*, Bk. I, § 1, 5:203.
151 It is worth noting that the definition this first moment yields does not define the beautiful, but rather provides a stipulation for what "is called beautiful" (*Critique of the Power of Judgment*, Bk. I, § 5, 5:211). The curious phrasing of this definition is further explored in the conclusion of the next chapter.

the *judging* of the object.¹⁵² That is, it will describe the way that the process works, which culminates in the act of declaring an object to have a certain aesthetic value. The end product of this process is the proclamation of a judgment. The *requirements* we are after, however, are those that stipulate *how* the power of judgment must operate so as to produce such a proclamation—i.e., how the act of aesthetically judging, itself, works. Thus, the analysis will focus on the mental processes at work and how the faculties relate to one another. From this it is clear that the moments of aesthetic judgment will *not* amount to an analysis of the grammar governing the proclamation, "This X is beautiful."

How, exactly, does the analysis of moments relate to the proclamation of something's beauty, one might ask. As observed above, this proclamation makes an unavoidable use of concepts. In essence, it states that this conceptualized object of experience is to be subsumed under the concept 'beautiful.' Although the term "moment" does not, itself, appear in the following section from the *Jäsche Logic*, what Kant says here is instructive for understanding the way in which the logical functions are used in such an analysis.

> Note: 2. It is a mere tautology to speak of universal or common concepts – a mistake that is grounded in an incorrect division of concepts into *universal, particular,* and *singular.* Concepts themselves cannot be so divided, but only *their use.*¹⁵³

This passage emphasizes the difference between logical functions and concepts. "Universal, particular, and singular" are the logical functions of Quantity, not the pure concepts of the understanding (i.e., categories, which would be: unity, plurality, totality). Furthermore, they are not used to modify concepts. What Kant says here suggests another grammatical analogy. Perhaps we could imagine the concepts as adjectives modifying nouns and the logical functions as adverbs that modify only verbs. Thus, the logical functions can modify the *use* of concepts, but not the concepts themselves. According to this analogy, the logical functions would be the adverb that modifies the verb of "judging,"

---

152 Although Kulenkampff and I disagree about whether the logical functions of judgment can be a useful guide for understanding Kant's analysis of aesthetic judgment, I am in agreement with him about the fact that this analysis is not directed at *objects* so as to determine which ones warrant a proclamation of beauty. Kulenkampff points out that in this respect Kant is in line with the commonly accepted ideas of the 18th century. He writes, "Kant teilt mit der Kritik an der sogenannten rationalistischen Ästhetik die Meinung, daß es nicht gelungen sei, eine hinreichend spezifische, objetive-deskriptive Bedeutung für "schön" anzugeben oder "Kriterien" zu formulieren, "wonach sich unser Geschmacksurteil richten müßte" (KdrV B 35, Anmerkung)" (Kulenkampff, *Kants Logik des ästhetischen Urteils*, 72).
153 *Jäsche Logic*, § 1, 91.

characterizing the way in which one judges. When a *Phänomen* results from such a judgment, then an intuition would be the noun that is the direct object of the judgment and the categories would be the adjectives that modify this noun. This means that in using the logical functions as our guide to analyze aesthetic judgment into its moments, we can expect nothing other than an analysis of how the logical functions work to give the form to the act of judging which will designate it as aesthetic.[154] This passage from the *Jäsche Logic* suggests an answer to the difficulty presented by the proclamation that concludes an aesthetic judgment. The logical functions do not modify the concepts in the proclamation "This X is beautiful." Rather, they modify the process that calls forth these concepts. The proclamation of beauty in which an aesthetic judgment may result, is not on the same level as our analysis of the moments of aesthetic judgment guided by the logical functions. The logical functions modify the underlying acts of thinking that give way to this proclamation.[155]

My interpretation of what it means to carry out an analysis of the moments of aesthetic judgment can be further supported by the precedence that form takes over matter for Kant. Longuenesse develops this point in the course of examining the concepts of comparison from the Amphibolies.[156] While building her

---

[154] In her article "Kant's Leading Thread in the Analytic of the Beautiful," Longuenesse makes a similar observation, commenting on "the striking shift of direction in Kant's analysis of judgments of taste, from an analysis of the explicit judgment about an object to an analysis of the implicit judgment about the judging subjects" (Longuenesse, "Kant's Leading Thread in the Analytic of the Beautiful," 194). Thus, "the leading thread of the elementary logical functions" concerns "the nature of the acts of judging at work in aesthetic judgments" so that we may investigate how "the functions of judging, *Function zu urteilen*, manifest in this form" (Longuenesse, "Kant's Leading Thread in the Analytic of the Beautiful," 195–196).

[155] Along with the concepts used to proclaim the empirical object's aesthetic value, the third-layer concepts of a further discursive harmony may be called forth by the non-discursive second layer activity of judging. I agree with Guyer, however, that this further harmony, which is described by Allison, need not be achieved in every case of aesthetic judgment (see Guyer, "The Harmony of the Faculties Revisited," 188). For an aesthetic judgment to occur the minimum requirement would be that the concepts necessary to state a verdict on the empirical object's aesthetic value are called forth.

[156] Longuenesse, *Kant and the Capacity to Judge*, 161. Here, Longuenesse makes an extended argument for attributing a much more crucial role to the logical functions in the table of judgements than is typically done. She argues that only by distilling out the workings of the logical functions, which often is not directly elaborated in Kant's text, can we make sense of the first *Critique*. More specifically, she defends the thesis that, "neither the argument of the Transcendental Deduction of the Categories, that is, the demonstration of the role of the pure concepts of the understanding in any respect of an object, nor the System of Principles of the Pure Understanding, can be understood unless they are related, down to the minutest details of their proofs, to the role that Kant assigns to the logical forms of our judgment, and to the manner

argument for how "the three pairs of the concepts of comparison" can help explain concept formation, Longuenesse increasingly emphasizes the "precedence [Kant] grants the form of thought over its matter."[157] She concludes that:

> The thesis that the concepts of comparison, "inner" and "outer," "agreement" and "conflict," "identity" and "difference," guide the formation of concepts from the sensible given is equivalent to saying that the *matter* of all thought (viz. concepts) is generated by the very activity that combines concepts in accordance with its proper *form* (the forms of judgment).[158]

Instead of entering into her analysis of the concepts of comparison, the resonance that I see here with my own analysis concerns the way that she details the relation between matter and form for the act of judging—the *moment* being the action of giving matter its form. Longuenesse further elaborates that this precedence of form over matter holds regardless of whether we,

> go further down, toward the determinable, and consider the *matter* for which the concepts themselves are the *form*, namely the object [...or] go further up, toward the determination, and consider the *form* for which judgments are the *matter*, namely forms of inference, and the form of a system in general.[159]

When directing our attention downwards, she describes two ways that form determines matter. First, "the forms of judgment determine the formation of concepts as the matter for judgments;" second, "they contribute to generating the representation of objects as the "matter" for concepts."[160] What I have in mind in suggesting that to analyze the moments of something is to look at how "the function of thinking"[161] governs the processes through which it takes shape is along the lines of the former. If "the forms of judgment determine the formation of concepts as the matter for judgments,"[162] then implicit in this is the idea that

---

in which he establishes the categories or pure concepts of the understanding according to the "guiding thread" of these logical forms" (5). Given the interest I share with her in emphasizing the much over-looked importance of the logical functions, I will repeatedly draw upon selected parts of her work, here, although a full engagement with the entirety of her detailed analysis is outside of the scope of this project, because, at heart, my interest is rooted in the third *Critique*, while her book is a detailed engagement with the first.

157 Longuenesse, *Kant and the Capacity to Judge*, 161.
158 Longuenesse, *Kant and the Capacity to Judge*, 162.
159 Longuenesse, *Kant and the Capacity to Judge*, 162.
160 Longuenesse, *Kant and the Capacity to Judge*, 162.
161 *Critique of Pure Reason*, A70/B95.
162 *Critique of Pure Reason*, A70/B95.

IV How Logical Functions Guide the Analysis of Moments for Aesthetic Judgment — 127

the components of a judgment must be *formed*, taking shape before judgment can use them to judge. This is more the level upon which I see an analysis of the moments of judgment to operate. It is not an analysis of the judgment statement produced in judging, but rather an analysis of how the logical functions are involved in forming the components that are necessary for the judging to occur—giving form to that which will become "the matter for judgments."[163]

This means that in the first moment we will be investigating the quality that the action of judging has, and not the determination of the qualities of the object of aesthetic judgment, because aesthetic judgment is "in" the subject, not the object. Thus, under the title of Quality, the Analytic aims to explicate our way of being interested in the object as an *interesselose* interest, which does not concern itself with the existence of the object, or with the goodness, or agreeableness that such an existence could provide. The analysis of the *moment* of quality for aesthetic judgment, is thus concerned with how, while lingering over an aesthetic judgment, the judging subject's conceptual processes function through specific negative, affirmative and infinite operations of thought.[164] Like the analysis provided in the second analogy, the *moments* will, thus, be the story of how this act of thinking is given the form that allows it to produce a judgment of beauty.[165]

---

163 Longuenesse, *Kant and the Capacity to Judge*, 162.
164 Donald Crawford says something similar to this, writing, "In essence, Kant maintains that the grammatical form of the judgment of taste is not its logical form. The logical form, considered under the heading of Quality, is affirmative. But it is not the affirmation of a concept to a particular; rather, it is analyzed by Kant as the affirmation of a feeling of pleasure the person doing the judging of the object—the object found to be beautiful—which is the grammatical subject of the judgment" (Crawford, *Kant's Aesthetic Theory*, 16). Here Crawford notes the schism between the proclamation in which an aesthetic judgment terminates, "This x is beautiful," and the judging subject towards whom the logical functions are directed in our analysis of the moments of aesthetic judgment. Although I will be disagreeing with Crawford that the Quality of aesthetic judgment can be simply identified with the affirmative in the next chapter, our views coincide regarding the way that logical functions relate to the activity of judging and are not determinations of the empirical object judged.
165 Further support for this interpretation of what it means to analyze aesthetic judgment into its moments will come forward in the third moment (Ch. 5), which will focus on the logical function of disjunction. Disjunction concerns a judgment which brings a number of judgments in relation to one another in order to "determine the true cognition in its entirety, since taken together they constitute the entire content of a particular given cognition" (*Critique of Pure Reason*, A74/B99). In discussing aesthetic judgment's relation to disjunction we will, thus, be focusing on how *judgments* relate to one another, and thus the question of how properties determine an empirical object will fall away even more fully, as such determination is the result of a subject-predicate relation and hence is established by a categorical, not disjunctive, judgment.

IV.A The Interrelation of Logical Functions in General

Over the course of analyzing the moments of aesthetic judgment, I will be uncovering a way that more than one logical function is operative in each quadrant. This will complicate and deepen each moment, with each of the functions relating either to different elements or in different manners, so as not to introduce a contradiction that makes the moment impossible. Thus, it is important to establish that the simultaneous operation of more than one logical function does not violate the way that Kant sees these functions as operating in the first place. Let us begin by examining how Kant is already doing something along these lines in the construction of the third entry in the table of categories. Kant writes,

> each class always has the same number of categories, namely three, which calls for reflection, since otherwise all *a priori* division by means of concepts must be a dichotomy. But here the third category always arises from the combination of the first two in its class.[166]

If the categories were to analyze objects of experience in a dichotomous manner, then we would have a rigid picture of the world. The third category breaks up this potential dichotomy, creating a way that the first two can be brought together, determining an appearance simultaneously. Kant specifies how this works for each quadrant in the table of categories:

> Thus **allness** (totality) is nothing other than plurality considered as a unity, **limitation** is nothing other than reality combined with negation, community is the **causality** of a substance in the reciprocal determination of others, finally **necessity** is nothing other than the existence that is given by possibility itself.[167]

Kant cautions us not to mistake this production of the third category through the first two for an indication that this third category is "merely derivative" and assures us that this combination "requires a special act of the understanding, which is not identical with the act performed in the first and second."[168] Thus, the third category is something new, standing in its own right, although it contains within it the workings of the first and second.

Since the table of the categories and the table of judgments are so closely interlinked with one another, the establishment of the third category through a combination of the first two gives good reason to believe that there could be

---

[166] *Critique of Pure Reason*, B110.
[167] *Critique of Pure Reason*, B111.
[168] *Critique of Pure Reason*, B111.

a similar dynamic at play among the logical functions, allowing the first and second logical function to be read as operative in the workings of the third. This possibility will be more thoroughly developed over the course of my analysis of the moments of aesthetic judgment.[169]

V Conclusion

Numerous scholars have dismissed Kant's decision to use the logical functions of judgment to guide his analysis, both in the first *Critique* where the categories are derived from them and in the third *Critique* where they are to have guided his search for "the moments to which this power of judgment attends in its reflection."[170] Guyer deems this an infelicitous decision that obscures Kant's intended

---

[169] Despite my fundamental disagreements with many aspects of Kulenkampff's approach, there is still a certain concurrence. He recognizes a "nur paradox faßbare Besonderheit des reinen Geschmacksurteils" and attempts to take account of it by understanding each of the moments as conditioning the others, so as to generate a richly complex conception of aesthetic judgment (Kulenkampff, *Kants Logik des ästhetischen Urteils*, 26). I, too, recognize that in a variety of ways aesthetic judgment risks slipping into paradoxes, and that this can only be taken account of if its structure is seen in full complexity. I find that doing so, however, does not involve the moments being brought to bear upon one another to form one moment, as Kulenkampff suggests, but rather, the logical functions in each moment conditioning each other, so as to form a moment with twists and turns that are not representable as the simple selection of one function in each quadrant.

[170] *Critique of the Power of Judgment*, Bk. I, § 1, 5: 203. It is not only in relation to aesthetic judgment that the usefulness of the table of judgments has been cast into doubt, but also in its original function as that from which the categories are derived. For criticisms of the latter see: Peter Strawson in *Bounds of Sense*, 82 ("The results of the appeal to formal logic are not merely meagre. Their meagerness is such as to render almost pointless any critical consideration of the detail of Kant's derivation of the categories from the Table of Judgments."); Smith, Norman Kemp, *A Commentary to Kant's 'Critique of Pure Reason'* (London: Macmillan, 1923) "Section I. The Logical Use of the Understanding.—This section, viewed as introductory to the metaphysical deduction of the categories, is extremely unsatisfactory. It directs attention to the wrong points, and conceals rather than defines Kant's real position"; and Martin Heidegger: "Not only are the categories not actually derived from the table of judgments, they cannot be so derived [...]" (Martin Heidegger, *Kant and the Problem of Metaphysics*, trans. J.S. Churchill [Bloomington: Indiana University Press, 1962], 58). Longuenesse skillfully carries out a detailed argument against these claims in *Kant and the Capacity to Judge* where she argues that not only the categories, but also the System of Principles of the Pure Understanding must be "related, down to the minutest details of their proofs, to the role that Kant assigns to the logical forms of our judgments" (Longuenesse, *Kant and the Capacity to Judge*, 5).

argument in the third *Critique*.[171] Jens Kulenkampff goes so far as to accuse Kant of not even having actually followed the guidance of the table of judgments in the first place.[172]

---

[171] "Since the logical functions of judgment describe difference in the contents of judgments, and the moments of aesthetic judgment describe quite different features of the status and ground of judgments, there is no reason why the order or even the number of the former should provide an appropriate framework for the analysis of the latter. In fact, Kant's sequential arrangement of the four moments as four "definitions" of the judgment of taste obscures the difference in function between those describing the requirement of intersubjective acceptability and those describing criteria by which such a requirement may be judged to be fulfilled" (Guyer, *Kant and the Claims of Taste*, 115). From our foregoing analysis, we see that Guyer is mistaken in his first line about the way that the logical functions of judgment work. By identifying them as describing content, he runs the risk of confusing them with the categories. That which the logical functions of judgment, *die logische Funktionen zu urteilen*, describe is not the content of an object, or idea, but rather the merely logical determinations that constitute the act of judging (*Critique of Pure Reason*, B128–129). Thus, if the "moments of aesthetic judgment describe [...] the status and ground of judgments," then there is, indeed, good reason to take the functions of judgment as "provid[ing] an appropriate framework for the analysis of the latter."

[172] Kulenkampff argues that the four moments do not examine four separate characteristics of aesthetic judgment, but rather that all four come together to constitute one particularity of aesthetic judgment. We see him develop this point as follows, "es fällt auf, daß sich die vier Bestimmungen auf eine, allerdings komplexe Eigenschaft reduzieren lassen" (Kulenkampff, *Kants Logik des ästhetischen Urteils*, 23); "Die Erörterungen zum ersten und zweiten Moment gehören zusammen und bilden eine einheit der Analyse. Die zweite Bestimmung ist als Weiterbestimmung zur ersten aufzufassen, indem sie nun auf ein mit der logischen Form des Urteils gegebenes Moment Rücksicht nimmt, in dessen Formulierung sich die verdeckte Paradoxie der ersten Erklärung deutlich wiederholt. Die zweite Erklärung erreicht erst die volle Charakteristik des reinen Geschmacksurteils, das damit verbundene philosphishe Problem und eine Skizze seiner Lösung" (Kulenkampff, *Kants Logik des ästhetischen Urteils*, 25); "...Wenn es aber so ist, daß die 1. und die 2.Folgerung zusammengesehen werden müssen, daß die 4.Folgerung nicht über die 2. hinausgeht und daß endlich die 3.Folgerung denselben Sachverhalt nur anders akzentuiert, so spricht das gegen Kants Selbstdarstellung, er habe "die Moments...nach Anleitung der logische Funktionen zu urteilen, aufgesucht" (3, Anmerkung); und die These ist gerechtfertigt, daß das Schema der Urteilstafel für die *Analytik der Schönen* äußerlich ist und das analytische Verfahren eher verdunkelt als erhellt" (Kulenkampff, *Kants Logik des ästhetischen Urteils*, 26). Consequently he argues that there is no particular reason to begin with quality instead of quantity and that Kant's statement about having followed the logical functions in the analysis of aesthetic judgment is entirely false: "Der Formenkatalog der Ureteilstafel enthält außerdem keinerlei Anhaltspunkte, daß eine bestimmte Reihenfolge der Subsumtion zu beobachten sei. Wie mit der Eigenschaft der Quantität könnte ebensogut mit der Eigenschaft der Qualität oder einer anderen begonnen werden. Und auch aus der Ureteilsform "dieses x ist schön" kann nicht einsichtig gemacht werden, warum die "Qualität...zuerst in Betrachtung gezogen" werden sollte" (Kulenkampff, *Kants Logik des ästhetischen Urteils*, 28). I find that Kulenkampff is in too much of a hurry to disregard Kant's own description of what he is doing. If he claims to follow the

Béatrice Longuenesse sets herself apart on this count. In her article, "Kant's Guiding Thread," she analyzes the moments of aesthetic judgment in relation to each quadrant in the table of judgments. She argues that the table provides a checklist of questions for aesthetic judgment to answer. Encouraged by her unwillingness to dismiss Kant's remark about the importance of this table, I find that the logical functions of judgment actually play an even more fundamental role for aesthetic judgment in general. It is their operation that enables the understanding to connect with the imagination, just enough so as to enter into a harmonious free play. Thus, commentators who found Kant's remark about the importance of the table of judgments inconsequential overlooked something of great importance, for it is only through the involvement of this very table that the understanding is able to engage in aesthetic judgment at all.

To analyze the *moments* of aesthetic judgment is to look at how "the function of thinking" [173] governs the processes through which it takes shape. Thus we should expect a rich investigation of the peculiarities characterizing the mental processes of aesthetic judging, and not of the object judged, nor of the discursive proclamation of beauty to which such judging may lead. This analysis of aesthetic judgment will reveal how the logical functions operate to give an aesthetic shape to this act of judging on each layer. It is through a particular operation of the logical functions in judging that this act of judging takes on an aesthetic form.

This reading sheds further light on the issue of how the faculties operate in aesthetic judgment without transforming it from indeterminate to determinate, and thus from aesthetic to cognitive. If aesthetic judgment acquires its characteristic features through the involvement of the logical functions of judgment, then insofar as a judgment is distinguished as aesthetic it is partially, but not fully, suitable to discursivity. Far from being an obstacle, the prominent role that Kant accords to the logical functions suits the indeterminate nature of aesthetic judgment perfectly. At the same time, it provides a potential link to discursive

---

guide of the logical functions, treats the four moments as each elaborating a particular aspect of aesthetic judgment and deviates from the typical ordering of his table to put quality before quantity, then we ought to thoroughly investigate whether there is a way of reading the Analytic that does justice to these moves before dismissing them altogether. My approach is to investigate how we can make sense of Kant's theory of aesthetic judgment, staying as close as possible to what he reports himself to be doing, and supplying further interpretation of how the system needs to function in order to achieve this in places where Kant did not further elaborate, but to avoid as much as possible a reading that comes into clear contradiction with what Kant, himself, tells us he is doing.

173 *Critique of Pure Reason*, A70/B95.

thinking, so that the harmony of the second layer may incite "much thinking" on the third. But this link is only enough for inspiration and not enough for the discursive thinking of the third layer to double back and subsume the second. No determinative grasp on the beautiful can obtain, as the absence of an empirical object prevents the concepts from finding application in the properly aesthetic layer.

The functions of judgment provide the understanding with enough access for it to be enlivened, but not enough for its determinative operations to take hold. If the categories allow the judging subject to bring together the understanding and sensibility by thinking something sensible, then their inapplicability in the properly aesthetic layer maintains a certain disconnect between these faculties, preventing the functions of judgment from becoming sensible in the properly aesthetic layer. Thus, the functions of judgment must direct themselves toward the act of judging—the judging subject's inner processes—instead of reaching out to determine the object.

Chapter Three:
Pleasure Without Interest: Affirming a Negated Interest Through the Infinite Logical Function of Quality

In the first chapter, I laid out the difficulties that one encounters when trying to make sense of the concept-independence of pure aesthetic judgments of taste. In the second chapter I offered my layered solution to this problem, showing concept-independence to be most fully displayed in the second, properly aesthetic layer of aesthetic judging where the harmonious free-play of the faculties arises. Since this layer concerns the transcendental workings of the faculties, no object to be categorically determined is involved here, and hence the concepts do not find application. This does not, however, indicate that the judging activity of this layer itself has no determinations, nor does it indicate that the imagination is active while the understanding lies dormant. As I discussed in the previous chapter, the logical functions of the understanding determine cognitive activity, and thus are active even on the second layer so as both to determine this pure aesthetic judging as a certain type of judging and to provide the necessary "relation to the understanding."[1] Now, I will begin outlining how the logical functions for judging determine the pure aesthetic judging of taste.

This chapter addresses the first moment of the judgment of taste: Quality. I will begin by explicating the logical functions found under the heading of Quality. This interpretation will then be used to investigate how the logical functions of Quality operate in the first moment so as to allow the feature of disinterested pleasure to take shape. Disinterest is of fundamental importance to the Analytic of the Aesthetic Power of Judgment, for it provides the crucial feature that allows us to distinguish between impure aesthetic judgments of the agreeable and pure aesthetic judgments of taste. I will show disinterest to be the affirmation of a negative characteristic and thus to take shape through the infinite logical function of quality. Reading disinterest through the infinite will allow us to pinpoint the specific sort of interest that is to be negated. Furthermore, I will examine how the infinite logical function is both beyond sensibility and discursivity, which will be useful for articulating the quality of aesthetic judging without this quality

---

[1] *Critique of the Power of Judgment*, § 1, 5:203. The sentence in full reads: "In seeking the moments to which this power of judgment attends in its reflection, I have been guided by the logical functions for judging (for a relation to the understanding is always contained even in the judgment of taste)."

being identified as a property of the object. After having put forward my reading of this moment, I will inspect Jens Kulenkampff's alternative interpretation, according to which disinterested pleasure characterizes aesthetic judgments with an *Indexlosigkeit*, or lack of indexicality. I will ultimately reject Kulenkampff's reading in favor of an alternative interpretation that shows the subject not to be disconnected from aesthetic pleasure in the way that he describes. In doing so, I will engage Rodolph Gasché's idea that aesthetic judgment involves a mood of pleasure. The chapter closes by considering a puzzle that arises for aesthetic judgment in the first moment and its solution.

I The Logical Functions of Quality

One might initially tend to see the entries listed under the title quality (*logical functions:* affirmation, negation, infinite; *categories:* reality, negation, limitation) as bearing little relation to *qualitative* features. Kant's elaboration of intensive magnitudes, however, demonstrates how it is through quality that such features are generated. Qualitative properties, such as color, tone and texture, manifest as specific degrees of intensity on a scale. The degree reached depends upon the extent to which the given quality is affirmed or negated. Thus, intensive magnitudes can be expected to have a general importance for aesthetic judgments, because these account for the perception of sensations in appearances.[2] Such magnitudes are generated through the synthesis of the productive imagination.[3] The intensive degree of the magnitude is determined through its place in the "contin-

---

2 *Critique of Pure Reason*, A170/B212. Melissa Zinkin also recognizes this relation between aesthetic judgments and intensive magnitudes, taking it a number of steps further. According to her analysis this relation supplies the answer to what it is about aesthetic judgments that precludes the application of concepts. She argues that in aesthetic judgments "the manifold is intuited as an intensive form of intuition" and since "concepts can only be applied to what is apprehended in an extensive form of time," concepts cannot be used to determine aesthetic judgments (Zinkin, Melissa. "Intensive Magnitudes and the Normativity of Taste," In *Aesthetics and Cognition in Kant's Critical Philosophy*, edited by Rebecca Kukla [Cambridge: Cambridge University Press, 2006], 139). She reads the third *Critique* as concerned with "a form of time in which intensity can be measured" and this "intensive form of time [...] cannot be thought by means of a concept" (146).
3 "Magnitudes of this sort can also be called flowing, since the synthesis (of the productive imagination) in their generation is a progress in time, the continuity of which is customarily designated by the expression "flowing" ("elapsing")" *Critique of Pure Reason*, A170/B212. See footnote #117, below, for the further implications that this has for pure aesthetic judgments of taste.

uous nexus of possible realities" that span "between reality and negation."[4] Thus, in the cognitive determination of quality, the category of limitation is operative as "reality combined with negation."[5] The particular shade of red in Claude Monet's *The Poppy Field, near Argenteuil* is determined by the place that this shade occupies on the scale between no perception of red and the complete reality of the color. This determination of the intensive magnitudes of the painting yields an empirical object with specific cognizable qualities, i.e., a certain shade of red. Determinations of this sort, however, belong to the initial, empirical layer of the judgment, discussed in the previous chapter. In investigating the proper aesthetic layer, we are not concerned with determining the discursively cognizable qualities of the painting themselves. What we are concerned with is the way that the logical functions work in our aesthetic engagement with these qualities. It is this active process of engagement that is governed by the functions on the table of judgment. I will argue that the logical functions of quality that determine the activity of pure aesthetic judging is the infinite, which emerges through the affirmation of a negative characteristic. The infinite function operates in this moment so as to allow Kant to be very specific about the sort of interest that is to be negated in aesthetic judgment, enabling him to navigate around the pitfalls that would ensue if disinterest were not recognized as a narrow, technical term. It is the infinite logical function that guides the qualitative dimension of aesthetic judging, so that *Interesslosigkeit* may pinpoint the absence of a specific sort of interest.

I.A Qualitative Complications

Under quality, aesthetic judgment presents us with two sorts of complications. The first is the more general logical difficulty of differentiating between negative and infinite judgments. The second is the particular aesthetic problem that, despite the disinterested nature of this judgment, not all sorts of interests appear to be negated. I will discuss the former difficulty in this section, and the latter more fully at the end of this chapter, where it emerges as the "puzzle." First, let us examine how the logical functions in this quadrant generally work.

Affirmative and negative judgments concern whether or not the predicate is attributed to the subject. They are directed at the copula relating that subject to the predicate, and determining whether this brings the two together, to make the

---

4 *Critique of Pure Reason*, A169/B211.
5 *Critique of Pure Reason*, A169/B211.

predicate an attribute of the subject, or holds them apart in opposition. In an infinite judgment, however, it is the predicate itself that is negative, while the copula is positive, affirming that the negative predicate belongs to the subject as an attribute. The *Jäsche Logic* elaborates this in spatial terms:

> In the *affirmative* judgment the subject is thought *under* the sphere of a predicate, in the *negative* it is posited *outside* the sphere of the latter, and in the *infinite* it is posited in the sphere of a concept that lies outside the sphere of another.[6]

This note offers further insight into how this works, offering the explanation that something,

> belongs in the sphere outside A, which is really no sphere at all but only *a sphere's sharing of a limit with the infinite,* or the *limiting itself.* Now although exclusion is a negation, the restriction of a concept is still a positive act. Therefore limits are positive concepts of restricted objects.[7]

Here we can see in a striking manner how the first two logical functions operate to form the third. An infinite judgment is not a simple affirmation, nor is it a simple negation. Rather, it is the affirmation *of* a negation, *through which* this negation acquires a status positive enough to allow it to be treated as an attribute (that is, to be affirmed). The fact that this is a *negative* attribute, however, means that it is a *less determined* attribute than a positive one. When a positive attribute is affirmed of something, then it supplies a definite determination of that thing. When a negative attribute is affirmed, however, the realm of possible positive attributes is left open to a great extent, the only determination being that one particular positive attribute from this realm has been eliminated. For this reason, Kant designates such a judgment as *infinite:* it places the subject "within the unlimited domain" of things that do not posses this attribute.[8] Thus, in stating that the soul is nonmortal, "nothing is said [...] but that the soul is one of the infinite multitude of things that remain if I take away everything that is mortal."[9]

The way that the procedure of determinate negation takes shape in Hegel's *Phenomenology of Spirit*[10] indicates certain similarities to Kant's infinite judge-

---

6 The *Jäsche Logic*, § 22, 104.
7 The *Jäsche Logic*, § 22, 104.
8 *Critique of Pure Reason*, A72/B97.
9 *Critique of Pure Reason*, A72/B97.
10 Within the confines of this chapter Hegel's *Phenomenology of Spirit* cannot be engaged with in all of its complexity, however, a cursory look at the contrast Hegel draws between mere and

ment, which can be helpful for further understanding the functioning of the latter. In his Introduction, Hegel contrasts "determinate negation" with "a merely negative procedure," writing:

> The necessary progression and interconnection of the forms of the unreal consciousness will by itself bring to pass the *completion* of the series. To make this more intelligible, it may be remarked, in a preliminary and general way, that the exposition of the untrue consciousness in its untruth is not a merely *negative* procedure. The natural consciousness itself normally takes this one-sided view of it; and a knowledge which makes this one-sidedness its very essence is itself one of the patterns of incomplete consciousness which occurs on the road itself, and will manifest itself in due course. This is just the skepticism which only ever sees pure nothingness in its result and abstracts from the fact that this nothingness is specifically the nothingness of that *from which it results*. For it is only when it is taken as the result of that from which it emerges, that it is, in fact, the true result; in that case it is itself a *determinate* nothingness, one which has a *content*. The skepticism that ends up with the bare abstraction of nothingness or emptiness cannot get any further from there, but must wait to see whether something new comes along and what it is, in order to throw it too into the same empty abyss. But when, on the other hand, the result is conceived as it is in truth, namely, as a *determinate* negation, a new form has thereby immediately arisen, and in the negation the transition is made through which the progress through the complete series of forms comes about of itself.[11]

Here, we see how the negation of something need not result in a "pure nothingness," and "empty abyss." The negation may bear a certain sort of determination insofar as "this nothingness is specifically the nothingness of that *from which it results*."[12] That is to say, that the negation of something simultaneously issues in a certain sort of limited determination ("*not* this"), which gestures beyond the item that is negated to the realm of all things that this negation does not negate —the realm of things that are, thus, still possible contenders for identity. We might imagine that the "pure nothingness" Hegel describes could result from a Kantian negative judgment. Here the copula is negated, so that the subject is fully severed from the predicate. The negative judgment causes the subject and predicate to part ways so that each becomes a free-floating term on its own, having nothing to do with the other. In an infinite judgment, however, the connective term is not negated. Thus the subject is held in an affirmative relation to a negated predicate. The negation is, consequently, not one that throws

---

determinate negation is helpful for understanding the difference between Kant's negative and infinite logical functions.
11 Hegel, *Phenomenology of Spirit*, trans. A. V. Miller (Oxford: Oxford University Press, 1977), 79, p. 50–51.
12 Hegel, *Phenomenology of Spirit*, 79, p. 51.

us into abstract nothingness, but rather one in which "this nothingness [...] specifically [as] the nothingness of that *from which it results*" [13] is clung to as a limited determination of the subject. Viewed in this manner, Kant's infinite judgment appears to be quite similar to a Hegelian determinate negation.[14]

---

13 Hegel, *Phenomenology of Spirit*, 79, p. 51.

14 The comparison intended above is between Hegel's "determinate negation" in the Introduction of the *Phenomenology of Spirit* and how Kant's logical function of the infinite relates the subject to that which lies beyond the negated predicate. We might also want to look at how Hegel's own conception of infinite judgment compares to Kant's infinite logical function. In *Hegel and Shakespeare on Moral Imagination*, Jennifer Ann Bates examines the negative element harbored in Hegel's infinite judgment. She writes that "there is always already an incommensurability in an infinite judgment" (Jennifer Ann Bates, *Hegel and Shakespeare on Moral Imagination*. (Albany: State University of New York Press, 2010), 147). Bates investigates how Hegel's treatment of infinite judgment in the *Philosophy of Right* and *Encyclopedia of Logic* takes shape in regards to possession, further developing her analysis to show that a *negative* infinite judgment "merely draws out that incommensurability between myself and the thing that was always there" (Bates, *Hegel and Shakespeare on Moral Imagination*, 147). T. M. Knox, cited in Bates, observes that when the incongruency of an infinite judgment develops into a Hegelian negative infinite judgment "the object must be altogether spurned or alienated. This is not a mere negative judgment, but a "negatively infinite judgment" which asserts a total incongruity between the subject (the will) and the predicate (the thing)" (Knox, cited in: Bates, *Hegel and Shakespeare on Moral Imagination*, 147). The absolute schism between the will and the thing that Hegel describes in a negative infinite judgment mirrors the logical form of the Kantian infinite function, where a relation can only be affirmed between the subject and predicate if the predicate has been fully negated. The important difference is that for Kant this remains an abstract determination of the act of judging that does not stipulate any determinations of a specific object. For Kant the logical functions "abstract from all content of a judgment in general, and attend only to the mere form of the understanding in it," describing the determinations that govern "the function of thinking" itself (*Critique of Pure Reason*, A70/B95). Kant's infinite logical function in and of itself only specifies *that* a negative quality is being affirmed without in any way specifying what this quality may be, let alone how it may relate to the will of the judging subject. That is, for Kant this dynamic could be applied to the will and the thing in possession, but it could just as well be applied to the subject human and predicate immortal, or soul and mortal, and a host of other terms. Hence, although the dynamic that Kant picks out with his infinite logical function resonates with that discussed by Hegel under infinite judgment, we cannot carry over Hegel's development of the latter in "the will's relation to the thing" regarding property and his specific description of how a certain behavior of the will can be describe through infinite judgement. No similar behavior of the will can be picked out in Kant's analysis of pure aesthetic judgments of taste (Hegel, cited in: Bates, *Hegel and Shakespeare on Moral Imagination*, 147). Indeed, the disinterested nature of pure judgements of taste signals that Kantian pure aesthetic judgments of taste bypass the faculty of desire and thus do not concern the will.

I.B The Interrelation of Logical Functions in Quality

From the above, it is clear that the infinite logical function allows us to affirm a negative characteristic, however, what remains unclear is why such an affirmation of a negation would be called "infinite." On the surface, the affirmation of a negation does not appear to have anything to do with the distinction between finite and infinite. To show how the affirmation of a negation does connect to the infinite, I will now revisit Longuenesse's sixth chapter of *Kant and the Capacity to Judge*. There she points out how this function indicates something that is beyond sensibility. I will further develop this insight to show that the infinite is not only beyond sensibility, but also beyond discursivity, making it the perfect logical function to determine the quality of pure aesthetic judgments of taste without reducing beauty to a quality of the object in the process.

Longuenesse traces out the relation between the concepts of comparison that Kant presents in the chapter on the Amphibolies and the logical functions from the table of judgments. She points out that under Quantity and Quality, the two sets of concepts of comparison offered correlate with the quadrant's first two logical functions, leaving the third function of each quadrant without a correlating comparative concept. That is to say, under quality *the affirmative* correlates with *agreement* and *the negative* with *conflict*, but *the infinite* goes without comment. She explains this omission, remarking that:

> There is a correlation between the fact that specific acts of comparison do not correspond to singular and infinite judgments, and the fact that, in Kant's view, these are not properly speaking distinct logical forms.[15]

Under quantity, she explains, the singular is not distinct, because it shares with the the universal the characteristic of not allowing for exceptions.[16] The infinite, as established above, integrates the affirmative copula with a negative predicate. Thus, in her analysis of singular and infinite functions as indistinct, Longuenesse is in agreement with my suggestion that infinite judgment is a new form of judgment generated through the fusion of negative and affirmative functions. Although she does not take this to be a logically distinct form of judgment, since

---

[15] Longuenesse, *Kant and the Capacity to Judge*, 139.
[16] This observation can be further supported by the *Jäsche Logic*, which reports that "[a]s to logical form, singular judgments are to be assessed as like universal ones in use, for in both the predicate holds of the subject without exception. In the singular proposition, Caius is mortal, for example, there can just as little be an exception as in the universal one, All men are mortal. For there is only one Caius" (Jäsche Logic, § 21, 599).

its characteristics were already covered by the other two forms, albeit not in this special combined form, Longuenesse finds the peculiarity of these third functions (the singular and the infinite) to consist in how they relate to the sensible—seemingly cutting around the discursive in order to do so. According to her analysis the singular and the infinite "refer concepts to what is beyond discursive capacity: the singular intuition in the first case, the whole of experience in the second."[17] Thus, the singular is "beyond" that which can be captured by discursive means.[18] Longuenesse argues, for this reason, that "no specific form of *discursive* comparison or comparison *of concepts* [...] corresponds to them," concluding that "they outline, at the extremes of discursive thought—the singular intuition, the whole of experience—the limits of discursive thought."[19] The infinite, thus, indicates the "whole of experience," but not by indicating something through its positive, determinative attribute. Rather, it does so by indicating the determinative attribute that it does *not* possess. This holds open the infinite range of things that are *not* this determinative attribute, which may then possibly be attributed to the thing in question. Through this single limitation, one indicates a realm of infinite possibility without going through the possibilities contained in it and conceptually grasping each one. We could almost think of this as a solution to a theoretical version of Zeno's paradox, which would run: If one cannot think through an infinite set of possibilities, then how can one have any conception of the infinite?[20] The answer being that one conceives of an infinite set of possible qualities through the affirmation of a negation. By concen-

---

[17] Longuenesse, *Kant and the Capacity to Judge*, 139.

[18] The issue of how the singular is "beyond" language, pointed out by Longuenesse, invites a certain parallel to Hegel's exploration of how the "sensuous This that is meant *cannot be reached* by language" (Hegel, *Phenomenology of Spirit*, 110, pg. 66, emphasis original). H. S. Harris offers a clear description of this issue encountered in Sense-Certainty, writing: "Sense-experience is infinitely *rich*, both in the sense that we keep on extending its range and in the sense that we can go farther and deeper into something that we have experienced already. But all we can ever *say* at the level of immediate awareness is: 'This *is*' and 'This is what I am aware of'" (Hegel, *Phenomenology of Spirit*, 23). Hence, the singular relates directly to the sensible, referring, as Longuenesse observes, "to what is beyond discursive capacity" (Longuenesse, *Kant and the Capacity to Judge*, 139).

[19] Longuenesse, *Kant and the Capacity to Judge*, 139.

[20] Aristotle reports Zeno's paradoxes concerning motion in which the infinite divisibility of space causes it to appear that, in any effort to reach a given point, there will always be some remaining magnitude to be overcome, because the distance that is left to be travelled can always be divided in half. Thus, "a moving object [will not be] moving because of having to reach the half-way point before it reaches the end," and "the slowest runner will never be caught by the fastest runner, because the one behind has first to reach the point from which the one in front started, and so the slower one is bound always to be in front" (Aristotle, *Physics*, VI:9 239b9–18).

trating on a negative picture of a determinate attribute, one acquires a sense of the infinite.[21]

In this manner, it seems as though Longuenesse only captures part of the picture when she says that the infinite indicates something beyond discursivity, because, unlike the singular, the infinite is by the very same token beyond *sensibility*. Just as all of the infinite possibilities cannot be discursively thought through, neither can they be sensibly experienced. Through the infinite, an infinitude of possibilities can be indicated without each of the individual possibilities in this infinite set being thought. Thus, the infinite allows us to work with possibilities that can be neither fully discursively, nor fully *sensibly*, present to us due to their open, indeterminate nature. Infinite judgment allows the indeterminate to be thought without being determined in the process, making it uniquely suitable to the needs of aesthetic judgment, which is to be carried out without involving conceptual determination, or reducing beauty to a quality of the object.

II The First Moment of Aesthetic Judgment: Pleasure without Interest

Now let us focus our attention on how the moment of quality allows the mental processes that characterize aesthetic judgment to take shape. The question is, thus, what is affirmed, what is denied, and is there an affirmation of a negation at work?

---

[21] Reinhard Brandt also emphasizes how the infinite logical function allows one to conceive of all possible predicates and compare the thing judged to this infinite sphere, when he writes, "Die Prädikate werden hier nicht nur logisch mit einander verglichen und im Urteil entweder bejaht oder verneint, "sondern das Ding selbst, (wird) mit dem Inbegriff aller möglichen Prädikate, transzendental verglichen" (A 573). Hierin liegt der Unterschied der bloß logischen Negation der Sterblichkeit in dem Urteil: "Die Seele ist nicht sterblich" von der transzendentalen Verneinugn, die in dem Prädikat der Unsterblichkeit ausgesprochen wird; mit ihm wird das Subjekt in die Sphäre dessen gestellt, was vom Inbegriff aller möglichen Prädikate, der omnitudo realitatis, übrigbleibt, wenn sie durch den Begriff der Nichtsterblichkeit eingeschränkt wird; "omnis (positio et) negatio est determinatio" – die hier kontradiktorischen Prädikate der Sterblichkeit und der Unsterblichkeit determinieren durch ihre Einschränkung des Inbegriffs aller möglichen Prädikate in gleicher Weise das Ding, von dem der Subjektbegriff gilt. – Dieser transzendentale Grundsatz gilt sowohl für Dinge (wie die Seele) wie auch für Gegenstände der Erscheinung (Cajus); die formale Logik abstrahiert von allem Inhalt der Erkenntnis" (Reinhard Brandt, *Die Urteilstafel. Kritik der reinen Vernunft A 67–76; B 92–101*. (Hamburg: Meiner Verlag, 1991), 74–75).

II.A Competing Readings

Reinhard Brandt argues that aesthetic judgment's analysis under quality works entirely differently than the analysis of epistemological or moral judgments. Namely, whereas other judgments are analyzed, in their own right, in terms of affirmation and negation, the qualitative analysis of aesthetic judgments, he argues, consists of comparing its pleasure to that of the agreeable and the good.[22] That is, he takes the question to be which similarities between these judgments are affirmed or denied, and not how affirmation and negation are at work in the process of aesthetic judgment, itself. Brandt's analysis is superior to that of Kulenkampff, who dismisses logical functions as merely relating to the statement that something *is* beautiful, but all the same, with Brandt's reading we lose sight of the way that Kant's comparative analysis serves to delineate the workings of these functions *in* aesthetic judgment, itself, through this contrast. Brandt's interpretation still fails to engage with the "moment" as described in chapter two, that is, the activity of judging as the mental processes that leads up to the proclamation that "X is beautiful."

I suggest instead that we understand the comparison between judgments of the beautiful, the agreeable, and the good as a method used to allow the workings of negation and affirmation *in* aesthetic judgment, itself, to come more clearly to the fore. The first moment is not a mere sectioning off of aesthetic judgment from judgments of the agreeable and the good, but rather a comparison undertaken so as to define the workings of affirmation and negation in the production of the *interesselose* pleasure peculiar to aesthetic judgments. This analysis is carried out by means of comparison, because, as I will argue, the primary logical function utilized here is the infinite. The infinite affirmation of a negative attribute (disinterest) can best be clarified by an elaboration of what is being negated, that is, of how the attribute functions in cases where it is *affirmed*. It is to this end that Kant gives so much attention to judgments of interest (the agreeable and the good).

Another interpretation of how this moment relates to the table of judgments is offered by Donald W. Crawford in his book, *Kant's Aesthetic Theory:*

---

[22] Brandt writes, "Kant hat in der *Kritik der Urteilskraft* das ästhetische Geschmacksurteil nach den Titeln der Urteilstafel bzw. der Kategorien neu exponiert; es folgt einer anderen Logik, so daß z. B. unter dem Titel der Qualität nicht die Bejahung oder Verneinung erscheint, sonder die Eigenschaft des ästhetischen Wohlgefallens im Gegensatz zu einem Erkenntnisurteil oder einem praktischen Wohngefallen." (Reinhard Brandt, "Zur Logik des ästhetischen Urteils." In *Kants Ästhetik, Kant, Kant's Aesthetics, L'esthétique de Kant*, edited by Hermann Parret, 229– 245 (Berlin and New York: Walter de Gruyter, 1998), 64, footnote: 31)

In terms of the Quality of judgments of taste, Kant does not even mention the obvious point that the judgment that something is beautiful is an affirmative judgment; instead, he attempts to specify precisely what is affirmed. He argues that what is affirmed in the judgment of taste is not a concept, but a feeling of pleasure; a feeling of pleasure is affirmed of the person making the judgment and not of the object judged.[23]

I agree that we must, indeed, establish what is being affirmed and surely this is a feeling. I disagree, however, with Crawford's intimation that this simple recognition exhausts the role of the logical functions in this moment. He overlooks the crucial aspect of *how* the feeling of satisfaction is affirmed, which is the crux of this moment, and which takes shape through the infinite function.[24] Moreover, what is being affirmed is not merely a feeling, but also the limited determination of that feeling through the affirmation of the negative predicate, disinterest. Thus, this moment does not yield the definition of taste as a faculty of judging merely through a satisfaction or dissatisfaction, but rather "through a satisfaction or dissatisfaction **without any interest**."[25] In this manner, the more crucial logical function with which this moment is engaged, is that of infinite judgment.

---

23 Crawford, *Kant's Aesthetic Theory*, 16.
24 It is not that Crawford overlooks the importance of disinterest, altogether, but rather that he overlooks the fact that the guiding thread of the logical functions leads us through the moment of disinterested pleasure. Thus, he makes no effort to connect his discussion of disinterest to the logical functions under quality. His limited view that in the first moment the logical functions indicate only that a feeling is affirmed, betrays a tendency in the literature to regard Kant's organization of his analysis according to the table of judgments as driven more by a neurotic urge to employ his architectonic than any real philosophical concern. Longuenesse strikes out strongly against this bias, stating that in the Analytic of the Beautiful, "[a]s always with Kant, architectonic considerations [...] play an essential role in the unfolding of the substantive argument" (Longuenesse, "Kant's Leading Thread in the Analytic of the Beautiful," 195). Despite the many similarities between Longuenesse's reading of this moment and my own, she, too, does not notice the involvement of the infinite. She writes, "As to quality, the form of the aesthetic judgments Kant is most directly concerned with (e.g., "this rose is beautiful") is affirmative, and there is no particular difficulty about that" (Longuenesse, "Kant's Leading Thread in the Analytic of the Beautiful," 196). Ultimately our accounts align, as she pushes beyond the proclamation of beauty to investigate what the predicate "beautiful" asserts about the subject's act of judging: "But the interesting question is: *What* is thus being affirmed? What is the content of the predicate 'beautiful' that is asserted of an object in aesthetic judgments?" (Longuenesse, "Kant's Leading Thread in the Analytic of the Beautiful," 196) I, however, contend that what is being asserted here is the affirmation of a negative predicate (disinterest), and as such it ought to be understood in relation to the infinite function of judgment, not merely the affirmative.
25 *Critique of the Power of Judgment*, § 5, 5:211, emphasis original.

Kant describes the sort of clarification that the first moment provides for aesthetic judgment:

> We can find no better way of elucidating this proposition, however, which is of the utmost importance, than by contrasting to the pure disinterested satisfaction in the judgment of taste that which is combined with interest, especially if we can be certain that there are not more kinds of interest than those that are to be mentioned now.[26]

If *disinterested* pleasure serves as the predicate in an infinite judgment about how aesthetic judgment functions, then its job is not to elucidate everything that aesthetic judgment is, but rather to erect a divide between that which it is not and the infinite realm of what it possibly could be. If we bring this into connection with the *Jäsche Logic*, then we see that insofar as disinterest is attributed to the subject through an infinite judgment, it will not provide "a real definition" which "suffices for cognition of the object according to its inner determinations."[27]

> Merely *negative* definitions cannot be called real definitions either, because negative marks can serve just as well as affirmative ones for distinguishing one thing from others, but not for cognition of the thing according to its inner possibility.[28]

That is to say that it is an affirmation of the negation of a given attribute (i.e. "interest"). Since this provides no real definition, only further interpretive work will be able to tease out the limited definitional potential this negated attribute provides. What it negates in negating interest can, thus, best be seen by establishing what an affirmation of interest looks like. To do so, the element that is being negated must be more fully described, so that we can see how, in Hegelian terms, "this nothingness is specifically the nothingness of that *from which it results*," so as to render it "a *determinate* nothingness, one which has a *content*."[29]

Kant does this by comparing judgments of taste (negated interest) with the two sorts of judgments that do affirm interest: the agreeable and the good. From this we see that the point of describing these other two sorts of judgment

---

26 *Critique of the Power of Judgment*, § 2, 5:205.
27 Real definitions are here defined as "ones that suffice for cognition of the object according to its inner determinations, since they present the possibility of the object from inner marks" (*The Jäsche Logic*, § 106, 143).
28 *The Jäsche Logic*, § 106, 144. The term "either" refers in the context of this passage to the fact that Kant just mentioned that "logical nominal definitions" are not real definitions.
29 Hegel, *Phenomenology of Spirit*, ¶79, pg. 51.

II The First Moment of Aesthetic Judgment: Pleasure without Interest

is not simply to negate aesthetic judgment's relation to them—indeed, the three sorts of judgments have important commonalities,[30] enabling the comparison in the first place—their elaboration, rather, allows the workings of interest to fully come into view, so that we can attain a greater level of clarity regarding what is and is not negated in aesthetic judgment *when* interest *is* negated.[31]

II.B Quality before Quantity

One cannot discuss the first moment without taking into account Kant's surprising choice to begin his analysis with Quality instead of Quantity, thus departing from the order presented in the table of judgments. Kant gives a brief explanation of this move, remarking in his footnote on the title of the first moment that "I have considered the moment of quality first, since the aesthetic judgment of the beautiful takes notice of this first."[32] This indicates that affirmation, negation and the infinite guide the power of judgment in the contemplation of the beautiful, shaping this form of judgment in a fundamental manner, designating it as a judgment of *taste*, as opposed to a judgment of the agreeable or the good.

The question is now what it is about the workings of quality that is so essential for this sort of judgment. This must pertain to the features affirmed, denied or negatively affirmed through the infinite. When examining the puzzle at the end of this chapter, I will discuss how this moment provides an affirmation of what we might term a "faculty-interest." The most prominent feature of the

---

[30] The comparison between moral and aesthetic judgment is invited by the fact that pleasure is somehow involved in the determining grounds for both. We see this for moral judgments insofar as "the determining ground of the faculty of desire is based on the feeling of pleasure or displeasure" and "reason, in the practical, has to do with the subject, namely with his faculty of desire." (*Critique of Practical Reason*, 5:26; 5:20; see also 5:22). There is also a further similarity, explored at the end of this chapter, insofar as both moral and aesthetic judgments relate to *Lebensgefühl*. The commonality between judgments of taste and judgments of the agreeable is easier to pick out, since they are both types of aesthetic judgments, the former being pure while the latter is impure.

[31] As mentioned above, it is on this point that my interpretation departs from Brandt's. He sees the logical functions as primarily directed at aesthetic judgment's relation to these other types of judgment, whereas I am suggesting that the infinite operates *within* aesthetic judgment, so as to yield the peculiar attribute of disinterest. The comparative analysis is, thus, only carried out in service of understanding what is being negated in this attribute and what it *means* for this to be negated. True, judgments of the agreeable and the good can only be compared to judgments of taste by means of affirming and negating certain features, but it is not the use of the logical functions of quality that governs the act of judging so as to characterize it with *disinterest*.

[32] *Critique of the Power of Judgment*, § 1, 5:203 footnote.

first moment, however, concerns satisfaction in the existence of the object judged, to which one relates through the infinite logical function.[33] It is this satisfaction in the existence of the object that Kant designates with his technical use of the term "interest."[34] In considering this feature, Kant is concerned with two things. On the one side, he is concerned with the extent to which the object, as an existing thing, is taken up in aesthetic judgment, on the other, he is concerned with the way of relating to the object. The moment of quality is crucial, because it answers two key questions. First, is the existence of the object one of the attributes involved in drawing us to it? Second, how do we relate to the representation of the object to which we are drawn? These issues are separate, although they intertwine insofar as the extent to which the object's existence is a primary feature conditions the way that one will relate to the representation.

By answering these questions, quality stipulates what sort of pleasure is to serve as the grounds for aesthetic judgement—that is, in what this pleasure is taken and how this pleasure manifests through the mental processes involved. This is the first and foremost feature that differentiates aesthetic judgment from other sorts of judgments, because, as discussed in the first chapter, whereas cognitive judgments use concepts as the predicate, aesthetic judgment has feeling as its grounds. To judge something aesthetically is to "relate it [...] to the subject and its feeling of pleasure or displeasure."[35] The sort of pleasurable feeling that is combined with the subject—grounding the judgment—will thus be fundamental in determining what sort of judgment it is. The pure aesthetic judgment of taste is not the only type of judgment that involves feelings of pleasure, thus the *specific* way that this pleasure arises and affects the activity of thinking will have to be clearly delineated.

In the first moment it quickly becomes clear that the essential thing about an aesthetic representation is that one can engage with it *without* a desire for its existence being affirmed. Thus, the sort of representation with which we are concerned is one that can be easily separated from its conditions of existence.

---

[33] Affirmations, such as that of a faculty-interest, are still possible in a moment that is predominately characterized by the infinite, because the infinite function leaves a great deal of space for the affirmation and negation of features that do not pertain to the negative attribute being affirmed. This will be further discussed below in section IV. B. of this chapter, entitled The Faculty-Interest.
[34] *Critique of the Power of Judgment*, § 4, 5:209.
[35] *Critique of the Power of Judgment*, § 1, 5:203.

II.C Separating Existence from Essence: Kant's Hundred Possible Thalers

The disinterested quality of aesthetic pleasure indicates that adding or subtracting existence to the aesthetic object will not affect the judgment, because insofar as one judges aesthetically one is indifferent to the existence of the object. When put in such a manner, this calls to mind Kant's discussion of the one hundred possible thalers.[36] This arises within the context of Kant's criticism of the ontological argument for God's existence. According to the ontological argument, our understanding of God as a perfect being proves his existence, since existence is one of the perfections that God, as a perfect being, must possess.[37] Kant, however, responds that existence is not a perfection, because:

> Being is obviously not a real predicate, i.e., a concept of something that could add to the concept of a thing. It is merely the position of a thing or of certain determinations in themselves.[38]

Consequently, conceiving of a perfect God does not necessitate that such a God exist *as* perfect. Kant buttresses his idea that existence is separable from our cognitive engagement with something through the example of the one hundred possible thalers:

> Now if I take the subject (God) together with all his predicates (among which omnipotence belongs), and say **God is**, or there is a God, then I add no new predicate to the concept of God, but only posit the subject in itself with all its predicates, and indeed posit the **object** in relation to my **concept.** Both must contain exactly the same, and hence when I think this object as given absolutely (through the expression, "it is"), nothing is thereby added to the concept, which expresses merely its possibility. Thus the actual contains nothing more than the merely possible. A hundred actual thalers do not contain the least bit more than a hundred possible ones. For since the latter signifies the concept of the former its object and its positing in itself, then, in case the former contained more than the latter, my concept would not express the entire object and thus would not be the suitable concept of it. But in my financial condition there is more with a hundred actual thalers than with the mere concept of them (i.e., their possibility). For with actuality the object is not merely included in my concept analytically, but adds synthetically to my concept (which is a determination of my state); yet the hundred thalers themselves that I am thinking of are not in the least increased through this being outside my concept. Thus when I think a thing, through which-

---

36 A thaler is a silver coin used in Europe from the 1500's to the 1800's.
37 Two of the most historically prominent versions of this argument are St. Anslem's *Proslogion* (1078) and René Descartes' *Fifth Meditation* (1639).
38 *Critique of Pure Reason*, A599/B627.

ever and however many predicates I like (even in its thoroughgoing determination), not the least bit gets added to the thing when I posit in addition that this thing **is**.³⁹

Regarding the inconsequentiality of existence, Kant's analysis of the "possible" thalers appears to have a great deal in common with the curious indifference he shows towards the aesthetic object's existence.⁴⁰ One adjustment, however, must first be made. In the course of making his argument, Kant insists that existence is not a real predicate, because it adds nothing *to the concept* of the object. It is worth noting here, that it is not *to the concept of the aesthetic object* that existence adds nothing in aesthetic judgment, because the concept of the object is not involved.⁴¹ It is rather *to the feeling* that existence adds nothing, because the feeling of pleasure or displeasure is what makes the judgment aesthetic.

This further ties in with the idea that in analyzing aesthetic judgment into its moments, we are not concerned with the proclamation that "X is beautiful" which aesthetic judging yields. We are engaging with aesthetic judgment on a level that will allow us to delineate the form taken by the underlying mental processes leading up to this statement. Thus, when translating the idea that existence "adds nothing to the concept of the object" of a determinative judgment into terms useful for our purposes, the "concept of the object" is not to be replaced by the grammatical subject ("X") of the judgment "X is beautiful." In the context of an analysis of the moments of aesthetic judgment, this should resonate instead with a mental *process*. Thus, in the first moment, the *activity* of judging is what should take the subject position so as to receive the limited determination provided by the negative predicate, disinterested pleasure.

Nicolai Hartmann explains Kant's argument regarding the thalers, clarifying what he takes to have been a terminological misstep in Kant's presentation of the objection. Hartmann argues that much hesitancy to accept Kant's argument⁴² stems from the fact that he conflated "two dimensions of opposition: the dimension of possibility and actuality with the dimension of essentia and existentia,

---

39 *Critique of Pure Reason*, A599-A600/B627-B628, emphasis original, translation edited from "dollars" to the original "thalers."
40 To the best of my knowledge, other commentators have not related Kant's comments on aesthetic judgment's disinterest in the existence of the object to the remarks he makes about existence when criticizing the ontological argument of the first *Critique*.
41 Or, rather, it is only involved in the properly aesthetic layer as a "deactivated" concept.
42 Hartmann highlights Hegel as particularly unwilling to accept Kant's objection to the ontological argument.

i.e. the dimension of ideal and real being."⁴³ Despite this infelicitous word choice, Hartmann contends that "Kant's refutation does not, by any means, mistake the meaning of this argument." He continues:

> If the terminological side is brought in order, then the refutation immediately becomes clear. It is not the derivation of 100 actual thalers from 100 "possible" thalers that is objectionable, but the derivation of the real presence of 100 thalers from the bare "essence" of 100 thalers. Just as in the ontological argument, it is not a deduction of the actuality of God from the possibility of God that is in question, but a deduction of the reality of God from the idea of God.⁴⁴

Though he himself does not make the connection, Hartmann's reading of this passage is also helpful for understanding what exactly Kant is getting at when he stipulates that,

> if the question is whether something is beautiful, one does not want to know whether there is anything that is or that could be at stake [...] in the existence of the thing, but rather how we judge it in mere contemplation.⁴⁵

The sort of existence to which the aesthetic judger is "indifferent"⁴⁶ is the *existentia* of the thing, which would designate it as *really* present. The *essentia* of the thing, however, which determines it as the specific sort of thing that it is, continues to be of the utmost importance for the judgment.

That said, it is also telling that the difference between thalers as *existentia* and *essentia* only acquires importance when we shift from an epistemological situation to a practical one. Although existence adds nothing to the *essentia* of the thalers, in a practical situation existence can make quite a difference to "my financial condition."⁴⁷

Hartmann's observation continues to be helpful as we redirect our attention back to Kant's third *Critique*. It is not just in regards to the hundred possible thal-

---

43 Hartmann, *Possibility and Actuality*, trans. Stephanie Adair and Alex Scott (de Gruyter: Berlin/Boston, 2013), 342. Hartmann explains further, "The ontological argument deduces real existence from essence. But Kant appears to refute a completely different deduction, namely, that of actuality from possibility. In this form, the refutation is in fact fallacious. The real possible is also really actual; and likewise, the essentially possible is also essentially actual" (*Ibid*).
44 Hartmann, *Possibility and Actuality*, 342–3.
45 *Critique of the Power of Judgment*, § 2, 5:204.
46 "One only wants to know whether the mere representation of the object is accompanied with satisfaction in me, however indifferent I might be with regard to the existence of the object of this representation" (*Critique of the Power of Judgment*, § 2, 5:205).
47 *Critique of Pure Reason*, A599/B627.

ers that Kant conflated "two dimensions of opposition: the dimension of possibility and actuality with the dimension of *essentia* and *existentia*, i.e. the dimension of ideal and real being."[48] Rather, this same issue crops up in his treatment of the first moment of the judgment of taste. Kant's assertion that pure aesthetic judgments are not interested in the existence of the thing judged should not be read in terms of the modal category of existence—indeed, discussion of the modality of pure aesthetic judgments belongs to the fourth moment. In the context of the first moment, existence should be understood in terms of the sensible materiality of the empirical object that triggers aesthetic judgment. As I established in the first two chapters, aesthetic judgment must begin with an experience of something that affords an intuitional excess. In so far as this is given to the judging subject, it can be asserted to have the modality of existence; it is actual. And this is so regardless of whether it belongs to real being (a painting) or ideal being (the imagery of a poem). Kant cannot be saying that the judging subject is indifferent to whether anything is actually given to her to occasion her judgment, because this would be tantamount to saying that it does not matter whether or not there is a stimulus to occasion aesthetic judgment. Such indifference would mean that one's faculties could just spontaneously enter a harmonious free play without any reception of an intuition—without anything actually being empirically given to the judging subject in that moment. Not only is it hard to picture how this would play out,[49] but furthermore, the great importance that Kant

---

48 Hartman, *Possibility and Actuality*, 342.

49 All of Kant's examples of aesthetic judgment begin with the experience of an empirical object (a flower § 33, foliage § 4, music § 16, a poem § 49, a painting § 14, a simple color § 14, a single tone § 14, to name a few). He never writes of an aesthetic judgment just spontaneously occurring without any *Anlass* being experienced by the subject. It is difficult to even imagine a pure aesthetic judgment of taste occurring without any empirical object (i.e. with neither an *Erscheinung* nor a *Phänomen* triggering the judgment). Perhaps the closest one could come to this would be if one were staring into complete darkness and one aesthetically judged the darkness to be beautiful. Even here, however, this staring into complete darkness would itself be the experience that animated the faculties into a harmonious free-play. Even if different judging subjects understand the complete darkness to work in different ways to occasion the judgment of taste, the fact remains that the experience of complete darkness would be considered necessary for occasioning this judgment across the board. Thus, the empirical object here is "complete darkness." As for Kant, he would likely argue that the key characteristic of complete darkness allowing it to occasion a judgment of taste was the purity of the color black, "The purity of a simple kind of sensation, however, means that its uniformity is not disturbed and interrupted by any foreign sensation, and belongs merely to the form; for in that case one can abstract from the quality of that kind of sensation (from whether and what color or whether and what tone it represents). Hence all simple colors, insofar as they are pure, are held to be beautiful; those that are mixed do not have this advantage since, precisely because they are not simple,

gives to intuition in aesthetic judgment indicates that no aesthetic judgment (pure or impure) could arise without intuition at all. Hence, I understand Kant's remarks about pure aesthetic judgment's indifference to existence as pertaining to material existence (real being) and not modality. To judge a painting or a poem to be beautiful, one need only receive it in intuition, experiencing the object and intuitional excess accompanying it. In such reception, the empirical object is *actually* something experienceable. Whether this actual thing exists as a real or ideal being, however, is of no consequence for judgments of taste. For existence to exert an influence upon the feeling of pleasure would knock us out of a contemplative engagement with the aesthetic object and into a practical one. The only issue of consequence is whether it is able to be given in intuition or not, because it is only that which can be given in intuition that can serve as an empirical object occasioning a pure aesthetic judgment.

One of the fundamental distinctions that Kant makes is between the a posteriori and the a priori: "although all our cognition commences *with* experience, yet it does not on that account all arise *from* experience."[50] Something that has its source in experience is empirical and a posteriori, whereas that which arises from a source independent from experience is pure and a priori.[51] Some may categorize a poem as a materially real object due to the physical form it takes when written on a page or when at a reading the sound waves enter one's ear. Others may point to the incorporeal nature of the ideas that constitute what is essential to poetry and thus categorize a poem as an ideal object.[52] Even if it is argued that a poem has ideal and not real being, it cannot be argued that a poem is a priori. Hence, a poem is to be understood as an empirical object for Kant regardless of how we understand its relation to materiality, because the poem is encountered

---

one has no standard for judging whether they should be called pure or impure" (*Critique of the Power of Judgement*, § 14, 5:224–5).

50 *Critique of Pure Reason*, B1, emphasis original.
51 Kant writes of "cognition independent of all experience and even of all impressions of the senses. One calls such cognitions a priori, and distinguishes them from empirical ones, which have their sources a posteriori, namely in experience" (*Critique of Pure Reason*, B2).
52 This view might be supported by Kant's remarks about how symbols are judged: "the power of judgment performs a double task, first applying the concept to the object of a sensible intuition, and then, second, applying the mere rule of reflection on that intuition to an entirely different object, of which the first is only the symbol" (*Critique of the Power of Judgement*, § 59, 5:352). It should also be noted that this passage fits well with my layered solution. The symbol belongs to the first layer as the phenomenon that is experienced, while that "of which the first is only the symbol" is reflected upon as the "second task" which occurs in the second layer.

empirically—a posteriori (when read or heard) and not a priori.⁵³ Thus, even when judging poetry, the judgment of taste starts with an encounter with an empirical object, which signifies that it begins with the reception of an intuition. This intuition is partially objectified, but also partially unable to be conceptualized and hence carries with it an intuitional excess. Curiously enough, although this first layer empirical object is something that "arise[s] *from* experience," the second layer harmonious free play of the faculties that it occasions is, in contrast, something that "commences *with* experience" but "arises from a source [...] independent from experience."⁵⁴ Thus, the first layer is rooted in the empirical, while the second is rooted in the a priori, but both are necessary for pure aesthetic judgments of taste to manifest.⁵⁵ What is so crucial to the way that something beautiful empirically affects the judging subject does not, however, have anything to do with the material existence (*existentia*) of the thing, but rather the form that its intuitional excess exhibits. Hence the distinction Kant draws with his term "disinterest" highlights how the form of something beautiful, to which one is receptive in intuition is all that matters, for it is this that constitutes its essence for contemplation, whereas the thing's existence does not interest the judgment of taste.

II.D Disinterest

In his article "On Kantian Notions of Disinterest" Nick Zangwill supplies a clear statement of what exactly Kant's technical term, "disinterest," indicates. Zangwill's article is prompted by the works of numerous anti-Kantian aestheticians who "have missed the mark in their criticisms of Kant's account of disinterest, because they don't understand what disinterest is supposed to mean."⁵⁶ Zangwill

---

53 Although Kant does not discuss it, this could be argued to apply equally to any other thing with ideal being that could be judged to be beautiful, such as a vision, hallucination or dream.
54 *Critique of Pure Reason*, B1; B2.
55 Kant speaks to this need for both an empirical and an a priori element to judgments of beauty when he writes, "Thus it is not the pleasure but the universal validity of this pleasure perceived in the mind as connected with the mere judging of an object that is represented in a judgment of taste as a universal rule for the power of judgment, valid for everyone. It is an empirical judgment that I perceive and judged an object with pleasure. But it is an *a priori* judgment that I find it beautiful, i.e., that I may require that satisfaction of everyone as necessary" (*Critique of the Power of Judgement*, § 37, 5:289). The next chapter discusses the universal validity of pure aesthetic judgments of taste in detail.
56 Zangwill, Nick, "UnKantian Notions of Disinterest," in *Kant's Critique of the Power of Judgment: Critical Essays*, ed. Paul Guyer (Lanham: Rowman and Littlefield, 2003), 63.

cautions such critics that this term is not meant to indicate, "the conscious mental state of being interested or of finding something interesting versus being bored, nor does it have to do with self-love or self-interest."[57] Rather, disinterested pleasure is "the kind of pleasure in a representation which is distinguished by a certain kind of independence from our desires or concerns with real existence."[58] Putting this in the terms of my analysis above, we can say that disinterest indicates that one does not take pleasure in the *existentia* of what is judged. Zangwill goes on to observe that "[i]nterestedness in some other sense may be compatible with Kantian disinterestedness."[59] This is one of the reasons motivating me to read the first moment through the infinite logical function. The infinite affirmation of the negation of interest in *existentia* of that which is judged, enables Kant to rule out a very specific sort of interest and not every possible sort of interest generally speaking. The implications of Zangwill's analysis can be further teased out with an example. Pierre-Auguste Renoir's *Le déjeuner des Canotiers* must, admittedly, exist in some form in order for it to occasion a pure aesthetic judgment. If we recognize this fact and consequently develop an interest to protect the painting in a museum—where photos are forbidden and humidity is carefully controlled—then this interest does not contaminate the aesthetic judgment that the painting occasions, because when exhibiting an interest in these measures one is not making an aesthetic judgment. To ground this moment on a careful limitation leaves it open to the affirmation of other sorts of interest, which fall outside of the negated sphere. Zangwill focuses on how aesthetic disinterest does not only preclude a specific sort of interest, but also a specific role for this interest in pure aesthetic judgment:

> Whether or not there are desires operative in the activity of perceptual attention or contemplation is irrelevant to the questions of whether the pleasures derived from such attention or contemplation are disinterested in Kant's sense. The existence of desires operative in attention or contemplation might be among the more distant causes of pleasure in the beau-

---

57 Zangwill, "UnKantian Notions of Disinterest," 65. We might add in support of Kant's remark that "the mind cannot reflect on the beauty of nature without finding itself at the same time to be interested in it," clarifying shortly thereafter that "this interest is moral" (*Critique of the Power of Judgment*, Bk. 1, § 42, 5:300). This, in turn, gives us reason to distinguish between the second and third layers of aesthetic judgment. If one cannot reflect on nature's beauty without taking a moral interest in it, and judgments of the moral good entail the sort of interest in existence that cannot contaminate pure aesthetic judgments, then we must distinguish between the activity of pure aesthetic judging and that which follows from it.
58 Zangwill, "UnKantian Notions of Disinterest," 65.
59 Zangwill, "UnKantian Notions of Disinterest," 65.

tiful without being involved with its ground, which is what Kant requires for interestedness.[60]

Disinterest does not mean that one has no desire for that which is judged beautiful to exist. It is, rather, that this desire does not serve as the grounds for the judgment of the thing's aesthetic beauty in any way. Thus, Zangwill's acknowledgment that an interest in the existence of the object "might be among the more distant causes of pleasure in the beautiful without being involved with its ground."[61]

Disinterested pleasure is a pleasure that is grounded on something that is not the existence of that which is judged. This serves as the negative predicate that is affirmed of aesthetic pleasure through the infinite logical function—specifying aesthetic judgment, while still leaving it open to an affirmative relation with other sorts of interests and ways of relating to existence that do not ground the judgment on *existentia*. While Zangwill's reading helps us work around the puzzle that although an interest in existence does not ground pure aesthetic judgment, one may still have a more remote, non-aesthetic interest in the existence of the object judged to be beautiful. Below, I will explore a further type of interest, the possibility of which is crucially left open by understanding the specificity of aesthetic disinterest, and this is what I will be terming faculty-interest.

II.E Different Ways of Taking Existence into Account: the Agreeable and the Moral

In contrast to pure aesthetic judgments, judgments of the agreeable and the good do take an interest in the existence of that which is judged. For both objects that correspond with the concept of their end and objects that gratify, the object's existence directly affects how it is valued. As Kulenkampff points out, the similarity between judgments of the agreeable and of taste—insofar as both are grounded on pleasure—not only qualifies both as aesthetic judgments, but furthermore situates judgments of agreeableness as a sort of prototype for pure judgments of taste.[62] Thus, let us first compare the importance that the agreeable object's ex-

---

60 Zangwill, "UnKantian Notions of Disinterest," 64–5.
61 Zangwill, "UnKantian Notions of Disinterest," 65.
62 Kulenkampff designates the "Lust am Angenahmen" as the "Prototyp von Lust," elaborating this a page later as he writes, "Gemäß der vorgängigen Typendisjunktion von Urteilen in: logishe – ästhetische; objektiv – subjektiv; Erkenntnisurteil – Urteil über das Gefühl der Lust und Unlust

istence has for impure aesthetic judgments to the insignificance that the object's existence bears for pure aesthetic judgments. Afterwards the same analysis will be carried out in relation to judgments of the good.

II.E.1 Impure Aesthetic Judgments of Agreeableness

For impure aesthetic judgments of gratification, the object must actually exist so that it may be consumed in some fashion. Above I described how something's existence and essence are to be distinguished from one another. Whether the hundred Thalers exist, or not, the essence remains the same. Thus, if judgments of gratification involve a "satisfaction that we combine with the representation of the existence of an object,"[63] then the pleasure supplied does not simply stem from the *essentia* of the object, but rather depends upon its existence as well. An example can quickly show how this is the case. To experience the pleasure of gratification in a rich chocolate mousse cake, it is not enough to know the details that constitute the essence of the cake (all of the ingredients and how they come together to give the cake its characteristic). The essence of the cake does not change if we add existence to it, but only a cake that exists with real, not ideal, being can gratify my desire for a scrumptious dessert, thereafter being honored with an impure aesthetic judgment that expresses my appreciation of its agreeableness. Just as existence does not change the essence of the hundred Thalers, although it does make quite a difference to "my financial condition,"[64] so too must existence accompany the object that is to generate gratification; the judgment of whether or not it is agreeable is generated through consuming the object in some form.[65] When the pleasure that grounds the judgment is aesthetic,

---

des Subjekts in gegebenen Weltbezügen, gehört das Urteil über das Schöne zur Klasse der ästhetischen Urteile, deren Prototyp das Urteil über das Angenehme ist" (Kulenkampff, 1994, 78). If this is not kept in mind, then the terminology Kant employs can lead to confusion. Aesthetic judgment is a class that includes judgments of two sorts: those pertaining to agreeableness and to taste. Judgments of agreeableness are impure aesthetic judgments, whereas judgments of taste are pure. It is the latter that can result in the statement "This x is beautiful," whereas the former merely allows one to conclude, "This x is agreeable to me." Thus, § 1 of the Analytic of the Beautiful clarifies what it is for a judgment to be aesthetic (i.e., one in which "the subject feels itself as it is affected by the representation," 5:204), and then § 2 supplies the criteria (disinterested pleasure) for distinguishing between the two different types of aesthetic judgment.
63 *Critique of the Power of Judgment*, § 2, 5:204.
64 *Critique of Pure Reason*, A599/B627.
65 In the contemplation of an idea one engages with essence, not existence. Existence, as discussed above, is not a predicate of the object and hence does not determine what the thing is. This is why Kant remarks that adding or subtracting existence from the idea of 100 Thalers or

but does not stem from the object's existence in this way, then it is a pure aesthetic judgment of taste.

Hence, a crucial factor differentiating impure aesthetic judgments from pure judgments of taste is how the agreeableness of gratification requires that the thing's existence be directly experienced, whereas pure judgments of taste do not involve consuming existence. In pure aesthetic judgments, the aesthetic object is engaged on a contemplative level that concerns representations and mental processes—that is, only in terms of how it affects the faculties of knowledge, *not* the bodily organs. Admittedly, both involve sense data being given to us through the senses, but the beauty of a wild flower is contemplatively observed, and the dependence on the bodily organs for its observation is limited. Good eyesight may be needed to read a poem by Goethe. But the material conditions of ink and eyesight, necessary for Goethe's poem to be read, hardly suffice for a judgment of its beauty. One does not revel in the beautiful poem by using one's eyes to consume the ink in a manner at all akin to how, in agreeableness, one uses one's mouth to consume an ice-cream sundae. The existence of the aesthetic object is not at issue in judgments of taste in the way that it is in those of agreeableness.

II.E.2 Judgments of the Good

Kant tells us that "if the question is whether something is beautiful, one does not want to know whether there is anything that is or that could be at stake, for us or for someone else, in the existence of the thing, but rather how we judge it in mere contemplation (intuition or reflection)."[66] Impure aesthetic judgments, on the other hand, have something at stake in the existence of the thing, because if the thing does not have real being, then one will be unable to use it to gratify oneself. What then is at stake in the existence of the thing in judgments of the good?

This question can be answered by looking at how satisfaction in existence arises in the judging of the good through the concept of an end, which has a relation to reason. Kant writes:

God does not change the idea itself. Kant's distinction between these two is further reflected in the way that he distinguishes modality from the other three quadrants on his table of judgment and of the categories. Quantity, quality and relation constitute "the content of a judgment," while modality takes the already constituted judgment as a whole and determines how this relates to "thinking in general" (*Critique of Pure Reason*, A74/B100). This is further discussed in chapter six.

66 *Critique of the Power of Judgment*, § 2, 5:204.

II The First Moment of Aesthetic Judgment: Pleasure without Interest

> That is good which pleases by means of reason alone, through the mere concept. We call something good for something (the useful) that pleases only as a means; however, another thing is called good in itself that pleases for itself. Both always involve the concept of an end, hence the relation of reason to (at least possible) willing, and consequently a satisfaction in the existence of an object or of an action, i.e., some sort of interest.[67]

Accordingly, the good involves "satisfaction in the existence of an object" because of how it "always involves the concept of an end," which indicates that it is always concerned with "the relation of reason to [...] willing."[68] When something is judged to be good—regardless of whether it is given this status because of being "good for something" or "good in itself"—this goodness arises from the correspondence between the concept of what the thing is and the concept of an end, that is, a concept of either what the thing should be in order to serve a purpose or what the thing should be in itself.[69] The importance of this correspondence indicates that the judging subject is not indifferent to whether this thing's state is such so as to correspond with the concept of its end or not. In judging the relation between the thing and the concept of its end one is willing the correspondence, desiring the thing to reveal itself to be good by fulfilling the concept of its end.[70]

Both the agreeable and the good exhibit an "interest in their object"[71] that the beautiful does not. This holds both for what is good because it is useful or perfect and,

> also [for] that which is good absolutely and in all respects, namely the morally good, which carries the highest interest with it. For the good is the object of the will (i.e., of a faculty of

---

67 *Critique of the Power of Judgment*, § 4, 5:207.
68 *Critique of the Power of Judgment*, § 4, 5:207.
69 This is the distinction between internal ends (perfection) and external ends (usefulness) indicating whether something is "merely mediately good or immediately good" (*Critique of the Power of Judgment*, § 4, 5:207), and it arises repeatedly in Kant's work. I discuss it further in chapter five (section II.A.1. The *nexus effectivus* and *nexus finalis*) where I investigate the different ways that something can be purposive.
70 Kant elaborates on how the imperative produced by reason functions as the determining ground of the will in the second *Critique* when he writes, "A practical rule is always a product of reason because it prescribes action as a means to an effect, which is its purpose. But for a being in whom reason quite alone is not the determining ground of the will, this rule is an *imperative*, that is, a rule indicated by an "ought," which expresses objective necessitation to the action and signifies that if reason completely determined the will the action would without fail take place in accordance with this rule. Imperatives, therefore, hold objectively and are quite distinct from maxims, which are subjective principles" (5:20).
71 *Critique of the Power of Judgment*, § 4, 5:209.

desire that is determined by reason). But to will something and to have satisfaction in its existence, i.e., to take an interest in it, are identical.[72]

Not only that which is good through usefulness or perfection, but also that which is morally good involves an interest in the existence of the object. As something that is good, it is simultaneously "the object of the will" and, hence, the object of a faculty of desire that is determined by reason.[73] Accordingly, something cannot be judged to be good without an interest in its existence being stimulated. For the good involves,

> a pure practical satisfaction, which is determined not merely through the representation of the object but at the same time through the represented connection of the subject with the existence of the object. Not merely the object but also its existence pleases.[74]

Although the way of being pleased in this object and its existence is through esteeming, approving and respecting it,[75] which contrasts starkly with the "pathologically conditioned satisfaction (through stimuli, *stimulos*)" of gratification in the agreeable, still, both involve an interest in the existence of the object, which is inextricably intertwined with the judgment itself.

Hence one cannot engage in the act of judging something to be agreeable or good in a merely contemplative manner, but rather the judging subject's faculty of desire intervenes with the representation on the empirical level. Kant writes,

---

[72] *Critique of the Power of Judgment*, § 4, 5:209.
[73] The idea that the morally good will be entangled with existence is not at odds with Kant's remarks in the second *Critique*. There, he repeatedly highlights how the attribution of reality in the *Critique of Practical Reason* distinguishes it from the *Critique of Pure Reason*, explaining that in the former "we have extended our cognition beyond the boundaries of the latter," because it is concerned with practical, and not theoretical, matters (*Critique of Practical Reason*, 5:50). Thus one may "deny objective reality to the supersensible use of the categories in speculation and yet grant them this reality with respect to the objects of pure practical reason [...]" (5:5). That is, because "the reality thought of here does not aim at any theoretical determination of the categories and extension of cognition to the supersensible but that what is meant by it is only that in this respect an object belongs to them, because they are either contained in the necessary determination of the will a priori or else are inseparably connected with the object of its determination; hence that inconsistency disappears because one makes a different use of those concepts than speculative reason requires" (*Critique of Practical Reason*, 5:5–6). For a further discussion of how the first and second Critiques differ from, and yet also build off of, one another, see *Critique of Practical Reason*, 5:42–57.
[74] *Critique of the Power of Judgment*, § 4, 5:209.
[75] The good is "what is esteemed, approved, i.e., that on which he sets an objective value;" it "extorts approval" and involves a "satisfaction that is related [...] to respect" (*Critique of the Power of Judgment*, § 5, 210).

II The First Moment of Aesthetic Judgment: Pleasure without Interest

"The agreeable and the good both have a relation to the faculty of desire, and to this extent bring satisfaction with them."[76] The faculty of desire is described in the second *Critique*, where Kant tells us that "'the matter of the faculty of desire' [is] an object whose reality is desired."[77] Hence, any connection to this faculty indicates a desire for the existence of some object. In the third *Critique* Kant describes judgments of the agreeable and the good in such a way that a desire for the existence of agreeable and good objects weaves through them, imposing itself upon the subject.

In the agreeable this takes the form of a pathologically conditioned inclination toward the object. Food is gratifying and forgoing this gratification is not an option. Thus the pleasure that one experiences in fulfilling one's desire for the agreeable is also tied up with the need to satisfy a desire.[78] One is compelled from within to satiate one's hunger.

In the good there is a similar constraint, for one wills the object under the imposition of reason. One's relation to the good is one of compulsion. Hence we see that the parallel between judgments of the good and judgments of the agreeable is not just carried out along the lines of interest, but also necessity. For the agreeable necessity arises as an inclination of the senses; for the good it is in an imposition of the principles of reason, determining the will, extorting approval so that "when the moral law speaks there is, objectively, no longer any free choice."[79] The expression of "one's moral mode of thinking contains a command and produces a need," while "people with a healthy appetite relish everything that is edible."[80] Both of these involve "a satisfaction [that] demonstrates

---

[76] *Critique of the Power of Judgment*, § 5, 5:209.
[77] *Critique of Practical Reason*, 5:21.
[78] Kant observes that taste differs from agreeableness on this point: "Concerning the interest of inclination in the case of the agreeable, everyone says that hunger is the best cook, and people with healthy appetite relish everything that is edible at all; thus such a satisfaction demonstrates no choice in accordance with taste. Only where the need is satisfied can one distinguish who among the many has taste or does not" (*Critique of the Power of Judgment*, § 5, 5:210).
[79] *Critique of the Power of Judgment*, § 5, 5:210. Kant elaborates on how the imperative produced by reason functions as the determining ground of the will in the second *Critique* when he writes, "A practical rule is always a product of reason because it prescribes action as a means to an effect, which is its purpose. But for a being in whom reason quite alone is not the determining ground of the will, this rule is an *imperative*, that is, a rule indicated by an "ought," which expresses objective necessitation to the action and signifies that if reason completely determined the will the action would without fail take place in accordance with this rule. Imperatives, therefore, hold objectively and are quite distinct from maxims, which are subjective principles" (*Critique of Practical Reason*, 5:20).
[80] *Critique of the Power of Judgment*, § 5, 5:210.

no choice in accordance with taste."[81] In both, the faculty of desire intervenes on the empirical level, so that the resulting satisfaction concerns the object as an existing thing—be this satisfaction through bodily gratification, or the practical satisfaction taken in recognizing that the object fits its external or internal end well.[82] Here, the feelings of the subject are stimulated not by a transcendental free play of the faculties, but by the idea of the existence of something agreeable, useful or perfect. Hence, the judging subject is not simply receiving the intuition passively and then feeling how this intuition stimulates the faculties of imagination and understanding "deeply buried"[83] within.

Judgements of taste take pleasure in the transcendental free play of the faculties, which is occasioned by the object, but does not have anything to do with this object as an existing thing. Indeed, this pure aesthetic free play must be free from the inclination of the agreeable and compulsion of the good. Hence, the relation to the object that occurs in these two "different relations of representa-

---

[81] *Critique of the Power of Judgment*, § 5, 5:210.

[82] Although Kant's main point in the first moment of the judgment of taste is to set pure aesthetic judgments apart from judgments of gratification and of the good, he also is careful to point out that a shared interest in the object's existence does not mean that the latter two types of judgments do not have crucial points of distinction. To ward off confusion, Kant also gives attention to how judgments of the agreeable are to be distinguished from those of the good. Whereas the gratification of something agreeable is felt immediately, for something to be judged to be good that thing "must first be brought under principles of reason through the concept of an end," only once this is done "can [it] be called good as an object of the will" (*Critique of the Power of Judgment* § 4, 5:208). Kant works out this difference using spicy food as an example. According to Kant, spicy foods are agreeable in the moment of gourmandization, but later judged not to be *good* when the body, presumably, has unpleasant reactions to the consumption of spices to which one is unaccustomed (although, Kant seems to assume that this is simply something that always happens when one eats spicy food). Another example Kant uses to highlight the difference between the agreeable and the good is health. Although health can be judged to be both agreeable and good, it is allotted each status for different reasons (agreeable, because of the absence of aches and pains; good, because it makes us fit for doing our work). If one were to judge only in terms of agreeableness, then one would think that the "greatest sum [...] of the agreeableness in life" is to be equated with the good of happiness (*Ibid.*). Reason, however, sees that this is not "all that is at stake," recognizing that it is "[o]nly through that which he does without regard to enjoyment, in full freedom and independently of that which nature could passively provide for him" that he "give[s] his being as the existence of a person an absolute value" (*Ibid.* 5:209). Thus, reason recognizes that the salient issue is not happiness through enjoyment, but making oneself good so as to become one whose existence has "an absolute value" (*Ibid.*).

[83] *Critique of the Power of Judgment*, § 17, 5:323.

tions to the feeling of pleasure and displeasure"[84] is inhospitable to judgments of taste, for, as Kant remarks:

> An object of inclination and one that is imposed upon us by a law of reason for the sake of desire leaves us no freedom to make anything into an object of pleasure ourselves.[85]

Taste, consequently, does not satisfy a need for gratification, nor does it prove itself to be useful or involve anything akin to moral compulsion. It is a sort of unanticipated pleasure that, as Kulenkampff observes, simply "continues as long as it continues."[86] One lingers over it. At every moment in this tarrying enjoyment it is complete, unencumbered by a need for anything beyond the representation and the pleasant harmonious play of the faculties in the subject. The disinterest that frees aesthetic judgment from any interest in the existence of the object also frees it from any further inclination, guaranteeing through this the freedom of its free play.

III The First Moment and the Risk of Indexlosigkeit

Now that I have put forward my reading of the first moment, let us look at an alternative interpretation. Kulenkampff presents a unique way of understanding disinterested aesthetic pleasure arguing that no subject is designated in pure aesthetic pleasure and this pleasure is thus *indexlos*. I will argue against this reading on two counts. First, it assumes that all key characteristics of the judgment of taste should be locatable in the wording of the final statement "This X is beautiful."[87] Second, the repeated emphasis that Kant puts on the judging subject's perception of the feeling of pleasure indicates that disconnecting the subject from aesthetic pleasure would crack the very foundation of judgments of taste.

---

84 *Critique of the Power of Judgment*, § 5, 209–210.
85 *Critique of the Power of Judgment*, § 5, 5:210.
86 My translation. In its entirey, the original reads: "Demgegenüber hat die Lust am Schönen kein solches Interesse zur Folge; sie ist *nur Lust an etwas*, die dauert, solange sie dauert, ohne auf dem Mechanismus von Erfahrung und aktiver Wiedergewinnung derselben Erfahrung zu beruhen" (Kulenkampff, *Kants Logik des ästhetischen Urteils*, 77).
87 As I argued in chapter two, the moments of aesthetic judgment describe the activity of aesthetic judging that underpins this statement. This does not, however, mean that every feature characterizing the activity of pure aesthetic judging will be found among the words of the final judgment statement that proclaims the object judged to have a certain aesthetic value.

Kulenkampff describes the complications that arise when trying to make sense out of disinterested pleasure:

> Now, according to Kant's own anthropological definition, pleasure implies the tendency to maintain, and displeasure, to alter. One can thus say that the state of the subject, who makes a positive aesthetic judgment, is certainly an *interested state:* the subject, who is endeavoring to extend the state of pleasure, takes an interest in the object towards which this pleasure is directed. And one can posit [*hinzusetzen*] that this is, by all means, the original meaning of pleasure and, in contrast, the idea of a pleasure that does *not* imply the interest in a thing is ultimately incomprehensible.[88]

For this reason, Kulenkampff is unwilling to accept the idea that disinterested pleasure could function just as any other pleasure, differing only insofar as it does not involve an interest in the existence of the object. This, in turn, motivates him to suggest a unique interpretive solution. It is not that this pleasure is simply disinterested in the object, but more so, that the pleasure is *disconnected* from the subject. In this manner, pure aesthetic pleasure naturally does not exhibit an interest on the part *of the subject*, to whom it cannot be ascribed:

> The analysis of this judgment must take into account the fact that the judgment "this x is beautiful" announces pleasure, insofar as it is aesthetic, and that it does not, however, designate a subject of this pleasure. Without such a designation, the announcement of pleasure in its original meaning would surely be incomprehensible. Due to this peculiarity of the judgment of beauty, however, which one could call *Indexlosigkeit* [lack of indexicality], it now depends on the distinct differentiation of the beautiful from the agreeable, but that is in such a manner that in both cases there can be an announcement of pleasure (§ 3 and § 5).
>
> It is for this purpose that Kant introduces a new terminology, so as to enable the thought of a *disinterested pleasure*. That is a thought, which was not at all present in the initial definition of "aesthetic judgment" and which now, on the other hand, is compelled through this structure of judgment about the beautiful, in which the indexical designating an experiencing subject is missing.[89]

---

[88] The translation is mine. The original reads: "Nun impliziert Lust nach Kants eigener anthropologisher Bestimmung die Tendenz, den lustvollen Zustand aufrecht zu erhalten, und Unlust, ihn zu ändern. Man kann deshalb sagen, daß der Zustand des Subjekts, den das positive ästhetische Urteil meint, sicherlich ein *interessierter Zustand* ist: das Subjekt, das bestrebt ist, den Zustand der Lust auszudehnen, nimmt ein Interesse an dem Gegenstand, auf den es bezogen ist. Und man kann hinzusetzen, daß diese Struktur duchaus der ursprüngliche Sinn von Lust ist und demgegenüber ist die Idee einer Lust, die *nicht* das Interesse an einer Sache impliziert, eigentlich unverständlich" (Kulenkampff, *Kants Logik des ästhetischen Urteils*, 73).

[89] The translation is mine. The original reads: "Die Analyse dieses Urteils muß dem Faktum Rechnung tragen, daß das Uretil "dieses x ist schön" Lust kundgibt, sofern es ästhetich ist, daß es aber nicht ein Subjekt dieser Lust bezeichnet. Ohne eine solche Bezeichnung wird jedoch

Concerning the very first sentence of this excerpt, it must be noted that both the announcement of "pleasure" and the designation of a subject who experiences this pleasure are *equally* absent from the proclamation "This x is beautiful." They are, however, both present in the mental processes that underlie this statement, allowing it to be made. As noted in chapter two (§ III.A.), Kulenkampff is mistaken if he expects to discover what is essential to each moment of the judgment of taste by analyzing the propositional statement of something's beauty to which pure aesthetic judging may give rise. In analyzing the four moments of the judgment of taste, we should be looking at how the logical functions determine the *activity* of judging—the mental processes leading up to the proclamation of beauty—and not the mere proclamation "This X is beautiful." Thus, Kulenkampff is wrong to be distracted by the way that this statement proclaims the object to be beautiful and not the subject to be experiencing pleasure. This proclamation of beauty is a final, third layer outcome of the activity of aesthetic judging. Disinterest pertains to how the activity of aesthetic judging is carried out, not how the judgment is worded. The activity of pure aesthetic judging needs to be such that it can stimulate a judgment worded in this manner, but since this judgment is produced on a different layer than the properly aesthetic harmonious free play, we cannot expect every peculiarity of pure aesthetic judging to be able to be derived from this final statement. True, "This X is beautiful" does not designate the subject experiencing aesthetic pleasure. This, however, does not in itself tell us anything about the relation the subject has, or does not have, to pure aesthetic pleasure. Despite how the final proclamation of beauty is worded, nothing prevents the experience of pleasure by the subject from being a major part of the processes that lead to this conclusion. Furthermore, if Kulenkampff were to continue along this line of argument, analyzing the wording of the judgment proclaiming something to be beautiful, then the fact that *pleasure* is no more mentioned in the statement "This x is beautiful" than the *judging subject* ("I") ought to lead him to conclude that this "missing" pleasure cannot be a criteria for this judgment, either. The idea that there is a *Lustlosigkeit*, running parallel to his *In-*

---

die Kundgabe der Lust in ihrem ursprünglichen Sinn unverständlich. Wegen dieser Eigentümlichkeit des Urteils über das Schöne, die man seine *Indexlosigkeit* nennen könnte, kommt es nun darauf an, das Schöne deutlich vom Angenehmen zu unterscheiden, aber doch so, daß in beiden Fällen von der Kundgabe einer Lust gesprochen werden kann (§§ 3 und 5). Kant führt zu diesem Zweck wie selbstverständlich eine neue Begrifflichkeit so ein, daß der Gedanke an eine *interesselose Lust* möglich wird. Das ist ein Gedanke, der in der ersten Bestimmung von "ästhetichem Urteil" gar nich gelegen war und der nun andererseits durch die Struktur des Urteils über das Schöne, in der der Index auf ein erfahrendes Subjekt fehlt, erzwungen wird" (Kulenkampff, *Kants Logik des ästhetischen Urteils*, 74).

dexlosigkeit, is, however, clearly something that he would be unwilling to accept.[90]

That said, let us now more fully explore Kulenkampff's reading by looking at the advantages he finds it to provide, before turning to the reasons for ultimately discarding it. Kulenkampff takes *Indexlosigkeit*, to be one of the key features of pure aesthetic pleasure that emerges through the contrast with the agreeable and the good. Aesthetic pleasure, he contends, does not pinpoint any subject of the pleasure. He draws out this point by distinguishing between the "realized or anticipated immediate *pleasure in something* [*Lust an etwas*] and the motivating desire, to do something, *pleasure to something* [*die Lust zu etwas*]."[91] It is readily apparent that the pleasure taken in the good involves the motivational desire *to do* something, insofar as it activates the will. He goes on to show that the pleasure of the agreeable involves an immediate,

> positive emotional reaction of the subject in its relation to the world [...] structured in such a manner that 'it excites a desire of objects of the same sort' (9) and thus is a pleasure to [*zu*] something, i.e., it implies interest, inclination or also will.[92]

By contrast, he suggests that pure aesthetic judgment involves a pleasure *an etwas* without also entailing any desire *zu etwas*. He writes,

> in consideration of the *Indexlosigkeit* of the judgment about the beautiful [...] the analysis achieves [...] the idea of a 'free pleasure' (15), in which no inclination grounded on affection is in play [...so that we may reach...] the idea of a *merely contemplative* or purely aesthetic judgment.[93]

---

[90] Indeed, the strategy of analyzing the proclamation of the judgment "This X is beautiful" to discover what is essential to the functioning of aesthetic judgment would quickly run into further, insurmountable problems. First of all, if we base our reading on the wording of this judgment then beauty would appear to be the property of an object. But Kant clearly states that this is not to be the case (*Critique of the Power of Judgment* § 15, 5:228). Furthermore, if this statement is not mitigated by a layered structure, then it would seem to be made on the basis of a concept of what beauty is, finding application this concept to be appropriate in the case of X.
[91] Kulenkampff, *Kants Logik des ästhetischen Urteils*, 74.
[92] Kulenkampff, *Kants Logik des ästhetischen Urteils*, 75; including a quotation from the *Critique of the Power of Judgment*, § 3, 5:207.
[93] My translation. The original reads in full "Die Analyse erreicht also in Rücksicht auf die Indexlosigkeit des Urteils über das Schöne und in Rücksicht auf den Sinn ästheticher Urteils im allgemeinen die Idee eines "freien Wohlgefallens" (15), in dem keine auf Affektion beründete Neigung im Spiel ist, und sie erreicht die Idee eines *bloß kontemplativen* oder reinen ästhetiche Urteils [...]" (76).

III The First Moment and the Risk of Indexlosigkeit — 165

This yields for aesthetic judgment "a pure, merely contemplative pleasure."[94] We might understand this pleasure to arise from the harmony of the faculties instead of from the "emotional reaction of the subject."[95] In this manner Kulenkampff's *Indeslosigkeit* might be understood as the contestation that this "merely contemplative" pleasure belongs more to the *faculties* "deeply buried in all human beings,"[96] since it arises in their transcendental free play,[97] than to any individual subject. Kulenkampff's point, accordingly, appears to be that, this faculty-pleasure[98] cannot properly be ascribed to the subject, rendering it a unique sort of subject-less pleasure, in which the "explicit relation to the emotionally responding subject [...] is precisely that which is missing."[99]

Kulenkampff finds two advantages to this reading. On the one hand, it helps differentiate the pleasure of taste from that of the agreeable, insofar as the latter places the "emotionally responding subject" front and center. On the other hand, it cleverly explains why this pleasure cannot have an interest in the existence of the thing, because for whom would this interest be? If he is right about the *Indexlosigkeit* of pure aesthetic judgments and no judging subject can be designated as the recipient of this pleasure, then there is no reason to believe that this subject would have an interest in the existence of the object judged.

While I agree with Kulenkampff that the pleasure of pure judgments of taste distinguishes it from other sorts by being merely contemplative—a sort of faculty-pleasure, if you will—I take issue with his claim that this plunges aesthetic judgments into an *Indexlosigkeit*.

The main problem for Kulenkampff's *Indexlosigkeit* I would like to address is that Kant does, in fact, repeatedly emphasize that the judging subject is of cru-

---

94 The translation is mine. The full original sentance reads: "So ergibt die Alanyse, daß es neben der ästhetichen Sinnenlust noch eine andere Form unmittelbarer Lust gibt, nämlich *reine, bloß kontemplative Lust, das interesselose Wohlgefallen*" (Kulenkampff, *Kants Logik des ästhetischen Urteils*, 77).
95 Kulenkampff, *Kants Logik des ästhetischen Urteils*, 75.
96 *Critique of the Power of Judgment*, § 17, 5:232.
97 This is described in detail in the next chapter (see §II The Second Moment of Aesthetic Judgment).
98 This is not a term Kulenkampff, himself, uses, but it does seem to suit his argument.
99 The translation is mine. A fuller quotation of the original reads: "[...] daß in ihm der explizite Bezug auf das emotional reagierende Subjekt—Konstituens in der Struktur des urteils über das Angenehme—gerade fehlt" (Kulenkampff, *Kants Logik des ästhetischen Urteils*, 78). Indeed, Kulenkampff goes on to describe aesthetic judgments as subject-independent [*subjektunabhängig*]. He explains, "Das Urteil über das Schöne hat eine kategorische Form ohne die Stelle für das Personalproneomen, durch das der explizite, einschränkende Bezug auf ein Subjekt geschehen könnte wie bei ‚dies ist mir angenehm'" (*Ibid.*, 87).

cial importance for pure aesthetic judgments. To make an aesthetic judgment "I must immediately hold the object up to my feeling of pleasure and displeasure [...]."[100] That "I" must do this and that they must be "my" faculties demonstrates that the pleasure serving as the grounds for the judgment cannot be experienced anywhere but within the subject, because it is only in the first personal position that we have access to *feelings*, and these can only ever be *one's own* feelings. In fact, this supplies an important point of contrast between one's conduct regarding the good and the aesthetic. Taste cannot be forced. Given that judgments of taste are grounded on feelings, if one does not have the appropriate feelings, but decides to imitate those who do have such feelings—in order to pretend to be making the same aesthetic judgment as them—then no matter how convincingly one acts *as if* one were judging the object to be beautiful, without *in fact* doing so on the grounds of a feeling of pleasure, one will never be making an aesthetic judgment.[101]

By contrast, Kant tells us that in moral matters the relation between feelings and virtues plays out quite differently. Here, "there are mores (conduct) without virtue, politeness without benevolence, propriety without honorableness."[102] Thus, one may do good action without having the proper feeling behind the action, but one cannot make an aesthetic judgment without feeling aesthetic pleasure, since the pleasure experienced firsthand in the subject serves as the grounds of the judgment, but the grounds of the moral action, i.e. of the free will, is not pleasure, but the moral law.[103] Thus, contrary to Kulenkampff's anal-

---

100 *Critique of the Power of Judgment*, § 8, 5: 215.
101 Admittedly, one may trick others into believing that one has made a judgment of taste when one has not, but one cannot *force* oneself to make such a judgment without the feeling necessary. So, judgments of taste can be faked interpersonally, but not intrapersonally. One can neither deceive oneself about having taste, nor force oneself into a particular judgment of taste.
102 *Critique of the Power of Judgment*, § 5, 5:210. The place in the second *Critique* where we find something comparable to the impossibility of deceiving oneself for aesthetic judgment concerns the moral feelings of humility and respect. Kant writes, "before a humble common man in whom I perceive uprightness of character in a higher degree than I am aware of in myself *my spirit bows*, whether I want it or whether I do not and hold my head ever so high, that he may not overlook my superior position. Why is this? His example holds before me a law that strikes down my self-conceit when I compare it with my conduct, and I see observance of that law and hence its *practicability* proved before me in fact" (*Critique of Practical Reason*, 5:76–77).
103 The observation that "a free will must find a determining ground in the law," leads Kant to conclude that "[t]he lawgiving form, insofar as this is contained in the maxim, is therefore the only thing that can constitute a determining ground of the will" (*Critique of Practical Reason*, 5:29). In the following Remark this is further developed: "It is therefore the *moral law*, of which we become immediately conscious (as soon as we draw up maxims of the will for ourselves), that *first* offers itself to us and, inasmuch as reason presents it as a determining ground

ysis, the subject is, indeed, indexically picked out as the individual subject of the pleasure of the aesthetic judgment, for this pleasure can belong to none other than she who makes the judgment. The pleasure must be experienced *in* this subject in order for her to be able to make an aesthetic judgment in the first place.[104]

III.A Harmony, Mood and Free Play

Whereas Kulenkampff saw the merely contemplative nature of aesthetic judgments as ultimately cutting the subject off from this pleasure, Rodolphe Gasché's reading of the harmony of the faculties can help explain what may appear to be a disconnect between the subject and feeling of pleasure without actually disconnecting the two. In his analysis of transcendental free-play, Gasché argues that the attunement (*Einstimmung*) of the faculties puts the faculties into the right mood (*Stimmung*) for cognition.[105] He reads the determining ground of aesthetic judgment as "constituted by the powers cohering in mood (*Stimmung*)."[106] This is a mood of pleasure, i.e., of "the pleasurable feeling of a furtherance of life that the beautiful directly brings with it."[107] If we read "the faculties' purposeful play itself" as having "the quality of a mood," then this means that the harmony "oc-

---

not to be outweighed by any sensible conditions and indeed quite independent of them, leads directly to the concept of freedom" (*Ibid*, 5:29–30).

104 One may initially expect that Kulenkampff's reading of *Indexlosigkeit* is necessitated by my adherence to the idea that the free play of the faculties on the second layer occurs without concepts, but this need not be the case. The transcendental unity of apperception is not the unity of the category of quantity: "Apperception is itself the ground of the possibility of the categories, which for their part represent nothing other than the synthesis of the manifold of intuition, insofar as the manifold has unity in apperception [...]. Hence of the thinking I [...] one can say not so much that it cognizes itself through the categories, but that it cognizes the categories, and through them all objects, in the absolute unity of apperception, and hence cognizes them through itself" (A401). Thus, Timothy Sean Quinn observes, "The basis for the synthetic activity of the categories is not a category of unity, but the unity of an 'original' self-consciousness, or transcendental unity of apperception" (Quinn, Timothy Sean, "Kant: The Practical Categories," In *Categories: Historical and Systematic Essays* [Catholic University of America Press, Washington, D.C.. 2004], 84). Accordingly, if on the second layer of pure aesthetic judgments of taste there is no object for the application of the categories, then the transcendental free play of the faculties can still be accompanied by the "I think" without invoking the categories. Here, there is only the activity of judging, determinable by the logical functions of judging.

105 Gasché, "Transcendentality, in Play," 301.
106 Gasché, "Transcendentality, in Play," 304.
107 Gasché, "Transcendentality, in Play," 304.

curs through a state of mind."[108] Not only does this description fall in line with how this harmony works in Kant's analysis and garner further etymological support from the fact that *Einstimmung* contains the root word *Stimmung*, but furthermore, it offers a way of accounting for the quasi-unconscious aspect of pure aesthetic pleasure that Kulenkampff picks out[109] without severing the pleasure from the subject in the process.

When in a mood, one knows oneself to feel a certain way without necessarily knowing *how* this mood took hold.[110] Although one can talk about how one feels, the exact way in which one was caused to feel this remains somewhat hidden. Often a specific event, or series of events, can be indicated as the trigger, but even then the exact relation of the *faculties* that brought about this feeling in the subject remains beyond one's discursive reach. If we assume a Kantian view of the faculties of mind, then it must be possible to tell, something like, a "faculties of mind causal story" about how a set of empirical events affected the faculties, causing one to enter a particular mood.[111] Of course, Kant does not employ his architectonic to pursue such an endeavor, because such an undertaking belongs to empirical psychology. Kant differentiates from psychology the work that he is carrying out in the third *Critique* as something that,

---

108 Gasché, "Transcendentality, in Play," 305.
109 Kulenkampff touches on this when he writes, "Sicherlich verweilen wir in Betractung des Schönen [...] aber dies Verweilen ist in einem gewissen Sinne bewußtlos und dauert einfach, solange die Betrachtung dauert" (Kulenkampff, *Kants Logik des ästhetischen Urteils*, 77).
110 The way that Gasché characterizes this mood of pleasure could in many ways be compared to a Heideggerian conception of mood [*Stimmung*]. For Heidegger *Dasein* always already finds itself in a mood, without necessarily being able to explain why. He writes: "In having a mood, Dasein is always disclosed moodwise [*stimmungsgemäßig*] as that entity to which it has been delivered over in its Being; and in this way it has been delivered over to the Being which, in existing, it has to be. "To be disclosed" does not mean "to be known as this sort of thing." And even in the most indifferent and inoffensive everydayness the Being of *Dasein* can burst forth as a naked 'that it is and has to be.' The pure 'that it is' shows itself, but the "whence" and the "whither" remain in darkness. The fact that it is just as everyday a matter for Dasein not to 'give in' to such moods [*Stimmungen*]—in other words, not to follow up their disclosure and allow itself to be brought before that which is disclosed—is no evidence *against* the phenomenal facts of the case, in which the Being of the "there" is disclosed moodwise [*stimmungsgemäßig*] in its "that-it-is"; it is rather evidence for it" (Heidegger, *Being and Time*, 173/ 134–5).
111 For Kant's discussion of the distinctions between emotion, affect and passion, see: *Critique of the Power of Judgment*,§ 29, 5:272–275, particularly the footnote at 5:272. Each represents certain "movements of the mind" (*Ibid*, 5:273).

elevates [aesthetic judgments] out of empirical psychology, in which they would otherwise remain buried among the feelings of enjoyment and pain (only with the meaningless epithet of a more refined feeling).[112]

Thus, over the course of the third *Critique*, we witness Kant's effort to place these feelings "in the class of those which have as their ground a priori principles, and as such to transpose them into transcendental philosophy."[113] It is not that ordinary feelings, and moods, *cannot* be understood in terms of the functioning of the faculties, but just that such a study is not of interest to the transcendental philosopher. It is the a priority of aesthetic feelings, which both grants them a subjective *necessity* and allows them to be *universally* communicable—setting them apart from more quotidian feelings, and making them a proper object of philosophical, not psychological, scrutiny.[114]

That said, understanding the harmony of the faculties as a mood of pleasure can help us understand how the subject relates to this faculty-pleasure. Kulenkampff's indexicalogical complaint is that a contemplative pleasure of the faculties cannot be properly ascribed to the subject. With Gasché's reading, however, we realize that the relation between the subject and this feeling is no more problematic than that of any other sort of feeling or mood. The problem appears for Kulenkampff, because he is comparing pure aesthetic pleasure to bodily pleasure. Accordingly, his argument seems to be that if a subject cannot ascribe the aesthetic pleasure to herself in the same way as she ascribes the pleasure taken in the taste of honey to *her* tongue, then she is not indexically picked out as the singular subject of this pleasure. But, if we shift the comparison to one with other sorts of moods, then things appear differently. If *Indexlosigkeit* does not thwart the ascription of humiliation, respect, love or fear to the subject,

---

112 *Critique of the Power of Judgment*, § 29, 5:266.
113 *Critique of the Power of Judgment*, § 29, 5:266.
114 The fact that aesthetic judgment could, when treated in this manner, become a proper object of investigation for transcendental philosophy was not apparent to Kant from the start of his philosophical career. His early engagement with aesthetics, thus, treats it more as a matter of empirical psychology, taking the beautiful to involve merely more "refined feelings," in the manner he now criticizes. This is particularly evident in *Observations on the Feeling of the Beautiful and the Sublime* (1763) where he casts an eye upon the field of the diverse "Empfindungen des Vergnügens, oder des Verdrusses" of humankind, and that is for an eye that is, "mehr das Auge eines Beobachters als des Philosophen" (*Über das Gefühl des Schönen und Erhabenen*, A1–2). He elaborates, "Das feinere Gefühl, was wir nun erwägen wollen, ist vornehmlich zweifacher Art: Das Gefühl des Erhabenen und des Schönen. Die Rührung von beiden ist angenehm, aber auf sehr verschiedene Weise" (A4). This contrasts starkly to the third *Critique* where Kant is concerned with the *judgment*, not feeling, of the beautiful and takes this to be a matter starkly divided from the agreeable.

then it should not create any more trouble for the ascription of a mood of pleasure.

Moreover, the complications involved in ascribing a feeling to the subject are not unique to moods. Indeed, even the ascription of bodily sensations can present complications similar to those that motivate Kulenkampff's verdict of *indexlos* and *subjektunabhängig*. For example, an undiagnosed anemic may experience a general sense of discomfort without being able to identify the cause as a deficient level of iron in her blood. This obscurity does not, however, confuse the anemic that it is *she* who is experiencing the discomfort. Nor does the disconnect cause the doctor, who identifies the cause, to declare there to be a "pain of the blood" that is *in*, but not *of*, the patient. Likewise, simply because the harmony of the faculties generates aesthetic pleasure in a manner not directly observable by the subject, this does not give us cause to say that insofar as pure aesthetic pleasure is a pleasure of the faculties, it is not one of the subject.

IV One Remaining Puzzle

I will now bring our discussion of the first moment to a close by inspecting one puzzling aspect of disinterested pleasure that remains. This is the difficulty presented by the fact that there *does* seem to be a way in which one *is* interested in the existence of the beautiful.

IV.B The Faculty-Interest

A certain difficulty is created by the way that this moment *is* intertwined with an interest in existence. I will now look at how one may appear to have an interest in the existence of the object insofar as it occasions a process that is purposive for our faculties.

Although the quality of disinterested pleasure clearly involves the negation of any "pathologically conditioned" or "pure practical" interest, setting beauty apart from the agreeable and the good,[115] it does not appear that all interest in the object as existing can be fully negated. The object must be encountered, at least as an *Anlass* or trigger, in order for an aesthetic judgment to ensue.[116]

---

115 *Critique of the Power of Judgment*, § 5, 5:209.
116 This is not to indicate that only the reproductive imagination is involved in pure aesthetic judgments of taste. Rudolf A. Makkreel points out that "the syntheses of the *Critique of Pure Rea-*

Thus, the object must exist. Aesthetic judgments are in the interest of the "optimal"[117] use of our faculties, because they bring about an "enlivening"[118] of the faculties of imagination and understanding through harmonious free-play.[119] In-

---

son are not merely formative in the sense of extending, gathering, and elaborating images, but productive of the fundamental unities necessary for representation to constitute experience" (Makkreel, *Imagination and Interpretation in Kant*, 25). Crawford comes to a similar conclusion. First he observes that although "association is the empirical ground for reproduction [...] this empirical ground (reproduction in imagination by means of association) must itself rest on some objective ground ("affinity"); otherwise, experience could not be coherent" (Crawford, *Kant's Aesthetic Theory*, 88). Crawford goes on to explain that the productive imagination "is a spontaneous faculty not dependent upon empirical laws but rather constitutive of them and hence constitutive of empirical objects" (Crawford, *Kant's Aesthetic Theory*, 88). Thus, the reproductive and productive functions of the imagination are to be distinguished from one another, but this does not mean that the experience of an empirical object should be understood as merely involving the reproductive and not the productive imagination. We also see this in quality, as mentioned above (see footnote#3 and the accompanying main text). Kant indicates that cognition of quality requires the productive imagination, since magnitudes of quality are experienced as "flowing," and this is achieved through "the synthesis (of the productive imagination) in their generation [which] is a progress in time, the continuity of which is customarily designated by the expression "flowing" ("elapsing")" (*Critique of Pure Reason*, A170/B212). Although the productive and reproductive imagination must both be involved in the constitution of experience, the first layer of aesthetic judgment is primarily concerned with receptivity of an intuition, whereas the harmonious free play of the faculties on the second layer is a spontaneous activity triggered by this intuition. The freedom of this free play indicates that the productive imagination is predominant here, as it is not constrained to the task of reproducing something that was given. Rather, this is "where the imagination in its freedom arouses the understanding, and the latter, without concepts, sets the imagination into a regular play [...]" (*Critique of the Power of Judgment* § 40, 5:296).

117 Referring to the proportion that the disposition of the powers of mind has in an aesthetic judgment, Kant writes, "[eine Proportion] in welcher dieses innere Verhältnis zur Belebung (einer durch die andere) die zuträglischste für beide Gemütskräfte in Absicht auf Erkenntnis (gegebener Gegenstände) überhaupt ist; und diese Stimmung kann nicht anders als durch das Gefühl (nicht nach Begriffen) bestimmt werden." (*Kritik der Urteilskraft*, B66/A65) The term "zuträglischste" is translated as "optimal" in Guyer. (*Critique of the Power of Judgment*, § 22, 5:238)
118 *Critique of the Power of Judgment*, § 9, 5:219.
119 The idea that Kant allows for faculty interest is further supported by a comment he makes in the *Critique of Practical Reason*: "To every faculty of the mind one can attribute an *interest*, that is, a principle that contains the condition under which alone its exercise is promoted. Reason, as the faculty of principles, determines the interest of all the powers of the mind but itself determines its own. The interest of its speculative use consists in the *cognition* of the object up to the highest a priori principles; that of its practical use consists in the determination of the *will* with respect to the final and complete end" (5:119–120, emphasis original). In the context of the third *Critique*, however, it is not the interest of the faculty of reason, but the interest of the faculties of imagination and understand that is under concern.

terest is defined by Kant as "the satisfaction that we combine with the representation of the existence of an object."[120] It is not the representation of the existence of the beautiful object which serves as the grounds for the pleasure felt in a judgment of the beautiful. Indeed, this pleasure is grounded on the harmonious free-play of the faculties. This free-play, however, is triggered[121] by the representation of the beautiful object, which must therefore exist in order to occasion the stimulation of the faculties into a harmonious free-play. If so, then although practical interests are negated, there would appear to be another sort of "faculty interest" in the object that is indirectly affirmed.

Brandt remarks on this same issue, putting it in terms of the relation between form and matter; subject and object.[122] He observes that even though aesthetic judgments are more concerned with form than matter—form being contributed by the subject and matter, by the object—they cannot be occasioned by *mere* form. That is to say, a subject could not just think up any form and then revel in aesthetic contemplation of it.[123] Matter is a necessary medium for the aesthetic object and is needed as an *Anlass* for aesthetic judgment. Hence, regardless of how heavily aesthetic judgment falls on the side of form, contributed by the subject, the object's side of matter cannot be altogether negated. The existence of the object is of a certain unavoidable interest to aesthetic judgment. We must, thus, understand Kant's assertion that the subject is not interested in the existence of the object in the context of his insistence that the existence of the object does not serve as the *grounds* for the pleasure of the judgment— the suppressed admission being that the object must exist in some way in order for it to be able to be encountered by the subject, enabling the possibility that an aesthetic judgment will be triggered.

Perhaps the layered solution from the previous chapter can help bring clarity to this. The aesthetic object is given to aesthetic judgment through an empirical

---

120 *Critique of the Power of Judgment*, § 2, 5:204.
121 That is, it has its "Anlass" in the representation of the object (*Kritik der Urteilskraft*, § 9, B31/A31).
122 Brandt, "Zur Logik des ästhetischen Urteils."
123 Brandt notes that, "Die Gegenstände können uns nur material, nicht aber mit ihrer Form affizieren; die Form ist also eigentlich Sache nur des Subjekts, nicht des Objekts" (Brandt, "Zur Logik des ästhetischen Urteils," 236). He further develops this point on the next page, where he writes, "Die Form gerät so in eine Schwebezustand zwischen Subjekt und Objekt; sie muß dem Subjekt zugehören, weil nicht die Form, sondern nur das Materiale uns zu affizieren vermag, eine andere Beziehung als die der Affektion aber zwischen Objekt und Subjekt nicht gedacht werden kann. Die Form muß andererseits dem Objekt angehören, denn der als schön deklarierte Gegenstand soll nicht nur der materiale Anlaß sein, eine Form im Subjekt zu entwerfen und diese als schön zu bezeichnen" (Brandt, "Zur Logik des ästhetischen Urteils," 237).

judgment of the initial layer. It is in this judgment that the object is synthesized as an object of experience and a surplus results. This surplus involves a way the subject is affected that is unable to be brought under a concept. In the second, properly aesthetic layer this aesthetic remainder of the intuitional excess is taken up. We could say that in the transition from the first to the second layer the *existentia* of the empirical object goes entirely out of focus and what is concentrated on is only the form. Thus, the existence of the object is not at issue in this layer of the judgment. The object was dealt with as an existing thing in the initial, empirical layer, but, once the properly aesthetic layer has been reached its existence has no more importance than that of an algebraic variable. Thus, we may work with the term, without concerning ourselves with it as an existing object.

Another way that faculty-interest can be demarcated from interest in the existence of something is by contrasting how aesthetic and moral judgments relate to the feeling of life. In the *Critique of the Power of Judgment,* Kant writes that when one is,

> conscious of [a] representation with the sensation of satisfaction [...] the representation is related entirely to the subject, indeed to its feeling of life [*Lebensgefühl*], under the name of the feeling of pleasure or displeasure [...].[124]

Rodolphe Gasché elaborates on this passage, writing that:

> The feeling of life predicated in judgments of taste is a non-cognitive awareness of being alive. The pleasure predicated of representations in judgments of taste is the pleasure of coming to life, as it were.[125]

Compare this aesthetic feeling of life now to what Kant writes in a footnote from the second *Critique:*

> **Life** is the faculty of a being to act in accordance with laws of the faculty of desire. The **faculty of desire** is a being's *faculty to be by means of its representations the cause of the reality of the objects of these representations.* Pleasure is the *representation of the agreement of an object or of an action with the* subjective *conditions of life,* i.e., with the faculty of the *causality of a representation with respect to the reality of its object* (or with respect to the determination of the powers of the subject to action in order to produce the object).[126]

---

[124] *Critique of the Power of Judgment,* § 1, 5:204.
[125] Gasché, "Transcendentality, in Play," 299.
[126] *Critique of Practical Reason,* 5:9–10.

In the practical sphere, the faculty of desire concerns the reality of objects. We desire a "satisfaction in the existence of an object or of an action"[127] when we judge something to be good and "relation of its existence to my state"[128] when we judge it to be agreeable. What one seeks to bring about in aesthetic judgment, however, is the harmonious free play of the faculties, *not* "the reality of the objects of these representations."[129] What one is *interested in* is an internal state of mind, *not* an external state of affairs. So, even if we believe aesthetic judgments to serve an internal faculty-interest, this interest is in no way comparable to the interest in the agreeable, because it does not directly involve an interest in something's existence. Hence, such an interest would not violate the disinterestedness of pure aesthetic judgments.[130]

V Conclusion

If infinite judgments supply partial determinations of the subject by affirming the relation of the subject to a negated predicate, then initially one might have expected this partial determination to be aimed at the object. On the contrary, when we look at the definition that concludes this moment, it is clear that what has been partially determined is "taste" as "the faculty for judging":

> Definition of the beautiful derived from the first moment.
>
> **Taste** is the faculty for judging an object or a kind of representation through a satisfaction or dissatisfaction **without any interest.** The object of such a satisfaction is called **beautiful.**[131]

---

127 *Critique of the Power of Judgment*, § 4, 5:207.
128 *Critique of the Power of Judgment*, § 3, 5:207.
129 *Critique of Practical Reason*, 5:9–10.
130 This accords with what Longuenesse observes when considering whether the involvement of *Lebensgefühl* links aesthetic judgment to the faculty of desire, thus contaminating it with an interest in the object. She concludes that this is not the case, because, "all we know is that by virtue of this pleasure, the mind tends to nothing more, and nothing less, than to *maintain itself in its own state*. Now, being the cause and effect of oneself is precisely Kant's characterization of life as a capacity of corporeal things. It thus seems quite apt to say that in aesthetic pleasure, the mind is cause and effect of *nothing but itself*, and so aesthetic pleasure is *Lebensgefühl* in this restricted sense: feeling of the life *of the mind* (of the representational capacities)" (Longuenesse, "Kant's Leading Thread in the Analytic of the Beautiful," 200).
131 *Critique of the Power of Judgment*, § 5, 5:211.

We see from this that the aesthetic judging is what occupies the subject position and is placed in an affirmative relation to the negated predicate ("without any interest"). This accords with how an analysis of something into its moments was portrayed in chapter two as an investigation into the mental processes that underpin this "thing." In an analysis of the moments of aesthetic judgment, this becomes an analysis of the form that the act of judging takes in the process leading up to the proclamation "X is beautiful." Aesthetic judgment does not determine the object. What does take a determinate form is its *way of engaging* with the representation of the object. The first determination of this form being that the act of judging aesthetically is carried out without the existence of the object grounding the satisfaction.

The moment of quality aims to establish what sort of interest we do and do not have in the object that occasions an aesthetic judgment, so that we can establish the limited involvement of the empirical world in this judgment. The object must be empirically given, but it is not the real empirical givenness (i.e., the existence) of the object that pleases. Thus, the definition that this moment yields is not one in which the *object* is known to *be* beautiful. Rather it is a definition of what occurs in "calling" an object beautiful—what determinations govern this *act of judging*, not the object.

Chapter Four:
The Universal Validity of a Singular Judgment

As I argued in chapters one and two, it is a mistake to read Kant's aesthetic theory in the one-dimensional manner that would assume all of the characteristics of aesthetic judgment to aim at generating the single judgment "this x is beautiful."[1] In chapter one, I showed how the assumption that there is only one layer to aesthetic judgment would prevent us from being able to make sense out of Kant's insistence that this form of judgment characteristically functions without concepts. Although an important part of aesthetic judgment occurs independently of concepts, this must be understood in a manner that still permits an empirically cognized object[2] with determinate features to be involved in occasioning the judgment. Moreover, one must be able to account for how aesthetic judgement opens up a realm of higher level moral appreciation. Neither of these things, however, could occur without any conceptual involvement. Thus, chapter two showed how a more satisfying way of resolving this difficulty can be offered by a stratified interpretation of Kant's system, separating the activity of judging that does use concepts for determination into different layers from that which does not. In chapter three we saw how taking this as our foundational structure for understanding Kant's system of aesthetic judgment allows us to make sense of the interests that are and are not taken in the empirical object judged, so as not to jeopardize the disinterestedness of this judgment. In the present chapter, we will see that aesthetic judgment is in an important sense both singular and universal, providing what Kant terms "the universal validity of a singular judgment."[3] As in the previous chapter, I will use my layered structure to resolve the complications that arise in connection to aesthetic judgment's quantity, which would introduce intolerable contradictions if left unresolved.

---

[1] On this point I am in agreement with Longuenesse, who emphasizes how there is a "turning around, in Kant's analytic of the Beautiful, from the manifest judgment about the object to the implicit judgment embedded in its predicate [...]" (Longuenesse, "Kant's Leading Thread in the Analytic of the Beautiful," 209). To fully understand how the logical functions operate in aesthetic judgment both the explicit and implicit judgments need to be taken into account.

[2] Designating an object as empirical does not specify its relation to materiality. Instead, what this indicates is that the object is given to us a posteriori through the intuition and thus cannot be cognized a priori. For a discussion of this see chapter three (section II.C. *Separating Existence from Essence: Kant's Hundred Possible Thalers*).

[3] *Critique of the Power of Judgment*,§ 31, 5:281.

I The Logical Functions of Quantity

Let us now begin by scrutinizing the logical functions that this moment concerns. The second title under which Kant brings "the function of thinking"[4] involved in aesthetic judgment is that of quantity, containing under itself the three moments of: universal, particular, singular. At first blush, quantity appears to be a straightforward matter, all of its logical functions having an immediately understandable meaning, unlike the "infinite" function of quality, which draws inquisitive attention right from the outset.

In the *Jäsche Logic* quantity is described as determining whether "the subject is either *wholly in*cluded in or *ex*cluded from the notion of the predicate or is only *in part in*cluded in or *ex*cluded from it."[5] When presented in this manner, it is difficult to see what precisely the difference is between quantity and quality, because Kant describes them in nearly identical terms. Quality determines the relation between the subject and predicate:

> In the *affirmative* judgment the subject is thought *under* the sphere of a predicate, in the *negative* it is posited *outside* the sphere of the latter, and in the *infinite* it is posited in the sphere of a concept that lies outside the sphere of another.[6]

Comparing this to the above, it is unclear what, if any, difference is to be recognized between the whole or partial inclusion or exclusion of the subject in the predicate (quantity) and the subject's being thought under the predicate's sphere (quality). Including or excluding would seem to be a function quite similar to thinking under or positing outside. The difference between these first two mathematical quadrants becomes more readily apparent if we double-back to § 8 entitled *Quantity of the extension of concepts*. Here, Kant states, "The more things that stand under a concept and can be thought through it, the greater is its extension or *sphere*."[7] The quantity of a judgment pertains to a ratio between the number of things standing under the subject-concept in total and the number of these that are being thought through this concept in the judgment at hand. Quality, on the other hand, is focused on whether "the subject is thought *under* the sphere of a predicate,"[8] and thus is concerned with the way that the judgment actively thinks the relation between the subject and predicate, and is thus

---

4 *Critique of Pure Reason*, A70/B95.
5 *Jäsche Logic*, § 21, 598.
6 *Jäsche Logic*, § 22, 600.
7 *Jäsche Logic*, § 8, 593.
8 *Jäsche Logic*, § 22, 600.

more concerned with how the copula relates the two.⁹ This difference becomes more apparent if we look at an example. Let us run through the different quantitative logical functions with the following judgment: All hummingbirds have spindle-like beaks (universal); Some hummingbirds live in North America (particular); This hummingbird is beautiful (singular). We might compare this to judgments exemplifying the qualitative logical functions: This hummingbird is beautiful (affirmative); This hummingbird is not red (negative); This hummingbird is asymmetrical (infinite). Changes to the quantity of the judgment were made through adjustments to the portion of hummingbirds to which the judgment applies. In contrast, changes to quality allow the subject concept to remain constant, since qualitative changes are primarily focused on the value of the copula.

The key role that the subject-concept plays in quantity explains both why Kant's table typically begins with quantity instead of quality and why this is reversed in the case of aesthetic judgment. That is, the table typically starts with the determination of the subject-concept, which is the foundational element from which the judgment begins.¹⁰ Quantity clarifies this concept, by telling us if the judgment will concern *all*, *some* or *just one* item falling under it. It seems natural to place this first, so as to clarify what the judgment is about before addressing the way that the designated portion of the subject-concept relates to the predicate. Aesthetic judgments, however, are *not* about the concept.¹¹ Thus, the first thing to be done is not to define the portion of the subject-concept to which the judgment will pertain. Aesthetic judgments do not supply a further determination of the concept of the subject. Thus, the moment of quantity, which is to lay out the relation of the concepts that make up the judgment, loses its nat-

---

9 This reading of the difference between the first two quadrants is in accordance with Reinhard Brandt's account: "Die Qualität bezieht sich auf den im Urteil quantifizierungsbedürfigen Begriff des Subjekts, die Qualität auf die Bejahung oder Verneinung, die dem Urteil als Urteil zukommt, und die Relation auf die noch ausstehende (notwendige) Verknüpfung der Materie von Begriffen oder Urteilen" (Brandt, *Die Urteilstafel. Kritik der reinen Vernunft A 67–76; B 92–101*, 62).

10 Reinhard Brandt explains this, writing "Das Urteil ist eine Erkenntnis durch Begriffe; Begriffe beziehen sich im Gegensatz zur Anschauung immer auf vieles, was unter ihnen begriffen wird. Das Erkenntnisurteil ist zur begrifflichen bestimmung der Vielheit, auf die sich die Begriffe beziehen, genötigt, d.h. es muß die Frage beantworten, ob das Prädikat von allem, von einigem oder von einem aus dem unbestimmten Feld des Vielen gilt, worauf sich der Subjektbegriff als bloßer Begriff bezieht. Daher die Notwendigkeit der Quantität als erstem Titel" (Brandt, *Die Urteilstafel. Kritik der reinen Vernunft A 67–76; B 92–101*, 5).

11 "Hence the judgment of taste is merely contemplative […]. But this contemplation itself is also not directed to concepts; for the judgment of taste is not a cognitive (neither a theoretical not a practical one), and hence it is neither grounded on concepts nor aimed at them" (*Critique of the Power of Judgment*, § 5, 5:209). And furthermore, "If one judges objects merely in accordance with concepts, then all representation of beauty is lost" (Ibid., § 8, 5:216).

ural place of fundamental importance if the judgment is aesthetic. Aesthetic judgments are about the feeling aroused in the judging subject. Through quality this feeling is carefully affirmed, and it is this that first catches the "notice"[12] of pure aesthetic judgment, thereby regulating into second position a quantitative analysis of the concepts which, in a crucial sense, are not aesthetically operative.

Before tackling the issue of understanding aesthetic quantity without concepts, let us establish how the logical functions of quantity operate in a typical, determinative judgment:

> In the *universal* judgment, the sphere of one concept is wholly enclosed within the sphere of another; in the *particular*, a part of the former is enclosed under the sphere of the other; and in the *singular* judgment, finally, a concept that has no sphere at all is enclosed, merely as part then, under the sphere of another.[13]

Quantity pertains to the scope of the spheres of the concepts involved. What is to be determined is the extent to which the subject-concept does or does not overlap with the sphere of the predicate-concept—or, in other words, what portion of the subject-concept's sphere is indicated by the predicate. Thus, in a case where the concept of the subject and predicate cover exactly the same sphere, all that falls under the subject-concept will be determined through the judgment, making the judgment universal (ex: "All humans are mortal"). When the concept of the predicate does not cover the entirety of the subject-concept's sphere, only some of what falls under the subject-concept will be determined by the judgment, which will thus be particular (ex: "Some humans are still alive"). When the subject-concept "has no sphere at all," it is to be identified as part of the predicate-concept's sphere, making the judgment singular. For example, in the singular judgment "Caius is mortal" the concept of Caius, as a singular individual, has "no sphere" because "there is only one Caius."[14] From this we see that something has a sphere insofar as it groups together different singulars by means of a common mark. The larger the group that is brought together by

---

[12] *Critique of the Power of Judgment*,§ 1, 5:203: footnote. My reading here aligns with that of Allison, when he observes: "since the judgment is aesthetic, it is based on feeling rather than concepts, so this must be the primary factor to be considered. Now, feeling may be considered either with regard to its quantity (strength) or its quality (kind), but clearly it is the latter that is crucial in determining what is distinctive about a judgment of beauty [...]. Moreover, [...] this appropriateness [of starting with quality] is reinforced by the fact that the quality of the feeling (its disinterestedness) is the key to the determination of the quantity of the judgment (its subjective universality)" (2001, 77).
[13] *Jäsche Logic*, § 21, 598.
[14] *Jäsche Logic*, § 21, 599.

this mark, "[t]he more things that stand under a concept and can be thought through it," hence, "the greater [...] its extension or *sphere*."[15] If there is only one singular instance to which the concept of the subject applies, then it will fail to *group* things under itself, and thus not constitute any sphere. In this case, the singular subject, Caius, is only being identified as having the mark of the predicate-concept, mortality. Since this predicate-concept has a sphere, while that of the subject does not, Caius is placed within the sphere of the predicate. Kant's discussion of cases in which the subject-concept has no sphere will be instructive in understanding the quantity of aesthetic judgment, which does not rely on concepts in a typical manner.

I.A Quantity in the first Critique

The *Critique of Pure Reason*'s discussion of the logical functions of quantity also grapples with the complexities that arise when one attempts to understand how quantitative logical functions are compared and contrasted with one another. This rests on the curious similarity between universal and singular judgments, also mentioned in the *Jäsche Logic*. In the first *Critique*, however, Kant seeks to specify in which cases the universal and singular do and do not coincide. He explains that "in syllogisms singular judgments can be treated like universal ones."[16] Thus, in his comment on the quadrant of quantity Kant seeks to explain why this is the case and, moreover, to defend his decision to present the singular and universal as two separate logical functions in his table. The fundamental factor that makes the equation of universal and singular possible in certain instances concerns the peculiarity of what was termed the sphere [*Sphäre*] of the singular in the *Jäsche Logic*, which is here discussed as the domain [*Umfang*].[17]

---

15 *Jäsche Logic*, § 8, 593.
16 *Critique of Pure Reason*, A71/B96.
17 This difference is more likely due to the fact that Kant commissioned Gottlob Benjamin Jäsche, a student of his, to prepare the *Jäsche Logic* from the manuscript Kant had used in lectures (see *Jäsche Logic*, Preface). Thus, I use this work when it elaborates on points that concur with the views expressed in the works Kant personally prepared for publication but are not as fully laid out there, leaving aside any remarks that are not supported in Kant's other writing. The *Jäsche Logic*'s reference to the *sphere* and the first *Critique*'s to the *domain*, thus, appears to be more an issue of "the clothing," which is "in part to be reckoned to [Gottlob Benjamin Jäsche's] account," but Kant personally commissioned him to prepare this work "with the expression of special, honorable confidence in [him], that, being acquainted with the principles of [Kant's] system in general, [he] would easily enter into the course of [Kant's] ideas, that [he] would not distort or falsify [Kant's] thoughts, but rather would present them with the required clarity

Although the terms used differ, the issue remains the same—namely, that the concept of a singular subject has no domain, no sphere:

> For just because they have no domain at all, their predicate is not merely related to some of what is contained under the concept of the subject while being excluded from another part of it. The predicate therefore holds of that concept without exception, just as if the latter were a generally valid concept with a domain with the predicate applying to the whole of what is signified.[18]

As was observed above, something singular has no domain, because it only applies to one singular case, and having a domain, or sphere, signifies that there is a range of things to which the concept applies. A universal logical function is applicable, when all of the items that fall under the concept exhibit the predicate. Thus, in such instances "[t]he predicate [...] holds of that concept without exception."[19] But, since the concept of something singular also holds of the singular thing "without exception," the singular and the universal operate in the same manner. All of this aligns with what was covered in the discussion of quantity in the *Jäsche Logic*. What comes to light in the first *Critique* is an answer to the question of why these are listed separately on the table of judgments.

Indeed, the rest of Kant's note aims to justify this move by explaining that there are two different uses in which the logical functions can be considered, and it is this use that determines whether the functions of universal and singular will appear as equal or be differentiated. The difference in use can be seen by bringing into focus the question that guides the consideration. The two functions are to be equated when the question being asked is whether anything that falls under the domain of the subject's concept does *not* receive the predicate. Suppose that while walking through the garden we happen across a singular hummingbird, laying on the ground with a broken wing. If we pose this question to ourselves, then we will find that none of the predicates that belong to *this* hummingbird fail to fall under the concept of "*this* hummingbird." The principle of non-contradiction would be violated if this were not the case. The broken wing that I observe as a predicate of this hummingbird belongs to my concept

---

and distinctness" (*Jäsche Logic,* Preface). For a study of the authenticity of the *Jäsche Logic,* see Terry Boswell's "On the Textual Authority of Kant's *Logic*" (1988). For concrete suggestions about how the *Jäsche Logic* can be used despite questions that may arise with Jäsche's editorial methods, see Huaping Lu-Adler's article "Constructing a Demonstration of Logical Rules, or How to Use Kant's Logic Corpus" (2015).
18 *Critique of Pure Judgment*, A71/B96.
19 *Critique of Pure Judgment*, A71/B96.

of this, singular bird with the same "internal validity"[20] as any predicates that hold universally of the concept hummingbird (ex. needle-like bill). Thus, neither the universal, nor the singular allow that which falls under the concept to *not* take the predicate. In this sense, they are the same.

The difference, which prevents these functions from fully converging, however, surfaces when we ask *how* the judgment achieves an exceptionless relation between concept and predicate. The universal achieves this because everything that falls under the concept takes the predicate (i.e. the predicate applies to the entire domain of the concept, without exception). The singular, however, achieves this by only pertaining to one, singular thing that takes the predicate from the start. Thus, it has "no" domain, insofar as the thing to which the concept applies is only that singular thing directly indicated in the judgment. The concept does not extend to anything beyond this.[21] The difference between the two becomes apparent when we adjust our focus from the "internal validity" that "is limited only to the use of judgments with respect to each other," so as to consider what the functions means "with respect to the quantity it has in comparison with other cognitions."[22] We might think of this as regarding the logical function within the wider context of cognition and whether it will have a bearing on any other judgments that might arise. Although a singular judgment has internal validity, this judgment in and of itself will not affect any other judgments. There is much that one could conclude from the fact that "This hummingbird has a broken wing," such as the fact that "The wings of hummingbirds can break," but this more general judgment reaches beyond the singular subject of the original judgment. The original singular judgment has no application beyond the scope of the singular thing about which it judges. This contrasts with the way that a more generally valid universal judgment contains within itself the potential for a nearly infinite line of application, because every time that something is identified as falling within the domain of the concept, the predicate will apply. It is for this reason that Kant suggests that when taken "merely as cognition" these two logical functions compare "as unity relates to infinity."[23] A singular cogni-

---

[20] *Critique of Pure Reason*, A71/B96.
[21] As discussed in the previous chapter, Longuenesse points out how this leads Kant to refer only to the universal and the particular in the Amphiboly of Concepts of Reflection at A262/B317–18 (Longuenesse, *Kant and the Capacity to Judge*, 139).
[22] *Critique of Pure Reason*, A71/B96–7.
[23] *Critique of Pure Reason*, A71/B96. When looking at this quotation in full, one is immediately struck by the way that Kant's language slips from a discussion of "universality" to the "general valid" in this comparison: "If, on the contrary, we compare a singular judgment with a generally valid one, merely as cognition, with respect to quantity, then the former relates to the latter as

tion can only provide unity to one judgment about one instance, but a cognition that makes use of the universal function will find application in an "infinite" number of instances. In this regard the singular is "therefore in itself essentially different from the [universal]."[24]

The differentiation of the particular from the singular and universal does not present similar complications. In the particular the predicate applies to some of the items that fall under the concepts of the subject. Thus, when we say that some birds are hummingbirds, we indicate "all birds" as the domain of our subject-concept and state that the predicate, "hummingbird," applies only to *some* of the birds within this domain. It is, rather, when we turn an eye to the categories that the particular retrospectively acquires a noteworthy relation to the other logical functions. This will be returned to when I address Guyer's objection that pure aesthetic judgments of taste ought to be understood as particular. For the moment, however, I will turn to the challenges faced by the second moment insofar as it must both elaborate a transition from the singular to the universal and do so without grounding the judgment on a concept.

---

unity relates to infinity, and is therefore in itself essentially different from the latter." This terminological slippage can be explained insofar as the transition to mere cognition is a transition from the logical form to the use of this form to cognize something. Use as a mere logical form pertains to general logic, which, as P. F. Strawson comments, "is not concerned with the relations of its forms to objects, but with the logical relations which hold between the forms themselves" (Strawson, *The Bounds of Sense*, 75). When matter enters the equation as that which is in fact being cognized, then a certain possibility for exceptions opens up. For example, the concept bird applies universally to creatures that have a certain set of defining characteristics, one of which is the possession of wings. In all actuality, however, there can be birds that lost their wings in some accident. The possibility of such birds means that strictly speaking the predicate "winged" will hold of the empirical concept "bird" with *general* validity, even though, when considered in a merely logical manner it holds with *universal* strength. This transition from universal to general validity with the introduction of matter is, however, not important to the parallel that Kant is drawing between these logical functions and the idea of unity and infinity. The real focus, here, is that when logical functions are considered in their actual use to generate cognitions, then a singular cognition can only be used to cognize one thing, unifying it, whereas the universal finds a seemingly infinite array of instances for its application.

[24] *Critique of Pure Reason*, A71/B96. Although the logical functions of universal and singular must be differentiable, they must also relate to one another. The relation between these two is of great importance to the second moment of the judgment of taste, since it is here that "the universal validity of a singular judgment" comes under examination (*Critique of the Power of Judgment*, § 31, 5:281). Hence, this relation will be scrutinized below.

II The Second Moment of Aesthetic Judgment

The second moment of aesthetic judgment is potentially threatened by a certain contradiction. Claudia Bickmann draws our attention to this, asking "How in aesthetic experience is a singular in its sensible fullness and presence to be rescued from the grips of a universalizing concept?"[25] With both the singular and the universal in play, how is the singular to maintain its singularity without melting into the universal? I will now turn to how my layered reading of Kant's aesthetic theory can allow us to account for the crucial roles played by both singularity and universality in this moment without losing the "sensible fullness" of the singular in the process.

Kant orients us to the second moment in the title of § 6: "The beautiful is that which, without concepts, is represented as the object of a universal satisfaction."[26] If we bear in mind the foregoing discussion of how logical functions of quantity work, then we quickly see there to be something very strange about the idea that universality may function without a concept. Kant acknowledges this peculiarity of the universal quantity of aesthetic judgment:

> One would think, however, that an *a priori* judgment must contain a concept of the object, for the cognition of which it contains the principle; the judgment of taste, however, is not grounded on concepts at all, and is above all not cognition, but only an aesthetic judgment.[27]

Since something singular has no domain, the idea of leaving aside any concept of this thing when engaging with it as singular does not present great difficulty. Thus, let us begin untangling the quantitative complications that arise with aesthetic judgment's universality before turning back to determine how the universality and singularity relate. The concept of the judgmental subject plays a key role in the very definition of what it is to judge the universal quantity of something. When those things that fall under the concept of the subject *all* take the predicate, then the proposition is universally valid. But, of pure aesthetic judgments, Kant writes "this universality cannot originate from concepts. For there is no transition from concepts to the feeling of pleasure or displeasure."[28]

---

25 Bickmann, "Kants 'Sinnliches Scheinen der Idee.' Die Einheit von Ethik und Ästhetik in Kants Kritik der Urteilskraft," 15, my translation. The original reads, "Wie soll in der ästhetischen Erfahrung ein Einzelnes in seiner sinnlichen Fülle und Präsenz vor dem Zugriff verallgemeinernder Begriff zu retten sein?"
26 *Critique of the Power of Judgment*, § 6, 5:211.
27 *Critique of the Power of Judgment*, § 32, 5:282.
28 *Critique of the Power of Judgment*, § 6, 5:211.

How, then, are we to make logical sense out of a universal that functions without a concept? How do we distinguish the domain of the judgmental subject, if there is no concept in play to determine this domain?

As daunting as the task of extracting concepts from a universal judgment may sound, it is not altogether impossible. As observed in the *Jäsche Logic*, the universal is not *itself* a concept, but rather a logical function that pertains to how a concept can be used.[29] We see this also in the discussion above. It is not that the universal *is* a concept, but rather, that the universal determines the portion of that which falls under the subject-concept to which the judgment pertains (i.e., whether the judgment is that *all* birds have wings, *some* birds have wings, or just *this* bird has wings). Even in a determinative judgment we can separate the concept from the quantitative determinations of its use. In an aesthetic judgment, consequently, the logical functions must operate so as to determine the pertinent portion of the domain of something that is not designated by a concept. We may take the determinative judgment that *all* birds have wings and analyze it into two parts: the quantitative determination of "all" and the concept of "birds." This allows us to regard the subject-concept as generated through the combination of these two (i.e., universal quantity + concept of birds = "all birds"). This suggests that if the judgment of taste is not grounded on a concept, then the quantitative logical function of universality may still be operative. The difference is that what is universal in a judgment of taste is not a concept, but a feeling. I will argue that the universality of judgments of taste arises from the feeling of a pleasure that is generated by the transcendental arrangement of the faculties and hence able to be universally felt by those who judge. This lends itself well to my layered solution, as it would then indicate that universality without a concept has its origin in the second layer, where no concepts are to be found. Moreover, this supplies further reason to favor my layered reading of the limitation Kant places on the use of concepts in aesthetic judgments, over Guyer's. Guyer suggests that Kant intended the application of concepts to be limited to the constitution of the judgmental subject, but kept out of the predicate.[30] When we read Kant's insistence that universality functions without a concept in conjunction with his first *Critique* description of how universality is typically used in relation to concepts, however, then it becomes evident that universality without concepts will directly affect the subject-concept. To take concepts out of the use of universality cannot mean anything but the removal of concepts from

---

29 "Note: 2. It is a mere tautology to speak of universal or common concepts – a mistake that is grounded in an incorrect division of concepts into universal, particular, and singular. Concepts themselves cannot be so divided, but only their use" (*Jäsche Logic*, § 1, 589).
30 Guyer, "The Harmony of the Faculties Revisited," 184.

the judgmental subject. If we are assuming that only one judgment (that "X is beautiful") is involved in aesthetic judgment, then we find ourselves caught in the disarray precipitated by the preposterous attempt to judge the aesthetic value of an empirical object without concepts, as described in the first chapter. Guyer's answer to this conundrum is to limit the use of concepts to the constitution of the subject. But, a universal without concepts speaks directly to the lack of a subject-concept, thus dismantling Guyer's solution. In my layered solution, however, this same problem would only occur if we took the use of universality without concepts to apply to the first layer of aesthetic judgment, in which the empirical object is cognized. There does not seem to be any good reason to do so, however, particularly because it is only the unconceptualized aesthetic excess that is generated on this layer which begins the aesthetic thread. It makes much more sense to look for the curious concept-independent functioning of the universal as originating in the second layer, where there is no object to be conceptualized.

Since the aesthetic universal is not used to describe the domain of a concept, perhaps what it describes is the functioning of pleasure. A close look at the definition that the second moment generates implies as much: "That is beautiful which pleases universally without a concept."[31] Here, we see that the adverb "universally" modifies that act of pleasing. This is instructive, because it suggests that the pleasure itself is what introduces the universality. Let us read this in conjunction with the following passage:

> First, one must be fully convinced that through the judgment of taste (on the beautiful) one ascribes the satisfaction in an object to everyone, yet without grounding it on a concept.[32]

It is in the ascription of this pleasure to all judging subjects that universality arises. There appear to be two aspects of universality involved here. First, no concept determines the portion of the domain to which the predicate is ascribed without exception, validating the employment of the universal. Rather it is in the pleasing itself that one realizes that this pleasure can be universally ascribed to all judging subjects. How such a thing is possible can be understood in terms of my layered solution. The pleasure first arises through the free-play of the faculties in the second layer. It is here that the universality of the pleasure originates, as one is pleased in a manner that is both internal and without any private inclinations as a basis. Thus, one perceives a transcendental feeling of pleasure through a free play that is enabled by the arrangement of the faculties for cog-

---

31 *Critique of the Power of Judgment*, § 9, 5:219.
32 *Critique of the Power of Judgment*, § 8, 5:214.

nition *in general*. This means that the conditions of the possibility for experience are supplied without being employed, in this case, to actually cognize any *thing*. This is both where aesthetic universality originates and where one feels this universal aesthetic pleasure.

On the third layer, a discursive interpretation of what was perceived without concepts is stimulated, so as to generate the judgment that all who judge will experience this pleasure. A number of commentators remark on this in different ways. Although he does not distinguish it into a separate layer, Guyer also notes that aesthetic judgment will need to reflect upon its pleasure in order to determine its origin, and thus identify whether this is a pure or impure source, "Aesthetic judgment then requires a process of reflection, guided by no determinate empirical concepts of objects, to determine the source of any given feeling of pleasure [...] and thus whether it satisfies the ideal of subjective universal validity—the universal that is sought."[33] Guyer, thus, gives a two-act, but not two-pleasure, interpretation of § 9, in which the process of aesthetic judgment begins with what he calls the aesthetic response. That is, one first engages in the "simple reflection or estimation of an object produci[ing] the harmony of imagination and understanding, thereby producing pleasure."[34] It is this "simple reflection [that] has pleasure as its consequence, and precedes it."[35] It is then the "reflection on that pleasure [that] can result in the judgment that it is universally communicable or valid."[36] Guyer argues that "[i]t is this complex model of reflection which is the 'key to the Critique of taste.'"[37] This is very close to my own layered solution, with a few crucial differences. In terms of my layered solution what Guyer terms the first pleasure of "simple reflection" is a combination of what I describe to occur on the first and second layers, with the additional caveat that in my interpretation it is not the *object* that causes the aesthetic response, but rather the aesthetic excess—that is, the part of the intuition that could not be subsumed under the concept of the object and thus cannot be properly called part of the object (i.e., *Phänomenon*). Guyer's second act of reflectively judging the simple reflection takes place in the third layer of my system, with my stipulation that it is not the reflection on the circumstances of the judging that cause the judgment to be universal; its universality originates in the second layer of the judgment. This is not, however, *articulated* until the reflective discursive activity

---

[33] Paul Guyer, *Kant's Critique of the Power of Judgment: Critical Essays*, (Lanham: Rowman and Littlefield), 33.
[34] Guyer, *Kant and the Claims of Taste*, 154.
[35] Guyer, *Kant and the Claims of Taste*, 159.
[36] Guyer, *Kant and the Claims of Taste*, 159.
[37] Guyer, *Kant and the Claims of Taste*, 159.

of the third layer. This distinction is acknowledged by Guyer, as well, and fuels the idea that there are, thus, two acts of reflection involved. Longuenesse emphasizes that without the reflection upon the "the first-order pleasure we take in the mutual enlivening of imagination and understanding" to determine that "the first-order pleasure it elicits, *could* and *ought to* be shared by all" we would not have the requisite "aesthetic pleasure of reflection."[38] Thus, she too identifies reflection upon the pleasure as a critical component of aesthetic judgment.

I will employ my layered structure to show that the third, discursive layer is where we find the *articulation*, but not the source, of aesthetic judgment's universality.[39] It is not discursive, logical reasoning that *grounds* the subjectively universal aesthetic pleasure. It is rather the non-discursive perception of such pleasure within oneself that gives rise to the discursively articulated judgment that there is such universal pleasure.[40] Let us take a closer look at this universal pleasure's origin in the second layer.

II.A The Curiosity of the Second Moment

The curiosity of the second moment is that the pleasure is grounded on neither internal inclinations nor external demands. This aspect initially surfaced in the first moment when the disinterested nature of aesthetic judgment was compared to judgments of agreeableness and the good. Thus, Kant observes right at the start of the second moment that the second moment's "definition of the beautiful

---

38 Longuenesse, "Kant's Leading Thread in the Analytic of the Beautiful," 207.
39 It is important not to lose sight of the crucial distinction between the nondiscursive source and the discursive articulation to which reflection on the source leads. Something that is not supposed to be a concept presents us with a certain difficulty, as we still need to form some concept of it in order to treat it philosophically. This problem is not unique to the third *Critique*, as is evidenced in the strange moment in the first *Critique* where Kant, in the midst of explaining that space is the *form* of intuition of outer sense, suddenly refers to it as a concept in the title of section three "Transcendental expositions of the concept of space" (*The Critique of Pure Reason*, A25/B40). This odd title does not signify that Kant was suddenly overtaken by misgivings about whether space is a concept. Rather it results from the fact that we must form a concept of space as an intuition in order to think about it philosophically. Likewise the transcendental arrangement of the faculties, which serves of the second-layer source of the universality of the judgment of taste, is nondiscursive, although the third-layer claim to universality it legitimates is.
40 The universality that arises is an aesthetic, and not logical, quantity. A logical quantity would be judged by transforming the aesthetic feeling "into a concept" through "the comparison of many singular" judgments, whereas the aesthetic quantity remains grounded on a feeling (*Critique of the Power of Judgment*,§ 8, 5:215).

can be deduced from the previous explanation of it as an object of satisfaction without any interest."⁴¹ There is no necessity involved in aesthetic judgment, neither in the form of private inclination (as in the agreeable), nor in the form of a command of the moral law (as in the good). This leaves one completely free regarding aesthetic satisfaction, but what is such freedom to mean? In the second *Critique* Kant writes of,

> a *comparative* concept of freedom (according to which that is sometimes called a free effect, the determining natural ground of which lies *within* the acting being, e. g., that which a projectile accomplishes when it is in free motion, in which case one uses the word "freedom" because while it is in flight it is not impelled from without; or as we also call the motion of a clock a free motion because it moves the hands itself, which therefore do not need to be pushed externally; in the same way the actions of the human being, although they are necessary by their determining grounds which preceded them in time, are yet called free because the actions are caused from within, by representations produced by our own powers, whereby desires are evoked on occasion of circumstances and hence actions are produced at our own discretion).⁴²

Although Kant discounts this as an inadequate explanation of human freedom in moral action, it does highlight how the identification of something as originating within the subject, rather than without, exhibits a certain sort of freedom. What is interesting in the case of pure aesthetic judgment, is that this freedom from external forces *also* entails an internal freedom from private inclinations, so that in contradistinction to the feeble account of freedom in human action, above, pure aesthetic pleasure cannot be understood as "caused from within, by representations produced by our own powers,"⁴³ because an aesthetic judgment that "immediately depend[s] on the representation through which the object is given,"⁴⁴ in this manner, "would be none other than mere agreeableness [...] and hence by its very nature could have only private validity."⁴⁵ Thus, "the person making the [pure aesthetic] judgment feels himself completely free with regard to the satisfaction that he devotes to the object," as he "cannot discover as grounds of the satisfaction any private conditions pertaining to his subject alone."⁴⁶

---

41 *Critique of the Power of Judgment*,§ 6, 5:211.
42 *Critique of Practical Judgment*, 5:96.
43 *Critique of Practical Judgment*, 5:96.
44 *Critique of the Power of Judgment*,§ 9, 5:217.
45 *Critique of the Power of Judgment*,§ 9, 5:217.
46 *Critique of the Power of Judgment*,§ 6, 5:211.

This raises the question: What could allow the satisfaction to occur so that it is not externally forced, feels internally free and yet strikes one as universal? This curious amalgam is explained by the generation of this pleasure through the free-play of the faculties enabled by their transcendental arrangement. We see this in passages such as the following,

> the determining ground of the judgment on this universal communicability of the representation [...] can be nothing other than the state of mind that is encountered in the relation of the powers of representation to each other insofar as they relate to a given representation to cognition in general [...]. Thus the state of mind in this representation must be that of a feeling of the free play of the powers of representation in a given representation for a cognition in general.[47]

Thus, it pertains to something that is *within* a person, but at the same time not a private, individually conditioned matter. Rather, since it manifests in the way that the faculties of mind relate to provide the conditions for the possibility of experience, it is something universal to all who judge.

The universal ascription of a response based upon the constitution of our cognitive faculties can be illustrated through an analogy to the biologically determined shivering response that humans have to cold weather. As warm blooded mammals, we need to keep our blood warm despite external temperatures. Thus our bodies are equipped with a shivering response:

> When muscles need to create ATP, their only energy source, they combine glucose with oxygen. This reaction also creates heat as a by-product. The body uses this heat to maintain normal body temperature. When the temperature of the body drops below normal, the brain signals the muscles to contract rapidly—what we perceive as shivering. The heat generated by these rapid muscle contractions helps to raise or at least stabilize body temperature.[48]

Although it is an external condition (the cold) that triggers this response, the response itself is not *forced* from the outside, even though it responds to external stimuli. That is, in shivering, one is not obeying the laws of an external force, or letting an external force command one's movements. The subconscious "decision" to shiver is internal, although the identification of the source of this "decision" is complicated, because one does not intentionally decide to shiver, so as to protect the warmth of one's vital organs. Thus, there is not any internal,

---

[47] *Critique of the Power of Judgment*,§ 9, 5:217.
[48] The Muscular System. (12 August, 2015). Retrieved from http://www.encyclopedia.com/doc/1G2-3437000017.html.

private ground upon which one decides to shiver, and moreover, all humans have a shiver response. In this regard, the shiver response can function as an illustrative analogy by representing something that is universally seen in humans due to an arrangement inherent to our biological systems.

Similar to how we, warm-blooded creatures, shiver to protect the warmth of our bodies, as judging subjects who are equipped with the transcendental arrangement of the cognitive faculties requisite for the conditions for the possibility of experience, an unconceptualizable intuitional aesthetic excess can stimulate these faculties, in their the proportional relationship, throwing them into the sort of free-play that will generate a universal aesthetic pleasure.[49] Thus, just as each living human body holds the condition for the possibility of shivering, so too does the mind of each judging human[50] subject hold the conditions for the possibility of aesthetic pleasure.[51] The exercise of this capacity, however, is

---

49 Kant describes this as: "A representation which, though singular and without comparison to others, nevertheless is in agreement with the conditions of universality, an agreement that constitutes the business of the understanding in general, brings the faculties of cognition into the well-proportioned disposition that we require for all cognition and hence also regard as valid for everyone (for every human being) who is determined to judge by means of understanding and sense in combination." (*Critique of the Power of Judgment*, § 9, 5:219). In aesthetic judgments this proportion "is optimal for the animation of both powers of the mind (the one through the other) with respect to cognition (of given objects) in general" (*Ibid*, § 21, 5:239–40). Melissa Zinkin remarks on the role that proportionality plays in aesthetic judgment: "When the cognitive powers are in a certain 'optimal' relationship, we have cognition. And when they are in a relationship with a different proportion of activity, this produces a judgment of taste. This proportion [...] occurs when the object given to the mind is one that is intuited by the imagination in an intensive form. The *sensus communis* is the faculty that makes possible the feeling of our mental state whatever the proportion of the relationship between the faculties. However, its capacity to make sensible this 'quickened' state of mind is the essential feature of the *sensus communis* and what explains its role as the necessary condition for universal communicability of judgments of taste" (Zinkin, "Intensive Magnitudes and the Normativity of Taste," 158).
50 Kant picks out aesthetic judgment as uniquely human, because it requires that the judging subject be both a sensible and intellectual creature: "Agreeableness is also valid for nonrational animals; beauty is valid only for human beings, i.e., animal but also rational beings, but not merely as the latter (e.g., spirits), rather as beings who are at the same time animal; the good, however, is valid for every rational being in general; a proposition which can receive its complete justification and explanation only in the sequel" (*Critique of the Power of Judgment*, § 5, 5:210).
51 Here one might use this parallel to object that both in the case of the biological shiver response and aesthetic pleasure these only hold with general, and not universal, validity. There are things that can go wrong with a particular individual's system, such as the build up of lactic acid in the muscles to the point where they stop working. This brings up the question of whether similar sorts of things could go wrong with the transcendental arrangement of the faculties so as

characterized by a curious freedom of the faculties to function entirely unencumbered, forced neither from without, nor from within. Rather they are *stimulated* from without, and their activity is *savored* from within, for the very arrangement of properly functioning faculties allows for this pleasure. And as such, this pleasure is universally valid for "those who judge."[52]

II.B The Peculiar Intertwinement of Quantitative Functions in Aesthetic Judging: Singularity Equated with Universality in Aesthetic Judgment

When investigating the first *Critique*'s discussion of the logical functions of quantity, above, we found that a certain equation can be made between the exceptionless application of the predicate to all that falls under the domain of a universal concept and the exceptionless application of the predicate to all that falls under a domainless singular concept. We are now at the point in our analysis where this can be applied to the singular aesthetic judgment that, nonetheless, has universal validity.

One of the peculiarities of aesthetic judgment is that both the judging subject and the object judged must be singular.[53] The judgment is related to an empirical object that has "no domain."[54] As a consequence of the empirical object's

---

to interfere with aesthetic pleasure. The suspicion that such problems could arise might be supported by aesthetic disagreement. Although the biological analogy is helpful for illustrating the universal origin of aesthetic pleasure, the issue of aesthetic disagreement involves nuances that do not find a place in the analogy. Whereas there may be unproblematic agreement about what external conditions elicit a shiver response in humans, the identification of which aesthetic objects ought to occasion a judgment of beauty is fraught with contention. At the end of this chapter I say a few words about how such disagreement may arise.

52 *Critique of the Power of Judgment*, § 8, 5:215.
53 "One wants to submit the object to his own eyes, just as if his satisfaction depended on sensation [...]" (*Critique of the Power of Judgment*, § 8, 5:216).
54 In the Introduction, Kant remarks that "empirical concepts do indeed have their territory [*Boden*] in nature, as the set of all object of sense, but no domain [*Gebiet*] (only their residence [*Aufenthalt*], *domicilium*); because they are, to be sure, lawfully generated, but are not legislative, rather the rules grounded on them are empirical, hence contingent" (*Critique of the Power of Judgment*, Introduction, § II, 5:174). Makkreel elaborates on this passage: "Nature as experienced by us can be said to be our territory [*Boden*]. This territory [*Boden*] of nature is a *domain* [*Gebiet*] to the extent that the concepts legislate to it. Categorial concepts such as *causality* have their domain [*Gebiet*] in nature because they necessarily apply to it. Empirical concepts simply have their *abode* [*Aufenthalt*] in nature because we have derived them from what we contingently find there" (Makkreel, "Reflection, Reflective Judgment, and Aesthetic Exemplarity," 228). Although aesthetic judgment does not engage with the part of the empirical object that

singularity, the internal validity of its judgment normally would not imply the validity of any further judgment—because when considered "with respect to the quantity it has in comparison with other cognitions," judgments of the singular and of the generally valid are to be starkly distinguished.[55] Aesthetic judgment does not, however, remain mired in singularity. The second layer concerns the faculties in general and no singular object, so that the first layer's inability to fully cognize the intuitional excess that is given with a singular empirical object triggers a transcendental reaction in the singular judger. It is when the singular and universal are regarded only in relation to their "internal validity" that they coincide by virtue of functioning without exception. The properly aesthetic, second layer is merely concerned with the harmonious free play of the faculties in a transcendental manner, without the involvement of concepts and hence no cognition through concepts. Thus, on this layer the singular inner perception of the singular judging subject intrinsically relates to nothing beyond its own inner validity. Indeed, since there is no *Phänomen* present on this layer, there are no concepts in play to have a domain. Hence, this layer ought to be regarded as a key instance where the universal and singular functions converge. Within this layer, no comparison between the transcendental free play and other cognitions is appropriate. Perception of pleasure arising in the harmonious free play of the faculties is simultaneously a singular pleasure of this singular judging subject and a pleasure that must arise in all singular judging subjects.[56]

On the first and third layers, however, concepts *are* involved. The discursive acts of judging in these layers can, thus, be meaningfully compared to other cognitions. On the first layer such a comparison would consider the singular empirical aesthetic object as cognized within the context of other empirical objects.[57]

---

has been conceptualized, it makes sense for our reading that empirical concepts have no domain [*Gebiet*], meaning that they "are not legislative," because the empirical is not imbued with the universality and necessity that can be found in the two domains of our cognitive faculty, "that of the concepts of nature and that of the concept of freedom," which are "*a priori* legislative" (*Ibid.*). In the *Jäsche Logic* this was communicated through the singular having no sphere [*Sphäre*], in the first *Critique* this was put into the terms of the singular having no domain [*Umfang*]. Thus, Kant's third *Critique* remark about empirical concepts does put this into slightly different terminology [*Gebiet*], however the point appears to be the same. The singular empirical object that occasions the aesthetic judgment has no domain [*Umfang*], and even its empirical concept lacks a *Gebiet*, denying it legislative power.

55 *Critique of Pure Judgment*, A71/B96.
56 "Must" should here be read with a hortatory tone conveying the subjective, not objective, nature of both the universality and necessity to which pure aesthetic judgments make claim.
57 This comparison with other cognitions provides for the sort of specificity that we find in aesthetic judgments. Guyer remarks on this, emphasizing how the verdict on something's aesthetic

On the third layer, the articulation of aesthetic judgment's subjective universality enters into the communicative context of discursive reflection on one's feelings. Hence, on the third layer, the judgments of others are taken into consideration and one may even engage in a discussion of one's feeling-response to the aesthetic object with others. Thus, on the first and third layers the aesthetic judging is naturally considered "as cognition in general, with respect to the quantity it has in comparison with other cognitions," and not merely "with respect to its internal validity."[58] For this reason the universal and singular are not to be equated on these layers, as there is an important difference between the judgment that "this rose is beautiful" and that "all roses are beautiful."

Indeed, Kant belabors this very point, so as to emphasize the difference between aesthetic judgments and the logical judgments that can be based upon them.[59] In order to differentiate the two, we ought not to merely consider whether things that allow for exception are admitted into the domain of the subject-concept. Rather, it is of the utmost importance that there is no other empirical object to which the judgment pertains than the singular one that the singular judger has before her. That is to say, no logically implied empirical object whose empirical intuition is not being given to the judging subject at that very moment can be aesthetically judged. Thus the singular object, constituted as an object of experience on the first layer, *remains* the only singular object that may be judged beautiful on the third.

II.C The Singular Judging Subject

The singularity of the *judging subject*, however, is more nuanced and complicated—as it is the judger's singularity that allows universality to seep into the structure of aesthetic judgment, so that the quantity of the judgment ultimately splits off onto two different routes in the third layer. On the one hand, we have the

---

value takes the form, "'This F is beautiful': this hummingbird, this sunset, this painting, this symphony, this part of the garden (but not the other), this façade of the building (but not its other elevations), or the public space of this hotel (but not its guest rooms)" (Guyer, "The Harmony of the Faculties Revisited," 179–180).

58 *Critique of Pure Judgment*, A71/B96.

59 "[B]y means of a judgment of taste I declare the rose that I am gazing at to be beautiful. By contrast, the judgment that arises from the comparison of many singular ones, that roses in general are beautiful, is no longer pronounced merely as an aesthetic judgment, but as an aesthetically grounded logical judgment" (*Critique of the Power of Judgment*, § 8, 5:215).

route of the object, which remains stubbornly singular.⁶⁰ On the other hand, we have the route of the singular judging subject, which finds a connection to the class of judging subjects through the subjective universality that emerges, so that "the judgment of taste carries with it an aesthetic quantity of universality, i.e., validity for everyone."⁶¹

Let us investigate how the equation of universal and singular on the second layer affects the judgments of the third. When the third layer is incited into thinking about the activity of the second, it is, on the one hand, still a judgment about the singular empirical object that generated the aesthetic excess, which occasioned a transcendental, aesthetic pleasure.⁶² On the other hand, however, the

---

60 "Hence, all judgments of taste are also singular judgments, since they combine their predicate of satisfaction not with a concept but with a given singular empirical representation" (*Critique of the Power of Judgment*, § 37, 5:289).

61 *Critique of the Power of Judgment*, § 8, 5:215.

62 One may wonder how such a concept-independent intuitional excess could obtain for poetry, since poetry uses a discursive medium. Kant speaks to this point in a footnote, where he writes that "The intuitive in cognition must be contrasted to the discursive (not the symbolic). Now the former is either **schematic**, by means of **demonstration**, or **symbolic**, as a representation based on mere **analogy**" (*Critique of the Power of Judgment*, § 59, 5:352). Even though poetry makes use of concepts to present its symbols, what is stirred up by this symbolic language is much more than what is conceptually denoted. The poem functions by "combin[ing] spirit with the mere letter of language" (*Critique of the Power of Judgment*, § 49, 5:315). Kant explains this, writing: "When the great king expressed himself in one of his poems thus: "Let us depart from life without grumbling and without regretting anything, leaving the world behind us replete with good deeds. Thus does the sun, after it has completed its daily course, still spread a gentle light across the heavens; and the last rays that it sends forth into the sky are its last sighs for the well-being of the world," he animates his idea of reason of a cosmopolitan disposition even at the end of life by means of an attribute that the imagination (in the recollection of everything agreeable in a beautiful summer day, drawn to a close, which a bright evening calls to mind) associates with that representation, and which arouses a multitude of sensations and supplementary representations for which no expression is found. Conversely, even an intellectual concept can serve as the attribute of a representation of sense, and so animate the latter by means of the idea of the supersensible; but only insofar as the aesthetic, which is subjectively attached to the consciousness of the latter, is used to this end [...]. In a word, the aesthetic idea is a representation of the imagination, associated with a given concept, which is combined with such a manifold of partial representations in the free use of the imagination that no expression designating a determinate concept can be found for it, which therefore allows the addition to a concept of much that is unnamable, the feeling of which animates the cognitive faculties and combines spirit with the mere letter of language" (*Ibid.*). Thus, in experiencing a poem one is receptive to spirit, the intellectual concepts in the poem "serve as the attribute of a representation of sense" (*Ibid.*). The "representation of sense" that the poem communicates is not reducible to the concepts that the poem uses, nor is it subsumable under the concepts the poem inspires in the judging subject. Brandt concurs, writing "Poems use concepts to create a surplus of meaning that

transcendental free play of the faculties in which the second layer's activity of judging inheres is the direct source of aesthetic pleasure. The latter is something we should be able to expect from all people insofar as the,

> subjective conditions of the possibility of a cognition in general, and the proportion of these cognitive faculties that is required for taste is also requisite for the common and healthy understanding that one may presuppose in everyone.[63]

This provides for the tension in Kant's account, which states on the one hand that "[i]n regard to logical quantity, all judgments of taste are singular judgments," while on the other hand "the judgment of taste carries with it an aesthetic quantity of universality."[64] Thus, the way that our faculties respond to what I have been calling "aesthetic excess" is a universal feature of judging human subjects, and it is this that provides the grounds for the subjective universality of aesthetic judgment.[65] This subjectivity is not simply to temper the universality

---

goes beyond the concepts, themselves" (Brandt, "Zur Logik des ästhetischen Urteils," 240). This active work of the subject of conceptually grasping after that which has been aesthetically judged is not what grounds the aesthetic judgment. The aesthetic judgment begins with the reception of an intuitional excess, even if this excess is encountered through the lines of a poem. The intuitional excess occasions a harmonious free play of the faculties. Ultimately, the understanding attempts to make conceptual sense of the second layer feeling. Although it cannot conceptually subsume the intuition, it is inspired by the second layer aesthetic judging to generate meaningful ideas.

63 *Critique of the Power of Judgment*, § 39, 5:292–3.
64 *Critique of the Power of Judgment*, § 8, 5:215.
65 One might object that this does not cohere with Kant's admission that there are people who somehow do not manifest the full response to beauty, as when he asserts that "to take an immediate interest in the beauty of nature (not merely to have taste in order to judge it) is always a mark of a good soul, and that if this interest is habitual, it at least indicates a disposition of the mind that is favorable to the moral feeling, if it is gladly combined with the viewing of nature" (*Critique of the Power of Judgment*, § 42, 5:298–9). For those who take such an interest we may "presuppose in him a beautiful soul" (*Ibid.* 5:300). In contrast, "we consider coarse and ignoble the thinking of those who have no feeling for beautiful nature (for this is what we call the receptivity to an interest in its contemplation) [...]" (*Critique of the Power of Judgment*, § 42, 5:302). To make sense of this difference between how judging subjects respond to beautiful nature, we must take notice of the word "interest." The interest discussed here is intellective, stirring up moral feelings. As such, it is not intrinsic to the workings of aesthetic judgment. The "beautiful soul" or alternatively "coarseness" evidenced in the judging subject's response has to do with how the third layer makes discursive sense out of the second layer feeling of transcendental aesthetic pleasure. Thus, a lack of intellectual interest in beautiful nature does not necessarily indicate that the second layer response failed to obtain, but rather that there are differences in how adept people are at glimpsing a higher level significance in beauty. Only when such significance is recognized does the "affinity with moral feeling" ensue (*Ibid.*, 5:301). Kant writes: "But,

of the judgment, but even more so to indicate its source—or, rather, to reveal what is universal about the judgment, so that it may "extend [...] over the whole sphere of those who judge."⁶⁶ Namely, it shows that what is universal about this judgment does not concern the object of the judgment, but rather the judging subject.

II.D Universal Communicability

Given Kant's characterization of aesthetic judgment as not cognitive,⁶⁷ the idea that it could be universally communicable is puzzling, as "[n]othing [...] can be universally communicated except cognition and representation so far as it belongs to cognition."⁶⁸ Communication functions by means of cognitions that are

---

first, this immediate interest in the beautiful in nature is not actually common, but belongs only to those whose thinking is either already trained to the good or receptive to such training; and then, even without clear, subtle, and deliberate reflection, the analogy between the pure judgment of taste, which, without depending on any sort of interest, allows a pleasure to be felt and at the same time to be represented *a priori* as proper for mankind in general, and the moral judgment, which does the same thing on the basis of concepts, leads to an equally immediate interest in the object of the former as in that of the latter – only the former is a free interest, the latter on grounded on objective laws" (*Ibid.*, 5:301). This final contrast between aesthetic pleasure's "free interest" and moral judgment's interest as "grounded on objective laws" indicates that the further "moral feeing" and "intellectual interest" arise from aesthetic judgment, without being an intrinsic part of its internal functioning. In this way they represent the intellectual counterpart to the social "empirical interest" one takes in the beautiful, as discussed in the preceding section, § 41. Hence, it is possible for one to respond to aesthetic excess with transcendental aesthetic pleasure, while failing to recognize what greater intellectual and moral significance could be made out of this.

66 *Critique of the Power of Judgment*, § 8, 5:215.
67 "If, then, the form of a given object in empirical intuition is so constituted that the apprehension of its manifold in the imagination agrees with the presentation of a concept of the understanding (though which concept be undetermined), then in the mere reflection understanding and imagination mutually agree for the advancement of their business, and the object will be perceived as purposive merely for the power of judgment, hence the purposiveness itself will be considered as merely subjective; for which, further, no determinate concept of the object at all is required nor is one thereby generated, and *the judgment itself is not a cognitive judgment*. – Such a judgment is called an aesthetic judgment of reflection" (*Critique of the Power of Judgment*, First Introduction, § VII, 20:221, emphasis added).
68 *Critique of the Power of Judgment*, § 9, 5:217. The way that *ordinary empirical* judgments are universally communicable is not puzzling, because the communication of an empirical object's shape and size depends upon a determination of that object through concepts and, even more fundamentally, through the categories a priori which thus provide for its universal cognizability.

articulated through the use of discursive concepts. That which is to be universally communicated from an aesthetic judgment, however, does not concern concepts at all. It is a feeling. Moreover, it would be decidedly wrong to imagine that this satisfaction could be discursively shared with the world of judgers through the communication of concepts, for "there is no transition from concepts to the feeling of pleasure or displeasure."[69]

In a certain sense, this means that aesthetic judgment involves a communication of the incommunicable. Claiming that a non-conceptual feeling can be communicated will thus have to mean something quite different than what we typically mean when we talk about communication.[70] That is, the feeling cannot be translated into concepts and an understanding of it cannot be transmitted from one person to another through discourse. For aesthetic judgment, the conceptual terms of the judgment cannot be responsible for communicability, because it is not knowledge of a feeling, but the feeling *itself* that is communicable. Others must submit the object to their own senses in order to *feel* for themselves the satisfaction communicated. And, thus, in order to understand the universal communicability of aesthetic judgments we must find an avenue for one to "assume his feeling to be universally communicable, even without the mediation of concepts."[71]

Thus, it is not a conceptualized judgment of some object that is communicated in aesthetic judgment, because "the determining ground of the judgment on this universal communicability of the representation is to be conceived merely subjectively, namely without a concept of the object."[72] Rather, what is communicated must be "the state of mind that is encountered in the relation of the pow-

---

69 *Critique of the Power of Judgment*, § 6, 5:211.
70 The same issue of universal communicability does not arise for the private feelings of agreeableness, because they are mired in singularity, making no claims to universality. Admittedly, we expect to be able to use conceptual language to allow others to understand how we feel, but this is not the sort of universal communicability of which Kant writes in the second moment of aesthetic judgment. When one successfully describes one's private feelings to another person, then the other person conceptually *understands* what is felt, but there is no transcendental structure in place to suggest the other person *must* be *able to feel* the feelings herself, neither through this understanding, nor if she actually found herself placed in a situation that stirs up these feelings in others. The universal communicability of aesthetic judgment, however, does involve the expectation that others will confirm one's own feeling, not by understanding it, but by *feeling* it themselves *when* beholding that which one has judged to be beautiful. Whether the same judgment of *agreeableness* will arise in different judgers, however, is dependent upon empirical similarities, in either their physical or psychological make up, if not both. Thus, only pure aesthetic judgments of taste carry subjective universality.
71 *Critique of the Power of Judgment*, § 39, 5:293.
72 *Critique of the Power of Judgment*, § 9, 5:217.

ers of representation to each other insofar as they relate a given representation to cognition in general."[73] This state of mind is "that of a feeling of the free play of the powers of representation in a given representation for a cognition in general."[74] Thus it concerns the transcendental operation of the faculties and not the cognition of the singular object presented in the first layer, for such a free play can only be achieved if "no determinate concept restricts [the faculties] to a particular rule of cognition."[75] It is this identification of the origin of aesthetic pleasure in the transcendental arrangement of the faculties, "the common ground, deeply buried in all human beings,"[76] that legitimates its subjective universality.

It is not that we communicate the pleasure of an aesthetic judgment through the discursive verbal attempts we make to discuss this pleasure, but rather that the perception of the pleasure is already there in anyone who has the transcendental arrangement of the faculties required as the conditions for the possibility of experience. It is "consequently universally communicable, just as any determinate cognition is, which still always rests on that relation as its subjective condition."[77] Thus, Kant's theory of the universal communicability of aesthetic judgment can be understood to involve two steps. In the first step, he is claiming that humans universally have the capacity to judge beauty, which generates pure aesthetic pleasure through the transcendental arrangement of the faculties. The second step adds the idea of communicability to this universality, which is not to say that the aesthetic pleasure can be communicated through discourse, but that one has a further capacity to recognize that the feelings of aesthetic pleasure do not originate in anything particular to the individual subject and thus must resonate with the feelings of others:

> Thus it is not the pleasure but the universal validity of this pleasure perceived in the mind as connected with the mere judging of an object that is represented in a judgment of taste as a universal rule for the power of judgment, valid for everyone.[78]

This lends a certain air of mystery to the communicability of aesthetic judgment. It is not that words communicate the feeling from one person to another. Rather communication only provides the limited service of enabling one to recognize signs in others of the same intimately individual aesthetic perception, that

---

73 *Critique of the Power of Judgment*, § 9, 5:217.
74 *Critique of the Power of Judgment*, § 9, 5:217.
75 *Critique of the Power of Judgment*, § 9, 5:217.
76 *Critique of the Power of Judgment*, § 17, 5:232.
77 *Critique of the Power of Judgment*, § 9, 5:218.
78 *Critique of the Power of Judgment*, § 32, 5:289.

was perceived in the depths of one's own faculties of mind.[79] Here "the representation [is] communicated, not as thought, but as the inner feeling of a purposive state of mind."[80]

Admittedly, disagreement often arises when aesthetic value is to be assigned to a specific object, but rather than undermine Kant's point, this can also support his argument. In order for such disagreement to be a disagreement that is actually about *aesthetics*, we must have a foundational agreement about what an aesthetic judgment is and all take such a judgment to be actually possible. Thus, people,

> do not find themselves in conflict over the possibility of such a claim, but only find it impossible to agree on the correct application of this faculty in particular cases.[81]

Thus, the agreement upon which aesthetic disagreement is predicated both enables the feeling to be universally communicable, and assumes that the capacity to perceive aesthetic pleasure is already transcendentally in place through the arrangement of our faculties. The communication of pure aesthetic judgment does not *institute* the capacity for such a judgment, for how could it? The capacity to judge aesthetically is not something learned as are mathematical rules, historical facts, or even linguistic terms, for these are all forms of knowledge acquired through concepts. Aesthetic judgment can only be trained and honed, which is done by practicing aesthetic judging with exemplary models of taste.[82] The capacity for aesthetic judgment must, however, already be there. It

---

79 Ameriks' reading is suggestive of such an account of communicability, insofar as he submits that "Kant probably holds the traditional theory that communication involves the having of matching subjective states. On this theory I understand you when the (inner) ideas I have are appropriately like the ones you have" (Ameriks, "How to Save Kant's Deduction of Taste," 298).
80 *Critique of the Power of Judgment*, § 40, 5:296. The purposiveness of aesthetic judgments will be the main topic of the next chapter.
81 *Critique of the Power of Judgment*, § 8, 5:214.
82 "Hence some products of taste are regarded as exemplary – not as if taste could be acquired by imitating others. For taste must be a faculty of one's own; however, whoever imitates a model certainly shows, so far as he gets it right, a skill, but he shows taste only insofar as he can judge this model himself" (*Critique of the Power of Judgment*, § 17, 5:232); "Succession, related to a precedent, not imitation, is the correct expression for any influence that the products of an exemplary author can have on others, which means no more than to create from the same sources from which the latter created, and to learn from one's predecessor only the manner of conducting oneself in so doing. But among all the faculties and talents, taste is precisely the one which, because its judgment is not determinable by means of concepts and precepts, is most in need of the examples of what in the progress of culture has longest enjoyed approval if it is not quickly

is the existence of this capacity that allows aesthetic pleasure to be universally communicable—its communicability not depending upon conceptual transmission, but rather signifying a recognition that, although we can neither feel the pleasure of *others*, nor encapsulate *our own* in a concept, when speaking of beauty we all refer to that same intimately individual perception of transcendental pleasure.

II.E Section 9

Kant hails the question that guides § 9 as the "key to the critique of taste."[83] The question is "whether in the judgment of taste the feeling of pleasure precedes the judging of the object or the latter precedes the former."[84] Although, from the outset, one might wonder why he places the discussion of this question right after his discussion of aesthetic judgment's universal communicability. This will become apparent through the presentation of my reading of § 9, which will take a two-pleasure interpretive route, identifying each pleasure as arising on a different layer.[85]

To answer § 9's question incorrectly would be to relate pleasure and judging in the wrong way. This would lead us into a contradictory account of aesthetic judgment, because "[i]f the pleasure in the given object came first, and only its universal communicability were to be attributed in the judgment of taste to the representation of the object" then we would end up with "[nothing] other than mere agreeableness in sensation."[86] This would not align with what we expect from a pure aesthetic judgment, because it would yield "only private validity" and not the subjective universal validity peculiar to judgments of taste.[87] Moreover, it would "depend on the representation through which the object is given."[88] This means that the pleasure would arise as a direct response to the representation of the object, however, the analysis thus far, along with my layered interpretation, has suggested that the representation is not directly respon-

---

to fall back into barbarism and sink back into the crudity of its first attempts" (*Critique of the Power of Judgment*, § 32, 5:283).
[83] *Critique of the Power of Judgment*, § 9, 5:216.
[84] *Critique of the Power of Judgment*, § 8, 5:216.
[85] Longuenesse also takes a two-pleasure reading, see: Longuenesse, "Kant's Leading Thread in the Analytic of the Beautiful," 207.
[86] *Critique of the Power of Judgment*, § 9, 5:217.
[87] *Critique of the Power of Judgment*, § 9, 5:217.
[88] *Critique of the Power of Judgment*, § 9, 5:217.

sible for pure aesthetic pleasure. More precisely, it is not what is represented (i.e. the representation constituted as an object of experience on the first layer), but rather that which is unrepresentable—the aesthetic excess that cannot be constituted into an empirical object—that triggers the faculties into a harmonious freeplay. Thus, the determinate representation is only indirectly involved insofar as it provides the occasion, but the harmony of the faculties is what produces the aesthetic pleasure that grounds the judgment.

It is notoriously difficult to discern Kant's answer to the question posed in § 9.[89] On the one hand, given the need to keep pure and impure judgments of taste separate, aesthetic pleasure cannot be the basis of the judgment. On the other hand, there does seem to be a judgment that is grounded on the feeling of aesthetic pleasure. My layered solution is helpful in making sense of this conundrum, suggesting a two pleasure reading in which one pleasure takes place on the second layer and the other on the third.

This works out in the following manner. On the first layer, the empirical object is constituted and the aesthetic excess escapes this constitution, stimulating the faculties into a second layer free play. This free play of the second layer is neither the cognition of an object, nor constitution of a representation. It is not even a response to the *Phänomen* constituted on the first layer, because that to which it actually responds is what escaped from being recognized in a concept on that layer. This free play generates transcendental pleasure. And this pleasure, generated from the judging activity of the second layer, inspires the judgments carried out on the third layer. It is on this third layer that one reflects upon the aesthetic pleasure, recognizing that although the pleasure is felt in an intimately private way, there are no private conditions causing one to feel this pleasure, and thus the pleasure is expected to be universally perceived. In this way, the first pleasure is an effect of the second layer judging and also the cause of the third layer judgment, which ascribes this pleasure to all who judge. It is from this third layer judgment about the subjective universal validity of aesthetic judging that the second pleasure emanates. Kant writes:

> That being able to communicate one's state of mind, even if only with regard to the faculties of cognition, carries a pleasure with it, could easily be established (empirically and psychologically) from the natural tendency of human beings to sociability.[90]

---

[89] See: Allison, *Kant's Theory of Taste: A Reading of the Critique of Aesthetic Judgment*, 110–118; Hannah Ginsborg, "On the Key to Kant's Critique of Taste," *Pacific Philosophical Quarterly* 72, (1991): 290–313; Guyer, *Kant and the Claims of Taste*, 151–160.
[90] *Critique of the Power of Judgment*, § 9, 5:218.

This is the further pleasure, which comes from judging the first pleasure of aesthetic judging to be universal. It stems from the universal communicability of aesthetic judgment, which thus needed to be clarified before the question of the relation between judging and pleasure could be taken up, thus explaining Kant's decision to wait until the second moment to discuss it.

Pure aesthetic judgment is special in its ability to recognize an intimately individual perception as held in common with others—allowing us, in turn, to feel that we find resonance with others in the intimate depths of our own subjectivity.[91] This is a connection that goes beyond any sort of superficial empirical agreement, indicating that we really do share a transcendental similarity in the arrangement of our faculties, which connects us with others in a much more intimate manner, bringing us close to confirming that our intimate experience of the world can be shared—a sort of aesthetic answer to solipsistic worries, supplying evidence that others are just as subjectively alive to the world as we find ourselves to be.[92]

---

91 See *Critique of the Power of Judgment*, § 60, 5:355. This important aspect of aesthetic judgment, won through its position as subjective and yet universally communicable, is overlooked by Karl Ameriks who struggles against any reading which would "condemn [aesthetic judgment] to revealing what is merely subjective," and thus, sets out to find a way of ascribing objectivity to it despite acknowledging what he terms "Kant's failure to draw this conclusion explicitly himself" (Ameriks, "Kant and the Objectivity of Taste," 14; 3).

92 This idea also finds expression in our culture at large. For instance, Kazuo Ishiguro's novel *Never Let Me Go*, describes a futuristic world in which human clones are raised to supply replacement organs for (the non-clone) society. Some who disagree with this practice seek to prove the humanity of the clones to be equal to that of the non-clones. They attempt to do so by having the cloned children create art. While living in the boarding school, the cloned children have only an inkling of the reasons behind their art classes. One recalls a teacher told them "that things like pictures, poetry, all that kind of stuff...revealed what you were like inside. She said they revealed your soul" (Kazuo Ishiguro, *Never Let Me Go* [London: Faber and Faber, 2006], 180). Once the children are grown, however, the motivation behind the art classes is finally clarified when some seek out a former teacher, who admits, "We took away your art because we thought it would reveal your souls. Or to put it more finely, we did it to prove you had souls at all" (Ishiguro, *Never Let Me Go*, 260). This echoes the Kantian notion that aesthetic judgment is something both uniquely and intimately human, which cannot be imitated or taught, but rather must spring forth from deep within on its own accord—with only the slight adjustment that what the teachers of Ishiguro's novel called the "soul," Kant would call the transcendental arrangement of the faculties of mind for cognition in general, or, as Christopher Janaway puts it, "a capacity contained in the very fabric of human mentality" (Janaway,"Kant's Aesthetics and the 'Empty Cognitive Stock,'" 69).

III Why Does Aesthetic Judgment Involve the Singular and Universal Instead of the Particular?

Now that an exposition of how the quadrant of quantity relates to aesthetic judgment has been supplied and the curious "universal validity of a singular judgment"[93] explained, let us turn to Paul Guyer's criticism of this moment. In answer to the question why some objects are judged to be beautiful, while others are not, Guyer identifies an operation of particularity at work in aesthetic judgment. I will argue that particularity only relates to aesthetic judgment extrinsically, that is, insofar as Kant is seeking to distinguish the features of aesthetic judgment that allow it to be set apart from other sorts of judgment as a *particular* sort of judgment.[94] As for the logical functions of quantity that are of intrinsic importance to aesthetic judgment, I will demonstrate how the above analysis reveals there to be no place for particularity here. I will then discuss how the emergence of aesthetic disagreement should be understood within Kant's system.

Guyer objects that in the second moment of aesthetic judgment, Kant overlooked the possibility that the singular judgment could apply to a particular group of *some* judgers, instead of to *all*.[95] This arises in the context of considering why "some but not all objects are beautiful."[96] Explaining this appears to leave us with a choice of either contending that all objects are beautiful, or searching for some factor that can introduce particularity. According to Guyer's view, such a factor must be either a characteristic of the object or a characteristic of the act of judging. The problem, as Guyer acknowledges, is that choosing ei-

---

[93] *Critique of the Power of Judgment*, § 31, 5:281.
[94] In this sense Kant neither overlooked the particular, nor sectioned off from it the singular and universal workings of aesthetic judgment. Aesthetic judgment distinguishes itself as a particular sort of judgment by bringing about the "universal validity of a singular judgment" (*Critique of the Power of Judgment*, § 31, 5:281). Thus, it is in the functioning of the singular and universal together in this form of judgment that a particular sort of judgment is generated: i.e. the aesthetic.
[95] Guyer, *Kant and the Claims of Taste*, 295–6. This particularization is one of the threats from which Ameriks seeks to save Kant's Deduction of taste. His strategy for doing so, however, is to identify "special objects or features and not special people or faculties that are primarily responsible for the fact that some experiences are harmonious and others are not" (Ameriks, "How to Save Kant's Deduction of Taste," 299). While this is close to my own view, there is an important distinction. Whereas Ameriks does this by locating in the object a differentiating feature that allows some objects, and not others, to be judged as beautiful, thus transforming Kant's aesthetic theory into something objective (i.e. combined in the idea of the object), my solution involves the part of the intuition that cannot be subsumed under a concept of the object and thus never becomes part of the object, hence saving the *subjectivity* of Kant's judgments of taste.
[96] Guyer, *Kant and the Claims of Taste*, 295.

III Why Does Aesthetic Judgment Involve the Singular and Universal Instead — 205

ther factor comes at a price. If it is a characteristic of the object, then the judgment loses its subjectivity. If it is a characteristic of the act of judging, then aesthetic judgment is not universal, because only some judging subjects are capable of it. Guyer chooses the second, thus sacrificing the universal validity of aesthetic judgment. He suggests that the difference between an object judged to be beautiful and one that is not does not stem from the object itself, but from "a psychological variation in the ease with which the unity of a given multiplicity may be detected."[97] He further elaborates:

> The ease with which any person may detect unity in his manifolds entails that each subject possesses the same facility in the perception of unity as any other. The ease with which any person may detect unity in his manifolds of intuition, or how well adapted any object is to produce the harmony of the faculties in any particular person, it might be contended, raises questions concerning contingent psychological similarities or differences among people [...]. Kant's use of the concept of proportion, then, suggests that his deduction of aesthetic judgment does not depend solely on transcendental principles of epistemology, but also rests on more particular psychological assumptions [...] if a unique ease or facility in synthesis is what is really connoted by Kant's concept of proportion, the difference between aesthetic response and cognition in general may be preserved, but the intersubjective validity of aesthetic response is then not entailed by the general communicability of cognitive capacity itself.[98]

Guyer raises an important question. Can particularity play an intrinsic role in aesthetic judgment for Kant? Building upon the analysis I developed above, I will show that the route through which aesthetic judgment acquires an aesthetic quantity beyond its logical singular quantity is only conducive to acquiring universality and could *not* lead to particularity. The subjective universality of aesthetic judgment has its determining grounds in "the state of mind that is encountered in the relation of the powers of representation to each other."[99]

Let us compare the path taken by judgments of taste to the path that the agreeable takes to acquire a quantity beyond the singular.[100] Idiosyncratic likings can only influence what is found to be agreeable to an individual, and not the way that the faculties relate to each other. Thus, judgments of agreeable-

---

97 Guyer, *Kant and the Claims of Taste*, 296.
98 Guyer, *Kant and the Claims of Taste*, 296–7.
99 *Critique of the Power of Judgment*, § 9, 5: 217.
100 This line of inquiry follows up on Allison's observation that all of the examples Guyer offers of how an aesthetic judgment could hold for only a particular group of people are due to an idiosyncratic characteristic that they share and thus "fall under the general rubric of the agreeable" (Allison, *Kant's Theory of Taste: A Reading of the Critique of Aesthetic Judgment*, 101).

ness are mired in their singularity,[101] at most only able to hope that polling the opinions of others will haphazardly reveal that a particular segment of the population happens to agree. This would send one off looking for empirical verification, "having to **grope** about by means of experience among the judgments of others and first inform himself about their satisfaction or dissatisfaction in the same object."[102] But, Kant makes it clear that aesthetic judgment's claim to universality is so much more than any merely empirically ascertained generality.

As an aesthetic judgment, pure judgments of taste begin with singularity, because concepts provide the domain that is the focus of quantitative logical functions, but since aesthetic judgments are based on a feeling, and not a concept, they must have the logical quantity of the only logical function that has no domain: the singular. It is the logical peculiarity, which allows the singular and universal to be equated when considered only in relation to their internal validity, in combination with the aesthetic peculiarity, according to which judgments of taste originate in the transcendental arrangement of the faculties. That is to say, "it is grounded only on the subjective formal condition of a judgment in general."[103] It is this that allows pure aesthetic judgments to rise above their logical singularity and acquire access to aesthetic universality. Thus, we see that the path taking us out of a singular quantity for pure aesthetic judgments can only bring us to a universal quantity and does not introduce anything that could constitutes a private inclination.[104]

Hence, a particular judgment does not fit the bill on two counts. First, unlike logical singularity and aesthetic universality, the particular does not offer any special way of getting around the use of a concept, for in the particular one requires a concept to distinguish between the portion of the subject to which the

---

[101] "[T]his claim to universal validity so essentially belongs to a judgment by which we declare something to be beautiful that without thinking this it would never occur to anyone to use this expression, rather everything that pleases without a concept would be counted as agreeable, regarding which everyone can be of his own mind, and no one expects assent to his judgments of taste of anyone else, although this is always the case in judgments about beauty" (*Critique of the Power of Judgment*, § 8, 5:214).

[102] *Critique of the Power of Judgment*, § 32, 5:282.

[103] *Critique of the Power of Judgment*, § 35, 5:287.

[104] "For since it is not grounded in any inclination of the subject (nor in any other underlying interest), but rather the person making the judgment feels himself completely free with regard to the satisfaction that he devotes to the object, he cannot discover as grounds of the satisfaction any private conditions, pertaining to his subject alone, and must therefore regard it as grounded in those that he can also presuppose in everyone else; consequently he must believe himself to have grounds for expecting a similar pleasure of everyone" (*Critique of the Power of Judgment*, § 6, 5:211).

III Why Does Aesthetic Judgment Involve the Singular and Universal Instead — 207

judgment pertains and that which is exempt. Second, supposing that this particularization could somehow take place without a concept, there is still no room in Kant's theory of aesthetic judgment for a particularizing inclination that allows "some" who fall under the domain of the judging subject to be affected differently than others.[105] All of the elements involved in the production of pure aesthetic pleasure are those necessary for experience and thus must be assumed to be the same *in all who have experience*.

This can also be put in the terms of the fourth note following the discussion of Quantity in the *Jäsche Logic*. Here particular judgments are described as judgments in which "the subject must be a broader concept [...] than the predicate."[106] If we were to say that: for some judging subjects this tulip is beautiful, then the domain of judging subjects would be broader than the domain of the judging subjects who find this beautiful. But, the pleasure that allows the tulip to be found beautiful is grounded on the transcendental conditions for the possibility of being a judging subject in the first place. Thus, it does not make any sense to think that subjects who meet the criteria to be qualified as judging will not experience the pleasure that is inherent in the act of aesthetic judging, as this merely involves the faculties of cognition entering the harmonious free play of judging without a concept—an activity that is foundational to the faculty of judgment to begin with.[107] Hence, recasting pure aesthetic judgment as particular would mean that there must be some difference between

---

[105] To argue that the "some" are those who empirically do judge a given object in a certain way would destroy the special characteristic that differentiates pure aesthetic judgments from the impure, "one cannot say, 'Everyone has his special taste.' This would be as much as to say that there is no taste at all, i.e., no aesthetic judgment that could make a rightful claim to the assent of everyone" (*Critique of the Power of Judgment*, § 7, 5:213). This would also shift us from an analysis of transcendental philosophy to the sort of empirical investigation that Kant clearly believes to belong to psychology: "So if the concern were to explain how that which we call taste first arose among human beings, why it was these objects rather than others that occupied them and brought about the judgment on beauty under these or those circumstances of place and society, by what causes it could have grown into a luxury, and so on, then the principles for such an explanation would have to be sought for the most part in psychology (by which is always meant in such a case empirical psychology)" (*Critique of the Power of Judgment*, First Introduction, § X 20:237). See also: *Critique of the Power of Judgment*, First Introduction, § X, 20:238; Bk. 1, § 29: General remark on the exposition of aesthetic reflective judgments, 5:277–78; § 39, 5:293.
[106] *Jäsche Logic*, § 21, 599.
[107] Kant tell us that "the state of mind in the free play of the imagination and the understanding" is one in which "they agree with each other as is requisite for a cognition in general" and thus "this subjective relation suited to cognition in general must be valid for everyone" (*Critique of the Power of Judgment*, § 9, 5:218).

those judgers imbued with the transcendental arrangement of the faculties necessary for experience and those who judge aesthetically—and this would involve a substantial rewriting of Kant's theory of aesthetic judgment.

Thus, the fact that people do make judgments of taste drawing differing conclusions about the aesthetic value of the same empirical objects cannot be understood as a violation of pure aesthetic judgment's universal validity. Rather, it would seem that some judgments are made in error. One of Kant's preoccupations throughout the Analytic of the Beautiful has been to differentiate the pure aesthetic judgment of taste from the other evaluative judgments with which it could be confused. Something that is judged to be agreeable or perfect may not be judged to be beautiful, but even if something could be correctly judged to be all three, to judge its beauty is not to judge its perfection, agreeableness, or goodness.[108] The judging activity leading to these differing evaluations is not interchangeable. As Kristi Sweet points out, "we do not have immediate or certain access to our mental states."[109] Hence, even though we "cannot be in doubt that we are in a state of pleasure [...] we can be in error as to the nature of that pleasure, namely, its source."[110] Consequently, if judging subject A has a tendency to mistake the agreeable for the beautiful, and judging subject B does not realize that "beautiful" is not a synonym for "perfect," then both will find that their assessments often disagree with those of judging subject C, who is not given to classificatory mistakes of either kind

---

108 For Kant's description of how the confusion of judgments of perfection with those of the beautiful can lead to disagreement, see: *Critique of the Power of Judgment*, § 16, 5:230 – 1. The possibility that judgments of the agreeable, the good and the beautiful could be wrongly confused with one another is suggested by Kant's discussion of the different sorts of pleasure each entails: "Pleasure is a state of the mind in which a representation is in agreement with itself, as a ground, either merely for preserving this state itself (for the state of the powers of the mind reciprocally promoting each other in a representation preserves itself), or for producing its object. If it is the former, then the judgment on the given object is an aesthetic judgment of reflection; however, if it is the latter, then it is an aesthetic-pathological or an aesthetic-practical judgment. It can be readily seen here that pleasure or displeasure, since they are not kinds of cognition, cannot be explained by themselves at all, and are felt, not understood; hence they can be only inadequately explained through the influence that a representation has on the activity of the powers of the mind by means of this feeling" (*Critique of the Power of Judgment*, First Introduction, § X, 20:230 – 31). Pleasure's status as a feeling, and not a cognition, leaves it "only inadequately explained" (*Ibid.*). Hence, it would not be the least bit surprising to find that the sorts of pleasure Kant carefully seeks to distinguish from each other *in theory* might be easily confused *in practice*.
109 Sweet, "Reflection: Its Structure and Meaning in Kant's Judgments of Taste," 74.
110 Sweet, "Reflection: Its Structure and Meaning in Kant's Judgments of Taste," 73.

and has instead a stable Kantian grasp of what the pure aesthetic judgment of taste entails.

But even our judging subject *C* is not infallible. "[F]or the beautiful presupposes and preserves the mind in **calm** contemplation,"[111] and thus is unamenable to overstimulation, like that which is caused by impure aesthetic pleasure. The overpowering pleasure of a particularly potent charm, for instance, may render one incapable of properly contemplating and reflectively judging in accordance with *pure* aesthetic pleasure. When this occurs there are two competing mental activities. It is not necessarily that the pleasure of agreeableness is more pleasant than the pleasure of beauty, but rather that the agreeable strikes one in a more immediate fashion, because it does not arise in contemplative reflection. Even our astute subject *C* could fall victim to this, mistakenly judging the sweet smelling lilac tree to offer only agreeableness and overlooking its beauty,[112] or alternatively, declaring the tree to be beautiful based only on its overpoweringly agreeable smell without actually having carried out a pure aesthetic judgment. That tendency that simultaneous affective states have to push each other out suggests that pain could also incapacitate one from making a successful judgment of taste. For example, standing over the Grand Canyon at sunset, judging subject *C* may be so overpowered by his allergy to sagebrush that—through the watery eyes, incessant sneezing and frantic itching—he fails to see anything the least bit remarkable about the canyon or sunset and is instead in a great hurry to get back in the car.[113] Since impure aesthetic pleasures

---

111 *Critique of the Power of Judgment*, § 25, 5:248.
112 Both gustatory and olfactory pleasures are pleasures of the senses that can lead to a judgment of agreeableness, but not of beauty. For further discussion of this, see chapter six, footnote 119.
113 Allison suggests a similar approach to understanding this sort of aesthetic error. I "may have simply failed to abstract completely from the factors that I believe myself to have set aside," and thus not have properly distinguished between "a judgment of taste simpliciter and a pure judgment" (Allison, *Kant's Theory of Taste: A Reading of the Critique of Aesthetic Judgment*, 109). He further elaborates: "To begin with, this distinction enables us to disambiguate the text in question by taking it to be saying that we can be certain about having made a judgment of taste and, perhaps even of having tried to have made a pure judgment, but we can never be certain that we have succeeded in making the latter. Accordingly, my consciousness of having separated out from my liking everything pertaining to the agreeable and the good concerns merely the attempt to make a pure judgment of taste. Being a sincere and discriminating lover of the beautiful, I make every effort to do this, because I recognize that it is a necessary condition of the conformity of my judgment to the universal voice. But, alas, I can never be certain that I have succeeded. For no matter how careful I may have been, there always remains the possibility either that my judgment has been corrupted by some quirky and unnoticed liking (perhaps of the kind suggested by Guyer in his critique of the argument of § 6), or that I have

and pains have private grounds, one's idiosyncrasies do have an influence on determining the situations in which one will be incapable of making a pure aesthetic judgment. But the involvement of idiosyncrasies in classificatory aesthetic errors does *not* indicate that they play a role in correctly conducted judgments of taste.

Having, ourselves, judged something to be beautiful, we expect that others will judge this thing in the same manner—and even "demand [...] it from them"[114]—but we do not *know* that they *will*, because their doing so requires that they actually engage in the act of pure aesthetic judging *in concreto*, and their ability to do so can be mitigated by various concomitant circumstances surrounding the empirical object's givenness, which are only to be known *a posteriori* in each concrete case.[115] That is, the judging is an act that must be per-

---

simply failed to abstract completely from the factors that I believe myself to have set aside. In either not very unlikely event, I have certainly made a judgment of taste (a claim of liking or disliking based on feeling) and have attempted to make a pure judgment, but I have simply failed with regard to the latter. Accordingly, the error is not, as Cohen suggests, in falsely believing that I have made a judgment of taste at all (it's difficult to conceive how one can be confused about that), but in claiming that my de facto judgment is pure" (*Ibid.*).

114 *Critique of the Power of Judgment*,§ 7, 5:213. One demands it of others, because one recognizes no private ground for the judgment in oneself, giving one the sense that beauty must be something that all who judge are able to perceive. Since Kant supposes this pleasure to originate in the structure of our faculties of cognition, his theory does not fall victim to a Nietzschean critique of the historicity of values, such as is to be found in the *Genealogy of Morals*. The pleasure that Kant deems pure aesthetic arises in the transcendental conditions for the possibility of cognition, which remain a constant throughout human history (i.e., as long as humans cognize). The factors to which Nietzsche directs his attention—such as history, culture and individual psychology—lead one to a judgment based on private grounds, and hence can only generate an impure aesthetic judgment or an erroneous claim to a pure aesthetic judgment of taste. The biases that characterize one's society may encourage one to misapply the term "beautiful" to something that merely fits that culture's concept of perfection, or to something that one finds agreeable due to how one's sense of agreeableness has habituated itself to the expectations of one's society. Regardless of what aggrandized claims the judging subject may incorrectly make, such a judgment cannot make a legitimate claim to beauty according to Kant's account.

115 Kant also remarks in the second *Critique* on the complications that arise when one seeks to understand how concrete cases connect to the a priori structure he is elaborating. We see this in the relation between pure practical judgment and concrete human action: "Now, whether an action possible for us in sensibility is or is not a case that stands under the rule requires practical judgment, by which what is said in the rule universally (*in abstracto*) is applied to an action *in concreto*. [...] [H]owever, all cases of possible actions that occur can be only empirical, that is, belong to experience and nature; hence, it seems absurd to want to find in this sensible world a case which, though as such it stands only under the law of nature, yet admits of the application to it of a law of freedom and to which there could be applied the supersensible

III Why Does Aesthetic Judgment Involve the Singular and Universal Instead — 211

formed, and transcendental philosophy cannot provide assurance that every individual judging subject will encounter the empirical object in a situation devoid of any factors that may block her from successfully entering into the activity of pure aesthetic judging.

III.A The Fundamental Particularization made by Kant's System at the Outset

I have argued that the only application which the particular finds in pure aesthetic judgment is that of picking out this particular form of judgment among others, allotting the particular no place in the intrinsic workings of this form of judgment itself. I would now like to consider a further role that the particular has in relation to pure aesthetic judgment which might initially appear to be intrinsic, but further scrutiny reveals as extrinsic. This role of the particular appears when we ask whether the designation "judging subject" holds universally or particularly of *humanity*.

The "judging subject" can only be a human who experiences the world in accordance with the necessary conditions for the possibility of experience. This means that we only count among "judging subjects" those humans who have the proper arrangement of the faculties to experience the world.[116] If this excludes anyone in the class of humanity, then it will be those who either have not developed sufficiently or have mental disorders that prevent the conditions for the possibility of experience from obtaining. This particularizing criteria is, however, not a special stipulation of aesthetic judgment, but rather a fundamental point of departure assumed by Kant's transcendental idealism from the start. Kant's system only pertains to those human subjects who have experience. A "healthy understanding" is assumed to be something that "has its foundation in human nature" and thus is "demanded" of "everyone."[117] Moreover, Kant acknowledges that "the common and healthy understanding" "is required for

---

idea of the morally good, which is to be exhibited in it *in concreto*" (*Critique of Practical Judgment*, 5:67).

116 Here I intend "experience" as the technical Kantian term, meaning to cognize an intuition by subsuming it under a concept, "through the categories alone is experience possible; only by means of them can any object of experience be thought [...]" (*Critique of Pure Reason*, A93/B126).

117 *Critique of the Power of Judgment*, § 29, 5:265. To quote this section more fully, it reads: "But just because the judgment on the sublime in nature requires culture (more so than that on the beautiful), it is not therefore first generated by culture and so to speak introduced into society merely as a matter of convention; rather it has its foundation in human nature, and indeed in that which can be required of everyone and demanded of him along with healthy understanding, namely in the predisposition to the feeling for (practical) ideas, i.e., to that which is moral."

taste," immediately following this with the assertion "that one may presuppose [this] in everyone."[118] Kant is only willing to consider as a "judging subject" those humans whose cognitive faculties are healthy enough to supply the conditions necessary for the possibility of experience, and only such subjects are to be designated by the term "everyone." This reveals that although "judging subject" may only pertain to a particular portion of humanity, this is a foundational particularization assumed by Kant's philosophical system from the outset, extrinsic to the workings of aesthetic judgment, itself.[119] Moreover, this extrinsic particularization is a far cry from the sort of aesthetic particularization sought by Guyer, for it does not supply any grounds for the judgment "This tulip is beautiful" to be corrected with the additional clause: *to me, and some others* within the class of judging subjects.

IV Conclusion: The Universal Voice

It is to this end that Kant introduces careful nuances into the subjective universality of aesthetic judgment. Subjective universality does not allow one to "postulate the accord of everyone" but rather only to "lay [...] claim to the consent of everyone" with a universal voice.[120] Thus, Kant takes the issue of aesthetic disagreement into account by clarifying what the aesthetic judgment "X is beautiful" really does assert and how.

---

[118] *Critique of the Power of Judgment*, § 39, 5:292–3. To quote this section more fully, it reads: "This pleasure must necessarily rest on the same conditions in everyone, since they are subjective conditions of the possibility of a cognition in general, and the proportion of these cognitive faculties that is required for taste is also requisite for the common and healthy understanding that one may presuppose in everyone."

[119] Ameriks poses the question whether the blind's inability to aesthetically judge visual arts circumscribes the universality of aesthetic judgments. If so, then this would present a genuine particularization among judging subjects, and not humanity at large. He responds to this by emphasizing that the universal communicability of aesthetic judgments does not require "that others actually do sense or are equipped to sense objects just as we do. Rather [...] it means that, given an act is cognition, we should believe that it has an objective ground; and if it is a perceptual cognition, then we should believe that the objective ground involves an appearance that all should be able to see if they are only normal and in appropriate circumstances" (Ameriks, "How to Save Kant's Deduction of Taste," 298). Although a blind person will not be stimulated into this faculty harmony through the visual arts, the same person is stimulated into that which is properly universal (the mental state) through other means, such as beautiful music. Hence, this does not limit the subjective universality of aesthetic judgment.

[120] *Critique of the Power of Judgment*,§ 8, 5:216.

It does not make claim to the empirical fact that every person who looks at this thing *will* find it beautiful, rather it claims that every judging subject should find it beautiful, because as a judging subject the object ought to trigger the pleasant transcendental free play of the faculties. One "demands" that others feel this, but as a demand this has a hortatory, rather than assertoric, characteristic.[121] To secure that this proclamation of the aesthetic worth of the object judged is understood in the right manner, Kant describes it as proclaimed through the *universal voice*. It is through the use of this voice that one lays claim to this peculiar breed of subjective universality.

How is the universal voice different from the normal voice we use typically? Perhaps we could say that we assert our personal likes and dislikes with a singular voice, and use an objective voice to declare judgments that have been combined in the object, and thus are objectively universally valid. The universal voice is different from these, insofar as it is based upon a private perception of pleasure, but, through the recognition that this private perception has no private grounds, it expects all other judging subjects to perceive the transcendental pleasure as well. It is this voice that is capable of proclaiming the subjectively universal validity of an aesthetic judgment and demanding the agreement of others without "postulating the accord of everyone."[122] The subjective characteristic of this universality must be preserved in the judgment itself, and this is done through the careful difference maintained between what the subjective universal

---

[121] "Hence he says that the thing is beautiful, and does not count on the agreement of others with his judgment of satisfaction because he has frequently found them to be agreeable with his own, but rather demands [*fordert*] it from them. He rebukes them if they judge otherwise, and denies that they have taste, though he nevertheless requires that they ought to have it" (*Critique of the Power of Judgment*,§ 7, 5:212–3). Such a "demand" might be understood as a cross between the conjecturing usage of "must have," as in "He *must have* been out when you called," and the more colloquial "You've *just must* try the flambé!" Rudolf Makkreel cautions against letting the sporadic appearance of demand [*fordern*] cloud our reading of the text. Taken too forcefully the demand tinging the universal voice "can evolve into an actual duty to which we must subordinate ourselves" ("Reflection, Reflective Judgment, and Aesthetic Exemplarity," 235, footnote #44). He takes exception to using "demand" as "a rather forceful translation of *Zumutung*, which Guyer and Matthews translate more appropriately as "expectation" and which [Makkreel] would render even more modestly as "presumption." We may merely presume that others will agree with our judgments of taste" (*Ibid.*). Guyer writes that the "imputation of pleasure or agreement in pleasure is not an induction, deduction, or postulation in any of their usual senses, but it is an "idea," a concept of objective but indeterminate validity" (Guyer, *Kant and the Claims of Taste*, 146). Longuenesse brings out a further dimension to this imputation, describing the aesthetic "demand" as "a peculiar kind of longing" (Longuenesse, "Kant's Leading Thread," 207).

[122] *Critique of the Power of Judgment*,§ 8, 5:216.

judgment *does* assert ("that everyone ought to so judge") and what it does not ("that everyone does so judge").[123]

---

[123] *Critique of the Power of Judgment*, First Introduction, §X, 20:238–9. To quote the section where Kant emphasizes the difference more fully, it reads: "Now aesthetic judgments of reflection [...] lay claim to necessity and say, not that everyone does so judge – that would make their explanation a task for empirical psychology – but that everyone ought to so judge, which is as much as to say that they have an *a priori* principle for themselves. If the relation to such a principle were not contained in such judgments, even though they lay claim to necessity, then one would have to assume that one can assert that a judgment ought to be universally valid because, as observation proves, it is universally valid, and, vice versa, that it follows from the fact that everyone does judge in a certain way that he too ought so to judge, which is an obvious absurdity."

Chapter Five:
Disjunctivity and the Form of Purposiveness

The third moment of aesthetic judgment is relation. A number of commentators have taken the relation of aesthetic judgment to be categorical,[1] because they focus their attention on how the assertion "This x is beautiful" is a categorical statement.[2] The categorical asserts a simple, direct relation between the predi-

---

[1] For instance, Jens Kulenkampff unabashedly asserts that the paradigmatic judgment of beauty, "this x is beautiful," is so easily seen to have a categorical relation that he offers no further explanation (Kulenkampff, *Kants Logik des ästhetischen Urteils*, 28). Béatrice Longuenesse also reads aesthetic judgment as categorical (Longuenesse, "Kant's Leading Thread in the Analytic of the Beautiful," 28). The reasoning behind her choice to do so is discussed below in footnote #2. Surprisingly, Henry Allison declines to make an effort to read the relation of the third moment through the logical functions of judgment. He writes: "Following the "guiding thread" of the table of judgments in the Critique of Pure Reason, the third moment in the Analytic of the Beautiful is that of relation. Unlike the logical functions of relation or the relational categories, however, the relation in question is between the judging subject and the object judged and/or its representation" (Henry Allison, *Kant's Theory of Taste*, 119). For an interesting reading of aesthetic judgment as entailing only *negated* relations see Simon, Josel,"Erhabene Schönheit: das ästhetische urteil als Destruktion de logischen." In *Kants Ästhetik, Kant, Kant's Aesthetics, L'esthétique de Kant*, edited by Herman Parret (De Gruyter: Berlin, 1998).

[2] We see a more sophisticated version of this in Longuenesse. She takes the assertion that "The judgment of taste has nothing but the *form of purposiveness* of an object (or of the way of representing it) as its ground" (*Critique of the Power of Judgment*, § 11, 5:221) to indicate that "the judgment is categorical," because "the ground of predication is to be found in the subject S of the judgment "S is P" (Longuenesse, "Kant's Leading Thread in the Analytic of the Beautiful," 210). I do not deny the categorical form of this judgment, however, I contest that this judgment is not the indeterminate activity of aesthetic judging that is given shape by the logical functions. The logical function guiding the third moment of aesthetic judgment should reveal how something is able to be represented as having the mere form of purposiveness, not how this mere form of purposiveness is, then, predicated of "a way of representing an object." In this chapter I show how the disjunctive logical function governs the judging activity that allows one to represent purposiveness without a purpose. As argued in previous chapters, the discursive statement of a judgment that this *is* the case (that "X *is* grounded in the form of purposiveness"; that "X *is* beautiful") is generated on the third layer as something that follows from the act of judging aesthetically, and although this gives us the ostensible aesthetic judgment, it is not properly a part of the activity of aesthetic *judging*, itself. This also holds in response to the further support that Longuenesses offers for the categorical nature of aesthetic judgment when she points out that "The implicit judgment embedded in the predicate [beautiful] ('all judging subjects, in apprehending this same object, ought to agree with my judgment') is a categorical judgment: the ground of predication is to be found in the subject of the judgment, 'all judging subjects'" (Longuenesse, "Kant's Leading Thread in the Analytic of the Beautiful," 212). Once again,

cate and subject. The key term explained in the third moment of pure aesthetic judgment under relation is, however, the curious notion of "*Zweckmäßigkeit, aber ohne Zweck.*"[3] To understand how purposiveness without a purpose can take shape thus requires a logical function that offers a relation of greater complexity—one capable of describing how the sense of having a purpose is obtained without any actual relation to a purpose being determined. The central task of the third moment is to articulate how this purposiveness both does and does not relate to a purpose.[4] To assist us in this task, we require a logical function of relation that describes how the subject can be characterized by the possibility of being something it is not. I argue that we find this in the disjunctive relation. I do not deny that both the empirical judgment "this is a tulip" and the final verdict "this tulip is beautiful" are categorical. I contend, however, that the judging *activity* enabling the second statement to be made is governed by another logical function of relation, the disjunctive. Kant describes the disjunctive relation as consisting "in the determination of the relation of the various judgments as members of the whole sphere of the divided cognition which mutually exclude one another and complement one another."[5] It is through this tension between parts which "mutually exclude" and simultaneously "complement" one another that the whole is constituted. I will show how this is of special importance for understanding the similarly peculiar being without purpose while still having a purposive form.

This chapter consists of three major sections. In the first section, I explicate the three logical forms of relation (categorical, hypothetical, disjunctive), comparing them with one another in terms of the matter of which they consist, the form that is given to this matter, the modality of judgment and judgmental structure (hierarchical or coordinative). Since I see aesthetic purposiveness as characterized by reciprocal causality, I close the first section by investigating the correspondence between the disjunctive logical function and category of community, commenting also on what differentiates the one from the other. In the second section, I bring this understanding of disjunctivity to bear on the third moment of aesthetic judgment. I first investigate what it means to have a purpose by looking at Kant's account of objective purposiveness in "The Critique

---

according to my layered structure, this categorical *assertion* of the subjective universality of aesthetic judgment belongs to the third layer and not the properly aesthetic second.

3 *Critique of the Power of Judgment*, § 15, 5:228.
4 Directly from the title of the third moment, we see that the relation under concern is to ends (i.e., purposes): "Third Moment of judgment of taste, concerning the relation of the ends that are taken into consideration in them" (*Critique of the Power of Judgment*, § 15, 5:219).
5 *Jäsche Logic*, § 28, 603.

of Teleological Judgment". Here Kant elaborates two causal networks that can make something purposive: the *nexus effectivus* and the *nexus finalis*. I then turn to the question of how a determinate purpose can be extracted from a purposive structure without purposiveness being destroyed as a result. Having highlighted how the *nexus finalis* functions through the category of community, I suggest that this can be done by shifting from an objectively purposive judgment that determines the object categorically to a subjectively purposive judgment through which only the activity of judging is determined.[6] This is accomplished through a judgment that, in contemplating beautiful nature and art, disjunctively holds together the idea of having and not having a purpose. In the final section, I offer a more detailed explanation of the observation made in chapter two that purposiveness without a purpose is the thread that runs through the layered structure of aesthetic judgment.

I The Logical Functions of Relation

The relation of a judgment describes how the "representations in judgment are subordinated one to another for the unity of consciousness."[7] Categorical, hypothetical and disjunctive relation can be distinguished from one another in a variety of ways. In this section, I lay the groundwork for understanding how purposiveness without a purpose can be meaningfully read through the disjunctive. To do so, I develop an understanding of how the logical functions of relation work by comparing them in terms of the matter of which they are comprised, the form that governs the judgment, the modality of the components of the judgment and the important difference between the hierarchical structure of the cat-

---

[6] It should be noted that—as was also the case with the foregoing moments of the judgment of taste—this difference between the categories and logical functions does not mean that the latter leads to an indefinite form of judgment. The logical functions give judgment a decisive, determined form. It is only that the determinations they supply are not carried over to determine anything other than the activity of judging itself (i.e., it does not determine an object of experience). It would be mistaken to think of disjunctive judgment as undecided or indeterminate. Despite the fact that a disjunctive judgment opens up multiple possibilities, it does so in a determinate manner. It is the decisive form through which an undecided matter is put forward for decision. A disjunctive judgment could take the form of a multiple choice question, in which case it may be unclear which answer is correct, however the judging subject's inability to discern which disjunctive limb should be selected does not affect the structure of the judgment itself. Despite the multiple possibilities presented in a disjunctive judgment, the disjunctive *form* of the judgment remains fixed.

[7] *Jäsche Logic*, § 23, 601.

egorical and the non-hierarchical structure of the disjunctive. To flesh out the non-hierarchical structure of the disjunctive further, I describe how this logical function resonates with its corresponding category, community.

I.A Matter

One of the most fundamental differences between logical functions can be seen when we identify the component parts related by each. A categorical judgment relates the *predicate* to the *subject*; a hypothetical judgment relates the *consequence* to the *ground*; and a disjunctive judgment relates the *concept to be divided* to the *"members of the division."*[8] As a consequence the number of judgments involved in each relation also differ. Whereas the categorical considers the relation between two concepts within one judgment, the hypothetical is between two judgments and the disjunctive is between two or more judgments.[9]

I.B Form

Each logical function provides the relation of the judgment with a distinct form. In a categorical judgment the form is supplied by the copula "through which the relation (of agreement or of opposition) between the subject and predicate is determined and expressed."[10] The relational term of hypothetical judgments is termed a *consequentia,* which connects the antecedent to the consequent—the ground to its consequence. The *consequentia* allows for a hypothetical logical function to bring two judgments together in a "relation of sequence," whereas the disjunctive brings judgments together in a relation "of logical opposition."[11] In disjunctive judgments "[t]he form of these judgments consists in the *disjunc-*

---

[8] *Jäsche Logic*, § 23, 601.
[9] See *Critique of Pure Reason*, A73/B99. It is worth noting that whereas subject and predicate make up the matter of categorical judgments, in a way categorical judgments constitute the matter of hypothetical and disjunctive judgments, as the judgments whose relation these specify are two or more categorical judgments (See *Jäsche Logic*, § 24, 601, Note). But one should not misunderstand this "as several logicians do" to mean that "hypothetical and disjunctive judgments are nothing more than various clothings of categoricals" (*Ibid.*). Although categoricals constitute their matter, hypothetical and disjunctive judgments offer something in their form, which specifies a certain way of relating the two matter-components together, and thus cannot be "traced back to" anything found in a categorical judgment (*Ibid.*).
[10] *Jäsche Logic*, § 24, 601.
[11] *Critique of Pure Reason*, A73/B99.

tion itself."¹² This relates the members that make up a sphere so that they simultaneously "mutually exclude one another and complement one another."¹³ In this manner a disjunctive relation situates the complementary terms within "the community of a sphere."¹⁴ Although the sphere is made up of all of the members taken together, a specific location is assigned to each complementary judgment within this sphere "through the restriction of the other [judgments] in regard to the whole sphere."¹⁵

I.C Modality

Another distinction between the logical functions of relation can be made in terms of the modality of the elements involved: "In categorical judgments nothing is problematic, rather, everything is assertoric, but in hypotheticals only the *consequentia* is assertoric."¹⁶ This ties in with the distinction between truth and validity. In a hypothetical judgment, the two judgments brought together may be false, while the judgment will still be valid, if they are connected in the correct manner (i.e., so that if the antecedent were true, then the consequent would follow). "[T]he correctness of the connection" indicates that "the form of the *consequentia*" is correctly applied, and it is upon this that "the logical truth of these judgments rests."¹⁷ The form of the relation "is only the implication that is thought by means of this judgment."¹⁸ In this respect hypothetical judgments differ from the categorical. Even if the categorical propositions making up the hypothetical judgment are false, the form may be valid.

In disjunctive judgments, the member judgments are all problematic, but underlying this disjunctive structure is also the conviction that "one of them must hold *assertorically*."¹⁹ Thus, disjunctive judgment does not have an indefinite, undecided form, but rather is the definite form that presents a set of mutually exclusive possibilities for decision. That is, since these *complementa* constitute

---

12 *Jäsche Logic*, § 28, 603.
13 *Jäsche Logic*, § 28, 603.
14 *Jäsche Logic*, § 28, 603, Note.
15 *Jäsche Logic*, § 28, 603, Note.
16 *Jäsche Logic*, § 27, 602, Note #2.
17 *Jäsche Logic*, § 25, 602, Note. Here, this is termed "logical truth," but it seems evident that logical validity is meant.
18 *Critique of Pure Reason*, A73/B98–9.
19 *Jäsche Logic*, § 29, 603. Kant explains, "the members of the disjunction are all problematic judgments, of which nothing else is thought except that, taken together, as parts of the sphere of a cognition, each is the complement of the other toward the whole."

220 —— Chapter Five: Disjunctivity and the Form of Purposiveness

the sphere, it cannot be the case that something outside of the sphere is what assertorically holds for the sphere. Kant illustrates this through an example: "The world exists either through blind chance, or through inner necessity, or through an external cause."[20] As disjunctive, the three *complementa* hold problematically as something that *could* be true. Since these *complementa* exhaust the possible answers to the question of how the world exists, the disjunctive judgment is underpinned by the conviction that "one of [the *complementa*] must hold *assertorically*."[21] That is, no judgment extraneous to this sphere (ex: "Water covers about 71% of the world's surface") could be what holds assertorically of *this* sphere (i.e., how the world exists). Moreover, since the *complementa* cover the entirety of the sphere by complementing (i.e., being opposed to) one another, nothing "more than one among them can be true."[22]

I.D Hierarchy

Categorical judgments exhibit a hierarchical relation between the sphere and its parts that is nowhere to be found in disjunctive judgments. In categorical judgments the representation of the thing "is considered as a part of the sphere of another."[23] Thus, the representation is subordinated to the sphere and "considered as contained under this, its higher concept."[24] Hence, the part of the sphere represented in the judgment is subordinated to the sphere.

In a disjunctive judgment, however, this is not the case. Through the *complementa*'s mutual exclusion, each of the parts is equal to the whole, and will be equated with the whole, if it is decided upon as the one that holds assertorically. Kant explains this in terms of the sphere of the concept, writing, "[w]hat is contained under the sphere of a concept is also contained under one of the parts of

---

20 *Critique of Pure Reason*, A74/B99.
21 *Jäsche Logic*, § 29, 603.
22 *Jäsche Logic*, § 29, 603. It is interesting to note the developing change in the expectations for each relation along the lines of truth and validity. Whereas the categorical judgment was either true or false and the hypothetical judgment could be valid despite containing false categorical judgments as its matter, the disjunctive judgment counts on all but one of its components being false.
23 *Jäsche Logic*, § 29, 603, Note. In the previous chapter we saw how the quantity of a judgment allows this hierarchical relation to take different forms with the entirety of the sphere of the subject-concept being indicated by the predicate in a universal judgment, or the subject whose concept has no sphere being identified as part of the sphere of the predicate-concept in a singular judgment.
24 *Jäsche Logic*, § 29, 603, Note.

this sphere."²⁵ Although the sphere of the concept of the whole is equivalent with the sphere of the concept of each of the *complementa*, the latter are "not in any way parts of one another."²⁶ This is what is meant by referring to the *complementa* as the "divided concept."²⁷ Categorical judgments, thus, subordinate the parts to the whole concept, whereas disjunctive judgments coordinate "all the parts of its sphere."²⁸ We can represent this contrasting relation through the diagram in the figures below:

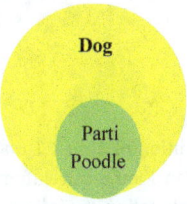
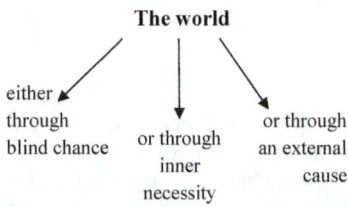

Fig. 1: A Parti Poodle is a dog. (Categorical Judgment)

Fig. 2: "The world exists either through blind chance, or through inner necessity, or through an external cause."²⁹ (Kant's example of a disjunctive judgment)

Kant concludes, "Here [in a disjunctive judgment] I think *many things through one concept*, there [in a categorical judgment, I think] *one thing* through *many concepts*, e. g., the *definitum* through all the marks of coordination."³⁰

I.E Correspondence Between the Disjunctive Logical Function and Categories of Community

The disjunctive logical function correlates with the category of community.³¹ Community is described as "the causality of a substance in the reciprocal deter-

---

25 *Jäsche Logic*, § 29, 603, Note.
26 *Jäsche Logic*, § 29, 603, Note.
27 *Jäsche Logic*, § 29, 604, Note.
28 *Jäsche Logic*, § 29, 604, Note.
29 *Critique of Pure Reason*, A74/B99.
30 *Jäsche Logic*, § 29, 604, Note.
31 Understanding how the disjunctive logical function and category of community relate is no easy task. Kant anticipated the difficulty that readers may have seeing the correspondence, and thus sought to assist us with a note (*Critique of Pure Reason*, B111–13). My understanding of how these two relate, developed in this section, draws on this note. Not all commentators, however,

mination of others."[32] The correspondence between this logical function and category can be seen in how the relation of *disjunction* must be thought within the *community* of the sphere that the disjunctive judgment concerns. Kant writes that disjunctive judgments contain the relation,

> of logical opposition, insofar as the sphere of one judgment excludes that of the other, yet at the same time the relation of community, insofar as the judgments together exhaust the sphere of cognition where the sphere of each part is the complement of that of the others in the sum total of the divided cognition [...].[33]

---

have found it convincing. Henry Allison revises his view in his second edition of *Kant's Transcendental Idealism* (2004), but in the first edition of his book he regarded Kant's correlation of disjunction with community as unsuccessful and the attempted explanation "a failure" (1983, 127; see also Allison's remarks on how "hopeless" it is to connect the schema of community to its category on 188). In the first edition, Allison argues that disjunctive judgment does not offer the reciprocity of community. On the contrary, I see the reciprocity between the *complementa* as constituting the entire sphere of the judgment in a manner that does accord with community. Admittedly, in community all of the parts exist for one another, while in a disjunctive judgment all of the parts must be held together only problematically. If in a disjunctive judgment any one part is taken assertorically, then this eliminates the possibility of the other parts. Were this to happen, however, then the disjunctivity of the judgment would be destroyed. In order for the judgement to be disjunctive, no single *complementa* can be taken assertorically. Despite this difference between disjunctivity and community regarding the modality of the parts, there is a similarity insofar as both describe how something is caused as a whole. In a disjunctive judgment, the parts must be held together to constitute the sphere of the judgment as a whole, whereas in community the parts must exist together grounding the reality of the whole. Hence, it is not just the modality of the parts that differs, but also the sort of thing that is being determined. The disjunctive logical function determines a judgment, while the category of community determines the object judged. The reciprocal causality through which the parts constitute the whole, however, is to be found both in disjunctivity as well as in community. Similar to how an organized being is constituted as a whole through its parts, so too can a disjunctive judgment only emerge as such if the judgmental parts of *complementa* are held together. In his second edition, Allison recognizes that "a connection between [disjunctivity and community] may be preserved," although he still finds Kant's defense to be "not entirely convincing because of an unclarity concerning the nature of the logical function involved" (2004, 151). Allison's revised position recognizes that the disjunctive logical function and category of community correspond, "if we take the logical function involved in disjunctive judgment to be coordination rather than exclusion. Moreover, there is support for this reading in the fact that Kant contrasts the relation of coordination expressed in judging under this form with that of the subordination operative in hypothetical judgment. As Kant suggests, this is analogous to the (ontological) coordination of items thought under the category of community" (2004, 151).

32 *Critique of Pure Reason*, B110–111.
33 *Critique of Pure Reason*, A73–4/B99.

This shows disjunctive relation to represent a curious form of holding together by holding apart, while also holding apart by holding together. For a relation can have disjunctivity only within the context of related *complementa* that together constitute the whole of the sphere of the judgment. If the relation to any of the members is lost, then the sphere as a whole is no longer indicated and nothing more than a simple categorical or hypothetical judgment can result. It is not possible to extract one *complementa* from its relation with the others and affirm it in isolation without destroying the disjunctive judgment in the process. Any such extraction would place the *complementa* outside the sphere of the divided concept altogether.³⁴

Kant anticipates that readers may have difficulty seeing the correlation between the disjunctive logical function and category of community. Thus, he devotes his third explanatory remark following the presentation of the table of categories to detailing this correspondence. He writes:

> The understanding follows the same procedure when it represents the divided sphere of a concept as when it thinks of a thing as divisible, and just as in the first case the members of the division exclude each other and yet are connected in one sphere, so in the latter case the parts are represented as ones to which existence (as substances) pertains to each exclusively of the others, and which are yet connected in one whole.³⁵

If the *complementa* were not related to one another disjunctively, then they would not be *complementa*. If it were not the case that each of the *complementa* could be equated with the whole of the sphere of the judgment, then they could not problematically hold of this sphere and the disjunctivity would be lost. Thus, it is the relation that holds both among the *complementa* and between each *complementa* and the whole that causes the judgment to have a disjunctive form. In this manner, we see that both community and disjunctivity involve a reciprocal causality in which "one member determines every other [...] insofar as they stand together in community as parts of a whole sphere of cognition."³⁶ A further similarity can be seen in how both community and disjunctivity function by *coordinating* the divided parts with one another and with the whole, rather than by

---

34 "To remove the cognition from one of these spheres means to place it in one of the others, and to place it in one sphere, on the contrary, means to remove it from the others" (*Critique of Pure Reason*, A74/B99).
35 *Critique of Pure Reason*, B112–3.
36 *Jäsche Logic*, § 28, 603, Note. The difference is that under community the parts of a natural product reciprocally cause an organic being, whereas under disjunctivity the *complementa* cause a disjunctive judgment. This is further discussed in the next paragraph.

subordinating one part of the judgment to another as occurs in the categorical logical function and its corresponding category of substance.[37]

The difference between disjunctivity and community is that as a category the reciprocal relation of the latter determines a cognized object.[38] As the disjunctive logical function, however, this is only a determination of the act of judging in which various elements are held together as conditioning one another and it is through this conditioning that they cause the judgment to be disjunctive. Whereas the cognition of an object through the reciprocal causality of community can enable us to see it as an organized being, it is a special type of *judgment* that takes shape through the logical functions of relation. Here, the reciprocal causality that holds sway over the *complementa* and scope of the judgment as a whole causes the disjunctivity of the judgment, thus allowing a disjunctive judgment to manifest. This logical determination of the relational form of the judgment does not carry over from the activity of judging to become a determination of that which is so judged.[39] In this manner, the logical function and category are both characterized by a certain reciprocal causality. The difference, however, between what a logical function determines (the judgmental activity, itself) and what a category determines (an intuition) has an important implica-

---

[37] "[T]hey do not determine each other unilaterally, as in a series, but reciprocally, as in an aggregate" (*Critique of Pure Reason*, B112). Longuenesse describes this shared feature of coordination in a way that also highlights a dynamic of exclusion that reverberates in community, writing, "in a logical disjunction, concepts are coordinated to each other, while at the same time excluding each other, just as in the relation of community, objects are coordinated in space according to universal attractive and repulsive forces" (Longuenesse, *Kant and the Capacity to Judge*, 376). It is noteworthy that logical disjunction requires the coordination of the concepts that make up the judgment as its *complementa*. Thus, it explains how the parts of the judgment relate to one another intrinsically so as to cause this specific form of judgment. The reciprocal causality of this form of judgment does not pertain to a relation that connects multiple disjunctive judgments to one another (that is, unless these judgments are taking the place of *complementa* in order to form one overarching disjunctive judgment on a greater scale).

[38] That is to say, community takes the role of a category that subsumes an intuition so as to cognize *Phänomen*, i.e., an object "in the concept of which the manifold of a given intuition is united" (*Critique of Pure Reason*, B137).

[39] This is in line with how Longuenesse reads the correspondence and difference between the disjunctive logical function and category of community in *Kant and the Capacity to Judge:* "Kant progresses from the context of the logical form to the context of the category when he progresses from characterizing a discursive relation of concepts (here, the form of disjunctive judgment) to characterizing the sensible manifolds reflected under concepts combined according to this discursive form (here, multiplicities of objects as coexisting in space and time). The category of community is the universal concept reflecting the *synthesis speciosa* by means of which we generate the representation of these sensible manifolds" (Longuenesse, *Kant and the Capacity to Judge*, 377). For Longuenesse's full account of how these two relate, see: Ibid., 378–87.

tion for how the disjunctivity of an act of judgment differs from the community of a cognized object. The former causes a certain sort of judgment, while the latter causes a certain sort of cognized object. This is further developed below when considering how purposiveness can be without a purpose.

II The Third Moment

To investigate the idea of purposiveness without a purpose, I will first look at what purposiveness *with* a purpose signifies and then explore how the purpose can be extracted from this.

II.A Purposiveness with a Purpose

It is in the Introduction that the third *Critique* first addresses purposiveness. Kant explains that, "we call purposive that the existence of which seems to presuppose a representation of the same thing."[40] This representation that seems to be presupposed by the purposive thing's existence is clarified as a concept of what the object both *is to be* and, in fact, *is:*

> the concept of an object insofar as it at the same time contains the ground of the reality of this object is called an end, and the correspondence of a thing with that constitution of things that is possible only in accordance with ends is called the purposiveness of its form [...].[41]

It is striking to recognize how many elements in this passage are not to be permitted in pure aesthetic judgment. The purity of such a judgment would be lost if it were to be grounded upon: "the reality of this object," "the concept of an object," or any "ends."[42] This suggests, right from the start, that the motivation for extracting purpose from aesthetic purposiveness will be to achieve a purely aesthetic form of purposiveness. Let us, however, put that aside for now and focus instead on what this passage says about purposiveness.

From the passage above, we can understand purposiveness of form as arising when something is constituted so as to have a form that "is only possible in accordance with ends." An object is constituted through its cognition under the

---

[40] *Critique of the Power of Judgment*, First Introduction V, 20:216.
[41] *Critique of the Power of Judgment*, Introduction IV, 5:180.
[42] *Critique of the Power of Judgment*, Introduction IV, 5:180.

concept that gives it unity.[43] When this concept is an end, however, a further element of causality enters the equation. It is not just that the concept provides unity to the object, so that it may be cognized as an object. Rather, the concept has a further function which goes above and beyond this: "at the same time [it] contains the ground of the reality of this object," setting it apart as a concept that is to be "called an end."[44] An end is a concept that does not just ground the cognition of the object, but also its "reality." Hence, as Kant remarks later on, "an end in general is that the concept of which can be regarded as the ground of the possibility of the object itself."[45]

The above passage from the Introduction immediately develops into a discussion of how,

> the principle of the power of judgment in regard to the form of things in nature under empirical laws in general is the purposiveness of nature in its multiplicity. I.e., nature is represented through this concept as if an understanding contained the ground of the unity of the manifold of its empirical laws [...].[46]

This reassures us that Kant's reference to "reality" is not to be understood as a reference to things-in-themselves. Rather, "reality" concerns "things in nature under empirical laws"[47] and "[b]y nature (in the empirical sense) we understand the combination of appearances as regards their existence, in accordance with necessary rules, i.e., in accordance with laws."[48] Kant further remarks that,

> the transcendental idealist is an empirical realist, and grants to matter, as appearance, a reality which need not be inferred, but is immediately perceived [...] in our system [...] these external things – namely, matter in all its forms and alterations – are nothing but mere representations, i.e., representations in us, of whose reality we are immediately conscious.[49]

From this it is clear that "reality" does not indicate something beyond appearance. But if this is the case, then how does the special use of a concept to ground an empirical object's reality as an end differ from the ordinary use of a concept to cognize, and thus ground it as an object (i.e., *Phänomen*)? From Kant's re-

---

43 See: *Critique of Pure Reason*, B137; A247/B304.
44 *Critique of the Power of Judgment*, Introduction IV, 5:180.
45 *Critique of the Power of Judgment*, § 15, 5:227.
46 *Critique of the Power of Judgment*, Introduction IV, 5:180.
47 *Critique of the Power of Judgment*, Introduction IV, 5:180.
48 *Critique of Pure Reason*, A216/B263.
49 *Critique of Pure Reason*, A371–2.

marks on ends, the answer appears to be that the latter might be somewhat arbitrarily applied to the empirical object, whereas the former plays an inherent role in making that thing what it is. When an end grounds something's reality, this involves "the correspondence of a thing with that constitution of things that is possible only in accordance with ends."[50] Kant elaborates that:

> An object or a state of mind or even an action, however, even if its possibility does not necessarily presuppose the representation of an end, is called purposive merely because its possibility can only be explained and conceived by us insofar as we assume as its ground a causality in accordance with ends, i.e., a will that has arranged it so in accordance with the representation of a certain rule.[51]

The importance of the "rule" will be explored below in my discussion of art as nature. But further clarity is first needed regarding exactly how an end can structure our conception of an object. The Critique of the Teleological Power of Judgment can be of great assistance in this, as it is here that Kant discusses contrasting forms of causality by drawing out the distinction between internal and external purposiveness.

II.A.1 The nexus effectivus and nexus finalis

In § 65, entitled "Things, as natural ends, are organized beings" Kant describes two types of causality. These two causal nexuses are: the *nexus effectivus* and *nexus finalis*. I will show the former to correlate with the category of causality and the latter with that of community. In this manner, the relation between the category of community and disjunctive logical function can be used to understand purposiveness without a purpose as a *nexus finalis* that is not directed at the object judged, but rather at the activity of aesthetic judging, itself. In this manner it allows one to hold together the *complementa* "with a purpose" and "without a purpose" as mutually conditioning one another and thus designating the entire sphere of aesthetic purposiveness.[52]

---

50 *Critique of the Power of Judgment*, Introduction IV, 5:180.
51 *Critique of the Power of Judgment*, § 10, 5:220.
52 Claudia Bickmann points out that purposiveness is always a determination of the reflecting power of judgment and not a determination of the thing itself: "*Soweit die idealtypische Rekonstruktion einer Sache in der Besonderheit ihrer Erscheinung, die Kant an jenes reflektierende Prinzip der Zweckmäßigkeit bindet, durch das allein unsere Urteilskraft, nicht aber die Dinge selbst bestimmt werden*" (Bickmann, "Die eingebettete Vernunft in Kants "Kritik der Urteilskraft": Wechselintegrationen vereint-entgegengesetzter Sphären," 25). My claim, above, is by no means at odds with this. What I seek to highlight in my distinction between what is determined

A nexus of efficient causes "is a connection that constitutes a series (of cause and effects)."[53] Here "the things themselves, which as effects presuppose others as their causes, cannot conversely be the causes of these at the same time."[54] Causality is "considered as a mere mechanism" which "is always descending" and the effects brought about are regarded as being "in the highest degree contingent."[55] The purposiveness that arises in such a nexus of efficient causes is one in which something is regarded as "a means for the purposive use of other causes."[56] This yields an "external purposiveness,"[57] which is called "usefulness (for human beings) or advantageousness (for every other creature), and is merely relative."[58] The work of the hypothetical logical function in the external purposiveness of a *nexus effectivus* surfaces in how there is only a "relative purposiveness [that] gives hypothetical indications of natural ends [but] justifies no absolute teleological judgments."[59]

A *nexus finalis*, on the other hand, presents "a special kind of causality" that characterizes "an internal purposiveness of the natural being."[60] For such beings the causal nexus is structured so that "as far as their existence and their form are concerned [they] are possible only through their relation to the whole."[61] We might say the *essentia* of the whole is manifest through its parts. This is suggested by how Kant likens the distinction between *nexus effectivus* and *nexus finalis*

---

by the disjunctive logical function and the category of community pertains to how the latter produces an, albeit regulative, concept of the object as an organized being, whereas the former determines only the activity of judging without producing a concept of the object. Bickmann appears to concur with this when she observes that after discussing the subjective purposiveness of aesthetic judgment, "geht Kant jedoch einen Schritt weiter: Er sucht nach der *inneren Zweckmäßigkeit* der gesamten natürlichen und sittlichen Ordnung: dh. nach den Prinzipien der objektiven Zweckmäßigkeit in dieser Welt, insofern sie zugleich aus inneren Quellen motiviert ist" (Bickmann, "Die eingebettete Vernunft in Kants "Kritik der Urteilskraft": Wechselintegrationen vereint-entgegengesetzter Sphären," 30 – 31). I add to this that the progression from the purposiveness of aesthetic judgment to that of teleological judgment involves a transition from the reflective use of disjunctivity to the reflective use of community.

53 *Critique of the Power of Judgment*, § 65, 5:372.
54 *Critique of the Power of Judgment*, § 65, 5:372.
55 *Critique of the Power of Judgment*, § 61, 5:360.
56 *Critique of the Power of Judgment*, § 63, 5:367.
57 *Critique of the Power of Judgment*, § 63, 5:368.
58 *Critique of the Power of Judgment*, § 63, 5:367.
59 *Critique of the Power of Judgment*, § 63, 5:369.
60 *Critique of the Power of Judgment*, § 63, 5:367.
61 *Critique of the Power of Judgment*, § 65, 5:373.

to that of "real causes" and "ideal ones."⁶² Whereas the real efficient cause explains how the thing came to exist, the ideal final cause describes how:

> a thing [...] contain[s] in itself and its internal possibility a relation to ends, i.e., is to be possible only as a natural end and without the causality of the concepts of a rational being outside of it [with] its parts [...] combined into a whole by being reciprocally the cause and effect of their form.⁶³

We see this particularly in products of nature and organisms, where a reciprocal causality is found both in the relation of parts to parts, parts to whole and whole to parts, as "each part is conceived as if it exists only through all the others, thus as if existing for the sake of the others and on account of the whole."⁶⁴

This structure of reciprocal causality should bring to mind the third entry under relation, the disjunctive logical function and category of community. Since the *nexus finalis* concerns the emergence of an organized being, here the reciprocal causality functions to determine this being and does not aim its determination of relation at the act of judging, itself. It is not that a disjunctive judgment gives rise to the cognition of a being as an organic whole, but that the reciprocal relation that presides over the *complementa* gives rise to the disjunctive judgment as a whole.⁶⁵ Hence, unlike how the disjunctive logical function merely allows a disjunctive initial constitution of the *judgment* as a whole to manifest, a *nexus finalis* allows for the determination of the *object* judged through the category of community. The inclusivity of the reciprocal conditioning of the parts is paramount. Kant re-elaborates how an "end" is to be defined within the context of the reciprocally causal network of a *nexus finalis*, writing:

> For the thing itself is an end and is thus comprehended under a concept of an idea that must determine *a priori* everything that is to be contained in it.⁶⁶

Thus, the concept of *what the thing is to be* functions as the end or purpose. The purposiveness of an organized being is comprehended as a purpose internal to this being. It is this purpose that determines the reciprocal causality of the being's parts and whole, exhibiting purposiveness of form—what this being must

---

62 *Critique of the Power of Judgment*, § 65, 5:373.
63 *Critique of the Power of Judgment*, § 65, 5:373.
64 *Critique of the Power of Judgment*, § 65, 5:373–4.
65 This underlying element of causality in disjunctivity that causes the judgment to be a specific sort of judgment as a whole will come more strongly to the fore when examining how purposiveness without a purpose arises in judgments of taste, below.
66 *Critique of the Power of Judgment*, § 65, 5:373.

be in order to be what it is. Pure aesthetic judgment, however, cannot have such a determined purposiveness of form as its grounds. Rather, a mere *form of purposiveness* must emerge in its place.[67]

II.B Taking the Purpose out of Purposiveness

Now let us investigate how the concept of an end—of a purpose—can be removed while allowing the form of purposiveness to remain. The purposiveness of form, described in the last section, is dependent upon the concept of what that something is to be. The "merely formal purposiveness" that serves as the principle of

---

[67] Both Guyer and Allison discuss the importance of distinguishing between a *form of purposiveness* and the *purposiveness of form* (which, as Allison points out, due to Guyer's differing translation of *Zweckmäßigkeit* in *Kant and the Claims of Taste*, is discussed by Guyer under the title "form of finality" and "finality of form"; I find Allison's rendering preferable). Allison remarks that "the operative contrast is between merely seeming purposive or being purposivelike, which occurs when this purposiveness is not connected with a determinate purpose, and actually being purposive or manifesting a purpose" (*Kant's Theory of Taste: A Reading of the Critique of Aesthetic Judgment*, 132). The latter, *purposiveness of form*, indicates the way that a given object can have objective purposiveness. That is, if it proves itself to be adequate for serving a purpose that the object can serve, then it has external purposiveness (i.e., usefulness or advantageousness). If it is found to correspond with the concept of what it is to be, in itself, then it has internal purposiveness (i.e., perfection). Both internal and external purposiveness involve the object being adequate to some concept, and thus neither fits precisely with what is exhibited in a pure aesthetic judgment. When one looks upon the object and sees that it is adequate to the concept of an end, then one recognizes that the object exhibits the *purposiveness of form*, meaning that a purpose is served by its very form. *Purposiveness of form* can be observed even if one does not *know* the concept of the purpose that this object's form serves. Kant makes this clear in a footnote where he writes of "the stone utensils often excavated from ancient burial mounds, which are equipped with a hole, as if for a handle, which, although they clearly betray by their shape a purposiveness the end of which one does not know, are nevertheless not declared to be beautiful on that account" (*Critique of the Power of Judgment*, § 17, 5:236, footnote). These archeological objects are judged to have *purposiveness of form* without one being able to determine what this purpose is. The obfuscation of this purpose does not yield aesthetic purposiveness without a purpose, because it is based upon a *purposiveness of form* (exhibiting a form that serves a purpose) and not the *form of purposiveness* (exhibiting the form of "merely seeming purposive," see Allison, 1998, 132). In the aesthetic purposiveness of form, there is the sense of purposiveness without any determinate purpose, not even an obscured one, being related to the object: "A flower, by contrast, e.g., a tulip, is held to be beautiful because a certain purposiveness is encountered in our perception of it which, as we judge it, is not related to any end at all" (*Critique of the Power of Judgment*, § 17, 5:236), footnote. In this next section, I explain how this *form of purposiveness* emerges through the special difficulties one encounters when seeking to relate a purpose to beautiful nature or beautiful art.

pure aesthetic judgment cannot, however, involve a concept of what the thing is to be, because the determining ground of such a judgment "cannot be a concept, and thus not a concept of a determinate end."[68] Kant's decision to extract purpose from aesthetic purposiveness naturally ensues from his adherence to the concept-independence of aesthetic judgment.

Even if concept-independence were not a concern, however, any judgment that involves the concept of an end still could not be aesthetic, because such judgments are *logical* and *objective*.[69] The fundamental distinction between aesthetic judgment as subjective and logical judgment as objective, thus, forecloses the possibility that any purposiveness found in aesthetic judgment involve a purpose.

II.B.1 Purposes in Art and Nature

The distinction that Kant draws between nature and art has to do with whether something was brought about by an intentionally acting cause, or not:

> 1) Art is distinguished from nature as doing (*facere*) is from acting or producing in general (*agere*), and the product or consequence of the former is distinguished as a work (*opus*) from the latter as an effect (*effectus*).
>
> By right, only production through freedom, i.e., through a capacity for choice that grounds its actions in reason, should be called art. For although people are fond of describing the product of the bees (the regularly constructed honeycombs) as a work of art, this is done only on account of the analogy with the latter; that is, as soon as we recall that they do not ground their work on any rational consideration of their own, we say that it is a product of their nature (of instinct), and as art it is ascribed only to their creator.[70]

Although there seems to be something like a concept of a finished hive towards which bees purposefully orient their activity, this cannot be purposive activity.

---

68 *Critique of the Power of Judgment*, § 15, 5:228.
69 "[T]he objective purposiveness of nature, i.e., the possibility of things as natural ends, the judgment about which is made only in accordance with concepts of these, i.e., not aesthetically (in relation to the feeling of pleasure or displeasure) but rather logically, and is called teleological. The objective purposiveness is grounded either on the internal possibility of the object, or on the relative possibility of its external consequences. In the first case the teleological judgment considers the perfection of a thing in accordance with an end that lies in it itself (since the manifold elements in it are related to each other reciprocally as end and means); in the second the teleological judgment about a natural object concerns only its usefulness, namely its correspondence to an end that lies in other things." *Critique of the Power of Judgment*, First Introduction XII, 20:250.
70 *Critique of the Power of Judgment*, § 43, 5:303.

Purposive activity is activity undertaken in order to realize an end. Before its actualization, the end exists as a concept in the mind of the intentionally acting agent, guiding her efforts. Kant, however, does not allow that the actions of animals or other natural forces are guided by concepts. Thus, nature itself cannot be determinatively judged to be purposive: "we do not actually **observe** ends in nature as intentional, but merely **add** this concept as a guideline for the power of judgment in reflection on the products of nature, they are not given to us through the object."[71] Consequently, what seems to be an element of purposiveness in nature, such as the bees' construction of their hive, must be understood as merely analogical to purposiveness. The bees are not capable of cognizing an end and hence their activity cannot be truly purposive.[72] Rather, their activity can only be seen as the result of an engrained instinctual drive pushing the animal to create its home without the involvement of cognition.[73] Kant elaborates further:

> In other cases too one sees an art in everything that is so constituted that a representation of it in its cause must have preceded its reality (as even in the case of bees), although it may not exactly have thought of the effect; but if something is called a work of art without qualification, in order to distinguish it from an effect of nature, then by that is always understood a work of human beings.[74]

Although nature cannot be judged as constituted according to a purpose, Kant acknowledges that in certain products of nature "a representation of it in its cause must have preceded its reality," as occurs with bees who do not accidentally happen to build a hive or birds who do not accidentally build a nest, but rather set out to do so. These are, however, merely "effect[s] of nature." Thus, nature offers a sort of shadow-purposiveness discernible in the way that causes and effects link together in a *nexus effectivus* without us being able to identify this as the work of an intentionally acting agent who strives to realize an end.

---

71 *Critique of the Power of Judgment*, § 75, 5:399, emphasis original.
72 This line of thought dates back to Kant's essay *On the Use of Teleological Principles in Philosophy* (1788), in which he writes, "**Ends** have a direct relation to **reason**, whether this is that of another or our own. But if we are to place them in the reason of another, then we must at least base this on our own as an analogue: because otherwise this cannot be represented at all. Now the ends are either ends of **nature** or of **freedom.** No one can see *a priori* that there must be ends in nature, although it can very well be seen *a priori* that there must be a connection of causes and effects in nature" (*Teleological Principles*, 8:182, emphasis original).
73 Marc Okrent analyzes the few remarks Kant makes on animals, showing that Kant's refusal to regard animals as capable of using concepts leads to an entirely unsatisfactory theory of animal sapience that in no way accords with what many a pet owner has observed to be true (2006). For further discussion of Okrent's article, see chapter one.
74 *Critique of the Power of Judgment*, § 43, 5:303

However, that which is mechanically brought about through a nexus of effective causes may still be entirely contingent.[75] It is only through the power of teleological judgment that we are able to regard this as having a *regulative* purposiveness, viewing nature *as if* it acted to intentionally bring about ends.

A work of art is to be distinguished from nature by the fact that it is the work of a human being, who intentionally acts to transform material "lent to us by nature [...] into something entirely different, namely into that which steps beyond nature."[76] Thus, the presence of a purpose cannot be denied in works of art, because they are the product of human action, whereas the presence of a purpose can neither be denied nor affirmed in the products of nature, because "[s]trictly speaking, the organization of nature is therefore not analogous with any causality that we know."[77] Moreover, knowledge of whether nature is the effect or an intentionally acting creator is beyond the limits of what humans can know. The recognition that one cannot know how purposes are or are not involved in the production of nature, coupled with the undeniable purposiveness of all human action, presents an initial obstacle for seeing how beautiful art and products of nature can be judged to be purposive without a purpose. I will now draw out the disjunctivity in aesthetic judging, which makes such an aesthetic purposiveness possible.

II.C What Purposiveness without a Purpose Means

The correspondence between the idea of what an object *should be* and what it *in fact is* yields objective purposiveness, but this "has nothing at all to do with the feeling of pleasure" that supplies the grounds for aesthetic judgment where

---

[75] This is why the antinomy of the Teleological Power of Judgment—which asks whether "all generation of material things is possible in accordance with merely mechanical laws" or "Some generation of such things is not possible in accordance with merely mechanical laws" (*Critique of the Power of Judgment*, § 70, 5:387)—resolves itself through the recognition that each holds as a regulative principle of the reflecting power of judgment, not a constitutive principle of the determining power of judgment. Kant observes that: "We can by no means prove the impossibility of the generation of organized products of nature through the mere mechanism of nature, because since the infinite manifold of particular laws of nature that are contingent for us are only cognized empirically, we have no insight into their primary internal ground, and thus we cannot reach the internal and completely sufficient principle of the possibility of a nature (which lies in the supersensible) at all" (*Critique of the Power of Judgment*, § 71, 5:389).
[76] *Critique of the Power of Judgment*, § 49, 5:314.
[77] *Critique of the Power of Judgment*, § 65, 5:375.

"such a concept is not necessary at all."[78] Instead, we find that "the representation of a subjective purposiveness of an object is even identical with the feeling of pleasure (without even involving an abstract concept of a purposive relation)."[79] This means that:

> Purposiveness can thus exist without an end, insofar as we do not place the causes of this form in a **will**, but can still make the explanation of its possibility conceivable to ourselves only by deriving it from a will [...].[80]

Hence, purposiveness and the concept of a purpose can be disentangled from one another if the form is not taken to be the product of a will—and yet one finds that the form can only be conceived of as if it were derived from a will. The disjunctive logical function gives us a way of holding these two mutually exclusive possibilities together so that they may condition one another.

Unlike the contemplation of an organic being, where the category of community determines the object, purposiveness without a purpose only involves the disjunctive logical function determining the act of judging and does not invoke the corresponding category in any determination of the object judged. Despite this crucial difference between the judgment of an organic being and aesthetic judging, the *nexus finalis* can provide an inroad for understanding purposiveness without a purpose. Kant, himself, suggests this when he writes regarding pure aesthetic judgment that, "we can at least observe a purposiveness concerning form, even without basing it in an end (as the matter of the *nexus finalis*), and notice it in objects, although in no other way than by reflection."[81] In a certain way, purposiveness without a purpose appears to have a structure very similar to that of the *nexus finalis*. The primary difference being that the structural similarity must be abstracted from the concept of an end. Thus, the description I provided above of how the category structures the *nexus finalis* (community) can help us now regressively work out how the logical function corresponding to this category (the disjunctive) provides the activity of judging with a structure analogous to that of the *nexus finalis*, which yields an aesthetic form of purposiveness for which there can be no purpose.

To see the aesthetic purposiveness, one must reflect disjunctively, retreating from any categorical assertion that the representation has or lacks a purpose. In-

---

[78] *Critique of the Power of Judgment*, First Introduction Remark, 20:228.
[79] *Critique of the Power of Judgment*, First Introduction, 20:228–9.
[80] *Critique of the Power of Judgment*, § 10, 5:219–220.
[81] *Critique of the Power of Judgment*, § 10, 5:220.

stead, one holds together the *complementa* that constitute the entire sphere of aesthetic purposiveness.

I will trace out the structure constituting[82] purposiveness without a purpose as follows: Two categorical judgments serve as the matter out of which two hypothetical judgments are formed, and these, in turn, are brought together in a disjunctively **chiasmic** relation. Let us begin with the two categorical component judgments. These are:

> Anything that is the product of the will has a purpose.
> Anything that is not the product of the will does not have a purpose.[83]

In the contemplation of aesthetic purposiveness, neither of these is asserted categorically. Rather, they are reformulated into two hypotheticals, where the antecedent is problematic so that whether the component "propositions in themselves are true remains unsettled"[84]:

> If nature is not a product of the will, then it does not have a purpose.
> If art is a product of the will, then it has a purpose.

As we saw above, unavoidable complications arise in the relation between products of nature and purpose. Nature cannot be determinatively judged to act intentionally towards an end.[85] The idea that nature is based on causes that act

---

[82] The fact that reflective aesthetic judgment does not constitute an object through concepts does not mean that the act of reflective aesthetic judging is not, itself, constituted through the logical functions. On the contrary, it has been my overarching argument over the course of this project that the logical functions govern the act of judging so as to make it into a determinate form of judgment even if this form of judgment is determined to be merely reflective and thus determined not to produce any determination of the object judged.

[83] These categorical propositions are derived from the § 10, discussed above.

[84] *Critique of Pure Reason*, A73/B99. Kant explains further, "It is only the implication that is thought by means of this judgment" (Ibid.).

[85] The most important feats of the teleological judgment of the second part of the third Critique must remain regulative and "in this way cannot be constitutive principles determining how the object is constituted [although, the regulative principles are] immanent and secure in their use and appropriate for the human point of view" (*Critique of the Power of Judgment*, § 76, 5:403). Thus, Kant does not allow that nature can be judged to be constituted through the will of an "intentionally acting cause" (*Critique of the Power of Judgment*, § 61, 5:360–1). He further elaborates on how the boundary of his philosophical system which prevents us from making a constitutive judgment of nature as based on intentionally acting causes shapes his analysis in the second part of the third *Critique:* "If, however, we were to base nature on intentionally acting causes, hence were to ground teleology not merely on a regulative principle for the mere judging of appearances, to which nature in its particular laws could be thought of as subjected, but rath-

intentionally is, however, a regulative judgment that must be conditionally asserted "for the sake of the cognition of natural laws in experience."[86] Thus, the relation between products of nature and purposes cannot be determinatively judged.

Rather than leading to frustration, this indeterminateness is precisely what makes nature the paradigmatic object for aesthetic judgments.[87] Here, the purposiveness *cannot* be determinatively judged through the concept of a purpose (i.e., the concept of an end towards which an intentionally acting cause oriented itself in the creation of this natural product). It is *possible* that there is an intentionally acting cause that created nature to serve a purpose (and, indeed, the teleological power of judgment takes hold of this possibility, so as to make a regulative use of it for reflective judgment), however this can only be entertained problematically and not taken assertorically. The problematic entertainment of the possibility that nature is purposive is reciprocally conditioned by the equally problematic judgment that nature is not purposive. Thus, the purposiveness of nature can only be judged disjunctively.

II.C.1 Nature as Art

The aesthetic judgment of beautiful nature is paradigmatic, because it embodies the disjunctivity towards a purpose that yields purposiveness without the ability to determine a purpose (i.e., to judge determinatively). In this manner the judging subject aesthetically judges beautiful products of nature by entertaining the mutually exclusive possibilities of having a purpose and of not having a purpose, these being "taken together [so as to] constitute"[88] the disjunctive community in which a purposiveness without a purpose can emerge.

---

er on a constitutive principle for the derivation of its products from their causes, then the concept of a natural end would no longer belong to the reflecting, but to the determining power of judgment; in which case, however, it would not in fact properly belong to the power of judgment at all (like the concept of beauty, as a formal subjective purposiveness), but rather, as a concept of reason, it would introduce a new causality into natural science, which, however, we merely borrow from ourselves and ascribe to other beings, yet without wanting to think of them as similar to ourselves" (*Ibid.*). From this, it is clear that nature cannot be simply asserted to be a product of the will.

86 *Critique of the Power of Judgment*, § 69, 5:386.
87 Kant indicates this when he discusses the "preeminence of the beauty of nature over the beauty of art" (*Critique of the Power of Judgment*, § 42, 5:300). Guyer remarks that it is as if the beauty of art is "borrowed" from nature (Paul Guyer, *Kant and the Experience of Freedom Kant and the Experience of Freedom* [Cambridge: Cambridge University Press, 1993], Ch. 7).
88 *Critique of Pure Reason*, A74/B99

Kant expresses this disjunctive judgment that gives rise to aesthetic purposiveness (this product of nature is either the effect of a will or it is not the effect of a will) through an analogy.

Of the beautiful,[89] Kant writes:

> Nature was beautiful, if at the same time it looked like art; and art can only be called beautiful if we are aware that it is art and yet it looks to us like nature.[90]

Nature can only be judged to be beautiful, when regarded in a manner that recognizes something analogous to art in it. Since art is known to be the product of the will, to see in nature something that looks like art is to see in it a form whose cause "we do not place [...] in a will, but can still make the explanation of its possibility conceivable to ourselves only by deriving it from a will."[91] Thus, to appear to us "like art" does not indicate a classificatory error in which a product of nature is *mistaken* for a human product. Rather, we are to be aware of what it is *while* we contemplate how it appears to be that which it is not. It must be either *art* or *nature*, and we know it to in fact be *nature*, but in judging it to be nature, we see nature as conditioned through the idea of art, although it is not *art*.

Kant makes it clear *that* beauty is judged in nature when nature is regarded as if it were art. *How* exactly this occurs (i.e., what it is about products of nature that trigger a feeling of purposiveness, leaving us unsatisfied by a merely mechanical account) is, however, not laid out in the Critique of the Aesthetic

---

89 Here, I outline how aesthetic purposiveness functions for the beautiful, and not the ugly. As Rodolphe Gasché notes, the pleasure taken in purposiveness without a purpose for the beautiful cannot simply be reversed so as to delineate the ugly as the beautiful in inverted form ("Transcendentality in Play"). He argues that there can ultimately be no aesthetic judgment of the ugly, because aesthetic judgment needs the universal communicability, but this communicability is only achieved through the harmony of the faculties. Thus, a disharmony of the faculties in an aesthetic judging of the ugly would fail to achieve the minimal harmony necessary for communicability. The resulting lack of an ability to communicate the judgment means that it is not a judgment of taste, for "[o]ne could even define taste as the faculty for judging that which makes our feeling in a given representation universally communicable without the mediation of a concept" (*Critique of the Power of Judgment*, § 40, 5:295). Furthermore, it should be observed that aesthetic judgments based on a feeling of displeasure appear to correlate with the sublime, not the ugly. The sublime circumvents the difficulties of communicability, because the "apprehension of an otherwise formless and nonpurposive object" (*Critique of the Power of Judgment*, § 30, 5:280) "awakens the feeling of a supersensible faculty in us" (*Critique of the Power of Judgment*, § 25, 5:268). Hence, the sublime "should properly be ascribed only to the manner of thinking, or rather to its foundation in human nature" (*Critique of the Power of Judgment*, § 30, 5:280).
90 *Critique of the Power of Judgment*, § 45, 5:306.
91 *Critique of the Power of Judgment*, § 10, 5:220.

Power of Judgment.[92] In the Critique of the Teleological Power of Judgment, however, Kant does leave hints of how something can strike us as purposive without any determinate purpose or intentionally acting agent discernable. Here, Kant begins with a description of how we occasionally encounter things in nature that strike us as more than a product of merely mechanical forces:

> If someone were to perceive a geometrical figure, for instance a regular hexagon, drawn in the sand in an apparently uninhabited land, his reflection, working with a concept of it, would become aware of the unity of the principle of its generation by means of reason, even if only obscurely, and thus, in accordance with this, would not be able to judge as a ground of the possibility of such a shape the sand, the nearby sea, the wind, the footprints of any known animals, or any other nonrational cause, because the contingency of coinciding with such a concept, which is possible only in reason, would seem to him so infinitely great that it would be just as good as if there were no natural law of nature, consequently no cause in nature acting merely mechanically, and as if the concept of such an object could be regarded as a concept that can be given only by reason and only by reason compared with the object, thus as if only reason can contain the causality for such an effect, consequently that this object must be thoroughly regarded as an end, but not a natural end, i.e., as a product of **art** (*vestigium hominis video*).[93]

Here, the hexagon presents signs of purposiveness that the judging subject is unable to ignore. One way that this sort of thing can occur is by an object appearing in such a manner that the judging subject cannot imagine it *not* to be the product of some intentionally acting agent who created it guided by the concept of an end. In this manner the object will appear purposive even if all contextual clues seem to indicate that it is not the product of an intentionally acting

---

92 For example, the following passage from the Critique of the Aesthetic Power of Judgment describes how a sense of purposiveness arises and clarifies that one does not need to be able to discern the end in order to sense this purposiveness: "An object or a state of mind or even an action, however, even if its possibility does not necessarily presuppose the representation of an end, is called purposive merely because its possibility can only be explained and conceived by us insofar as we assume as its ground a causality in accordance with ends, i.e., a will that has arranged it so in accordance with the representation of a certain rule. Purposiveness can thus exist without an end, insofar as we do not place the causes of this form in a will, but can still make the explanation of its possibility conceivable to ourselves only by deriving it from a will. Now we do not always necessarily need to have insight through reason (concerning its possibility) into what we observe. Thus we can at least observe a purposiveness concerning form, even without basing it in an end (as the matter of the *nexus finalis*), and notice it in objects, although in no other way than by reflection" (*Critique of the Power of Judgment*, § 10, 5:220). This passage does not answer the question of *how* something in nature can strike us as purposiveness despite the fact that, due to its status as a product of nature, no purpose can be determinately judged.
93 *Critique of the Power of Judgment*, § 64, 5:370.

agent. Thus, a perfect hexagon drawn in the sand causes us to doubt our initial impression that the island is uninhabited. Similarly, a farmer unable to imagine that any human could ever bypass the security measures protecting his field, may take the spontaneous appearance of designs in these crops to indicate the involvement of an intentionally acting non-human agent.[94] These two examples illustrate how something may seem unexpectedly purposive despite the fact that it appears in a natural context. In both cases the intention involved in forming the sand, or crops, in accordance with a given geometrical concept or cognizable design is identified as the purpose that guided the production of the shape. Consequently, the judging subject finds that—despite all contextual clues to the contrary—this thing is not a product of nature, but of an intentionally acting agent (i.e., a product of art).

From this Kant moves on to instances where the recognition of purposiveness cannot lead one to the unequivocal conclusion that an intentionally acting agent is responsible for the purposiveness of the object. These are cases in which something is recognized beyond a doubt to be a product of nature, but it is cognized with purposiveness and thus appears to be a natural end. This arises for a natural product, such as a tree, which "must be related to itself reciprocally as both cause and effect."[95] In judging something to be a natural end, the judging subject is struck by an impression of purposiveness that has an effect similar to that of the hexagon drawn in the sand. Kant lists three ways that a natural product is seen to involve purposiveness and thus to be a natural end:

> First, a tree generates another tree [...] and so it generates itself as far as species is concerned [...]. Second, a tree also generates itself as an individual. This sort of effect we call [...] growth [...]. Third, one part of this creature also generates itself in such a way that the preservation of the one is reciprocally dependent on the preservation of the other.[96]

When we look at a tree and recognize these features, we see it as "an organized and self-organizing being" and, hence, call it "a natural end."[97] Thus, a natural

---

[94] Hence, the geometrical figure drawn in the sand represents the same sort of situation that leads some farmers who wake to find that their crops have been pressed into a design to believe that extraterrestrial life forms were at work. Such a farmer recognizes in the shapes a design that can only be the result of an intentionally acting agent and since the farmer somehow has an unquestionable conviction that no human agent was involved, this is concluded to have been the result of a non-human intentionally acting agent.
[95] *Critique of the Power of Judgment*, § 65, 5:372.
[96] *Critique of the Power of Judgment*, § 64, 5:371.
[97] *Critique of the Power of Judgment*, § 65, 5:374.

product can present itself as something purposive, even though it cannot be determinatively cognized as the product of an intentionally acting agent. Admittedly, Kant does not develop this line of thought concerning natural ends in the Critique of the Aesthetic Power of Judgement, presumably because it pertains to explicitly causal concerns in the cognition of an *object*, which is the central issue for teleological, not aesthetic, judgment. Whereas the teleological power of judgment is used to reflectively judge a natural end as an object, the purposiveness of this same natural end stimulates the aesthetic power of judgment into the activity of reflectively judging with taste.

Kant, himself, remarks on the fact that both the teleological judgment of natural ends and the judgment of taste pertain to natural products:

> Beauty in nature, since it is ascribed to objects only in relation to reflection on their **outer** intuition, thus only to the form of their surfaces, can rightly be called an analogue of art. But **inner natural perfection**, as is possessed by those things that are possible only as **natural ends** and hence as organized beings, is not thinkable and explicable in accordance with any analogy to any physical, i.e., natural capacity that is known to us; indeed, since we ourselves belong to nature in the widest sense, it is not thinkable and explicable even through an exact analogy with human art. [98]

Both respond to a purposiveness that is detected in natural products, the difference being that when judged in a pure aesthetic manner the purposiveness reflected "on their outer intuition" stimulates one into a harmonious free play of the faculties, which are not brought to a halt by any determinate concept, but when judged teleologically one makes reflective use of a concept to cognize the "inner natural perfection" [99] of the object. The purposiveness without a purpose that is encountered in judgments of taste is to be seen insofar as nature appears *as if* it were art, although it is not. Only through this analogy can we understand how beautiful nature appears to be purposive, despite the fact that it is not determinable through a purpose. It looks as if it were art, but actually is nature.

II.C.2 Art as Nature

Although art's relation to a purpose would initially seem to be unproblematic, further scrutiny reveals this not to be the case. Just as beautiful nature needs an analogy to art for its aesthetic purposiveness to be understood, so too does art require an analogy to nature. We can see this need of analogy if we first

---

[98] *Critique of the Power of Judgment*, § 65, 5:376.
[99] *Critique of the Power of Judgment*, § 65, 5:372.

look to the conditions for the production of beautiful art (genius), and then build upon this to hone in on what it is to which one is responding when judging a work to be beautiful.

Just as beautiful nature can only be seen through an analogy to art, beautiful art can only be seen through an analogy to nature:

> In a product of art one must be aware that it is art, and not nature; yet the purposiveness in its form must still seem to be as free from all constraint by arbitrary rules as if it were a mere product of nature.[100]

The analogy to nature, allows for the neutralization of the purpose one assumes to guide human action so that the requisite form of purposiveness without a purpose can manifest. Only if this neutralization of the purpose through an analogy to art is achieved can an artwork be judged to be beautiful. This is clearly stated in the very section title: "§ 45. Beautiful art is an art to the extent that it seems at the same time to be nature."[101]

I will now show that the contemplation of art as analogous to nature is not merely some trick in the mind of the judging subject. Rather, Kant develops a theory of artistic production, which shows that it is only through the intertwinement of art and nature that a human agent is capable of producing beautiful art.

II.C.2.i Creating Art: Genius

As Kant observes, "art always has a determinate intention of producing something."[102] In the creation of beautiful art, however, the natural talent of genius is what causes the artwork to come out beautiful. This talent is instilled in the artist by nature, not training, and guides the artist's creative actions in an intuitive, not discursive, manner. Thus, although the artwork has an intentionally acting human agent as its cause, it is more that which is unintentional *in* this agent (i.e., natural) that is responsible for the beauty of the piece. These conditions of aesthetic creation also have implications for aesthetic judgment. When one judges an artwork to be beautiful, this is because one can see that the piece offers something beyond mechanical art "which can be grasped and followed according to rules."[103] It is "the originality of his talent [that] constitutes one [...] essen-

---

100 *Critique of the Power of Judgment*, § 45, 5:306.
101 *Critique of the Power of Judgment*, § 45, 5:306.
102 *Critique of the Power of Judgment*, § 45, 5:306.
103 *Critique of the Power of Judgment*, § 47, 5:310. Kant suggests that beautiful art does have something of the mechanical in it, altough its beauty is something that no mechanism can pro-

tial element of the character of the genius."[104] This originality cannot be simply attributed to the intentional actions of the artist, because even to the artist its origin remains mysterious: "no Homer or Wieland can indicate how his ideas, which are fantastic and yet at the same time rich in thought, arise and come together in his head, because he himself does not know it and thus cannot teach it to anyone else either."[105]

It is nature in the artist that provides the genius that allows for the creation of beautiful art. For this reason, Kant defines genius as "the talent (natural gift) that gives the rule to art."[106] Kant elaborates that genius "is a **talent** for producing that for which no determinate rule can be given, not a predisposition of skill for that which can be learned in accordance with some rule, consequently that **originality** must be its primary characteristic."[107] This talent is "an inborn productive faculty of the artist, [which] itself belongs to nature."[108] Thus, the talent of genius is instilled by nature in the artist.[109] Hence, the originality that exhibits genius is the product of a part of nature in the artist. It is for this reason that the artist cannot explain whence this originality comes, for the cause acting to bring it about is "the inborn predisposition of the mind (*ingenium*),"[110] and it is through this that "nature gives the rule to art."[111] Kant summarizes:

> For every art presupposes rules which first lay the foundation by means of which a product that is to be called artistic is first represented as possible. The concept of beautiful art, however, does not allow the judgment concerning the beauty of its product to be derived from any sort of rule that has a concept for its determining ground, and thus has as its ground a concept of how it is possible. Thus beautiful art cannot itself think up the rule in accordance with which it is to bring its product into being. Yet since without a preceding rule a product can never be called art, nature in the subject (and by means of the disposition

---

duce. Accordingly, even the genius is in need of some training in order to produce tastefully beautiful art: "Genius can only provide rich material for products of art; its elaboration and form require a talent that has been academically trained, in order to make a use of it that can stand up to the power of judgment" (*Ibid.*).
104 *Critique of the Power of Judgment*, § 47, 5:310.
105 *Critique of the Power of Judgment*, § 47, 5:310.
106 *Critique of the Power of Judgment*, § 46, 5:307.
107 *Critique of the Power of Judgment*, § 46, 5:307–8, emphasis original.
108 *Critique of the Power of Judgment*, § 46, 5:307.
109 Bickmann writes that "Im Genie nun findet Kant diejenige Instanz, durch die sich die Natur einem empfänglichen Gemüte in ihrer inneren Zweckmäßigkeit offnebart" (Bickmann, "Die eingebettete Vernunft in Kants "Kritik der Urteilskraft": Wechselintegrationen vereint-entgegengesetzter Sphären," 30–31).
110 *Critique of the Power of Judgment*, § 46, 5:307.
111 *Critique of the Power of Judgment*, § 46, 5:307.

of its faculties) must give the rule to art, i.e., beautiful art is possible only as a product of genius.[112]

Art, broadly construed, is "a skill of human beings" through which humans use their "practical faculty" to produce things.[113] It "operates only technically (in accordance with its own laws)."[114] Kant grapples with the way that beautiful art must "presuppose [...] rules," but the rule that nature gives to art can be neither conceptual nor determining. It must be distinguished from the determinate, stylistic rules that are presupposed, taking a distinct form that is not typically assumed by rules. The atypicality characterizing this rule is addressed in the latter half of the passage quoted above:

> The concept of beautiful art, however, does not allow the judgment concerning the beauty of its product to be derived from any sort of rule that has a **concept** for its determining ground, and thus has as its ground a concept of how it is possible. Thus beautiful art cannot itself think up the rule in accordance with which it is to bring its product into being.[115]

In another passage, Kant further notes that "If one judges objects merely in accordance with concepts, then all representation of beauty is lost. Thus there can also be no rule in accordance with which someone could be compelled to acknowledge something as beautiful."[116] These two passages describe the rule that nature gives to art as having the following peculiarities: It is a rule that can neither describe the mechanics of how beautiful art is to be produced. It is a rule that cannot be grounded on a concept. It is a rule that cannot be used as a measure for determining which works of art are beautiful. Further evidence for the non-discursive, indeterminateness of the rule that nature gives to art is supplied by Kant's characterization of how this rule does not,

> itself describe or indicate scientifically how it brings its product into being, but rather that it gives the rule as **nature**, and hence the author of a product that he owes to his genius does not know himself how the ideas for it come to him, and also does not have it in his power to think up such things at will or according to plan, and to communicate to others precepts that would put them in a position to produce similar products.[117]

---

112 *Critique of the Power of Judgment*, § 46, 5:307.
113 *Critique of the Power of Judgment*, § 43, 5:303.
114 *Critique of the Power of Judgment*, First Introduction XII, 20:248.
115 *Critique of the Power of Judgment*, § 46, 5:307.
116 *Critique of the Power of Judgment*, § 8, 5:215–6.
117 *Critique of the Power of Judgment*, § 46, 5:308.

The rule is something that manifests in the work of genius without being articulated or later becoming articulable by the artist. It is a nondiscursive rule that can only be given by nature, thus one artist cannot state it for others to follow.

Admittedly, there are determinate rules that govern each art form and beautiful art is not created in ignorance of these. Kant notes this writing:

> Although mechanical and beautiful art, the first as a mere art of diligence and learning, the second as that of genius, are very different from each other, still there is no beautiful art in which something mechanical, which can be grasped and followed according to rules, and thus something **academically correct**, does not constitute the essential condition of the art. For something in it must be thought of as an end, otherwise one cannot ascribe its product to any art at all; it would be a mere product of chance. But in order to aim at an end in the work, determinate rules are required, from which one may not absolve oneself.[118]

These determinate rules that provide for academic correctness are not, however, to be equated with the rule given to art from nature. It is the inarticulable rule given by nature that makes beautiful art beautiful. The creation of art that skillfully embodies this rule, however, requires the articulable rules: "Genius can only provide rich **material** for products of art; its elaboration and **form** require a talent that has been academically trained, in order to make a use of it that can stand up to the power of judgment."[119] On the other hand, art that is *merely* created in accordance with the articulable determinate set of rules will be mechanical. Kant writes that "one cannot learn to write inspired poetry, however exhaustive all the rules for the art of poetry and however excellent the models for it may be."[120] Rules of style govern the technique, while the rule given by nature enables genius to infuse the work with spirit. Genius exhibits the talent,

> which is called spirit, for to express what is unnamable in the mental state in the case of a certain representation and to make it universally communicable, whether the expression consist in language, or painting, or in plastic art—that requires a faculty for apprehending the rapidly passing play of the imagination and unifying it into a concept (which for that very reason is original and at the same time discloses a new rule, which could not have been deduced from any antecedent principles or examples), which can be communicated without the constraint of rules.[121]

---

118 *Critique of the Power of Judgment*, § 47, 5:310.
119 *Critique of the Power of Judgment*, § 47, 5:310.
120 *Critique of the Power of Judgment*, § 47, 5:308–9.
121 *Critique of the Power of Judgment*, § 49, 5:317.

Whereas the rules of technique and style can be clearly articulated, carefully practiced and hence taught, development of artistic ability in accordance with the rule given to art by nature is more complicated:

> Since the gift of nature must give the rule to art (as beautiful art), what sort of rule is this? It cannot be couched in a formula to serve as a precept, for then the judgment about the beautiful would be determinable in accordance with concepts; rather, the rule must be abstracted from the deed, i.e. from the product, against which others may test their own talent, letting it serve them as a model not for copying but for imitation. How this is possible is difficult to explain. The ideas of the artist arouse similar ideas in his apprentice if nature has equipped him with a similar proportion of mental powers. The models of beautiful art are thus the only means for transmitting these to posterity, which could not happen through mere descriptions [...].[122]

The creation of beautiful art stems from something in the artist (genius) that the artist has not acquired through training, nor can access through conceptual thinking. Rather it is this gift of nature instilled in the artist that guides the artistic creation. The rule found only in beautiful art does not appear as something that could be clearly articulated and then followed. Rather, it can only be glimpsed in its state of inextricable intertwinement with the artistic work in which it manifests. The rule that resides in this gift of nature cannot be conceptualized, but is *expressed* in beautiful art. In this manner beautiful art exhibits "the unsought and unintentional subjective purposiveness in the free correspondence of the imagination to the lawfulness of the understanding presupposes a proportion and disposition of this faculty that cannot be produced by any following of rules, whether of science or of mechanical imitation, but that only the nature of the subject can produce."[123] Through genius, nature gives the rule to art.

II.C.2.ii Judging Art

Beautiful art is then analogous to nature, because its essential cause is not the intentionality of the artist, but rather the natural inborn gift that the artist possesses. This does not only affect the creation of beautiful art, but rather has further implications for the act of judging art. When judging art to be beautiful, one is responding to something in the artwork that is known to be art, but seems to be nature:

---

[122] *Critique of the Power of Judgment*, § 47, 5:309–310.
[123] *Critique of the Power of Judgment*, § 49, 5:317–8.

> Thus the purposiveness in the product of beautiful art, although it is certainly intentional, must nevertheless not seem intentional; i.e., beautiful art must be regarded as nature, although of course one is aware of it as art. A product of art appears as nature, however, if we find it to agree punctiliously but not painstakingly with rules in accordance with which alone the product can become what it ought to be, that is, without the academic form showing through, i.e., without showing any sign that the rule has hovered before the eyes of the artist and fettered his mental powers.[124]

Beautiful art "appears as nature" through the seeming effortlessness with which it all comes together, as if it could have simply grown together, although the judging subject knows this not to be the case.[125]

By no means is art's appearing as nature merely some sort of mind trick in the judging subject. Rather, in aesthetically judging beautiful art one must disjunctively hold together the mutually exclusive ideas that the art does and does not have a purpose. Although art is the product of human action, that which is beautiful in art stems from nature in the artist. Thus, the relation between beautiful art and purpose is just as mysterious as it was for beautiful nature. In nature, the way that nature is analogous to art afforded beauty. In art, the way that art can be seen as emerging from a gift of nature makes it beautiful. The judging subject, however, need not know the details of the art's creation. What is judged to be beautiful in the artwork is that which is effortlessly achieved, just as nature effortlessly produces the delicate petals of a tulip.[126]

---

124 *Critique of the Power of Judgment*, § 45, 5:306–7.

125 This connection between art and nature is further emphasized in Kant's description of genius, the natural talent through which beautiful art is created. The artistic genius represents a point of juncture between nature and art, where the artist who wills to create the art is guided by an inborn, natural talent. The set of conceptualized rules is needed to train the talent, helping it to find the appropriate "elaboration and **form**" (*Critique of the Power of Judgment*, § 47, 5:310), but the beauty of art does not originate in the compliance with such rules. Indeed, genius is "a talent for producing that for which no determinate rule can be given" (*Critique of the Power of Judgment*, § 46, 5:307).

126 Admittedly, there are also atrocities that are produced by nature, and even misshapen tulips arise now and again. Hence, the claim is not that all products of nature are beautiful, nor is it that all products of nature are effortlessly produced, but rather that *beautiful* nature is produced "punctiliously, but not painstakingly," and thus the effortlessness with which a beautiful artwork expresses the rule that nature gives to art indicates a further parallel in the art/nature analogy.

II.C.3 Chiasmus

If we take into consideration the reciprocity of the analogy between beautiful art and nature, then a complex chiasmic structure is generated. For something to be art is for it to appear as nature, although beautiful nature appears as art—art, that is, which in turn appears beautiful when it is as if it were nature.[127] We must hold art and nature together, so that they mutually condition one another—beautiful art being understood as such insofar as it could be seen both as being and as not being nature; nature being beautiful insofar as its relation to a purpose—and hence its status as art—can never be determinately judged.

The crisscrossing logic connecting art and nature in the beautiful can be described through a disjunctive relation, which exhibits,

> logical opposition, insofar as the sphere of one judgment excludes that of the other, yet at the same time the relation of community, insofar as the judgments together exhaust the sphere of cognition proper; it is therefore a relation of the parts of the sphere of a cognition where the sphere of each part is the complement of that of the others in the sum total of the divided cognition [...].[128]

As disjunctive, the two possibilities can be held together, undermining any simplistic classification of the object judged to be beautiful as squarely situated in the realm of art or nature. At the same time, doing so disjunctively allows one to avoid the violation of the principle of noncontradiction which would ensue upon an assertion that the object is *both* art *and* nature at the same time and in the same way. It is as if the determinative judgment that would organize the tulip under the category of nature is undone, partially rewound—so that we may enter an indeterminate moment of judging, problematically entertaining that the tulip is either art or nature. There is a tension in the mutually reciprocal relation of art and nature created by the logical opposition that weaves them together, while also keeping them apart. Thus, it remains a disjunctively governed act of judging that does not settle into any determination of the object as *actually*

---

[127] If we trace the inverted parallels that ensue from the reciprocally analogical structure that holds between beautiful art and nature, then we see that this in no way fosters any categorical claim that art *is* nature, nor does it indicate a casual relation in which art *causes* nature or nature *causes* art. There is a certain causality here, but it is not the linear causality of the *nexus effectivus*. Rather, this mutual reciprocity is analogous to that of the *nexus finalis*, in which an essence is ideally caused. Unlike the *nexus finalis* of an organized being (through the category of community), the beautiful does not "provide objective reality for the concept of an **end** [...] of **nature**" (*Critique of the Power of Judgment*, § 65, 5:376, *emphasis original*).
[128] *Critique of Pure Reason*, A73–4/B99.

being both nature and art through the category of community.[129] To do so would not only violate the law of non-contradiction,[130] but also transform the judgment so that it supplies a further determination of the object judged, which would be in clear conflict with how Kant describes aesthetic judgment:

> I have already pointed out that an aesthetic judgment is of a unique kind, and affords absolutely no cognition (not even a confused one) of the object [...] and does not bring to our attention any property of the object, but only the purposive form in the determination of the powers of representation that are occupied with it.[131]

Here, we see that it is of special importance that the logical function of disjunctivity structures the relation conceived in the *act of aesthetic judging*, that is "the purposive form in the determination of the powers of representation," and not the objects judged.[132] Aesthetic judgment, thus, does not determine the object as having its reality grounded on a reciprocal relation of community between its whole and parts. Rather, it holds together mutually exclusive judgments, so as to perceive "the purposive form in the determination of the powers of representation that are occupied with it." That is, aesthetic purposiveness reveals the capacity of our powers of representation to generate the form of purposiveness independent of the concept of an end.[133]

---

129 It may be argued that the presence of the natural gift of genius in the artist fuses nature and art together, but this should be understood as an interweaving, in which the identity of each remains intact, and not a homogenizing fusion that blends them together so that they become undifferentiable. Even if we identify something of nature in the artist, then the accordingly identified part will be *nature* that *guides* the artist's creative work; the art that results will not itself be nature. In beautiful nature, the way in which it seems as if the tulip had been created through artistic intent does transform nature into art, because no artist of nature can be determinately judged to have taken action.
130 Despite the way that Kant uses the regulative idea of a technique of nature for reflective judgment, nature and art are still defined in antithetical terms. Hence, neither side of the dialectic of teleological judgment can be determinately asserted as a constitutive judgment. Rather, regulative use must be made of both.
131 *Critique of the Power of Judgment*, § 15, 5:228.
132 Remarks such as this further support my reading of aesthetic judgment as guided by the logical functions to determine the act of judging, rather than by the categories, which would determine an object.
133 It is through the contemplation of beauty that we become receptive of a sense of purposiveness and practice judging it. This, in turn, builds up our ability, readying us so that we may learn to regulatively infuse the world with purposiveness through the power of teleological reflective judgment. It is in this manner that I see the second book of the third *Critique* building upon the first. The Critique of Aesthetic Judgment describes how we become aware of the mere form of purposiveness. This prepares us to apply the form of purposiveness objectively so as to reflective-

III Layers

In chapter two I suggested that purposiveness without a purpose is the thread that runs through the layered structure of aesthetic judgment, exerting a higher level of influence on our cognitive faculties with each layer. It begins to take shape on the first layer where the cognition of an empirical object allows a part of the intuition to escape—not because of an attempt at cognition was unsuccessful, but rather because no attempt to cognize this part of the intuition could ever be successful.[134] The intuitional excess is simply not the sort of thing that can be cognized. Hence, it will always escape cognition, *effortlessly*, like water passing through a sieve. Thus, we might say that the reception of the intuition occasioning the judgment of taste is grounded on its independence from a concept, and thus also from a purpose. It is in lingering over the intuitional excess, however, that the sense of aesthetic purposiveness arises.

This occurs in the feeling of the free play of the faculties. It is not that the intuitional excess is judged to be purposive, as serving the purpose of stimulating our faculties. To conceive of it along these lines would be to ascribe an external purpose to it (usefulness), regarding it as a sort of intellectual *nexus effec-*

---

ly judge purposiveness *with* a purpose in the teleological judgments of nature discussed in The Critique of the Teleological Power of Judgment. In the former we discover our ability to see purposiveness in the world and in the latter we apply it. Thus, the third *Critique* traces out a developmental story of sorts: "By a formal technique of nature, I understand its purposiveness in intuition; by its real technique, however, I understand its purposiveness in accordance with concepts. The first provides purposive shapes for the power of judgment, i.e., the form in the representation of which imagination and understanding agree mutually and of themselves for the possibility of a concept. The second signifies the concept of things as ends of nature, i.e., as such that their internal possibility presupposes an end, hence a concept which, as a condition, grounds the causality of their generation" (First Introduction IX, 20:232). Aesthetic judgment allows us to hone our sense of purposiveness, so that we are later ready to make teleological judgments in which we judge according to objective purposiveness "as a principle of the possibility of the things of nature" (*Critique of the Power of Judgment*, § 61, 5:360). Kant appears to have ordered the books in this manner to highlight the process in which the sense of purposiveness arises, first as subjective appreciation and then growing strong enough to be applied objectively to nature.

[134] "An aesthetic judgment in general can therefore be explicated as that judgment whose predicate can never be cognition (concept of an object) (although it may contain the subjective conditions for a cognition in general). In such a judgment the determining ground is sensation. However, there is only one so-called sensation that can never become a concept of an object, and this is the feeling of pleasure and displeasure. This is merely subjective, whereas all other sensation can be used for cognition" (*Critique of the Power of Judgment*, First Introduction, VIII., 20:224.).

tivus. Rather, when I say that the purposiveness, not the purpose, arises in the free play of the faculties, then what I mean is that this "harmonious play of the two faculties of cognition in the power of judgment, imagination and understanding"[135] is precisely the *feeling* of aesthetic purposiveness.[136] Since the free play does not yield any determination of the object, determinate concept or knowledge, it is not that the intuitional excess serves as the material for the production of some *thing*. Rather it stimulates our faculties into the mutual furthering of each other's activity, so that we have the feeling of purposiveness—the feeling of the conditions for the possibility of something being produced—without any determinate thing actually being produced. This is not, however the frustrating feeling of something that should and could be produced, but is blocked from taking shape—as Guyer describes in his apt example of a multiple choice test where all of the choices appear possibly correct, but the test-taker knows only one to be actually correct.[137] It is, instead, the pleasant feeling of boundless meaning, significant possibility without any worry of settling into actuality. This feeling of boundless meaning and significant possibility underpins creative production, but in the judging subject it arises without any need to struggle with the material medium so as to actually produce.

In this manner a compelling sense of purposiveness takes hold through the enlivening free play of the faculties of imagination and understanding on the second layer. This compelling feeling of purposiveness without a purpose incites discursive thinking on the third layer, allowing one to grasp the form of purposiveness as a concept that can hover before one's mind in the absence of any determinate purpose. On the third layer, purposiveness without a purpose comes into its own, facilitating the emergence of aesthetic ideas, "an inexponible rep-

---

135 *Critique of the Power of Judgment,* First Introduction, VIII., 20:224.
136 "The consciousness of the merely formal purposiveness in the play of the cognitive powers of the subject in the case of a representation through which an object is given is the pleasure itself, because it contains a determining ground of the activity of the subject with regard to the animation of its cognitive powers, thus an internal causality (which is purposive) with regard to cognition in general, but without being restricted to a particular cognition, hence it contains a mere form of the subjective purposiveness of a representation in an aesthetic judgment [...]. [I]t has a causality in itself, namely that of maintaining the state of the representation of the mind and the occupation of the cognitive powers without a further aim" (*Critique of the Power of Judgment,* § 12, 5:222).
137 Guyer, "The Harmony of the Faculties Revisited," 177. One might reformulate the multiple choice analogy to say that it is more that all of the possible answers must be held together to create the whole of the question, while, at the same time no one answer can be selected as correct. Clearly not the sort of question that belongs on any standardized test.

resentation[s] of the imagination (in its free play)."[138] Armed with our newly discovered ability to judge the beautiful "in accordance with the purposive disposition of the imagination for its correspondence with the faculty of concepts in general,"[139] one may make a different use of this same ability to judge nature teleologically. Through aesthetic judgment one creates in oneself the idea of a purposiveness without a purpose. This sets the stage so that one may later look upon the world and infuse it with purposes.[140] In this manner one may reflectively judge nature as purposeful, although such a judgment can never become determinate and constitutive.

---

138 *Critique of the Power of Judgment*, § 57, Remark I, 5:343. A further relation of reciprocal causality between nature and morality is described by Bickmann, who writes that aesthetic judgment functions as the "erster Schauplatz der gesuchten wechselseitigen Integration von natürlicher und sittlicher Ordnung" (Bickmann, "Das unskeptisches Fundament der Erkenntniskritik. Kants "schlechterdings notwendige Voraussetzungen" bei den wesentlichen Zwecken der menschlichen Vernunft," 144). She elaborates, "Kunst gilt Kant als erster Indikator jener Wechselintegration [...]. Die ästhetische Idee indiziert das Zusammenspiel der Kräfte, indem sie vereint und trennt, tielhat am Bedingten wie am Unbedingten gleichermaßen [...]. So ist die Sphäre der Kunst ein erstes Indiz für die sinnlich-übersinnliche Doppelstrukture unseres Weltbezugs" (*Ibid.*, 144). As suggested in earlier chapters, I view this as an activity of judgment that emerges on the third layer of aesthetic judgment, serving the intellectual interests that follow upon the pure aesthetic judging of the second layer, so that "the mind cannot reflect on the beauty of nature without finding itself at the same time to be interested in it. Because of this affinity, however, this interest is moral, and he who takes such an interest in the beautiful in nature can do so only insofar as he has already firmly established his interest in the morally good" (*Critique of the Power of Judgment*, § 42, 5:300).

139 *Critique of the Power of Judgment*, § 57, Remark I, 5:344.

140 Kant writes in the Introduction, "the purposiveness of a thing, insofar as it is represented in perception, is also not a property of the object itself (for such a thing cannot be perceived), although it can be derived from a cognition of things" (*Critique of the Power of Judgment*, Introduction, 5:189). This shows that even objective purposiveness is not a property perceived in the object, but rather something added to the object in the cognition of it. Kant continues, "Thus the purposiveness that precedes the cognition of an object, which is immediately connected with it even without wanting to use the representation of it for a cognition, is the subjective aspect of it that cannot become an element of cognition at all" (*Critique of the Power of Judgment*, Introduction, 5:189). Hence, the Critique of the Aesthetic Power of Judgment elaborates how a "purposiveness that precedes the cognition of an object" can take shape through "the cognitive faculties that are in play in the reflecting power of judgment" (*Critique of the Power of Judgment*, Introduction, 5:190). In The Critique of the Teleological Power of Judgment, this capacity of the power of judgment to generate a "purposiveness that precedes the cognition of an object" is used to judge nature with the concept of an end, although only regulatively. Such a judgment uses the idea of a detachable sense of purposiveness to cognize nature as if it were purposive and conceive of "an end of nature" (*Critique of the Power of Judgment*, § 66, 5:376–7).

I see the common aesthetic thread of purposiveness as running through the layers of aesthetic judgment so that in the first layer one is receptive to an intuition that cannot be subsumed under any concept, including that of an end (barring the intuition from any possible purpose); in the second layer the feeling of purposiveness emerges through the harmonious free play of the faculties within a context where the possibility of a purpose eliminated on the first layer, must be held disjunctively together with the impossibility of there not being a purpose. This free play then inspires the discursive thinking of the third layer, which can also include a creative wielding of the concept of purposiveness as something that the judging subject infuses (regulatively, not determinately) into the world. Thus, the purposiveness without a purpose quintessential to aesthetic judgment occurs on the second, properly aesthetic layer, but this both is importantly contextualized within the first layer cognition that eliminates the possibility of a purpose from the start and feeds into the third layer, enabling the judging subject to discover a new relationship to (and power over) the idea of purposiveness.

The way that the layers relate to one another can also be put in terms of the logical functions of relation. Although the hypothetical relation is not the proper one to characterize purposiveness without a purpose, itself, this function does appear to express the causal relation that holds sway between the layers. So that, if the right sort of intuitional excess is given, then the faculties can be stimulated into a free play. And if the faculties are stimulated into a harmonious free play, then the categorical proclamation of the object's beauty and discursive thinking of the third layer can be stimulated. Importantly, just as it is described for the hypothetical, the causal direction of the relation between the layers cannot be reversed. That is, one cannot begin with judgments that proclaim the aesthetic value of an empirical object and then work back from this to a feeling of pleasure in contemplating it and, finally, to a recognition that there appears to be some intuitional excess that escapes. To do so would be in clear contradiction with Kant's insistence that no one can be talked into an aesthetic judgment or make an aesthetic judgment by adopting those of others.[141]

---

[141] Kant does suggest that aesthetic judgment can be further developed by practicing judging those works that judgers of exceptional taste have judged to be exemplary: "Hence some products of taste are regarded as exemplary – not as if taste could be acquired by imitating others. For taste must be a faculty of one's own; however, whoever imitates a model certainly shows, so far as he gets it right, a skill, but he shows taste only insofar as he can judge this model himself" (*Critique of the Power of Judgment*, § 17, 5:232). If it were to be possible for one to judge beautiful art in a backward manner (starting with the assumption that it is beautiful and then looking for what is beautiful in it) then the judgment would begin with the concept of beauty, rather than

IV Conclusion

Now the full import of the definition provided by the third moment, the relation, of aesthetic judgment can be understood: "Beauty is the form of purposiveness of an object, insofar as it is perceived in it without representation of an end."[142] The "form of purposiveness" is purposiveness without a purpose, that is, "perceived [...] without representation of an end." In beautiful nature this arises, because *as* nature it cannot be determinately judged to have a purpose (i.e., to be the product of an intentionally acting cause). However, one still sees in the beautiful piece of nature something that can only be made conceivable to us "by deriving it from a will."[143] Thus, we judge nature to be beautiful through an analogy to art, so as to take pleasure in the purposefulness observable in something that cannot be judged to have a purpose. This delicate balance is achieved by problematically holding the *complementa* of having a purpose and not having a purpose in a disjunctive judgment of nature. Art, on the other hand, is created by an intentionally acting agent, however that which is beautiful in art comes from the gift of genius that nature has instilled in the artist. Hence, the purpose that sparked the creation of the art, is not the spark that ignites the beauty of the work as "nature in the subject [...] must give the rule to art."[144] Thus, beautiful art must likewise be conceived through an analogy to nature, since the purpose that the art must have as the product of a will is disjunctively held together with the beauty that takes shape under the governance of a rule that is given by nature—a force that cannot be determinately judged as acting intentionally, and thus cannot constitute purposes.

---

with the feeling of pleasure, making the judgment cognitive rather than aesthetic. The exemplarity of certain products of taste does not indicate that these products are to be aesthetically judged to be beautiful *before* aesthetic pleasure is felt. It is, rather, along a pedagogical line that exemplary objects can be helpful. Something exemplary is sure to supply the judging subject with the proper stimulus for a correct aesthetic judgment of beauty. The student must then, however, do the work of contemplating the exemplary beautiful object and judging it. Exemplary works are helpful for training one's taste, because if the work is exemplary, it is more likely to lead the student to a pure aesthetic judgment. Hence, training one's taste through the judgment of exemplary aesthetic objects does not indicate any reversibility of the hypothetical relation the layers of aesthetic judgment exhibit towards one another. The role of the exemplary in aesthetic judgment is further discussed in the next chapter.
142 *Critique of the Power of Judgment*, § 17, 5:236.
143 *Critique of the Power of Judgment*, § 10, 5:220.
144 *Critique of the Power of Judgment*, § 46,5:307. Hence, "beautiful art cannot itself think up the rule in accordance with which it is to bring its product into being" (Ibid.).

Here, in aesthetic judgment, the purposiveness that reigns is crucially without any determinate purpose. Aesthetic judgment puts us in touch with an inchoate feeling of purposiveness that can take hold without any determinate purpose being judged. This feeling of purposiveness may, in turn, be wielded teleologically, revealing a human capacity to infuse the world with purpose. Such creation of purpose happens in teleological, not aesthetic, judgment. This ability to create purposes being something *further* that can indirectly result from aesthetic judgment.

Chapter Six:
An Exemplary, Conditioned Necessity

Kant picks out the modality of judgments as "a quite special function."[1] The "content of the judgment" has been exhausted by quality, quantity and relation.[2] Quality specifies whether the relation between the subject and predicate is to be affirmed, denied, or if the judgment affirms the subject's relation to a negated predicate (infinite). Quantity specifies whether the judgment pertains to all (universal) or some (particular) of that which falls within the scope of the subject-concept, or if the singular subject alternatively has no scope and thus falls within the scope of the predicate-concept. Relation further specifies the form of connection between the judgmental components as categorical, hypothetical or disjunctive, which in turn indicates whether the subject and predicate positions are filled by mere subject and predicate concepts (categorical) or two judgments, one being the ground and the other the consequence (hypothetical), or multiple judgments that come together as the parts of a whole (disjunctive).

Hence, once quantity, quality and relation have been addressed, there is "nothing more that constitutes the content of a judgment."[3] One final, overarching aspect, however, does remain to be elaborated and this is how "the relation of the whole judgment to the faculty of cognition is determined."[4] With the internal structure of the judgment fully detailed, we must now describe how the judgment as a whole fits into the context of "thinking in general."[5] The judgment locates itself in relation to "thinking in general" through "the value of the copula."[6] This value is that of quality, which describes whether the relation between the parts comprising the judgment is affirmed or negated. This extrinsic concern pertains to how the judgment fits into the cognitive landscape of judgments. It is this distinction from the other three quadrants that gives modality its special status.

Although the fourth moment's importance is generally accepted, some commentators have questioned whether the necessity of aesthetic judgment indicates anything that was not already stipulated through its universality. Karl Ameriks writes that "[t]he second and fourth moments are practically indistin-

---

1 *Critique of Pure Reason*, B99.
2 *Critique of Pure Reason*, B99.
3 *Critique of Pure Reason*, A74/B100.
4 *Jäsche Logic*, § 30, 604.
5 *Critique of Pure Reason*, A/74B100.
6 *Critique of Pure Reason*, A74/B100.

guishable."⁷ Although Guyer recognizes that the fourth moment of aesthetic judgment presents new and essential elements that did not come to the fore in the second, he does not see any reason to read these developments in terms of modality, regarding the universality and necessity discussed in the second and fourth moment, respectively, as "ultimately plac[ing] the same demand on the judgment of taste."⁸

Guyer takes the necessity to show that aesthetic pleasure "is connected with a necessary rather than a contingent feature of the subject."⁹ If this were what was necessary, then he would be correct that the universality and necessity of aesthetic judgments coincide. I do not, however, see this to be the case. Kant's exploration of the universality of aesthetic judgment was an investigation into the transcendental arrangement of the faculties in which this universality originates through transcendental pleasure. The modality of aesthetic judgment, in contrast, pertains to how a judgment that is internally constituted so as to contain subjective universality fits "in relation to thinking in general."¹⁰ That is, how "the value of its copula" relates to that of the other judgments making up the cognitive landscape.¹¹ Thus, I will show there to be an important difference between the elements that the universality and necessity of aesthetic judgment pick out, since the former pertains to the internal workings of such judging and the latter to the status that the judgment has as a whole after the judgment

---

7 Ameriks, "Kant and the Objectivity of Taste," 1983, 3.
8 Guyer, *Kant and the Claims of Taste, Second Edition*, 144. Guyer elaborates that "Both require that a person calling an object beautiful rationally expect that others will take pleasure in it, unless he has in fact erred in assigning his own pleasure to its proper source. This demand can be met only if the pleasure is attributed to a ground which is neither private nor contingent, but is instead a necessary constituent of human nature [...]. The attribution of pleasure to the harmony of the faculties to answer the demand for subjective universal validity thus furnishes precisely what Kant takes the moment of necessity to require—namely, a "subjective principle [...] which determines what pleases or displeases, through feeling and not through concepts, but yet with universal validity" [*CPJ*, § 20]" (Guyer, *Kant and the Claims of Taste, Second Edition*, 144–145). Longuenesse disagrees with such a reading. She does not take modality to be "parallel to that of quantity," because whereas in quantity the singular judgment about the object lead to a universal judgment about the judging subject, in modality "the necessity of the latter (the implicit judgment about the judging subject) seems to ground the necessity of the former (the manifest judgment about the object): Because all judging subjects ought to judge as I do, the relation of the predicate 'beautiful' to the subject of the manifest judgment can legitimately be asserted as necessary" (Longuenesse, "Kant's Leading Thread in the Analytic of the Beautiful," 213).
9 Guyer, *Kant and the Claims of Taste, Second Edition*, 145.
10 *Critique of Pure Reason*, A74/B100.
11 *Critique of Pure Reason*, A74/B100.

itself has been fully formed.[12] Hence, the second moment pertained to the non-conceptual, transcendental "common ground, deeply buried in all human beings"[13] from which this subjective universality springs forth. This pertains to the content of the judgment, legitimating the claim to universality, whereas the modality of the judgment is the actual making of this claim.[14]

As discussed in chapter four, aesthetic judgment cannot make a bald claim to objective universality. The judgment must instead be characterized as a *subjective* universality. This also impacts the manner in which the claim to such university is to be made. Thus, in the fourth moment of the judgment of taste Kant describes a necessity that is modified by the terms 'exemplary' and 'conditioned'. In this chapter I will examine what exemplary and conditioned necessity is, how its claim to universality differs from that of objective necessity and what role the common sense plays in enabling the necessity of pure aesthetic judgment.

I begin by exploring how the special status differentiating modality from the three proceeding quadrants impacts the way that the logical functions and categories relate here. I then develop a reading of the special sort of modality that arises in judgments of taste. On the one hand, these judgments clearly have necessity, but, on the other hand, this can only be a necessity that is tempered by subjectivity. It is to this end that Kant develops the idea of a specifically aesthetic necessity that has an *exemplary, conditioned* status. To better understand what the conditioned nature of such necessity indicates, I compare aesthetic judgments to mathematical judgments, the latter serving as a prime example of judgments whose necessity is not conditioned. I then examine the subjective principle of the common sense, which allows this subjective necessity to be represented as if it were objective. Kant's reliance on the idea of a common sense also allows us to get a better idea of what it is that is being judged. Whereas the bodily senses allow for us to judge how we are affected by corporeal stimuli, the common sense allows us to sense "that proportion which is suitable for

---

[12] Reinhard Brandt describes this shift as "die Cäsur zwischen den ersten drei Titeln und dem vierten Titel" (Brandt, "Zur Logik des ästhetischen Urteils," 62 footnote #23). He further specifies that "Quantität, Qualität und Relation den Inhalt eines Urteils ausmachen" (Brandt, "Zur Logik des äesthetischen Urteils," 5). In contrast, "Der titel der Modalität fügt zum Urteil nichts Neues hinzu, lokalisiert es aber in der methodus der Erkenntniss" (*Ibid.*, 6).
[13] *Critique of the Power of Judgment,* Bk. 1, § 17, 5:232.
[14] Allison also draws a difference between the first three moments of aesthetic judgment and the fourth. For his reading of this difference in terms of *quid facti* and *quid juris*, see 2001, 67–85; 144–145; 160–195.

making cognition out of a representation."¹⁵ Thus, even if judgments of taste are typically triggered by some stimulation of the bodily senses on the first layer, what is key to the second, properly aesthetic layer is the way that the *cognitive* faculties are stimulated. Hence, it is the common sense that serves as the subjective principle for aesthetic judgment, and not the bodily senses.

I The Logical Functions of Modality

Whereas quality provides the affirmation or negation of a judgment, modality tells us how "one regards [this] assertion or denial" of the judgment.[16] Let us consider Kant's example. When discussing hypothetical relations, Kant considered the proposition "If there is perfect justice, then obstinate evil will be punished."[17] Now, under modality, he looks at the *antecedens* of this hypothetical: "There is a perfect justice."[18] Admittedly, the modality of the judgment could be communicated by switching out the copula "is" for a term that communicates a lower or higher grade of certainty (i.e., "might be" or "must be," respectively), but this need not always be done in this manner. For example, despite the fact that the verb "is" appears within the *antecedens* of the hypothetical judgment, the judgment is understood as "not [being] said assertorically, but only [being] thought as an arbitrary judgment that it is possible that someone might assume, and only the implication is assertoric."[19] Thus, the modality of a judgment can be altered without altering any of its internal components. A change in modality signals a change in how the judgment is "said" and not *what* the judgment says.[20] It remains the case that the existence of perfect justice is being categorically affirmed, regardless of whether this affirmation is taken to be possible, actual or necessary. Thus, we see that modality really is about how the judgment is to be positioned within the greater context of thinking, because positioning this judgment differently (by adjusting its modal intensity) can be done without altering any of the judgmental components themselves.[21] Even if it were deemed

---

15 *Critique of the Power of Judgment*, § 21, 5:238.
16 *Critique of Pure Reason*, A74/B100.
17 *Critique of Pure Reason*, A73/B98.
18 *Critique of Pure Reason*, A75/B100.
19 *Critique of Pure Reason*, A75/B100.
20 *Critique of Pure Reason*, A75/B100.
21 Brandt describes modality as "die Lokalisierung des Erkenntnisurteils im Erkenntnisprozeß" (Brandt, "Zur Logik des ästhetischen Urteils," 86). Under modality the judgment, whose content has already been determined by quantity, quality and relation, is "fertig übernommen und im

impossible for "there [to be] a perfect justice," the judgment, itself, would remain the same. Only the subject's reflection on how this judgment relates to other judgments changes.

I.A The Problematic, Assertoric and Apodictic

The three forms of modality allowing one to position a judgment are: the problematic, assertoric and apodictic. The *Jäsche Logic* describes these as follows:

> The problematic ones are accompanied with the consciousness of the mere possibility of the judging, the assertoric ones with the consciousness of its actuality, the apodictic ones, finally, with the consciousness of its necessity.[22]

This underscores how modality does not describe the content of the judgment, but rather how this judgment is situated in relation to the faculty of cognition by putting modality into the terms of the sort of consciousness that accompanies the judgment—the consciousness with which it is thought. Noteworthy is how this consciousness situates the judgment within a context of possibility, actuality and necessity. These are not, however, logical functions, but rather categorical terms:

4. Of Modality
Possibility – Impossibility
Existence – Non-existence
Necessity – Contingency[23]

The description of the logical functions of modality in the *Critique of Pure Reason* likewise connects them with categorical terms:

Erkenntnistotum verortet" (Brandt, "Zur Logik des äesthetischen Urteils," 84). It is necessary that judgment be "im Kontinuum der Erkenntnisurteil verortet" through its modality, because "es gibt kein isoliertes Urteil, das eine Erkenntnis wäre" (*Ibid.*, 71).

22 *Jäsche Logic*, § 30, 604. Although the English translation by J. Micheal Young reads "apodeictic" instead of "apodictic," there is no reason to take this as signifying a discrepancy with the discussion of modality in the first *Critique*, since the German original reads "apodiktischen" and I have adjusted the quotation above to reflect this.

23 *Critique of Pure Reason*, A80/B106. Admittedly, "actuality" [*Wirklichkeit*] does not appear on this table. Its resonance with existence and non-existence [*Dasein–Nichtsein*], however, is stronger than with the assetroic [*Assetorische*] logical function.

> **Problematic** judgments are those in which one regards the assertion denial as merely possible (arbitrary). **Assertoric** judgments are those in which it is considered actual (true). **Apodictic** judgments are those in which it is seen as necessary.[24]

In an effort to understand how the internal workings of aesthetic judgment can occur without concepts and yet involve a harmonious free-play of the imagination with the understanding,[25] I have concentrated on the logical functions of the understanding, which determine merely the activity of judging itself. Only when this activity of judging is the judging of an object do the logical functions pass over into the categories, so as to produce determinations of the object judged. In the second layer, where there is no object to be determined, the logical functions merely determine the activity constitutive of the act of judging itself, and thus the categories cannot be applied to an object that is not given. Accordingly, my discussion of quality, quantity and relation focused on how the logical functions determine the activity of judging in aesthetic judgment with the categories being discussed only insofar as they can help draw out a further characteristic of the correlating logical function.

Now, however things are quite different. Modality does not determine the content of the act of judging, itself. It determines the relation this judgment has to something beyond itself. If the categories emerge in the cognition of an object, then it appears that the quadrant of Modality from the Table of Judgments takes the judgment in its entirety as the object to be categorically determined.[26] Thus, the logical functions of modality tell us whether the judgment is thought as relating to the conditions of experience in a manner that makes this judgment possible, actual or necessary.

In the second chapter, I described how the logical functions have an explanatory role towards the categories.[27] Whereas the categories are the pure concepts of the understanding used to cognize content, the logical functions "abstract from all content of a judgment in general, and attend only to the mere form of the understanding in [judgment]."[28] Hence, the logical functions "explain" the categories, because they describe the mere "function of thinking" itself, better positioning us to understand how thinking functions when applied to content.

---

24 *Critique of Pure Reason*, A74/B100.
25 For Kant's remarks on the concept-independence of aesthetic judgment, see: *Critique of the Power of Judgment*, First Introduction XII, 20:250; § 6, 5:211; § 17, 5:231; § 40, 5:296; § 42 5:300.
26 This could not be done by the proceeding logical functions, because they govern the activity constitutive of the judgment, hence allowing this judgment to arise in the first place.
27 See chapter two, sections II. E. and F.
28 *Critique of Pure Reason*, A70/B95.

One of the curiosities of modality, however, is that this relation between the logical functions and categories as explainer and explained reverses itself.[29]

The modal categories are invoked to explain the logical functions in the fourth quadrant, as evidenced in the passages quoted above. This can be understood to result from modality's unique feature of describing how the judgment as a whole is related to other judgments. Since modality pertains to the already constituted judgment, and not to the activity of judging that internally constitutes the judgment, it determines an object (i.e., the constituted judgment, "This X is beautiful") and not an activity. Hence, modality takes the judgment as its object, whereas the other logical functions are operative in the judging activity of this judgment and consequently do not have an object in the same way. We can see this in the course that our analysis of the moments of the judgment of taste has taken up to here. Quality determines that the activity of judging is without interest. Quantity determines that the harmonious free play of the faculties is universal, because this free play is grounded upon the transcendental arrangement of the faculties. Relation determines that the representations of having a purpose and of not having a purpose will be disjunctively held together in the process of judging so that a sense of purposiveness without any determinate purpose may arise. All three of these modify the activity of judging, itself. In this manner, they do not further determine something that has already been formed, but rather supply determinations for the constitutive activity of judging that allows a judgment of taste to take shape. Modality pertains to a judgment of taste that has already been formed in this manner so as to determine its place in the cognitive landscape. Whereas the first three logical functions govern the cognitive acts that produce a judgment of taste, modality takes a given judgment of taste as its object, supplying a further determination for it. Thus, modality naturally takes an object (i.e. a formed judgment) in a way that the preceding log-

---

29 Kant suggests that the logical functions under quantity, quality and relation have an explanative role towards the corresponding categories when he writes, "The logical functions of judgment in general – unity and multiplicity, affirmation and negation, subject and predicate – cannot be defined without falling into a circle, since the definition would itself have to be a judgment and therefore already contain these functions of judgment. The pure categories, however, are nothing other than the representations of things in general insofar as the manifold of their intuition must be thought through one or another of these logical functions: Magnitude is the determination that must be thought only through a judgment that has quantity (*judicium commune*); reality, that which can be through only through an affirmative judgment; substance, that which, in relation to the intuition, must be the ultimate subject of all other determinations" (*Critique of Pure Reason*, A245–6/B302). For a further discussion of how the logical functions and categories relate, see chapter two, section II.C – E.

ical functions do not, since they pertain to the judging activity that bring about the formation of the judgment in the first place.

It is for this reason that we must understand the logical function of modality through the categories of modality. Kant gives a fuller description of the modal categories in The Postulates of Empirical Thinking in General:
1. Whatever agrees with the formal conditions of experience (in accordance with intuition and concepts) is possible.
2. That which is connected with the material conditions of experience (of sensation) is actual.
3. That whose connection with the actual is determined in accordance with general conditions of experience is (exists) necessarily.[30]

The categories of modality describe the level of agreement and connection that something has with the conditions of experience. Just like the logical functions of modality, the categories of modality are not about constituting content, as "they do not augment the concept to which they are ascribed in the least," rather, they "express only the relation to the faculty of cognition."[31] It is for this reason that Kant famously declares that "No further determinations in the object itself are hereby [through the categories of modality] thought."[32] This is significant for our purposes, because if the categories of modality do not determine the *internal* working of a judgment, then the way that they are unavoidably woven into the logical functions of modality will in no way affect the inner constitution of the judgment itself. Thus, the reflective nature of pure aesthetic judgment is safeguarded from any risk of becoming determinative through the involvement of the pure concept of necessity in its modality.[33]

---

30 *Critique of Pure Reason*, A218/B265–6.
31 *Critique of Pure Reason*, A219/B266.
32 *Critique of Pure Reason*, A219/B266.
33 This means that the categories of modality can be applied to a judgment of taste without bringing about the determination that would occur if the categories of quantity, quality or relation were to be operative in this same judgment. To involve the latter would impact the intrinsic constitution of the judgment, transforming it into a judgment that determinatively "think[s] an object" (*Critique of Pure Reason*, A80/B106). This would be a far cry from the reflective judgment of taste which engages the activity of pure aesthetic judging and allows us to conclude that a tulip is beautiful. The involvement of the categories, would yield a judgment that determines "objects of intuition" (*Critique of Pure Reason*, A70/B105). This constitutive judgment could determine the tulip to be a totality of petals, pistil, stamen, leaves and stem (quantity) that has reality (quality) and is an organism characterized by the reciprocal causality of a community (relation). It could not, however, generate pure aesthetic pleasure. Naturally, there is a determinative judgment at work in one's aesthetic experience of a beautiful tulip overall, since the judg-

I The Logical Functions of Modality —— 263

If we bring together the sections quoted above that offer Kant's definition of the logical functions of modality (problematic, assertoric and apodictic) with his description of the modal categories (possibility, actuality and necessity)—using the latter to explain the former—then we find that:
- A *problematic* judgment is considered to agree "with the formal conditions of experience (in accordance with intuition and concepts)" [34] and thus to be "arbitrary." [35]
- An *assertoric* judgment is considered to connect "with the material conditions of experience (of sensation)" [36] and thus to be "true." [37]
- an *apodictic* judgment is considered to be "determined in accordance with general conditions of experience" [38] and thus "(exists) necessarily." [39]

We can, thus, expect that the fourth moment of aesthetic judgment will take up the subjective universality belonging to the content of pure aesthetic judgment, which arises in the second layer of aesthetic judging, and discern how such a judgment relates to the conditions of experience. This subjective universality of aesthetic judgment should be situated in the cognitive landscape in a manner that pushes beyond a mere agreement with the "formal conditions of experience." It is not just that the "sensation" of pure aesthetic pleasure is judged to be "true." Rooted in the very arrangement of the faculties of cognition that makes experience possible, subjectively universal aesthetic pleasure is "deter-

---

ment of experience constitutes the object on the first layer as a phenomenon. What is essential to the judgment of taste, however, is the intuitional excess that does not become part of the objective object. Rather, it stimulates the faculties into the activity of pure aesthetic judging, which is a determinate activity, but does not determine any object. Since the categories of quantity, quality and relation all determine an object, they cannot be involved in the judgment of taste. But since "[n]o further determinations in the object itself" are thought through modality, the category of necessity may determine how the judgment of taste fits into the cognitive landscape without converting this judgment into a determination of an object, namely because it neither introduces an object nor pertains to the internal workings of the judgment (*Critique of Pure Reason*, A219/B266).

34 *Critique of Pure Reason*, A218/B265 – 6.
35 "Problematic judgments are those in which one regards the assertion denial as merely possible (arbitrary)" (*Critique of Pure Reason*, A74/B100).
36 *Critique of Pure Reason*, A218/B265 – 6.
37 "Assertoric judgments are those in which it is considered actual (true)" (*Critique of Pure Reason*, A74/B100).
38 *Critique of Pure Reason*, A218/B265 – 6.
39 "Apodictic judgments are those in which it is seen as necessary" (*Critique of Pure Reason*, A74/B100).

mined in accordance with general conditions of experience" and thus "(exists) necessarily."[40]

In this manner we see that although the second and fourth moments closely relate to one another, this relation is such that the former feeds into the latter, the latter being far from a mere feeble echoing of the former. The subjective universality of aesthetic judgment describes how this universality arises in the act of judging itself; the conditioned necessity describes how such a judging fits into the conditions of experience.

As we will see in this chapter, the communicability of aesthetic judgment is involved in both moments. Since aesthetic universality arises in the activity of judging within the subject, it has the potential to connect subjects to one another in a special way—directly through the feeling to be communicated, springing over the concepts that would typically be used to communicate such a feeling. The "general conditions of experience," in accordance with which aesthetic judgment is to necessarily exist, are not the objective conditions of experience, but rather the subjective and *inter*-subjective conditions. The modality of aesthetic judgment is not only about taking one's own judgment as exemplary.[41] It reaches beyond this, so as to make a claim about how the judgment ought to relate to the general conditions that make the experience of all judging subjects possible, and thus claiming that we really are connected to each other as feeling, judging sub-

---

[40] *Critique of Pure Reason*, A218/B265–6. Although, as I discuss below, there are good reasons why aesthetic judgment cannot be regarded as fully apodictic (see *Critique of the Power of Judgment*, §18, 5:237), judgments of taste push in this direction. We can see this if we scrutinize Kant's remark that "the apodictic proposition thinks of the assertoric one as determined through these laws of the understanding itself, and as thus asserting a priori, and in this way expresses logical necessity" (*Critique of Pure Reason*, A75–6/B100–1). On the one hand, this resonates strongly with how pure aesthetic judgment is determined through the transcendental arrangement of the faculties, itself, giving it an a priori status. On the other hand, this is no determination through the "laws of the understanding itself," and hence the necessity of aesthetic judgment must be of a certain sort that cannot fully coincide with the apodictic logical function.

[41] This view, contrary to my own, is put forward by Hannah Ginsborg, who contends that "in the case of a judgment of taste [...] there is no antecedently specifiable content to the demand. Instead, it is purely self-referential. I claim that everyone else ought to judge the object just as I do, without any specification of how the object is to be judged beyond its being the way that I am judging it in making this very claim" (Ginsborg, "On the Key to Kant's Critique of Taste," *Pacific Philosophical Quarterly* 72 [1991]: 290–313; 306). While I find helpful Ginsborg's explanation of the exemplary nature of aesthetic judgment as a self-referential claim that others should "judge the object just as I do," I am not satisfied with the "thin and abstract" reading (*Ibid.*, 309) that results when she takes this as essentially the sole determination of the activity of aesthetic judging. Rather, I see exemplary necessity as one determination among the many that are supplied over the course of the four moments of the judgment of taste.

jects. With the second moment, the idea of normativity arises as a driving force internal to the judging itself, asserting that all judging subjects *should* feel this same aesthetic pleasure.[42] With the fourth moment the judgment settles into the cognitive landscape so that the judging subject affirms the agreement of all judging subjects as necessary due to our shared transcendental conditions for the possibility of experience. The fourth moment thus pertains to the third layer necessity with which the judgment proclaiming something's aesthetic value is pronounced.

II The Fourth Moment of Aesthetic Judgment

In the last three chapters I have shown quality, quantity and relation each to be a richly complex moment of aesthetic judgment that can only take shape through an equally complex involvement of the logical functions. This does not change for modality even though the content of a judgment is not concerned. Here, too, we find that a simple identification of aesthetic judgment as necessary is insufficient for understanding how aesthetic judgment positions itself in relation to thinking in general. A full analysis of the moment is required to reveal the nuances of its modality.

Kant begins the fourth moment by identifying the mode to which aesthetic judgment most strongly relates, casting this in contrast to judgments of the agreeable and the good, which are made in accordance with the other two modes. "Every representation" can be said to have at least a *possible* combination with pleasure.[43] Thus, the way in which the representations involved in pure aesthetic judgment admit of this possibility does not describe any modal particularity, because in this respect it is like any other judgment. Kant goes on to identify the agreeable as that which "**actually** produces a pleasure in me."[44] Hence, actuality is the highest modality that impure aesthetic judgments

---

[42] Makkreel describes this as a "normative reflective judgment that projects a felt agreement with other subjects. It is not a descriptive *Urteil*, but a prescriptive *Beurteilung*. What is the source of this normativity? For Kant, it is transcendental. The aesthetic judgment transforms an empirical determinant judgment about an object into a disinterested reflective judgment that expresses a subjective assessment [...]. Aesthetic appreciation is a free evaluative response to the object's formal purposiveness, which does nothing more than allow the cognitive faculties to operate in harmony with each other. Aesthetic pleasure is the feeling of this equilibrium" (Makkreel, "Reflection, Reflective Judgment, and Aesthetic Exemplarity," 237).
[43] *Critique of the Power of Judgment*, § 18, 5:236.
[44] *Critique of the Power of Judgment*, § 18, 5:236.

reach, when someone grounds the judgment "on a private feeling" and "says of an object that it pleases him."[45] A judgment grounded in this manner cannot reach beyond the assertoric, because it is "restricted merely to his own person,"[46] depending entirely on "the taste of the [individual's] tongue, palate, and throat" as well as "that which may be agreeable to someone's eyes and ears."[47] Kant concludes, "thus with regard to the agreeable, the principle Everyone has his own taste (of the senses) is valid."[48]

In a pure aesthetic judgment of taste, there is certainly a recognition that something "actually produces a pleasure in me,"[49] as this judgment is grounded upon the feeling of pleasure—a feeling which, thus, must be actually felt in order for the judgment to be made. Unlike impure aesthetic judgments, however, judgments of taste go beyond this mere assertion of one's own pleasure, because "one thinks that [the beautiful] has a necessary relation to satisfaction."[50] This necessity, however, cannot be the apodictic necessity of "an objective and cognitive judgment" that can "be derived from determinate concepts."[51] Thus, the modality of pure aesthetic judgment cannot fit neatly into a modal function that accurately captures its unique character. When making a pure aesthetic judgment of taste one both can and does attach pleasure to the representation, meaning that the judgment is both possible and actual, both problematic and assertoric.[52] In order to understand the necessity of such a judgment, however, the correlation between the apodictic logical function and category of necessity must be partially dismantled: "Since an aesthetic judgment is not an objective and cognitive judgment, this necessity cannot be derived from determinate concepts, and is therefore not apodictic."[53] Kant distances the one from the other by describing aesthetic necessity as attenuated by its exemplary, conditioned status.

---

45 *Critique of the Power of Judgment*, § 7, 5:212.
46 *Critique of the Power of Judgment*, § 7, 5:212.
47 *Critique of the Power of Judgment*, § 7, 5:212.
48 *Critique of the Power of Judgment*, § 7, 5:212.
49 *Critique of the Power of Judgment*, § 18, 5:236.
50 *Critique of the Power of Judgment*, § 18, 5:236.
51 *Critique of the Power of Judgment*, § 18, 5:237.
52 Kant describes modalities that hold with higher strength as already incorporating those that hold with less strength, and that an increase in modal strength belongs to the process of incorporating the representations into the understanding (*Critique of Pure Reason*, A76/B101). Thus, something actual will also be possible, and something necessary will be both actual and possible. How this can be meaningfully brought in relation to the layered structure of aesthetic judgment is explored below.
53 *Critique of the Power of Judgment*, § 18, 5:237.

II.A Exemplary Necessity

Exemplary necessity is "a necessity of the assent of all to a judgment that is regarded as an example of a universal rule that one cannot produce."[54] Like the subjective universality of the second moment, we see that aesthetic necessity "extends [...] over the whole sphere of those who judge"[55] as subjective, and not over the sphere of objects judged as objective.

When one makes a judgment of taste, one regards the final judgment produced as exemplary. That is to say, much as an exemplary artwork is a perfect example of the sort of thing that can occasion an aesthetic judgment, an exemplary aesthetic judgment is a perfect example of this sort of judging. Thus, in regarding one's aesthetic judgment to be exemplary, one reflects upon the process of judging as a whole and affirms that it is precisely the judging activity in which a pure aesthetic judgment should engage. It is not a perfect adherence to any rules of aesthetic judging that award the judgement an exemplary status. In pronouncing one's judgment as exemplary, one is well aware that the universal rule it exemplifies cannot be produced.[56] It does not imitate the rule, but rather embodies it. It is in the exemplary judgment that the unproducible rule finds expression.[57]

II.B Conditioned Necessity

The modality of a judgment tells us how the judgment is pronounced, but the pronouncement of aesthetic judgment's modality must itself be modulated. It is not just a matter of the judgment "This tulip is beautiful" being pronounced with *necessity*, but also a matter of how this necessity is itself pronounced, namely *conditionally*.

The recognition that pure aesthetic judgments are grounded on the transcendental arrangement of the faculties, which can be assumed in all judging subjects, means that the pleasure of this judgment applies to all judging subjects as well, hence grounding its subjective universality. The subjective universal characteristic of the *content* of the judgment (i.e., the pure aesthetic pleasure) provides for the judgment to be pronounced as necessary, because the transcen-

---

54 *Critique of the Power of Judgment*, § 18, 5:237.
55 *Critique of the Power of Judgment*, § 8, 5:215.
56 *Critique of the Power of Judgment*, § 18, 5:237.
57 *Critique of the Power of Judgment*, § 22, 5:239.

dental arrangement of the faculties that generates this pleasure is the same transcendental arrangement of the faculties that supplies the conditions for the possibility of experience. Hence, pure aesthetic judgment's "connection with the actual is determined in accordance with general conditions of experience."[58] The internal workings of pure aesthetic judgment that make it subjectively universal already determine that it will fit into the cognitive landscape as necessary. This necessity, however, does not stipulate that no judging subject can fail to accord with this judgment. Rather, it only creates the conditions for stipulating that they *should*, and "[t]he should in aesthetic judgments of taste is thus pronounced only conditionally."[59]

II.B.1 Differentiating between Conditional and Unconditional Necessity

A necessity that is not conditional can be found in mathematical judgments. Although the judgment must be synthesized by a judging subject,[60] "properly mathematical propositions are always *a priori* judgments and are never empirical, because they carry necessity with them, which cannot be derived from experience."[61] Hence, a mathematical judgment is a priori as a "cognition independent of all experience and even of all impression of the senses."[62] At the same time, they are synthetic, for one must "add to the concept of the subject a predicate that was not thought in it at all, and could not have been extracted from it through any analysis."[63]

This means that the proper synthesis of one mathematical concept with another is something that the judging subject must bring about. As a synthesis in accordance with the rules of the understanding, however, mathematical judgments are determinative, conceptual and constitutive. There is only one way that five and seven can be brought together in accordance with the rules of the understanding, and in this sense regardless of how many individuals make the judgment, "it is still only a singular proposition [...]. [T]he synthesis here can take place only in a single way [...]."[64] The addition of five to seven

---

[58] *Critique of Pure Reason*, A218/B265–6.
[59] *Critique of the Power of Judgment*, § 19, 5:237.
[60] In, say, the equation $7 + 5 = 12$, "[t]he concept of twelve is by no means already thought merely by my thinking of that unification of seven and five," because "no matter how long I analyze my concept of such a possible sum I will still not find twelve in it" (*Critique of Pure Reason*, B15).
[61] *Critique of Pure Reason*, B15.
[62] *Critique of Pure Reason*, B2.
[63] *Critique of Pure Reason*, A7/B11.
[64] *Critique of Pure Reason*, A164/B205.

must be carried out by a judging subject in order to be synthesized as twelve, but the validity of the equation "5 + 7 = 12" does not depend upon any one subject's correct synthesis of five and seven. Judging subjects who mathematically miscalculate do not affect the validity of this "singular" mathematical propositions. According to Kant "[m]athematical cognition [is rational cognition] from the construction of concepts."[65] This is carried out by "exhibit[ing] *a priori* the intuition corresponding to [the concept]."[66] This requires a "non-empirical intuition" that "as intuition, is an individual object" and it must "express in the representation universal validity for all possible intuitions that belong under the same concept."[67] Kant elaborates,

> Thus I construct a triangle by exhibiting an object corresponding to this concept, either through mere imagination, in pure intuition, or on paper, in empirical intuition, but in both cases completely *a priori*, without having had to borrow the pattern for it from any experience [...] mathematical cognition considers the universal in the particular, indeed even in the individual, yet nonetheless *a priori* and by means of reason [...] the object of the concept [...] must [...] be thought as universally determined.[68]

Mathematical judgments are objective; they are synthesized in the idea of the object that corresponds to their concept, universally determining this object.

It is here that we can locate the essential source of the difference between unconditioned and conditioned necessity. If mathematical judgments are synthesized in the idea of a mathematical object, then, even though this synthesis must be carried out by the judging subject, for the subject to judge mathematically, the validity of a mathematical proposition does not depend upon all judging subjects individually synthesizing it correctly, because it is combined in the object and not in the subject. In mathematics "an objectively universally valid

---

65 *Critique of Pure Reason*, A713/B741.
66 *Critique of Pure Reason*, A713/B741.
67 *Critique of Pure Reason*, A713/B741.
68 *Critique of Pure Reason*, A714/B742. Just before this, Kant makes a remark that can be used to bring out contrasts of further interest: "The form of mathematical cognition is the cause of its pertaining solely to quanta. For only the concept of magnitudes can be constructed, i.e., exhibited *a priori* in intuition, while qualities cannot be exhibited in anything but empirical intuition" (Critique of Pure Reason, A713–4/B742–3). This indicates a key difference between mathematical judgments of quantity and pure aesthetic judgments, as the latter center on quality and must begin with some sort of empirical intuition. The subject is receptive to something that is given *a posteriori*, be it something empirically seen, heard, read, or simply felt. Unlike the quantitatively grounded mathematical judgments, the qualitatively grounded judgments of taste require an empirical sensation to occasion them, although what the transcendental free play of the faculties and feeling of pure aesthetic pleasure occasioned thereby is *a priori*.

judgment is also always subjectively so, i.e., if the judgment is valid for everything that is contained under a given concept then it is also valid for everyone who represents an object through this concept."⁶⁹ The validity of pure aesthetic judgments contrasts starkly to this, because these judgments are combined in the subject, not the object. Aesthetic pleasure bursts forth in the very activity of aesthetic judging itself. This judgment centers on the combination of an intuition with pleasure in the subject, not the concept of the object:

> But from a subjectively universal validity, i.e., from aesthetic universal validity, which does not rest on any concept, there cannot be any inference at all to logical universal validity; because the first kind of judgment does not pertain to the object at all. For that very reason, however, the aesthetic universality that is ascribed to a judgment must also be of a special kind, since the predicate of beauty is not connected with the concept of the object considered in its entire logical sphere, and yet it extends it over the whole sphere of those who judge.⁷⁰

The unconditioned necessity of mathematical propositions indicates that their validity is not affected by any mistakes that a novice might make in calculation, because the proposition, itself, inheres in the mathematical object that exhibits it. They are made in accordance with "a determinate objective principle" and, hence, lay claim to "unconditioned necessity."⁷¹ Pure aesthetic judgments, however, are made in accordance with "a subjective principle."⁷² Although this subjective principle provides for universal validity, as subjective it depends upon being combined in the subject so as to generate certain feelings of pleasure and displeasure. It is the *a priori* arrangement of the faculties that allows the feelings grounding aesthetic judgment to arise, but for this to occur a specific judging subject must subject a singular aesthetic object to her faculties and judge it in a pure aesthetic manner. That is to say, in a manner appropriate to the pure aesthetic judgment of taste so that "the mere representation of the object is accompanied with satisfaction in me"⁷³ and not to the impure aesthetic judgment of the agreeable that "pleases the senses in sensation."⁷⁴ Thus, this will have to happen *in* each subject—i.e., the faculties of imagination and under-

---

69 *Critique of the Power of Judgment*, § 8, 5:215.
70 *Critique of the Power of Judgment*, § 8, 5:215.
71 *Critique of the Power of Judgment*, § 20, 5:237–8.
72 *Critique of the Power of Judgment*, § 20, 5:238.
73 *Critique of the Power of Judgment*, § 2, 5:205.
74 *Critique of the Power of Judgment*, § 3, 5:205.

standing will have to enter a harmonious free play, *in concreto*[75] and thus actually generate the transcendental pleasure that grounds aesthetic judgment.[76] One cannot know that all judgers will, in fact, do so any more than one can know that all students of mathematics will in fact correctly calculate 5+7 to equal 12. The key difference is that since 5+7=12 is also combined in the object, any particular student's failure to calculate it correctly does not affect the necessity with which this judgment holds at all. The case of aesthetic judgment is more complicated,

---

[75] With the term *in concreto* I do not mean to indicate that this process of aesthetic judgment can only begin with the experience of a concrete (i.e., physical) empirical object. The process must begin with the experience of an empirical object, but the question of this object's material existence is of no concern to aesthetic judgment, as Kant makes clear in the first moment (§ 1–5). I use the term *in concreto* in relation to the *activity* of aesthetic judging to indicate that one must *actually* engage in an act of judging for the judgment to manifest as there is no rule that can appear in abstraction from the act of judging itself. This is also how I understand Kant's use of the term when he writes "Now, whether an action possible for us in sensibility is or is not a case that stands under the rule requires practical judgment, by which what is said in the rule universally (*in abstracto*) is applied to an action *in concreto*." (*Critique of Practical Judgment*, 5:67). And then again, "If we cannot have insight into universal propositions in their universality without cognizing them *in concreto*, then they cannot serve as a standard and hence cannot hold *heuristically* in application, but are only assignments to investigate the universal ground for that with which we first became acquainted in particular cases" (*Jäsche Logic*, § 21, 599).

[76] Ginsborg remarks on something similar when contrasting the validity of aesthetic judgments with those that are universally valid through a concept. She writes, "In making a judgment of taste, I take it that there is something that all other perceivers of the object ought to do, that is, that they should judge the object as I do. Thus I think of my judgment as laying down a "universal rule" which everybody ought to follow. But the "rule" cannot be specified without reference to my own judgment. In contrast to the case of cognitive judgment, in which I have in mind some determinate way in which the object ought to be judged (e. g. as containing a movable drop of water), my claim to universal agreement does not specify a concept. Instead, I judge that all others should judge the object as I do, where the only way of pointing to how the object is to be judged (and thus to the "universal rule" implicit in my judgment) is through the example of my judgment itself" (Ginsborg, "On the Key to Kant's Critique of Taste," 306). The point that I am making about how the necessity of the judgment is conditioned by the fact that the person pronouncing the judgment with necessity is the same as the one who actually engaged in the act of aesthetic judging bears a great deal of similarity to the point Ginsborg makes here about how the "rule" governing aesthetic judgment can only be presented "through the example of my judgment itself." Thus, the conditional and exemplary nature of this necessity intertwine. The necessity only appears upon the condition of the actual exercise of aesthetic judgment in a manner that can be taken as an example of the proper use of this faculty. I differ with Ginsborg, however, insofar as she appears to take universality and necessity as essentially the same thing, as is evidenced in how she leads into this discussion of universality by quoting a passage at § 18 that discusses "exemplary necessity." Moreover, Ginsborg seeks to totalize all of the moments of aesthetic judgment under this universal, necessary self-referentiality, whereas I have argued that each moment describes a different determination of the activity of aesthetic judging.

however, because two variables are involved. On the one hand, the judgment is generated by an interaction of the faculties in their transcendental use, but on the other hand, what these faculties generate, grounding the judgment, is a pleasure that only exists in a state of *being felt* in the subject.⁷⁷ Thus the concrete question of whether or not pure aesthetic pleasure is *actually* felt occupies a position of inescapable importance in the aesthetic judgment of taste.

Thus, the actual execution of aesthetic judgment is important to this form of judgment in a way that it is not to judgments based on an objective principle. Pure aesthetic judgment is conditioned by the special difficulty tied up in its subjective structure so that one is not entirely "sure that the case [will be] correctly subsumed under that ground as the rule of approval,"⁷⁸ primarily because this rule can never be produced and the judging is not through the determination of a cognized object, but rather "determines what pleases or displeases only through feeling."⁷⁹ As a consequence, the actual activity of judging that is carried out in the judging subject *in concreto* attenuates the necessity of the pure aesthetic judgment of taste. One way of capturing this is to say that there is an important way in which the necessity of aesthetic judgments seems contingent, only coming into force when pure aesthetic judging actually occurs.⁸⁰

---

77 "For in the power of judgment understanding and imagination are considered in relation to each other, and this can, to be sure, first be considered objectively, as belonging to cognition (as happened in the transcendental schematism of the power of judgment); but one can also consider this relation of two faculties of cognition merely subjectively, insofar as one helps or hinders the other in the very same representation and thereby affects the **state of mind**, and [is] therefore a relation which is **sensitive** (which is not the case in the separate use of any other faculty of cognition)" (*Critique of the Power of Judgment*, First Introduction VIII, 20:223, emphasis original).
78 *Critique of the Power of Judgment*, § 20, 5:237.
79 *Critique of the Power of Judgment*, § 21, 5:238.
80 The contingency of aesthetic necessity has been noted by a number of commentators. Guyer remarks that for reflecting judgment "we posit systematicity precisely to lend an appearance of necessity to otherwise contingent judgments, Kant's account of our response to the beautiful stresses that the harmonious free play of imagination and understanding that a beautiful object induces in us must seem contingent: an object appears beautiful to us precisely when in response to a given representation "the imagination [...] is unintentionally brought into accord with the understanding," and "this agreement of the object with the faculties of the subject is contingent" (*CPJ*, VIII, 5:190)" (Guyer, *Kant's Critique of the Power of Judgment*, 31). Rudolf A. Makkreel offers an interesting account of how modality can be correlated with Kant's discussion of the "different regions in which we can locate or frame objects" in the second section of the Introduction to the third *Critique* (Makkreel, "Reflection, Reflective Judgment, and Aesthetic Exemplarity," 2006, 225 – 233). Makkreel correlates field (*Feld*) with the possible, territory (*Boden*) with the actual, domain (*Gebiet*) with the necessary and abode (*Aufenhalt*) with the contingent (*Ibid.*, 228). He then locates reflective judgment as operating in the abode: "The abode of the

Whereas the objective validity of mathematical judgment entails subjective validity, since aesthetic judgment is only subjectively valid, even though grounded on the transcendental arrangement of the faculties, inhering in the structure of judging itself, its validity must be individually generated through each instance of judging. Hence, unlike mathematical judgments, aesthetic judgments cannot lay claim to a necessity that holds sway even when this judging activity is not being carried out. Rather, the necessity of aesthetic judgments can only be asserted by a judging subject who actually is feeling transcendental pleasure while engaging in the activity of aesthetic judging. Thus, the modality of aesthetic judgment stipulates that the judgment is pronounced as necessary only under the condition that the judging subject making this pronouncement has actually engaged in a pure aesthetic judgment. This is what is meant by *conditional* necessity.

II.C The Subjective Principle of Common Sense

The way that the common sense perceives the mind's self affection resonates with the historical roots of the term in Aristotle. To see better how Aristotle could be used to bring out this specific aspect of the commons sense, we will first look at how Aristotle describes his form of the common sense in Book III of *De Anima*. Although there is this initial resonance with Aristotle, as one looks further into how Kant develops this term, one recognizes features of this common sense that can find no reference in Aristotle. More specifically this is the role that Kant's common sense plays in supporting the universal communicability of judgments of taste. I will use a short exploration of Aristotle's common sense to think about how Kant's use of the common sense picks up this thread, but goes on to develop something else out of this—the foundation upon which the universal communicability of the judgment of taste rests.

---

contingent involves a collocation of facts that we happen to come across and that demonstrate no objectively necessary connection. What reflective judgment looks for then is a subjective necessity[...]. A systematic order of nature demands a rational coherence that is intrinsically contingent from the standpoint of the understanding[...]. Kant makes it evident that this concept of a purposiveness of nature is nothing more than a subjective mode of representing nature, or, to use more contemporary language, of interpreting it" (*Ibid.*, 229).

II.C.1 Aristotle on the Sensus Communis

The need for a *sensus communis* becomes evident in the context of Aristotles's discussion of each sense as having "special-objects." [81] This is the object that each of the fives senses is specifically able to sense (e.g. color for sight, flavor for taste). In connection to the idea of the special-objects, two questions arise: how are we able to judge that characteristics perceived by different senses belong to one and the same object; how are we able to perceive things which are not among the "special-objects" of any of the five senses, such as motion and magnitude? The idea of a *sensus communis* allows both of these difficulties to be answered. Let us look at each issue in more detail.

First, if sight perceives color and not flavor, and taste perceives flavor and not color, then how is it that we are able to recognize that something both has a certain taste and a certain color? Aristotle explains that:

> Each sense, therefore, is concerned with the subject perceived by it, being present in the sense-organ, *qua* sense-organ, and it judges the varieties of the subject perceived by it, e.g. sight for white and back, and taste for sweet and bitter; and similarly for the other senses too. Since we judge both white and sweet and each of the objects of perception by reference to each other, but by what do we perceive also that they differ? This must indeed be by perception; for they are objects of perception. From this it is clear also that flesh is not the ultimate sense-organ; for if it were it would be necessary for that which judges to judge when it is itself touched.[82]

Individual sense organs taken as working in isolation from one another cannot fully account for our experience of perceiving. Each individual sense organ can judge "the varieties of the subject perceived by it," but this does not provide the distinction between "white and sweet". For this, as commentator Ronald Polansky notes, the five senses must "join to form a common sense."[83] By being common to both taste and sight, the common sense perceives the gustatory- and visual-perceiving with a consciousness that allows the subject to judge one to be the perception of color and the other to be the perception of taste, and furthermore recognize when the two are different perceptions of one and the same object.[84]

---

[81] Aristotle, *De Anima*, (Translated by D. W. Hamlyn. Oxford: Clarendon Press, 2002), 425a14.
[82] Aristotle, *De Anima*, 426b8.
[83] Polansky, Ronald, *Aristotle's De anima: A Commentary* (Cambridge: Cambridge University Press, 2007), 379. "These five senses do not stand isolated from each other...but they join to form a common sense [...]. The full discriminative power of sense requires five senses as subfaculties of a central sense power" (*Ibid.*).
[84] Polansky explains this similarly writing: "A sense does not perceive the proper objects of another sense as it does its own proper sensibles, and were the five senses completely distinct rath-

II The Fourth Moment of Aesthetic Judgment —— 275

Let us turn now to the second difficulty that indicates a need for the common sense. Some perceptions cannot be traced back to any one of the five senses. Aristotle calls these "the common-objects which accompany {the special-objects}, e.g. movement, magnitude and number."[85] These perceptions "accompany" the sense-specific perceptions. For example, color and magnitude invariably accompany each other, since we perceive colored things as physical objects with magnitude.[86] Aristotle writes that "since the common-objects are present in the objects of another sense too, this makes it clear that each of them is distinct."[87] The common sense is needed as a way of gathering together the data from the five senses. Thus it is not only to enable one to identify when differing qualities inhere in a single perceptible that we need the common sense, but furthermore to put these differing qualities in relation to one another and perceive "movement, magnitude and number."[88]

In summary we find from the first difficulty that to judge "that sweet is different form white [...] both must be evident in one thing" and both must be present in the same sense while their distinction is nonetheless maintained.[89] Thus, even though "there is no other sense apart from the five (and by these I mean sight, hearing, smell, taste, and touch),"[90] these five senses must be able to unite into a common sense so as to perceive the perceptions. In this manner, one may judge the perceptions of the five senses in relation to one another, because "it is not possible to judge separate things by separate means."[91] The common sense is accordingly described by Aristotle as the sense "which is concerned with itself."[92] As such it can be "concerned with sight" while at the same time

---

er than unified as subfaculties of a common sense faculty, there would be no way at all to perceive the objects of other senses. Each sense could perceive exclusively its own proper objects. Yet because the senses are connected as subfaculties of the common sense faculty, and because several sorts of proper sensibles inhere in one substratum, the senses can perceive the objects of the other senses accidentally. This is the first striking appearance of the view that the senses are unified in a single sensibility. We may perceive something, such as bile, as bitter and yellow, requiring no further faculty beyond sense to give unity since the five senses are united in the central sensorium (a31–425b2)" (Polansky, *Aristotle's De anima: A Commentary*, 376).

85 Aristotle, *De Anima*, 425b4.
86 Polansky remarks that: "Not merely the common sensibles are disclosed through several senses but also the accidental sensibles as bodily beings with magnitude, figure, rest, and motion" (Polansky, *Aristotle's De anima: A Commentary*, 378).
87 Aristotle, *De Anima*, 425b4.
88 Aristotle, *De Anima*, 425b4.
89 Aristotle, *De Anima*, 426b17.
90 Aristotle, *De Anima*, 424b22.
91 Aristotle, *De Anima*, 426b17.
92 Aristotle, *De Anima*, 425b15.

being "different from sight,"⁹³ and likewise for the other five senses. It is through this sense that "we perceive *that* we see and hear."⁹⁴ We must first see and hear through sight and hearing, and then mediate these perceptions through the common sense which "must both think [...] and perceive[...].⁹⁵

II.C.2 Kant on the Sensus Communis

Aristotle describes the common sense as a sense that is not linked with any particular sense but rather common to all. Through this one acquires the capacity to perceive common objects beyond the special-objects.⁹⁶ There are certain ways in which this resonates with the aesthetic common sense of Kant. The idea that the common sense is not located in any one sense organ but capable of allowing the subject to become reflectively aware of sense organ perception suits the way that, for Kant, the mind senses its own activity through merely reflective aesthetic judgment. We see this similarity particularly in Kant's discussion of the role that sense organs play in the perception of a beautiful color or beautiful tone. Here, he carefully differentiates mere sensation from reflection, the latter being what is essential to the pure aesthetic judgment of taste:

> If one assumes, with Euler, that the colors are vibrations (*pulsus*) of the air immediately following one another, just as tones are vibrations of the air disturbed by sound, and, what is most important, that the mind does not merely perceive, by sense, their effect on the animation of the organ, but also, through reflection, perceives the regular play of the impressions (hence the form in the combination of different representations) (about which I have very little doubt), then colors and tones would not be mere sensations, but would already be a formal determination of the unity of a manifold of them, and in that case could also be counted as beauties in themselves.⁹⁷

This passage is suggestive of Aristotle's common sense, particularly in how the mind perceives the vibrations of air constituting color and sound by sense, but then perceives the beauty of color and sound by reflection upon what is sensed. In Aristotelian terms we might say that beauty does not come to us through the special-objects of the senses, or the proper sensibles, but rather through common objects or common sensibles. Hence, thinking of the common sense as a

---

93 Aristotle, *De Anima*, 425b15.
94 Aristotle, *De Anima*, 425b12, *emphasis added*.
95 Aristotle, *De Anima*, 426b17.
96 Or, as Polansky renders it "the common sensibles that accompany the proper sensibles" (Polansky, *Aristotle's De anima: A Commentary*, 378).
97 *Critique of the Power of Judgment*, § 14, 5:224.

means for reflecting upon perceptions helps us to understand how beauty is not a particular property of the object perceived. In this respect, it can be informative to trace Kant's notion of the common sense back to Aristotle.

There are, however, also important ways that Kant departs from Aristotle. First of all, Kant does appear to treat the common sense as another "sense apart from the five,"[98] giving it the autonomous identity Aristotle denied. Furthermore, Kant develops his notion of the common sense so that it is tailored to fit the needs of his aesthetic theory. His most detailed discussion of the common sense appears in **§ 40. On taste as a kind of *sensus communis*.** Here, Kant writes that,

> taste can be called *sensus communis* with greater justice than can the healthy understanding, and that the aesthetic power of judgment rather than the intellectual can bear the name of a communal sense [*den Namen eines gemeinschaftlichen Sinnes*],* if indeed one would use the word "sense" of an effect of mere reflection on the mind: for there one means by "sense" the feeling of pleasure. One could even define taste as the faculty for judging that which makes our feeling in a given representation **universally communicable** without the mediation of a concept.[99]

From this passage we see that the word "sense" indicates "an effect of mere reflection on the mind,"[100] which aligns well with the Aristotelian use of the term as indicated above. Aristotle's use of the term did not, however, involve the idea that this sense is also communal. For Kant, this "mere reflection on the mind"[101] is not just a *sensus communis* but "a communal sense"[102] to be directly linked to "the faculty for judging that which makes our feeling in a given representation **universally communicable.**"[103] I will now investigate how the common sense fits into Kant's aesthetic theory, showing that the further *communal* role it plays—supporting taste's claim to subjective universality—interrelates with its role of reflecting upon what is sensed.

In the passage cited above the phrase "a communal sense" directs us to a footnote in which Kant differentiates between two different types of *sensus communis*:

---

98 Aristotle, *De Anima*, 424a22.
99 *Critique of the Power of Judgment*, § 40, 5:295.
100 *Critique of the Power of Judgment*, § 40, 5:295.
101 *Critique of the Power of Judgment*, § 40, 5:295.
102 *Critique of the Power of Judgment*, § 40, 5:295; 293.
103 *Critique of the Power of Judgment*, § 40, 5:295.

* One could designate taste as *sensus communis aestheticus*, common human understanding as *sensus communis logicus*.[104]

Sensus communis aestheticus pertains to "the inner feeling of a purposive state of mind"[105] that arises when one judges something beautiful, sensing an "agreement of the two powers of mind"[106] that occurs without cognition through concepts. When this agreement is sensed *with* cognition through concepts, then it is *sensus communis logicus*, giving us the feeling of common human understanding (so that something "makes sense" or just "seems right"). Both of these forms of *sensus communis* arise through reflection upon perceptions and involve a type of consciousness of the perceiving that cannot be assumed in the direct act of perceiving itself. It is, hence, not merely seeing the tulip that gives one pure aesthetic pleasure, but the reflective activity of judgment that is performed upon this seeing. The focus accordingly shifts from reflecting on the thing perceived to reflecting on the way that the mind is affected in the act of perceiving itself. Kant specifies the work of the *sensus communis* as *aestheticus*, when "the word 'sense' [indicates] an effect of mere reflection on the mind: for there one means by 'sense' the feeling of pleasure."[107] This direct linkage between the *sensus communis* and the feeling of pleasure is a further aspect not found in Aristotle's usage of the term.

From § 40 we can discriminate three ways that the common sense specifically serves pure aesthetic judgment:

1. It is the common sense that feels "the agreement of the two powers of mind," which occurs when "the imagination in its freedom arouses the understanding" and the understanding "sets the imagination into a regular play."[108]

---

104 *Critique of the Power of Judgment*, § 40, 5:295.
105 *Critique of the Power of Judgment*, § 40, 5:296.
106 *Critique of the Power of Judgment*, § 40, 5:295. To quote this section more fully: "The aptitude of human beings for communicating their thoughts also requires a relation between the imagination and the understanding in order to associate intuitions with concepts and concepts in turn with intuitions, which flow together into a cognition; but in that case the agreement of the two powers of the mind is lawful, under the constraint of determinate concepts. Only where the imagination in its freedom arouses the understanding, and the latter, without concepts, sets the imagination into a regular play is the representation communicated, not as a thought, but as the inner feeling of a purposive state of mind" (*Ibid.*, 5:295–296).
107 *Critique of the Power of Judgment*, § 40, 5:295.
108 See *Critique of the Power of Judgment*, § 40, 5:295–296. In terms of my layered interpretation, I see the stimulation of the understanding as playing out in the "much thinking" of the third layer (*Critique of the Power of Judgment*, § 49, 5:314; 315). The play of the imagination on

2. It is in this manner, that "the representation [is] communicated, not as a thought, but as the inner feeling of a purposive state of mind."[109] The common sense must exist in all who cognize, since without it there would be problems for cognition,[110] and due to its necessary existence in all judging subjects, the common sense can serve as the grounds for universal communicability. All must thus be able to feel the agreement between the faculties of mind, imbuing this feeling with subjective universality. Furthermore, since this is a feeling and not a thought, it can be universally communicable without the mediation of a concept.
3. The perception of this universally communicable feeling of agreement between the cognitive faculties (#1 and #2) is thus carried out by "a **communal** sense, i.e., a faculty for judging that in its reflection takes account (*a priori*) of everyone else's way of representing in thought, in order **as it were** to hold its judgment up to human reason as a whole."[111]

These three roles of the common sense are interrelated, building off of one another. The feeling of "the agreement of the two powers of mind"[112] is necessary for universal communicability without the mediation of a concept, and it is this that gives rise to the "inner feeling of a purposive state of mind"[113] felt by judging subjects in pure aesthetic judgments of taste, which in turn supplies a communicable representation that is felt not thought.[114] One recognizes that this pleasure of "the agreement of the two powers of mind" does not stem from "subjective private conditions,"[115] but rather from the arrangement of the faculties necessary for the possibility of experience, and as such it is in accord with "everyone else's way of representing in thought" *a priori*.[116]

---

the second layer is regulated through the operation of the logical functions which determine cognitive activity but do not generate a determinate cognition.
109 *Critique of the Power of Judgment*, § 40, 5:296.
110 Some of these problems are elaborated above by Aristotle. The others that would arise specifically for Kant pertain to "that proportion which is suitable for making cognition out of a representation," discussed in sections II.D and II.E. below (*Critique of the Power of Judgment*, § 21, 5:238).
111 *Critique of the Power of Judgment*, § 40, 5:293.
112 *Critique of the Power of Judgment*, § 40, 5:295.
113 *Critique of the Power of Judgment*, § 40, 5:296.
114 See chapter four, section II.D. for my analysis of how the judgment of taste allows for the communication of the incommunicable.
115 *Critique of the Power of Judgment*, § 40, 5:293.
116 *Critique of the Power of Judgment*, § 40, 5:293.

II.E The Proportion Sensed by the *Sensus Communis Aestheticus*

Thus, the common sense does not directly judge the bodily senses. Instead, it judges the activity of the faculties of imagination and understanding. The common sense is how we judge what is cognitively underway in our faculties of mind. Unlike the bodily senses, the "sense-data" perceived by the common sense is entirely immaterial. The common sense is, thus, not subject to material differences in the sense organs of individuals, nor is the "play of the powers of representation" it perceives *merely* subjective.[117] What it senses arises from a

---

117 *Critique of the Power of Judgment*, § 21, 5:238. The proportion felt by the common sense is thus better suited for pure aesthetic judgment than are unmediated sensations supplied directly from the bodily senses. Moreover, not every bodily sense can ultimately occasion a purely aesthetic, reflective judgment through the common sense. As Kant remarks, "The beautiful arrangement of corporeal things [...] is also given only for the eye [...]; the sense of touch, however, cannot furnish any intuitable representation of such a form" (*Ibid.*, § 5:323). The pleasure of touch is designated as a "sensory sensation" pleasure, and the pleasure of a sensory sensation "comes into the mind through the senses and we are therefore passive with regard to it, [thus, it] can be called the pleasure of enjoyment" (*Ibid.*, § 39, 5:291). This is held in contrast to the pleasure of pure aesthetic judgment. Touch is not the only sensory sensation pleasure. Both gustatory and olfactory pleasures are too dependent upon the sense organs for Kant to discuss the possibility of beautiful tastes or smells. The "taste of the tongue, palate, and throat" yield only an *impure* aesthetic judgments of *agreeableness* (*Ibid.*, § 7, 5:212). They are too immediate to be judgments of beauty. They respond directly to a sensory sensation and not to the proportion achieved in the harmonious free play of the faculties (be this as it may *occasioned* by an intuitional excess to which one is receptive by means of the senses). Tastes and smells do not supply the reflective distance necessary for the pure aesthetic judgment of taste. Indeed, Kant uses gustatory pleasure to illustrate how impure aesthetic judgments of the agreeable are "ground[ed] on a private feeling" and thus "restricted merely to [one's] own person" whereas pure aesthetic judgments of beauty are not (*Ibid.*). He observes that one "is perfectly happy if, when he says that sparkling wine from the Canaries is agreeable, someone else should improve his expression and remind him that he should say 'It is agreeable **to me**'" (*Ibid., emphasis original*). Kant also clarifies that it is not the olfactory pleasure of flowers that allow them to serve as a paradigmatic example of natural beauty: "On account of the agreeableness of [the flower's] smell it has no claims [to everyone's satisfaction] at all. For one person is enraptured by this smell, while another's head is dizzied by it. Now what should one infer from this except that the beauty must be held to be a property of the flower itself, which does not correspond to the difference of heads and so many senses, but to which instead the latter must correspond if they would judge it? And yet this is not how it is. For the judgment of taste consists precisely in the fact that it calls a thing beautiful only in accordance with that quality in it by means of which it corresponds with our way of receiving it" (*Ibid.*, § 32, 5:281). The "difference of heads and so many senses" allows one person to be "enraptured by this smell, while another's head is dizzied by it." Smells, and other responses of the senses, are dependent upon one's physical constitution. Some people are physically structured "with heads" that respond positively to the smell of flowers. Others have allergies that

"mental state" common to all judging subjects, that is "the disposition of the cognitive powers for a cognition in general."[118] Although *a posteriori* stimulation of our bodily senses on the first layer is what occasions the second layer free play of the faculties of cognition, the common sense which feels this free play is sensing something that begins with—but does not arise from—experience and, hence, something that is *a priori*.[119] What is sensed in this common mental state is "that proportion which is suitable for making cognition out of a representation."[120] It is important to note that this is the *proportion required* to make a representation into a cognition and not the *actual making* of a representation into a cognition itself. This proportion is present in all cognition,[121] but it is most potently sensed in pure aesthetic judgment, namely, because here it is present *without* the representation actually being made into a cognition. When the representation is made into a cognition, this proportion is eclipsed by the resulting cognition. The cognition attracts all of our attention, obfuscating the proportion that allowed it to come about; we are immediately caught up in the determinative cognitive activity that ensues upon cognition of an object. It is only when this process is stopped in its tracks by the understanding's inability to supply a determinative concept that we are truly able to linger over the proportion itself, tarrying in the feeling of an enlivening interplay of imagination and understanding. Here the proportion is "one in which this inner relationship is optimal for the animation of both powers of the mind (the one through the other) with respect to cognition (of given objects) in general; and this disposition cannot be determined except through the feeling (not by concepts)."[122] Here there is no push rushing us past this proportion to cognition. With the road to cognition

---

cause a painful response to the very same smell. Something that depends upon the way that one's physical constitution will only ever be able to make claim to a singular judgment. The claim will only hold for the person whose sense organ judges the sensory pleasure, and thus the judgment cannot express "the universal validity of a singular judgment" (*Ibid.*, § 31, 5:281, See chapter four, section II). Hence, when an empirical object is judged immediately through the sensory sensation, and not mediately through the proportion, an impure aesthetic judgment of agreeableness is underway.
118 *Critique of the Power of Judgment*, § 21, 5:238.
119 "But although all our cognition commences with experience, yet it does not on that account all arise from experience" (*Critique of Pure Reason*, B1).
120 *Critique of the Power of Judgment*, § 21, 5:238.
121 As Kant observes, "this actually happens every time when, by means of the senses, a given object brings the imagination into activity for the synthesis of the manifold, while the imagination brings the understanding into activity for the unification of the manifold into concepts" (*Critique of the Power of Judgment*, § 21, 5:238).
122 *Critique of the Power of Judgment*, § 21, 5:238–9.

blocked by the inability to supply a suitable concept, the common sense comes into view as more than a mere cog in the machinery of determinative judgment. In pure aesthetic judgment the common sense comes into its own as a full-fledged sense that *feels* the concordant relation of the faculties, basking in the pleasant sensation of a harmonious free-play.

In our discussion of the second moment of aesthetic judgment, the intersubjective validity of aesthetic judgment did not arise through conceptualization of the feeling of aesthetic pleasure and discursive transmission from one subject to another.[123] Rather, a sheen of mystery remains, for that which is communicated in aesthetic judgment does not follow a discursive route. Similarly, the workings of the common sense in the fourth moment is to be assumed and not determinatively established. We have a number of good reasons to presume that there must be a common sense—that is, a sense common to the cognitive faculties of a judging subject and thus shared by all subjects who judge. But this cannot be proven, because it pertains to the conditions for the possibility of cognition, and as such can only be argued for in a retrograde fashion. We can only begin with the cognitions we *do* have, working back form this to the conditions for the possibility for these cognitions. As a condition for the possibility of cognition, however, it cannot appear to us as an object in cognition and consequently cannot have its existence proven in that manner.

In chapter four we saw that the second moment describes a universal communication of the incommunicable insofar as we come to recognize that we all share in the common pleasure of pure aesthetic judgment. As something that is felt deep within, this is unable to be fully conceptualized and thus cannot, in turn, be discursively communicated. Since it is something in which all share, however, we feel a reverberation of aesthetic judging allowing us a certain pure aesthetic communion with those who judge in a manner that does not need to be discursively communicated. In the fourth moment we find that "since the universal communicability of a feeling presupposes a common sense, the latter must be able to be assumed with good reason [...] as the necessary condition of the universal communicability of our cognition, which is assumed in every logic and every principle of cognitions."[124] The fourth moment accordingly takes up the content of universal communicability determined in the second moment, so as to determine regressively how such judgmental content would have us locate the judgment as a whole in the faculties for cognition

---

[123] See chapter four, section II. D.
[124] *Critique of the Power of Judgment*, § 21, 5:239. From this description logic seems to feed right into the common sense.

in general. The answer is that this universally communicable judgment must be situated within a sense common to all cognitive activity and to all cognizing subjects. The common sense fits this perfectly, as it is where the proportion necessary for cognition is felt. Such a sense can be assumed to be actively sensing in all relations of the understanding and imagination in all judging subjects, thus locating where the subjective universality of pure aesthetic judgment resides in the cognitive landscape of judging subjects.

II.F The Common Sense and the Representation of Subjective Necessity as Objective

It is the presumption of the common sense that allows us to represent subjective necessity as objective.[125] This sense functions like a bridge that allows us to move from the intimately private, non-conceptual feeling of pure aesthetic pleasure, arising in the act of aesthetic judging, to the realm of all judging subjects—subjects for whom we can presume this private sensation to be commonly sensed. It is for this reason that we take the feeling that grounds pure aesthetic judgment "not as a private feeling, but as a common one."[126] As has been observed for subjective universality and conditioned necessity, there is once again a nuance that offsets the absoluteness one would expect from a "common" feeling. The feeling is common, and should arise in all judging subjects, but it will only *in fact* arise in subjects that actually engage in the activity of pure aesthetic judging. If one's judging deviates from that which is purely aesthetic—by, for example, confusing the cognitive judgments of perfection and imperfection with aesthetic judgments of beauty, or mixing in impure sensations—then one may in all actuality fail to agree, even though one *should* agree. The normative dimension of a "should" cannot be grounded upon experience. The common sense thus functions as an "ideal norm" which allows us to "ascribe exemplary validity" to our judgments of taste, so as to assert that our making of this judgment exemplifies exactly how a pure aesthetic judgment is to be carried out.[127] The common sense is "an idea necessary for everyone" without which the proportional relation between the faculties of understanding and imagination—nec-

---

[125] Kant states this in the title of § 22 "The necessity of the universal assent that is thought in a judgment of taste is a subjective necessity, which is represented as objective under the presupposition of a common sense" (5:239).
[126] *Critique of the Power of Judgment*, § 21, 5:239.
[127] *Critique of the Power of Judgment*, § 22, 5:239.

essary for cognition—could not be felt.[128] If we concern ourselves only with the realm of judging subjects, we see that the "demand [for] universal assent" holds with just as much universality and necessity as any "objective one."[129] There is, however, a hesitation that must hold us back from assigning unconditional necessity to any particular pure aesthetic judgment, and this is rooted in the fact that we can never be entirely "certain of having correctly subsumed" the representation judged under the rule for pure aesthetic judgment—a rule that can never be supplied.[130] Thus, no matter how much this judgment pushes towards objectivity, it must always be restrained by subjectivity; the "norm of common sense" must remain "indeterminate."[131] It cannot be determinately proven. Instead, it must always be "presumed" due to the necessity of its existence—a necessity which is revealed when we regressively consider the conditions necessary for grounding the judgments we do in fact make.[132]

This indeterminate and presumed character of the common sense leaves open the disjunctive possibility that it may be either "a constitutive principle of the possibility of experience," or that "a yet higher principle of reason" might only make "it into a regulative principle for us first to produce a common sense in ourselves for higher ends."[133] This is the disjunctive possibility that common sense either be "an original and natural faculty, or only the idea of one that is yet to be acquired and is artificial."[134] If it is the latter, then the "expectation of a universal assent" to a given judgment of taste would become "a demand of reason to produce such a unanimity in the manner of sensing."[135] The "should" would accordingly, "signif[y] only the possibility of coming to agreement about this, and the judgment of taste only provid[e] an example of the application of this principle."[136] Far from deciding between these *complementa*, Kant is content to allow this matter to remain problematic, as our task "for now" is "only to resolve the faculty of taste into its elements and to unite them ultimately in the idea of a common sense."[137] The role that the presumption of a common sense plays in pure aesthetic judgment is not changed by regarding this idea of a com-

---

[128] *Critique of the Power of Judgment*, § 21, 5:239.
[129] *Critique of the Power of Judgment*, § 21, 5:239.
[130] *Critique of the Power of Judgment*, § 21, 5:239.
[131] *Critique of the Power of Judgment*, § 21, 5:239.
[132] *Critique of the Power of Judgment*, § 21, 5:239.
[133] *Critique of the Power of Judgment*, § 21, 5:240.
[134] *Critique of the Power of Judgment*, § 21, 5:240.
[135] *Critique of the Power of Judgment*, § 21, 5:240.
[136] *Critique of the Power of Judgment*, § 21, 5:240.
[137] *Critique of the Power of Judgment*, § 21, 5:240.

mon sense as an original part of the faculties for cognition, in general, or as something brought about for the sake of cognition. Without determining the status of the common sense any further, we are able to attain the definition that is to be "drawn from the fourth moment," namely: "That is beautiful which is cognized without a concept as the object of a necessary satisfaction."[138]

III Conclusion: Modality in Terms of the Layers

When discussing modality in the first *Critique*, Kant observes that the higher the modal level a judgment obtains, the more modes it has traversed:

> Now since everything here is gradually incorporated into the understanding, so that one first judges something problematically, then assumes it assertorically as true, and finally asserts it to be inseparably connected with the understanding, i.e., asserts it as necessary and apodictic, these three functions of modality can also be called so many moments of thinking in general.[139]

In this manner, we might regard the layered structure of aesthetic judgment as telling a similar modal story of how something only problematically entertained as possible in the first layer is then sensed as actual in the second, but only declared to have conditioned necessity in the third where one discursively analyzes its grounds.[140] Kant suggests such a reading with his opening remarks to the fourth moment:

> Of every representation I can say that it is at least **possible** that it (as a cognition) be combined with a pleasure. Of that which I call **agreeable** I say that it **actually** produces a pleas-

---

138 *Critique of the Power of Judgment*, § 21, 5:240.
139 *Critique of Pure Reason*, A76/B101.
140 With each layer we see the development of an increasingly higher grade of modality. By no means, however, do I intend to imply with this that a higher modality can be derived from a lower one, as "*a posse ad esse non valet consequentia* (there is no valid inference from possibility to actuality)" (*Critique of the Power of Judgment*, § 41, 5:296). It is noteworthy that both quantity and modality allow for this sort of development, whereas quality and relation generally do not. If something holds universally, then this will also hold for both singular instances and particular cases falling under the universal. Something that is necessary is also possible and actual. Quality and relation differ in this respect. An affirmative judgment cannot be negative, and the categorical, hypothetical and disjunctive are distinct relational forms. One might still pick out one way in which the logical functions within each of these quadrants overlap. The infinite logical function of quality consists of the affirming a negated predicate (see chapter three). Hypothetical and disjunctive judgments describe relations among two or more judgments and these component judgments can be categorical (see chapter five).

ure in me. Of the **beautiful**, however, one thinks that it has a necessary relation to satisfaction.[141]

The necessary relation is discursively thought, whereas the production of pleasure must be actually sensed. On the first layer the relation between the representation that involves an intuitional surplus and pure aesthetic pleasure is problematic ("at least possible"). On the second layer this relation is actualized as one perceives that the free play of the faculties occasioned by contemplation of the intuitional excess is in fact accompanied by pure aesthetic pleasure. On the third layer one reflects discursively upon the second-layer activity of judging; and when this judging is recognized to have been carried out only through the arrangement of the faculties, without private grounds, then one recognizes how this allows one to lay claim to the conditioned necessity of this pleasure for all judging subjects. Thus, the final verdict is declared with necessity on the third layer, although the grounds allowing one to make such a claim pertain to the activity of judging that occurred on the second layer.

Necessity, as discussed at the beginning of this chapter, is a pure concept of the understanding and not a logical function. Furthermore, as a modality it designates how an already constituted, whole judgment fits into the cognitive landscape. This means that it does not operate within the judgment itself to determine the judgment's content. Thus, it is the intrinsic characteristics of the judging arising on the second layer that entitle the judgment to claim conditioned necessity. The claim of necessity itself, however, is extrinsic to the content of the judgment and consequently made on the third layer. In this manner the common sense, operative on the second layer, allows this claim to be made about the necessary status of the judgment as a whole.[142]

As Kant observes, this claim of the third layer must fall short of obtaining apodictic status, as "this necessity cannot be derived from determinate concepts."[143] It does, however, come close enough to apodicity to obtain precisely the sort of exemplary necessity befitting a judgment grounded upon a universally communicable feeling. This necessity is tempered with a certain contingency. Cognition of the necessity of the third layer is contingent upon actually having felt the transcendental pleasure of the second that entitles one to make such a claim.

---

141 *Critique of the Power of Judgment*, § 18, 5:237.
142 This bears similarity to how the transcendental pleasure that allows judgments of taste to be universally communicable arises on the second layer but is articulated on the third layer, as discussed in chapter four, section II.B.
143 *Critique of the Power of Judgment*, § 18, 5:237.

Concluding Remarks

I The Project

This project defends an understanding of Kant's theory of the judgment of taste as detailing an operation of the faculties that does not violate the cognitive structure laid out in the first *Critique*, even though it would not be easily anticipated from the standpoint of that work, nor would it initially be expected to be of transcendental interest to Kant. My orientation has been primarily epistemological, elaborating the determinations that govern the activity of pure aesthetic judging, specifying it as the judgment of taste. In the course of doing so, a picture has emerged of how the world is not just cognizable in a Kantian framework but also becomes charged with human feeling, acquiring an inexhaustible, inchoate meaningfulness that incites "much thinking."[1] The universal communicability of aesthetic pleasure serves as the foundation that grounds robust intersubjective relations, enabling genuine connection to others through a shared a priori feeling.

II Looking Back

The first two chapters tackled the question of concepts, thereby setting the foundation for my analysis of the four moments of the judgment of taste. Kant repeatedly remarks on how the judgment of taste "is neither grounded on concepts nor aimed at them."[2] To understand such remarks as an indication that judgments of taste are completely concept-independent would run into the three obstacles I describe in chapter one. First, despite Kant's insistence that beauty is not a property of the object, various passages explicitly relate aesthetic judgment to an object of experience. Such an object is, however, to be understood as "that in the *concept* of which the manifold of a given intuition is united,"[3] and thus involves concepts. Second, an empirical concept of the object judged inevitably occupies the subject position in the final aesthetic judgment that is generated (i.e., "This *tulip* is beautiful"). Third, aesthetic judgment "sets the faculty of intellectual ideas (reason) into motion," which "aesthetically enlarges the concept itself."[4]

---

[1] *Critique of the Power of Judgment*, § 49, 5:315.
[2] CPJ, AA05: 209.
[3] *Critique of Pure Reason*, B137, emphasis added.
[4] *Critique of the Power of Judgment*, § 49, 5:315.

I respond to these difficulties in chapter two with a layered solution that contextualizes pure aesthetic judging within a larger judgmental process. This allows me to explain how the properly aesthetic harmony of the faculties on the second layer relates to the empirical object constituted on the first layer and incites the thinking of the third without, however, becoming a determinate, cognitive judgment in the process. Streamlining the activity of pure aesthetic judgment allows us to recognize the context in which this judging takes place and thus specify the contextual layers that do involve concepts and the pure aesthetic layer that does not. Having established my layered solution as an interpretive foundation, I then analyze how each moment relates to the corresponding logical functions.

The first moment ushers us on to the track for pure aesthetic judging. The quality of the judgment of taste clarifies that it is not the existence of the empirical object that is aesthetically judged. The empirical object as an existing thing is encounterable on the first layer of aesthetic judgment. The disinterest of the judgment of taste indicates, however, that the encounter with the object is only as an *Anlass*, occasioning the activity of pure aesthetic judgment—stimulating the faculties in a way that could not occur without experience but does *not* arise *from* experience. This activity of pure aesthetic judgment is not grounded upon the thing as existing; it is stimulated by the intuitional excess that was apprehended in the givenness of the object, but not recognized in its concept.

Quantity elaborates how the sphere of the subject-concept relates to that of the predicate-concept.[5] The importance of the concept to the very definition of quantitative logical functions presented a potential complication for the concept-independent nature of the second, properly aesthetic layer. This difficulty was, however, overcome because what acquires universal status in the judgment of taste is not a concept, but rather, the *feeling* of pure aesthetic pleasure. Hence, aesthetic "universality cannot originate from concepts. For there is no transition from concepts to the feeling of pleasure or displeasure."[6] It is not that an intuition is recognized in a concept that finds universal application, but that a feeling perceived first hand by the judging subject is recognized in all other judging subjects. Hence, judgments of taste are subjectively universal.

The third moment of relation, is where the purposiveness *without* a purpose of pure aesthetic judgment is explicated. Similar to quantity, relation brushes up against the threat of impermissible concept involvement. For something to have

---

[5] "In the *universal* judgment, the sphere of one concept is wholly enclosed within the sphere of another; in the *particular*, a part of the former is enclosed under the sphere of the other; and in the *singular* judgment, finally, a concept that has no sphere at all is enclosed, merely as part then, under the sphere of another" (*Jäsche Logic*, § 21, 598).
[6] *Critique of the Power of Judgment*, § 6, 5:211.

a purpose is for it to relate to the concept of an end. How a pure purposiveness of form is to be understood without it being grounded on any concept of a determinate purpose thus arose as an issue to be addressed. Kant's way of understanding nature indicates the path that takes us out of this difficulty. Concepts arise through cognition, but Kant maintains that nature cannot be known to be cognizant. Thus, no concept of an end can be determinatively attributed to nature. Consequently, the aesthetic purposiveness of beautiful nature arises *without* the concept of an end, i.e. without a purpose. The beauty of nature is seen when the natural product is regarded as if it were aiming at an end even though it cannot be determined to aim at any concept. In other words, nature *qua* nature is unable to be determined as having ends, but *qua* beautiful nature it still *appears* to aim at something, and thus appears *as if it were* art. Beautiful art is alternatively known to have been created by an intentionally acting agent (and thus to aim at an end), and yet it appears to have arisen in a natural manner, free from the constraint involved in acting intentionally to achieve a purpose. It is the disjunctive function that allows us to hold these contradictory possibilities together without asserting one or the other, charging the air with an indeterminate purposive possibility—a sense of purposiveness unconstrained by any determinate purpose.

With the "content of the judgment" exhausted by quality, quantity and relation, modality emerged as the "special function" that describes "the relation of the whole judgment to the faculty of cognition."[7] Pure aesthetic judgments of taste fit into the cognitive landscape as judgments that have a carefully attenuated claim on necessity. The judging subject who feels pure aesthetic pleasure recognizes this pleasure to arise neither from private grounds, nor from obligation, but rather to be a free pleasure stemming from the very arrangement of the faculties, the transcendental conditions for the possibility of cognition, themselves. This pure aesthetic pleasure is both actual for the individual subject making the judgment and recognized to be possible for every other judging subject. The empirical circumstances surrounding any specific encounter with a given aesthetic object, however, are not determined a priori. Thus, an element of contingency is unavoidable in aesthetic necessity, yielding a subjective necessity to be "pronounced only conditionally."[8]

Thus we have seen that the oddities of each intrinsic moment—quality's *disinterest* in existence, quantity's *subjective* universality, relation's purposiveness *without* a purpose—reveal determinations of the activity of pure aesthetic judging

---

7 *Jäsche Logic*, § 30, 604.
8 *Critique of the Power of Judgment*, § 19, 5:237.

that do not determine any object and are not grounded upon a concept. Without a qualitative interest in the existence of the object, we are free to enter the second layer of pure aesthetic judgment where the feeling of transcendental free play is enabled by the a priori arrangement of the faculties. The specification of aesthetic quantity as *subjective* assures that universality pertains to a *feeling* ascribable to all judging *subjects*, circumventing universality's typical mode of operation by determining the extent of a concept's application. Since the purposiveness sensed in judgments of taste does not entail a purpose, it is not predicated upon the obtainment of any relation to the determinate concept of an end.

III Looking Ahead

It would be interesting to investigate how this layered structure can be used to inform Kant's theory of the other type of pure aesthetic judgment, the sublime. The judgment of the sublime would seem to naturally lend itself to being structured by the first and second layers. In the sublime we see something quite similar to what I have described in the judgment of taste as the reception of an intuitional excess. The judgment of the sublime begins when one encounters something in nature endowed with either a greatness or a power that surpasses our capacity to such an extent that it not only reveals our limitation, but becomes "contrapurposive for our power of judgment."[9] Whereas the intuitional excess of the judgment of taste was entirely pleasant, the sublime actively resists our attempts to cognize it in a manner that does "violence" to our faculties of mind.[10] This initially causes pain—or "negative pleasure,"[11] as Kant terms it— but then proceeds to "awaken [...] the feeling of a supersensible faculty in us"[12] and "reveal [...] a superiority [that we have] over nature."[13]

One can imagine how these sublime feelings that are awakened could be understood in a manner similar to the pleasure taken in beauty—that is, emerging inchoately on the second layer and then stimulating discursive attempts at articulation on the third. The positive pleasure would accordingly seem to be two-fold arising in a manner similar to that of the judgment of taste. The pleasure of sensing a greater capacity within oneself would manifest on the second

---

9 *Critique of the Power of Judgment*, § 23, 5:244.
10 *Critique of the Power of Judgment*, § 23, 5:244.
11 *Critique of the Power of Judgment*, § 23, 5:245.
12 *Ibid.*, § 25, 5:250.
13 *Ibid.*, § 28, 5:261–2.

layer, and then the pleasure of articulating and reflecting upon this power discursively would come forth on the third layer.

Whereas the judgment of taste only entails positive pleasure, it would be interesting to investigate how exactly the negative pleasure of the sublime works. Perhaps my layered solution could provide further detail concerning how the transition from negative to positive pleasure takes place, so that the initial negative response does not entirely dissipate when the positive response takes hold, but rather remains and continues to condition the positive pleasure.

Works Cited

Allison, Henry. *Essays on Kant.* Oxford: Oxford University Press, 2012.
Allison, Henry. "Is the *Critique of Judgment* 'Post-Critical'?" In *The Reception of Kant's Critical Philosophy: Fichte, Schelling, Hegel,* edited by Sally Sedgwick, 78–92. Cambridge: Cambridge University Press, 2000.
Allison, Henry. *Kant's Theory of Taste: A Reading of the Critique of Aesthetic Judgment.* Cambridge, MA: Cambridge University Press, 2001.
Allison, Henry. *Kant's Transcendental Idealism: An Interpretation and Defense.* New Haven, CT: Yale University Press, 1983.
Allison, Henry. *Kant's Transcendental Idealism: An Interpretation and Defense.* 2nd ed. New Haven, CT: Yale University Press, 2004.
Ameriks, Karl. "Kant and the Objectivity of Taste." *British Journal of Aesthetics* 23 (1983): 3–17.
Ameriks, Karl. "How to Save Kant's Deduction of Taste." *Journal of Value Inquiry* 16 (1982): 295–302.
Ameriks, Karl. "New Views on Kant's Judgment of Taste." In *Kants Ästhetik, Kant, Kant's Aesthetics, L'esthétique de Kant,* edited by Hermann Parret, 431–47. Berlin: Walter de Gruyter, 1998.
Aristotle. *De anima.* Translated by D. W. Hamlyn. Oxford: Clarendon Press, 2002.
Aristotle. *Nicomachean Ethics.* Translated by Terence Irwin. Indianapolis: Hackett Publishing, 1999.
Aristotle. *Physics.* Translated by Robin Waterfield. Oxford: Oxford University Press, 1996.
Bates, Jennifer A. *Hegel's Theory of Imagination.* Albany: State University of New York Press, 2004.
Bates, Jennifer A. *Hegel and Shakespeare on Moral Imagination.* Albany: State University of New York Press, 2010.
Beck, Lewis White. *Essays on Kant and Hume.* New Haven: Yale University Press, 1978.
Beck, Lewis White. "Did the Sage of Königsberg have No Dreams?" In *Essays on Kant and Hume.* New Haven: Yale University Press, 1978.
Bernstein, J. M. *The Fate of Art.* University Park: Penn State University Press, 1992.
Bernstein, J. M. "The Bernstein Tapes." The New School for Social Research, New York. Lecture Recording from 10.17.2007. Course Title: GPHI 6030 Kant's Critique of Judgment. Online.
Bickmann, Claudia. "Das unskeptisches Fundament der Erkenntniskritik. Kants 'schlechterdings notwendige Voraussetzungen' bei den wesentlichen Zwecken der menschlichen Vernunft." In *Transzendentalphilosophie heute,* edited by Andreas Lorenz, Königshausen & Neumann: Breslauer, 2004.
Bickmann, Claudia. "Die eingebettete Vernunft in Kants "Kritik der Urteilskraft": Wechselintegrationen vereint-entgegengesetzter Sphären." In *Philosophische Schrifte,* Band 68, edited by Reinhard Hiltscher, Stefan Klingner and David Süß, 19–39. Freiburg/Br.: Germany, 2006.
Bickmann, Claudia. *Differenz oder das Denken des Denkens. Topologie der Einheitsorte im Verhältnis von Denken und Sein im Horiyont der Tranzendentalphilosophie Kants.* Hamburg: Felix Meiner, 1996.

Bickmann, Claudia."Kants 'Sinnliches Scheinen der Idee.' Die Einheit von Ethik und Ästhetik in Kants Kritik der Urteilskraft." In *Das Geistige und das Sinnliche in der Kunst. Ästhetische Reflexion in der Perspektive des deutschen Idealismus*, edited by Dieter Wandschneider, 13–27. Würzburg: 2005.

Boswell, Terry. "On the Textual Authority of Kant's *Logic*." In *History and Philosophy of Logic* 9–2 (1988): 193–203.

Brandt, Reinhard. *Die Urteilstafel. Kritik der reinen Vernunft A 67–76; B 92–101*. Hamburg: Meiner Verlag, 1991.

Brandt, Reinhard. "Zur Logik des ästhetischen Urteils." In *Kants Ästhetik, Kant, Kant's Aesthetics, L'esthétique de Kant*, edited by Hermann Parret, 229–245. Berlin and New York: Walter de Gruyter, 1998.

Cohen, Ted & Paul Guyer, eds. *Essays in Kant's Aesthetics*. Chicago, IL: University of Chicago Press, 1982.

Crawford, Donald W. *Kant's Aesthetic Theory*. Madison: University of Wisconsin Press, 1974.

Descartes, René. *Meditations on First Philosophy*. Translated by Donald Cress. Indianapolis: Hackett Publishing, 1639.

Gasché, Rodolphe. *The Idea of Form*. Stanford, CA: Stanford UP, 2003.

Gasché, Rodolphe. "Transcendentality, in Play," In *Kants Ästhetik, Kant, Kant's Aesthetics, L'esthétique de Kant*, edited by Hermann Parret, 431–47. Berlin: Walter de Gruyter, 1998.

George, Rolf. "Vorstellung and Erkenntnis in Kant," In *Interpreting Kant*, ed. Moltke S. Gram. Iowa City: University of Iowa Press, 1982.

Ginsborg, Hannah. "Kant on the Subjectivity of Taste," In *Kant's Aesthetik, Kant's Aesthetics, L'estéthique de Kant*, edited by Hermann Parret, 448–65. Berlin: Walter de Gruyter, 1998.

Ginsborg, Hannah. "On the Key to Kant's Critique of Taste," *Pacific Philosophical Quarterly* 72 (1991): 290–313.

Guyer, Paul. "The Harmony of the Faculties," In *Kant and the Claims of Taste, First Edition*. Cambridge, MA: Harvard University Press, 1979.

Guyer, Paul. *Kant and the Claims of Taste, Second Edition*. Cambridge, MA: Harvard University Press, 1997.

Guyer, Paul. *Kant and the Experience of Freedom*, Cambridge: Cambridge University Press, 1993.

Guyer, Paul. *Kant's Critique of the Power of Judgment: Critical Essays*. Lanham: Rowman and Littlefield, 2003.

Guyer, Paul. *Knowledge, Reason, and Taste: Kant's Response to Hume*. Princeton: Princeton University Press, 2008.

Guyer, Paul. *Value of Beauty: Historical Essays in Aesthetics*. Cambridge: Cambridge UP, 2005.

Guyer, Paul. "The Harmony of the Faculties Revisited," In *Aesthetics and Cognition in Kant's Critical Philosophy*, edited by Rebecca Kukla. Cambridge: Cambridge University Press, 2006.

Hartmann, Nicolai. *Aesthetics*. Translated by Eugene Kelly. Berlin: de Gruyter, 2014.

Hartmann, Nicolai. *Possibility and Actuality*. Translated by Stephanie Adair and Alex Scott. Berlin/Boston: de Gruyter, 2013.

Harris, H. S. *Hegel: Phenomenology and System*. Indianapolis: Hackett Publishing, 1995.

Hegel, G. W. F. *Phenomenology of Spirit*. Translated by A. V. Miller. Oxford: Oxford University Press, 1977.
Hegel, G. W. F. *The Encyclopaedia Logic: The Encyclopaedia of Philosophical Sciences 1 with the Zusatze*. Translated and edited by Theodore F. Geraets, W. A. Suchting & H. S. Harris. Indinapolis: Hackett Publishing, 1991.
Heidegger, Martin. *Being and Time*. Translated by J. Macquarrie and E. Robinson. New York: Harper & Row, 1962.
Heidegger, Martin. *Kant and the Problem of Metaphysics*. Translated by J.S. Churchill. Bloomington: Indiana University Press, 1962.
Ishiguro, Kazuo. *Never Let Me Go*. London: Faber and Faber, 2006.
Janaway, Christopher. "Kant's Aesthetics and the 'Empty Cognitive Stock'" In *Kant's Critique of the Power of Judgment: Critical Essays*. Lanham: Rowman and Littlefield, 2003.
Jennings, Carolyn Dicey. "Consciousness without Attention," Journal of the American Philosophical Association 1–2 (2015): 276–295.
Kant, Immanuel. *Critique of the Power of Judgment*. Translated by P. Guyer and E. Matthews. Cambridge: Cambridge University Press, 2000.
Kant, Immanuel. *Critique of Practical Reason*. Translated by Mary Gregor. Cambridge: Cambridge University Press, 2005.
Kant, Immanuel. *Critique of Pure Reason*. Edited and translated by P. Guyer and A. Wood. Cambridge: Cambridge University Press, 1997.
Kant, Immanuel. *Gesammelte Schriften*. vols. 1–29, Berlin: DeGruyter/Reimer, 1902.
Kant, Immanuel. *Groundwork of the Metaphysics of Morals*. Translated by H. J. Paton. New York: Harper & Row, 1964.
Kant, Immanuel. *Jäsche Logic. The Jäsche Logic, Lectures on Logic*. Translated by Michael Young, 521–640.
Kant, Immanuel. *Kritik der reinen Vernünft*. Hamburg: Felix Meiner Verlag, 1998.
Kant, Immanuel. *Kritik der Urteilskraft*. Frankfurt: Suhrkamp, 1974.
Kant, Immanuel. *Metaphysical Foundations of Natural Science,* AK. IV, 474.
Kant, Immanuel. *Observations on the Feeling of the Beautiful and the Sublime*. Translated by J. T. Goldthwait. Berkeley: University of California Press, 2004.
Kant, Immanuel. *Prolegomena to any Future Metaphysics*. Translated by Lewis White Beck. Indianapolis: Bobbs-Merrill, 1950.
Kant, Immanuel. "On the Use of Teleological Principles in Philosophy." In *Anthropology, History, and Education.* translated by Robert B. Louden and Günter Zöller. Cambridge: Cambridge University Press, 2007.
Kulenkampff, Jens. *Kants Logik des ästhetischen Urteils*. Frankfurt am Main: Vittorio Klostermann, 1978.
Lacan, Jacques. *On Feminine Sexuality: the Limits of Love and Knowledge: Encore*. 1972–1973. Ed. Jacques-Alain Miller. Translated by Bruce Fink. New York: Norton, 1998
Longuenesse, Béatrice. *Kant and the Capacity to Judge*. Princeton, NJ: Princeton UP, 1998.
Longuenesse, Béatrice. "Kant's Leading Thread in the Analytic of the Beautiful." In *Aesthetics and Cognition in Kant's Critical Philosophy*. edited by Rebecca Kukla. Cambridge: Cambridge University Press, 2006.
Lu-Adler, Huaping. "Constructing a Demonstration of Logical Rules, or How to Use Kant's Logic Corpus." In *Reading Kant's Lectures*, edited by Robert Clewis. Berlin: Walter de Gruyter, 2015.

Lurz, Robert W. *The Philosophy of Animal Minds*. Cambridge: Cambridge University Press, 2009
Makkreel, Rudolf. *Imagination and Interpretation in Kant*. Chicago, IL: University of Chicago Press, 1990.
Makkreel, Rudolf. "Reflection, Reflective Judgment, and Aesthetic Exemplarity," In *Aesthetics and Cognition in Kant's Critical Philosophy*. edited by Rebecca Kukla. Cambridge: Cambridge University Press, 2006.
Manning, "The Necessity of Receptivity: Exploring a Unified Account of Kantian Sensibility and Understanding." In *Aesthetics and Cognition in Kant's Critical Philosophy*, edited by Rebecca Kukla. Cambridge: Cambridge University Press, 2006.
Nietzsche, Friedrich. *Zur Genealogie der Moral: Eine Streitschrift*. In *Kritische Studienausgabe*, vol. 5, II. Berlin: de Gruyter, 1999.
Okrent, Mark. "Acquaintance and Cognition," In *Aesthetics and Cognition in Kant's Critical Philosophy*, edited by Rebecca Kukla. Cambridge: Cambridge University Press, 2006.
Palmquist S. R. "Six Perspectives on the Object in Kant's Theory of Knoweldge." In *Dialectica* 40:2 (1986): 121–151.
Pippin, Robert B. *Kant's Theory of Form, An Essay on the Critique of Pure Reason*. New Haven and London: Yale University Press, 1982.
Plato. *Plato: Five Dialogues: Euthyphro, Apology, Crito, Meno, Phaedo*. Translated by G. M. A. Grube. Indianapolis: Hackett Publishing, 2002.
Polansky, Ronald. *Aristotle's De anima: A Commentary*. Cambridge: Cambridge University Press, 2007.
Quinn, Timothy Sean. "Kant: The Practical Categories," In *Categories: Historical and Systematic Essays*. Catholic University of America Press, Washington, D.C.. 2004.
Strawson, P. F. *Bounds of* Sense. London: Methuen, 1966.
Strawson, P. F. "Kantian Aesthetics Pursued." In *Philosophy* 69.268 (1994): 248–251.
Simon, Josel."Erhabene Schönheit: das ästhetische urteil als Destruktion de logischen." In *Kants Ästhetik, Kant, Kant's Aesthetics, L'esthétique de Kant*, edited by Herman Parret, 246–274. De Gruyter: Berlin, 1998.
Smith, Norman Kemp. *A Commentary to Kant's 'Critique of Pure Reason'*. London: Macmillan, 1923.
Sweet, Kristi. "Reflection: Its Structure and Meaning in Kant's Judgments of Taste." In *Kantian Review* 14–1 (2009) 53–80.
Trebels, Andreas Heinrich. *Einbildungskraft und Spiel: Untersuchungen zur Kantischen Ästhetik*, Bonn: Bouvier, 1967.
Walsh, W. H. *Kant's Criticism of Metaphysics*. Edinburgh: Edinburgh University Press, 1975.
Zangwill, Nick. "UnKantian Notions of Disinterest." In *British Journal of Aesthetics* 32.2 (1992): 149–152.
Zinkin, Melissa. "Intensive Magnitudes and the Normativity of Taste," In *Aesthetics and Cognition in Kant's Critical Philosophy*, edited by Rebecca Kukla. Cambridge: Cambridge University Press, 2006.

Abstract

The Aesthetic Use of the Logical Functions in Kant's Third *Critique*

I defend an understanding of Kant's theory of *Geschmacksurteil* as detailing an operation of the faculties that does not violate the cognitive structure laid out in the first *Critique*, even though one would not easily anticipate it from the standpoint of that work, nor would one initially expect aesthetic judgment to be of transcendental interest to Kant. My orientation is primarily epistemological, elaborating the determinations that govern the activity of pure aesthetic judging so as to specify it as a *bestimmte* type of judgment without transforming it into *einem bestimmenden Urteil*. I focus on identifying how the logical functions from the table of judgments operate in the pure aesthetic judgment of taste to reveal "the moments to which this power of judgment attends in its reflection" (*Critique of the Power of Judgment*, § 1, 5:203). In the course of doing so, a picture emerges of how the world is not just cognizable in a Kantian framework but also charged with human feeling, acquiring the inexhaustible, inchoate meaningfulness that incites "much thinking" (*Critique of the Power of Judgment*, § 49, 5:315). The universal communicability of aesthetic pleasure serves as the foundation that grounds robust intersubjective relations, enabling genuine connection to others through a shared a priori feeling.

Index

Aesthetic Harmony   14, 83, 98, 110, 288
Affirmative   9, 17, 108, 115, 127, 135–137, 139, 143f., 154, 175, 177f., 261, 285
Agreeable   12, 18, 26, 96, 133, 142, 144f., 154f., 157–160, 162, 164f., 169f., 174, 189, 195, 205f., 208–210, 213, 265f., 270, 280, 285
Allison, Henry   11, 18, 22–24, 30f., 39, 43, 53–59, 62f., 65, 67, 79, 102–105, 109f., 125, 179, 202, 205, 209, 215, 222, 230, 257
Ameriks, Karl   85, 200, 203f., 212, 255f.
Apodictic   9f., 259f., 263f., 266, 285f.
Aristotle   6f., 121, 140, 273–279
Assertoric   9, 115, 213, 219, 258–260, 263f., 266

Bates, Jennifer A.   28f., 138
Beck, Lewis White   30, 37, 58
Bickmann, Claudia   4, 69f., 76f., 82, 99f., 109, 113, 184, 227f., 242, 251
Boswell, Terry   22, 181
Brandt, Reinhard   141f., 145, 172, 178, 195f., 257–259

Categories   11, 19f., 29f., 37f., 40, 43, 45, 53, 55–63, 67, 73, 99f., 102–111, 121f., 124–126, 128–130, 132, 134, 156, 158, 167, 183, 197, 211, 215, 217, 221, 223, 248, 257, 260–263
Cohen, Ted   31, 210
Common Sense   19, 257f., 273–286
Community (Category of)   128, 216–219, 221–225, 227–229, 234, 236, 247f., 262
Concept   1–7, 10, 12–16, 18, 20, 24–26, 28–38, 40–43, 45–55, 57–74, 77–80, 82–89, 91–108, 110–115, 118, 122, 124–128, 132–134, 136, 139f., 143, 146–148, 151, 154, 156–158, 160, 164, 167, 171, 173, 176–189, 192–202, 204–207, 210f., 213, 218, 220f., 223–226, 228–232, 234–240, 242–245, 247–252, 255f., 260, 262–264, 266, 268–271, 273, 277–279, 281f., 285–290
Conditioned Necessity   19, 255, 257, 264, 267, 269, 283, 285f.
Crawford, Donald W.   17, 31, 127, 142f., 171
Creation   91f., 97, 236, 241f., 244–246, 253f.
Critique of Practical Reason   145, 158f., 166, 171, 173f.
Critique of Pure Reason   4–6, 9, 11, 13, 24, 28, 35, 39–41, 44, 49, 53–55, 57, 59–61, 63, 65, 68f., 72, 84, 99–101, 103, 105–108, 110, 115–117, 119–122, 126–131, 134–136, 138, 147–149, 151f., 155f., 158, 171, 177, 180, 182f., 188, 211, 215, 218–224, 226, 235f., 247, 255f., 258–264, 266, 268f., 281, 285, 287

Descartes, René   147
Disinterest   17, 133, 135, 142–145, 148, 152–154, 161, 163, 288f.
Disjunctive   9, 19, 84, 127, 215–224, 227–229, 234, 236f., 247, 253, 255, 284f., 289

Essence   33, 82, 137, 147, 149, 152, 155, 176, 247
Exemplary Judgment   19, 267
Exemplary Necessity   19, 264, 267, 271, 286
Existence   17, 58, 75f., 117, 127f., 146–162, 165, 170, 172–176, 223, 225f., 228, 258f., 271, 279, 282, 284, 288–290

Faculty-Interest   146, 170
Form   7, 10–15, 17f., 19, 24, 30, 37, 40, 42, 49f., 53f., 67–69, 71, 75, 79–81, 96–100, 102–105, 108, 110, 116, 121f., 125–127, 130–131, 134–140, 143, 148, 150–153, 165f., 172f., 179, 182f., 188f., 191, 194, 197, 215–220, 222–231, 234f., 237–244, 246, 248–250, 253, 255f., 259f., 263f., 269, 272–276, 278, 280, 285, 288f.

Index

Free Play 7, 13 f., 25, 31, 65 f., 68 f., 81, 83, 85 f., 88 f., 91, 93, 95, 97, 100, 105–112, 131, 150, 152, 160 f., 163, 165, 167, 171, 174, 186, 190, 193, 196, 199, 202, 207, 213, 240, 249–252, 261, 269, 271 f., 280 f., 286, 290

Gasché, Rodolphe 134, 167–169, 173, 237
Gegenstand 22–24, 43, 56 f., 67, 109, 162, 172
Ginsborg, Hannah 202, 264, 271
Guyer, Paul 7, 10, 18, 31, 37, 39, 77, 79–83, 125, 129 f., 152, 171, 183, 185–188, 193 f., 202, 204 f., 209, 212 f., 230, 236, 250, 256, 272

Harmony of the faculties 7, 31, 37, 79–83, 102, 115, 125, 165, 167, 169 f., 185, 194, 202, 205, 237, 250, 256
Hartmann, Nicolai 14, 84, 90–92, 148 f.
Hegel, G. W. F. 11, 22 f., 28 f., 136–138, 140, 144, 148
Heidegger, Martin 33, 129, 168

Impure Aesthetic Judgment 50, 76, 133, 155 f., 210, 265 f., 270, 280 f.
Indexlosigkeit 134, 161–165, 167, 169
Infinite 9, 17, 127, 133–146, 153 f., 174, 177 f., 182 f., 233, 255, 285
Interest 12, 17, 72, 75 f., 106, 127, 133, 135, 141–146, 152–154, 157–162, 164 f., 169–176, 189, 196 f., 206, 251, 261, 269, 290
Intertwinement 192, 241, 245
Intuition 1 f., 4–6, 13 f., 24–26, 28, 30–43, 45 f., 48, 50–54, 57–62, 65, 68–70, 79, 84 f., 92 f., 95, 98–101, 103–114, 125, 134, 140, 150–152, 156, 160, 167, 171, 176, 187 f., 194, 196 f., 204 f., 211, 224, 240, 249, 252, 261–263, 269 f., 278, 287 f.
Intuitional Excess 16, 25, 42, 85, 87, 92–97, 113 f., 150–152, 173, 193, 195 f., 249 f., 252, 263, 280, 286, 288, 290

Janaway, Christopher 77, 107 f., 203

Jäsche Logic 15, 19–22, 36, 38, 40, 43–45, 48, 52, 55, 61, 122, 124 f., 136, 139, 144, 177, 179–181, 185, 193, 207, 216–221, 223, 255, 259, 271, 288 f.

Kulenkampff, Jens 11, 17, 115 f., 124, 129 f., 134, 142, 154 f., 161–170, 215

Layered Solution 14, 16, 31, 33, 40, 49, 57, 67, 73–84, 88 f., 114, 133, 151, 172, 185–187, 202, 288, 291
Logic 20–22, 33, 43, 103 f., 116, 129, 138, 181, 183, 247, 282
Logical Functions 1, 9–11, 13–18, 20, 32, 43, 59, 75, 97–110, 115, 121–131, 133–139, 142 f., 145, 163, 167, 176–185, 192, 204, 206, 215, 217–219, 224, 235, 248, 252, 257–263, 265, 279, 285, 288, 296
Longuenesse, Béatrice 1–5, 15, 17, 24 f., 29 f., 37, 41, 45, 62, 110, 125–127, 129, 131, 139–141, 143, 174, 176, 182, 188, 201, 213, 215, 224, 256
Lu-Adler, Huaping 20–22, 43, 181

Makkreel, Rudolf 1–3, 5 f., 29 f., 37, 170 f., 192, 213, 265, 272
Matter 96, 116, 118–120, 125–127, 159, 172, 183, 216–218, 220, 226, 234 f., 238, 267 f.
Modality 9 f., 12, 19 f., 108, 122, 150 f., 156, 216 f., 219, 222, 255–267, 272 f., 285 f., 289
Moments of the Judgment of Taste 9, 11 f., 17, 108, 163, 217, 261, 264, 287
Mood 134, 167–170
Moral Good 153

Negated Interest 17, 133, 144
Negative 9, 23, 127, 133, 135–139, 141–144, 146, 148, 154, 177 f., 285, 290 f.
Nietzsche, Friedrich 210

Objective 10, 19, 22–24, 38 f., 41 f., 44–46, 48–51, 54–58, 60 f., 63–65, 74 f., 81, 87, 101 f., 107, 109, 121, 157–159, 171, 193, 197, 204, 212 f., 216,

230f., 233, 247, 249, 251, 257, 263f., 266f., 269f., 272f., 283f.
Objekt 22–24, 43, 56f.
Okrent, Mark 25, 34–36, 45f., 48, 52, 70, 232

Particularization 18, 204, 207, 211f.
Plato 92, 101
Pleasure 7f., 10, 16–18, 31, 36, 47, 50–52, 62, 64, 71, 76, 82, 85f., 91–93, 95, 97, 101, 109, 114, 120, 127, 133f., 141–148, 151–155, 159–170, 172–174, 184–193, 195–203, 206–210, 212f., 231, 233f., 237, 249f., 252f., 256, 262f., 265–273, 277–283, 285–291, 296
Polansky, Ronald 274–276
Proportion 171, 191, 196, 205, 212, 245, 257, 279–281, 283
Pure Aesthetic Judgment 12–15, 17–19, 25f., 41, 46, 49f., 76, 85f., 92, 94–96, 112–114, 133f., 138f., 146, 150–156, 160, 164–167, 170, 174, 179, 183f., 189, 193, 198, 200f., 203, 206–211, 216, 225, 230f., 234, 253, 257, 262–270, 272f., 276, 278–284, 288–290, 296
Purposiveness with a Purpose 225, 249
Purposiveness without a Purpose 11, 18, 87, 96f., 215–217, 225, 227, 229f., 233–237, 240f., 249–253, 288f.

Quality 8–10, 17, 57, 81, 88, 91, 96, 108, 117, 119, 122, 127, 130f., 133–135, 138f., 141–143, 145–147, 150, 156, 167, 170f., 175, 177–179, 255, 258, 260–263, 265, 269, 280, 285, 288f.
Quantity 9f., 12, 18, 108, 118, 122, 124, 130f., 139, 145, 156, 167, 176–182, 184f., 188, 192–196, 204–207, 220, 255f., 258, 260–263, 265, 269, 285, 288–290
Quinn, Timothy Sean 167

Reflective Aesthetic Judgment 1, 3, 7, 62, 235, 276

Relation 9–14, 18–20, 23, 35, 46, 48–52, 60–62, 64, 81f., 84, 91, 98–102, 106–108, 111, 115, 122f., 126f., 137–139, 154–157, 159f., 163–166, 168f., 172, 174–178, 182f., 190, 198f., 203, 205–207, 210f., 214–224, 227–229, 231f., 234–236, 240, 246–248, 251–253, 255–266, 271f., 275, 278, 282f., 285–290, 296

Section 9 62, 108, 187, 191, 201–205
Sensus Communis 191, 274, 276–278
Sensus Communis Aestheticus 278, 280
Singular Judgment 18, 114, 139, 176, 179f., 182f., 195f., 204, 220, 256, 281, 288
Smith, Norman Kemp 129
Strawson, P. F. 104, 129, 183
Subjective Principle 19, 157, 159, 256–258, 270, 273
Subjective Validity 49, 273
Sublime 68, 85, 94, 169, 211, 237, 290f.
Sweet, Kristi 47, 91, 208f., 274f.

Teleology 235
Transcendental Concept 99, 107, 111–114

Universal Communicability 50f., 190f., 197–199, 201, 203, 212, 237, 273, 279, 282, 287, 296
Universal Validity 18, 53, 114, 152, 176, 183, 187, 192, 199, 201f., 204–206, 208, 213, 256, 269f., 281
Universal Voice 209, 212f.

Validity 23, 54, 56, 61, 107, 111f., 114, 182f., 189, 191, 193–195, 201, 205f., 213, 219f., 269–271, 273, 282f.

Walsh, W. H 4

Zangwill, Nick 152–154
Zinkin, Melissa 134, 191

www.ingramcontent.com/pod-product-compliance
Lightning Source LLC
Chambersburg PA
CBHW061933220426
43662CB00012B/1893